SECRET MISSION
TO MELBOURNE
— NOVEMBER 1941 —

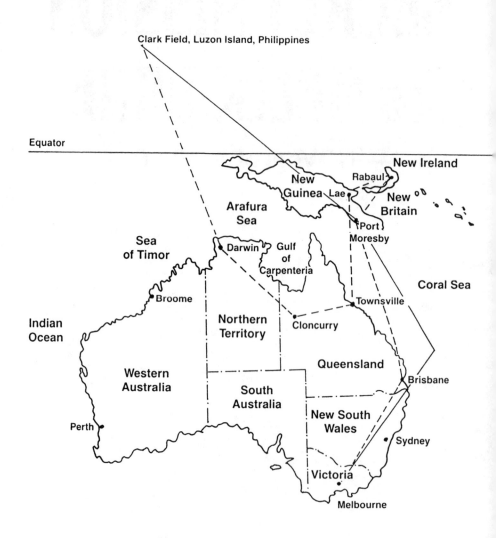

SECRET MISSION TO MELBOURNE

— NOVEMBER 1941 —

by Sky Phillips

Sunflower University Press®
1531 Yuma (Box 1009), Manhattan, Kansas 66502-4228, USA

© 1992 by Sky Phillips

Printed in the United States of America on acid-free paper.

ISBN 0-89745-148-1

Layout by Lori L. Daniel

*To the sweetheart
I met at Randolph Field
and married during World War II,
whose love and support
made this book possible.*

Actual Persons

Major General Lewis Hyde Brereton, Commander, U.S. Air Forces, Far East
Lieutenant Colonel Eugene Eubank, Commander, 19th Bombardment Squadron
Captain Norman I. Llewellyn, senior aide to Brereton
Major Charles H. Caldwell, also an aide-de-camp
Captain Allison Ind, the Air Intelligence Officer, Philippines
Captain Harold E. (Lefty) Eads, Jr., Corps of Engineers
Group Captain Scherger, CO of RAAF Station Darwin
Lieutenant Floyd (Slugger) Pell, USAAC, later killed over Darwin
Captain William E. McDonald, B-17 pilot, stranded in Darwin
Brigadier D. V. J. Blake, CO of Darwin AIF garrison
Air Commodore F. W. F. Lukis, Air Officer Commanding NE Area
Commander Eric A. Feldt, RAN, Director of the Coastwatchers
Brigadier Basil M. Morris, Australian Army Commander, Papua, NG
Squadron Leader C. W. Pearce, RAAF Commander, Port Moresby
Flying Officer Robinson, detachment of No. 24 Squadron based at Rabaul
Dr. Edward Thomas Brennan, Public Health Administrator, Papua, NG
Mrs. Shaughnessy, Manager of Lennon's Hotel, Brisbane

Colonel Van S. Merle-Smith, U.S. Military Attaché in Melbourne
Air Chief Marshal Sir Charles Burnett, RAF, Chief of the Australian Air Staff
Sir Keith Murdoch, Director-General of Information
John Curtin, Prime Minister of Australia
Robert Menzies, leader of the Liberal Party
Lieutenant General Vernon A. H. Sturdee, CGS, AMF
Hubert Vere Evatt, Minister for External Affairs
Donald Rogers, Curtin's secretary
The Reverend Donald Robinson
Bishop Mannix

Fictional Characters

Jim Davis, a P-40 pilot, 21, born and reared in the Philippines
David, his younger brother, in a Jesuit high school in Manila
Leda Hogan Davis, their Irish-Cherokee mother, a teacher
Alexander Drexel Davis, their father, a scholar
Daphne Light, Jim's romantic interest in Singapore
Punch Bartrock, the handsome bad boy who grew up next door in Manila
Mariluz Martinez, the girl in the mansion on Manila Bay
Sergeant Werner Fredericks, RAAF, retired
Flight Lieutenant Wesley Popkins, RAAF
Flight Officer Penny Parker, WAAF
Arthur Reginald Evans, named for the Coastwatcher who rescued John F. Kennedy
Flight Officer T. W. L. Griffin, RAAF
Anthony Lightbody, Assistant Manager, Papua Hotel, Port Moresby, NG
Gail and Fiona, young women of Brisbane
Albion Birdsall, a young widow in Melbourne
Lieutenant Robert H. O'Daniel, member of U.S. Consulate staff, Melbourne

Author's Note

During my long years of research for a series about Bataan's gallant "Bamboo Air Force" and its aftermath, I've received superb assistance from Ex-POWs and "Bataan Angel" nurses, who characteristically helped me "above and beyond the call of duty."

My public thanks to those individuals must wait, however, for this is not yet their story, but only the prologue to their Greek tragedy.

My research led me southward, after I came across brief accounts of General Lewis Brereton's trip from the Philippines to Australia on the eve of World War II. That mission, kept out of the news then and quickly overtaken by events, was barely mentioned in postwar memoirs by two of the main protagonists: General Brereton gave it about five pages, while Allison Ind (by then Colonel) recounted it in eight.

Their wide-ranging diplomatic and strategic assignment (which so soon produced enormously valuable results) was accomplished by a handful of Air Corps officers masquerading as civilians but traveling by B-17 bomber, without any preliminary staff studies, and without a single computer!

Convinced that their undertaking deserves to be better known, I have tried to follow the mission's chronology and events as accurately as possible — as they might have been shared by a fictional young pilot.

Sky Phillips
Alexandria, Virginia

Acknowledgments

In writing this story, I've been extremely lucky to have had help and encouragement — in person or via correspondence — from many wise and kind individuals, whom I wish to thank.

Dr. Robin Higham, President of Sunflower University Press, and Carol A. Williams, Associate Publisher, have been receptive and cooperative all the way. Irving Brick, M.D., is not only a fine squash player, but also off-court gave me information about the Solomon Islands, where he served as a medical officer during World War II. The superb historian Walter D. Edmonds has honored me with his support through letters over the years and generously gave permission to use his own hand-drawn maps. Major General Eugene L. Eubank, the pilot and second in command of the mission, graciously answered my questions.

Commander Philip F. Eckert (USN-Ret.), a submariner in the Pacific war, shared his knowledge of Commander Feldt. Steve Gerson gave me maps of the Solomons, and Bill Graham (Colonel, USAF-Ret.) described his missions over Rabaul.

Mary Z. Gray, my friend since high school and a professional writer, over the course of an entire year nobly responded to monthly installments of my manuscript with cogent-but-not-cutting critiques. Bruce Hoy, former curator of New Guinea's Air Museum, wrote of Amelia Earhart's last takeoff. The late General George C. Kenney answered my queries warmly and thoughtfully, and James M. Keys, Ph.D., taught me how to put my intuition to work.

Dr. Robert S. Laubach wrote to me about his father's literacy work on

Mindanao. The librarians at the National Air and Space Museum, the Embassy of Australia, and the U.S. Naval Historical Center were unfailingly helpful. Donald S. Lopez, Deputy Director of the National Air and Space Museum, lent me his own manual for the P-40 airplane (which he had flown with success in China during World War II).

From the 19th Bombardment Group, Colonels Edward M. Jacquet and Austin W. Stitt, and the late Generals Emmett "Rosie" O'Donnell and Hewitt "Shorty" Wheless gave me firsthand information. Lieutenant General Joseph H. Moore, CO of the 21st Pursuit Squadron at Clark Field in December 1941, welcomed me to his home for an interview. The British military writer Eric Morris taught me techniques of interviewing retired veterans and accompanied me to the Army Military History Institute at Carlisle Barracks, Pennsylvania, whose library personnel gave us perceptive assistance.

Morton J. "Jock" Netzorg, BIP (Born in the Philippines), with his wife Petra presides over the bottomless Cellar Book Shop in Detroit. He is a human encyclopedia who generously shares his knowledge of sources concerning World War II in the Pacific, and it would have been impossible for me to write this book without his guidance. Richard R. Slater, an expert on the aircraft and air activity of the period, has freely given me the benefit of his research.

Jean Clagett Thorne, both daughter and wife of Air Corps officers who experienced Japan's attack on the Philippines, has helped me by mail. Manette Villamor, widow of the Filipino pilot-hero Jesus Villamor, has given me faithful encouragement. Fay Gillis Wells, charter member of the Ninety-Nines, has been generous with personal information about her friend Amelia Earhart (although Fay disapproves of speculation about AE's disappearance). John C. Woodward II (Lieutenant Colonel, USAF-Ret.) knowledgeably answered my questions about radio reception over the Pacific.

Proceeding alphabetically has brought me to Shirley Yarnall, although chronologically she was the first to tell me (in her seminar at American University), "You can write a novel."

Finally, I am indebted to Ken Scott of the Pentagon Officers' Athletic Center Pro Shop, for my "data storage banks." For perhaps ten years he saved for me the best and biggest (size 10-13) of the boxes discarded by Pentagon jocks who replaced their worn-out athletic shoes with new ones. Those Adidas, Brooks, Nike, Reebok, and Tiger boxes, holding the index cards with my scrawled research notes, somehow seem appropriate for this low-tech, 1941 narrative.

My deep thanks go to all of these, and to all my beloved family members and friends who have loyally stood by me during this effort.

Any errors are, of course, solely my own.

Contents

Actual Persons		vii
Fictional Characters		ix
Author's Note		xi
Acknowledgments		xiii
Preface		xix
Prologue		xxi
Chapter 1		
Part 1	To Darwin	1
Part 2	Instrument Check	8
Part 3	Early Birds	16
Part 4	Navigation Lesson	23
Part 5	Timor!	26
Chapter 2		
Part 1	Desolate Darwin	32
Part 2	On Amelia's Trail	44
Part 3	Wirraway Ride	51
Chapter 3		
Part 1	To Townsville	61
Part 2	Tropical Townsville	74
Part 3	Coastwatcher Commander	81
Part 4	Penny	87

Chapter 4
- Part 1 To Papua, New Guinea 95
- Part 2 Miserable Moresby 110
- Part 3 Seven Mile 116

Chapter 5
- Part 1 Over the Owen Stanleys 132
- Part 2 New Britain 146
- Part 3 To Rabaul 150
- Part 4 Rotten-Egg Rabaul 158

Chapter 6 A Dining-In 167

Chapter 7
- Part 1 To Brisbane 173
- Part 2 "Beaut" Brisbane 180

Chapter 8
- Part 1 South to Melbourne 190
- Part 2 Sydneyside 193
- Part 3 Over the Capital 197
- Part 4 Misty Melbourne 200

Chapter 9
- Part 1 Buckley's or Nothing 208
- Part 2 *Rainbow* Revealed 210
- Part 3 Dreamtime 216
- Part 4 "Franksgiving" Dinner 221
- Part 5 Barracks Bedtime 231

Chapter 10
- Part 1 A Run in the Royal Domain 235
- Part 2 John Curtin, PM 241
- Part 3 A Gift of Time 253
- Part 4 Very Little Theater 255

Chapter 11
- Part 1 Flemington Racecourse 258
- Part 2 Royal Park Zoo and Chloe's 261

Chapter 12
- Part 1 St. Paul's Problem 264
- Part 2 Royal Melbourne Hospital 267
- Part 3 Port Phillip Bay 272
- Part 4 Decision Time 277

Chapter 13
    Part 1   Farewell to Australia   280
    Part 2   Bad News in Brisbane   283
Chapter 14   Farewell to New Guinea   285
Chapter 15   Clark Field Confrontation   290
Epilogue   292
Aftermath   293
Sources   294
Permissions to Quote   295

Maps

Route of the Brereton Party, November 1941   ii

The Pacific — Showing the route of the 19th Group Squadrons, Hawaii to Clark Field, and also the ferry routes later used, Hawaii to Australia.   xviii

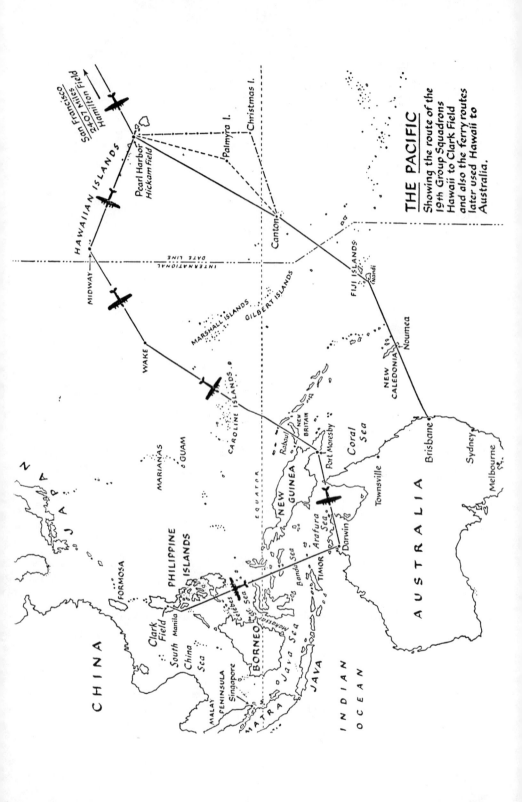

Preface

On November 6, when Saburo Kurusu left Tokyo as a special envoy to assist the Japanese Ambassador Nomura in negotiations with the U.S., he told his American-born son: "Maybe I will not be able to come back. Look after the family." In Washington it was reported that the chances for a settlement were about one in ten. In Manila — 4,800 miles nearer to Tokyo than to Washington — the chances seemed to be about one in ten thousand. Stopping over night in Manila, Kurusu told friends that there was "not much hope" that his mission to Washington would be successful.

The same day that Kurusu passed through Manila, General MacArthur ordered me to proceed by air to Australia for the purpose of surveying the Trans-Pacific Air Ferry Route from Australia to the Philippines and Java, which also included a project for extending the route to Singapore and China. My instructions were to begin preparation of bases in Northern Australia and throughout the Malay Barrier from which American Air Forces could operate. . . . if a campaign in the Philippines was unsuccessful, it would be essential for the Pacific campaign to provide adequate air defense of Northern Australia, the Dutch Indies, and the Malay Peninsula.

— Major General Lewis Hyde Brereton, *The Brereton Diaries*

Prologue

Clark Army Air Field, Luzon Island, Philippines
1230 Hours. Monday, 8 December 1941
(Sunday, 7 December, in U.S. and Hawaii)

"Good God Almighty!" Jim's crew chief yelled, pointing to the northwest sky. "Yonder they come! JAPS!"

Second Lieutenant James T. Davis, on Cockpit Alert status in his Curtiss P-40B, shot a glance downwind over his shoulder. Against the tropical blue, above the Zambales Mountains, he saw the most thrilling, most terrifying sight of his 21 years.

The meridian sun glinted on a spearhead of silver flecks approaching in such precision that they formed a single entity. Lightning logic told Jim that those three Vs, comprising that vast silver V, were bombers — nine in each V — flown by pilots as human as himself; but in its inexorable progression, the formation fused itself into one machine with but one aim: to kill him.

Prologue

Chapter 1

Part 1 — To Darwin

Japan must have oil. If the Netherlands East Indies and America do not agree to deal with her in quantities sufficient to keep her reserves intact, she will act. She will drive to the Netherlands East Indies. And she will take them.
— Ernest Hemingway, in Manila, May 1941

Aboard B-17D No. 40-3097
Clark Army Air Field, Luzon Island, Philippines
0300 Hours. Armistice Day, 11 November 1941

Lucky me! thought Second Lieutenant James Thomas Davis. *Even a hot pursuit pilot can appreciate a rare ride in a Flying Fortress.*
. . . And this promises to be **some** *ride — all the way Down Under, on a secret mission in civilian togs — and home via Singapore and adorable Daphne. . . .*

Not necessarily a comfortable ride, he realized already. At the moment, however, he was occupying one of the best seats in the aircraft, directly behind the pilot and copilot. The flight engineer's jump-seat — in the absence of a flight engineer — allowed Jim room to stretch his lanky legs.

Just over six feet tall, he was accustomed to being cramped in the cockpit of his "own" Curtiss P-40; but that was a small price to pay for the privilege of flying it, he thought. This bomber made him appreciate his good fortune in having been selected for the single-engine specialty during his Flying Cadet training — before the rumored new restrictions took effect, limiting pursuit/ fighter pilots to a height of 5'10" or less.

Besides, it's **personality,** not height, that creates a fighter pilot — and we aggressive, daring, bright and sexy types come in all sizes. To condemn a man to fly monstrous multi-engine planes just because he's tall would be "cruel and unusual punishment." Driving a bomber would be like flying a bus — including the awful responsibility for the safety of your riders. . . . This Fortress is a nice plane to visit, but — ! Right now, for example: that audible check-and-double-checklist going on in the cockpit — who in hell wants to go through all that rigmarole every time, before you can take off? Give me the fighter pilot's credo: "Have faith in your Crew Chief, read the Form One, and when faced with an unfamiliar type of plane, just climb into the cockpit and push buttons till something meaningful happens."

The pilot of the B-17D, Lieutenant Colonel Eugene Eubank, already had used a flashlight to make a walk-around inspection, covering every foot of the plane's nearly 68-foot length.

Now Jim heard Eubank tell the copilot, in his warm southwestern accent: "Gear switch neutral. . . ."

Where's the damned airspeed indicator in that multifarious mass of dials?

Jim searched again. Eubank had assigned him a small duty; but now the dial seemed smaller and the responsibility larger.

As the checklist litany continued, the copilot reached over with his right hand, touched something in the array of instruments, and said what sounded like, "Intercoolers cold."

And they call this flying?

Jim had hated the early prototype of the B-17 for killing a man he loved, the father of a childhood friend, Petey Hill. Three years ago, however, he had seen the huge silver bombers in the movie *Test Pilot,* with Clark Gable and Spencer Tracy — and in his eyes even Myrna Loy's cool charm faced stiff competition from the stunning sky giants. But those had been Boeing's early models of the Flying Fortress. This D-model, with improvements like the engine-cooling cowl flaps, was the almost-perfected version. The Series E, now in production in Seattle, promised even further refinements.

By next year, the War Department promised that scores of beautiful new B-17Es would be flying to the Philippines from Stateside factories . . . via a New Guinea-Australia ferry route that the men on this plane would recommend.

This is the ultimate bomber, Jim thought. *The only way any four-engine plane could possibly surpass this job would be by installing comfortable seats.*

The first nine B-17s had landed on Clark Field in September — after a record-breaking overwater mass flight led by Major Emmett C. ("Rosie")

O'Donnell — and the most recent ones, only a week ago. These were the first land-planes ever to reach the Philippines under their own power; during Jim's lifetime of 21 years in the islands, all previous military aircraft had arrived on shipboard in crates.

Now Clark Field boasted 34 of these four-engine bombers, out of 35 that had left California in the five squadrons of the 19th Bombardment Group. The absent B-17 had run into trouble in Australia en route to Clark; it needed two new propellers — which were now being carried to the stranded pilot on this plane, lashed down in the bombless bomb bay.

No bombs, no guns — and no trained bomber crew — were aboard B-17D No. 40-3097 for this pre-dawn takeoff. The only man aboard who had had any experience in a B-17 was the pilot.

By reputation, however, Eubank was "a pilot's pilot" and more than equal to the usual crew of nine. It was he who had led the second flight of three B-17 squadrons safely from Albuquerque Field, New Mexico, across the Pacific to Clark Field: a journey of more than 10,000 miles, most of it over uncharted seas, and over Pacific islands held by unfriendly Japanese forces in the area where Amelia Earhart had disappeared. The unprecedented movement of the 19th Bombardment Group had been made without publicity, but each member of every crew had been awarded the Distinguished Flying Cross.

Deservedly, Jim thought, contemplating the 14-hour, overwater journey in store for him this day.

The Fortresses had flown the 2,407 miles from Hamilton Field, California, to Hickam Field, Honolulu, in about 13 hours. Today's trip would cover 1,702 miles, but Eubank's fuel calculations allowed for 14 hours in the air.

En route to the Philippines, the 19th Bombardment Group had landed to refuel at Port Moresby, New Guinea, and Darwin, Australia. Now Eubank was flying that course in reverse, on a top-secret assignment for his important passenger: Major General Lewis Hyde Brereton, the highest-ranking officer in the U.S. Army Air Forces that had ever been stationed in the Philippines.

This will be a secret flight, not a silent one. Noisy as hell, Jim thought, as the Wright radial engine in the right inboard position roared into life with the power of 1,200 horses, followed by the No. 1 engine, the farthest on the left. Even though the triple-bladed propellers were idling, they shook the huge plane, trying to pull it forward from its chocks. Now the left inboard engine, and finally No. 4, the right outboard, joined in the synchronized thunder.

Brakes unlocked . . . Tabs . . . Flaps . . . Run-up . . . Taxi. . . .

"Tailwheel locked. Light out. Gyros," said the copilot.

"Gyros set," responded Colonel Eubank. Palm up, his sturdy right hand grasped all four throttle handles and smoothly advanced them, as the engines responded in a crescendo and 4,800 horses tugged toward their starting gate.

"Generators!" yelled the copilot.

As the great plane began its takeoff run, Jim leaned forward to call out the speed from the airspeed indicator dial, as Eubank had instructed him.

"Sixty-five, seventy, seventy-five, eighty, eighty-five, ninety, ninety-five. . . ."

The ship raced east toward Mount Arayat, whose familiar cone expanded, garishly stage-lit by a searchlight of the anti-aircraft battery on the airfield. At last, the 15 tons of metal left the bumpy sod and floated.

Jim felt the prickling hair on his neck and down his spine, the thrill that he always experienced during that leap of faith when a plane cast itself on the air. He could see the stars through the Plexiglas windshield, and he thought, *I'm trading my old familiar Philippine stars for the adventure — and maybe romance — of the Southern Cross. . . .*

He felt the thump as the huge wheels folded up into their wells. Eubank peered out and said, "Landing gear up left."

"Landing gear up right," the copilot verified on his side.

This was Jim's cue for his next move in the role of surrogate flight engineer. He got up and went back into the fuselage, hunching over more as the space closed in, and finally crawling to the rear. He tested the tailwheel assembly with the hand crank, then tested it again, thinking, *What if I did something wrong and caused the death of every man aboard? Not to mention wiping out Uncle Sam's two hundred fifty thousand dollar airplane!*

Finally, he felt it was safe to report to the cockpit over the intercom radio, "Tailwheel up, Sir!"

Flying south in the dark, Eubank's course would parallel the jungled Zambales range on their right. Before the range ended on the rugged tip of Bataan Peninsula, the plane would swing eastward over Manila Bay, keeping well clear of Bataan's formidable extinct volcanoes.

The engines' roar would not disturb the sleeping city lying in the curve of the Bay — though Jim suspected that his mother might be awake and listening for it.

Extending eastward from Manila, a necklace of lights still glittered along the Bay's edge, marking the elegant night clubs and gambling casinos of palm-bordered Dewey Boulevard. Tourists and rich Manilans who frequented the famous strip seldom came as far east of the city as the suburb of Pasay.

Dewey Boulevard ended before it reached Pasay, a district that was fashionable only on its southern flank beside the bay. Behind the beachfront mansions sprawled a jumble of unfenced Filipino barrios and walled housing *kampongs* where Americans lived. Inland from these lay the U.S. Army's Nichols Field, whose noisy airplanes added to Pasay's unfashionable status.

Many families in Pasay's low-rent compounds belonged to two groups of ManilAmericans who were poorly paid but socially respectable: schoolteachers and military families. As a BIP (Born in the Philippines) American, the son of two teachers, Jim had spent most of his growing years in a two-story concrete house in the compound called the Court of Roses, although rosebushes never survived the mildews of humid Manila. His playmates were "Army Brats" whose military-officer fathers were dashingly unlike his own quiet, scholarly father.

Jim's mother, Leda, a feminist of Irish-Cherokee lineage from Oklahoma, also was dashingly unlike Jim's father, Alexander — a Yale graduate whose Philadelphia Main Line parents had disapproved of his marriage to Leda. The unlikely pair had met in the Philippines in 1919, new members of a continuing corps of idealistic Americans who had come out by ship since the turn of the century: teachers, facing the hazards of tropical diseases, typhoons, brigands, and lonely islands of their nation's farthest frontier "to educate the Filipinos for democracy."

Now Leda and Alexander were part of a respected remnant of the teacher corps who had made the islands their permanent home, seeing their dream fulfilled as they were being replaced by Filipino teachers who had been their pupils.

David, Jim's younger brother, would be asleep down there in the Court of Roses. Deep in the untroubled sleep, Jim thought, of a high school senior who's a basketball whiz, who could blow a trumpet like Clyde McCoy, and who has his heart set on becoming a Jesuit priest.

Both brothers were tall, but their features revealed different strains of their mother's ancestry. Jim's straight black hair, dark brown eyes, aquiline nose, and bronze complexion bespoke Cherokee genes, while David wore "the map of Ireland on his face." Jim thought his brother resembled a young Spencer Tracy.

Next door stood the house Jim still thought of as "Punch's house," although many other military families had lived there since Punch and his sister and their strange parents had moved on. Punch's father, Captain Bartrock, a martinet whom all the neighborhood kids hated, had returned to the States when his tour was up, taking his daughter. Mrs. Bartrock and Punch had remained in Manila, but not in the Court of Roses. Eventually, Punch had gone to the States, graduated from MIT, and now had returned as an Air Corps second lieutenant.

Leda had forbidden Jim, age 12, to enter the Bartrocks' house after he innocently had mentioned that Punch's mother must be the cleanest lady in Manila, because she was always wrapped in a towel — obviously going to or coming from a shower — whenever he saw her.

Punch (so nicknamed by his English mother because, she said, he was conceived while she was under the influence of Artillery Punch) was a favorite of all the other mothers because of his fine manners, his rosy-cheeked, blond good looks, and his always-clean appearance. All the boys disliked him, but they put up with him because he knew the dirtiest jokes and had a huge collection of lowdown cartoon joke magazines like *Ballyhoo* and *Uncle Billy's Whiz-Bang*.

Punch had a one-track mind, the boys said, and he was born with a stiff prick. At age 14, frustrated by the moral strictures of Manila's American girls and the heavily-chaperoned young Filipinas, he'd had his way with the Bartrocks' housegirl by threatening to accuse her of theft. Captain Bartrock had put the pregnant young woman on an inter-island steamer to return to her family on Panay Island, but she never arrived. Another passenger had seen her, distraught and *desgrasyada*, slip over the side in the night.

The Court of Roses contained seven houses built in a semicircle around an eighth, all surrounded by a high concrete wall. A giant mango tree stretched its heavy branches over the wall toward Manila Bay. One branch even extended over the next wall — topped with wicked shards of jewel-colored glass — enclosing the bayfront estate of Don Abelardo Martinez and his wife, a poet and artist. Their daughter Mariluz was Jim's longtime friend; for most of his life, he had visited Mariluz by dropping over the wall into her parents' lush garden. Since childhood, the two had planned similar careers as physicians, and now Mariluz was enrolled in Pre-Med courses at the University of the Philippines.

Because of what he considered a point of honor, Jim had left Bishop Brent High School without graduating; and after the U.S. Army Air Corps no longer demanded a diploma as a requisite for flying school, he had passed the equivalency tests and won his wings. He still intended to go through medical school after the present war scare was over, but he felt he could become a more useful physician as a "flying doctor" to remote islands of the archipelago.

Now he wondered if Mariluz, in her sleep, was hearing the Fortress' song. Because of the secrecy of this trip, he had not been able to say goodbye to her, his best friend and confidante. *I'll write her a long letter from Australia*, he promised himself.

Nichols Field was dark now. On Sunday night Jim had partied there, in the seedy old wooden Officers' Club, with friends who epitomized the fighter-pilot personality — and were not too tall, either. It was the 27th birthday of Jesus "Jess" Villamor; his 6th Pursuit Squadron of the Philippine Air Force had thrown a wing-ding of a party for their "old man." In duty hours, their only pursuit planes were obsolete P-26s (small enough to fit under a wing of this Fortress) — but they flew them hell-for-leather, with skill and daring. Jess was even brave enough to serve as a flying instructor; earlier, he had given lessons to two members of General MacArthur's staff: Lieutenant Colonels Eisenhower and Sutherland.

At the bay's entrance, the little emerald island of Corregidor would now have slipped beneath the plane, and the B-17, like the ancient Spanish galleons, would depart Luzon over the South China Sea.

"A Fort almost flies itself," the newly-arrived B-17 pilots had told Jim. "After takeoff, the pilot can fly it solo." Encouraged by such remarks and by the glimpses he had seen of the jovial Eubank, he had dreamed of serving for a spell as copilot during some of the long flights in store for this journey. It would be fun to enter that experience in his embryonic Log Book. To assure Eubank of his all-weather proficiency, he had brought along his Green Card, recently updated by a blind-flying check ride with his squadron commander, Captain Joe Moore of the 20th Pursuit Squadron. Jim had first earned his Instrument Certification Card at Kelly Field, Texas, piloting an AT-6 Texan while "under the hood," and he was proud of it.

Now, however, gazing at that formidable instrument panel, he felt inept and inadequate. *If Nature had intended me for a bomber pilot,* he thought, *she'd have given me several more pairs of eyes.*

Adding to his qualms: Some of Colonel Eubank's worshipful bomber pilots had told Jim of "the old man's" insistence that they all must become expert navigators themselves, not depending entirely on the specialist assigned to navigate each B-17. Indeed, there was no "star-gazer" on this flight, and Eubank had told Jim, "No deadheads fly with me. I expect you to take a turn at every position on this ship — except bombardier, gunner, and airplane commander!"

Now, as he considered assuming the duties of flight engineer, navigator, or copilot, every glance into the cockpit, with all its dials, gauges, and switches, made his stomach tighten. He had not felt so awkward and incapable since his first days as a Flying Cadet.

Just look at all that crap: The pilot's control panels and pedestals, controls to left of him, controls to right of him, controls to copilot's right, controls on the goddam ceiling. . . . On the Automatic Pilot alone I count more than forty gadgets to worry about! The only items I'm sure of are those four above the windshield: a compass and compass card, the de-icer pressure gauge, and a clock. To be honest, there's really only one position I could step right into, and manage confidently — radio operator. . . . But, for a thousand air-miles today, this plane will be out of range of any transmitter or receiver.

Part 2 — Instrument Check

INSTRUMENT CHECK

Filed and posted at Post Operations
Nichols Field, Manila, PI, June 1941

MANEUVER

Level Flight..............................OK
90 Degree Turns.....................OK
180 Degree Turns...................OK
Fast Turns...............................OK
Spiral Climb............................OK
Glides......................................OK
Stalls.......................................OK

<u>RECOVERY</u> Spirals, Spins & Stalls
(Link Trainer)..........................OK

RADIO BEAM
Following.................................OK
Cone of Silence......................OK
Orientation..............................OK

Chapter 1 — Part 2 — Instrument Check 9

TO: Operations Officer.

I certify that <u>Davis, James Thomas,</u> has this date <u>20 June 1941</u> passed the instrument test as prescribed in Air Corps Circular 50-1.

(signed) <u>Joseph H. Moore, Capt.</u> (Check pilot)

In Jim's view, the best part of this trip would begin after the group left Australia and headed northwest. In the hope of appeasing President Roosevelt's anxiety to keep beleaguered China from falling to Japan, MacArthur had directed Brereton to ascertain the feasibility of sending U.S. supplies to China by flying them as far as Singapore, via Australia (in further violation of the Neutrality Act). That project would give Jim a chance to renew his summer romance with Daphne Light, the young blonde Englishwoman he had met in Singapore in July.

Brereton had landed in the Philippines only the previous week, on 3 November, to take command of the newly-named Far East Air Force. His arrival had been delayed by a typhoon that forced the *Philippine Clipper,* Pan American World Airways' westbound flying boat, to remain at Wake Island for three additional nights, with another day's delay on Guam. Since his splashdown in Manila Bay, the wry joke had spread: *Brereton brought the typhoon with him!*

In six days this short, dapper, dark-haired officer had visited every U.S. Army Air Forces flying field in the islands — all the way down to the pineapple plantation at Del Monte on Mindanao, 500 miles south of Manila. He was not happy with what he had found: "No spare parts of any kind; no anti-aircraft defenses at any airfield; air-warning service pitifully inadequate; no spare engines for either bomber or fighter aircraft; few tools of any kind for even rudimentary repairs and maintenance — and not so much as an extra washer or nut for a Fortress."

Brereton had abolished peacetime schedules: no more free afternoons; no more siestas; training routines would be speeded up and intensified. He had put the Philippine Air Depot on a 16-hour work day, against the protests of the Civil Service personnel; and on the seventh day he had not rested.

Now, in the copilot's seat, Brereton was still complaining to Eubank. Nothing had been improved, he said, since his first brief tour in the Philippines in 1916-1917. Then — while he was on a temporary assignment back in the States, to test some new seaplanes and return with them to Corregidor — "We got into the Big War, and I got my orders changed to go to France."

"Well, this time we stayed out of France — for better or worse," Eubank said.

"This time, we don't have to go to Europe to get into a war. General MacArthur told me we can expect the Japs to make a serious move in April. How the hell can I get the Far East Air Force battle-ready by then?"

* * * * *

"*Brereton?* Of course I know 'Lousy Lewie' Brereton!" Jim's mother, Leda, had told him. "Lewie commanded the 12th Aero Squadron, in the Vosges sector, when I was setting up canteens around there."

In 1918 Leda, with other Smith College alumnae, had responded to a call for volunteers from Mrs. Theodore Roosevelt, Jr., in Paris. "Young women of good character" were asked to serve with the American YMCA in Europe, arranging "wholesome activities" for the morale and morals of American troops on Occupation duty after the World War. (Leda's sailing for France, however, was delayed by her imprisonment in Virginia for picketing the White House on behalf of Women's Suffrage.)

"'Brereton,'" mused Alexander, Jim's father. "Another name steeped in British history. Like 'Sutherland' and 'Richard Marshall,' appropriate for another disciple at King MacArthur's Table Round."

"Don't kid yourself," Leda had retorted. "Lew Brereton's nobody's disciple but his own. He didn't get to be a Major General without stepping on some heads, I betcha. . . . Douglas MacArthur knew him in France, too. In the spring of 1919, Douglas was Chief of Staff for the 42nd Division — my doughboys — while Lew's squadron was supporting them. . . . Hells bells, Jim, the best thing I remember about Lew is that he graduated from Annapolis. If Douglas wanted a 'fighting general' for you flyboys, he's got himself a fighter by the tail now. Lewie Brereton will fight with *anybody!*"

"And so would you, my dear mama," Jim had said. "Maybe the man has mellowed. I'll keep an open mind, and judge him with eyes unclouded by inherited prejudices."

* * * * *

Jim respected Brereton for being a Command Pilot like Colonel Eubank; each had flown more than 5,000 hours as an Army pilot. In addition, each was a Command Observer, having flown more than 5,000 hours in military aircraft as a non-pilot. Only longevity could achieve those totals, for during the Depression the shortage of funds for fuel had limited even the most eager pilots to 100 flying hours annually. These two ranked high in Jim's pantheon of heroes because they were part of the holy remnant of the 13,800 Americans trained as pilots for the World War; they were among the 149 who were retained by the postwar Army Air Corps. He gave them each ten points for

Chapter 1 — Part 2 — Instrument Check

surviving as Canvas Falcons.

Today's passengers included other pilots, and Jim was thankful that they were experienced in flying multi-engine aircraft, if not B-17s. Two members of Brereton's personal staff were aboard who had come with him from Tampa, where he had commanded the 3rd Air Force.

Brereton's senior aide, Captain Norman I. Llewellyn, was, in Captain Ind's words, "a good-natured blond giant." His other aide was Major Charles H. Caldwell. Previously, Jim had noted that the long-faced Caldwell wore on his uniform the coveted silver wings topped by a wreath-encircled star; he, too, was a Command Pilot. In his anonymous khaki flying suit, Caldwell's experience was displayed only in his sure responses on the controls, during a stint beside Eubank as copilot. He was no longer wearing his Class of 1925 West Point ring, either; regulations forbade crew members' wearing a safety hazard that could lead to loss of a ring finger.

So what if I never got my high school diploma? Hell — I'm the only one aboard who's lived in the Philippines for over twenty years. None of the others have been here even twenty months, and most of them haven't been here even ten days. So, in flying suits, we're all equal. . . .

On this trip, at least in public, the officers would pretend to be equal. Because Australia had declared war on Germany simultaneously with England two years earlier, any aid given to Australia would be in violation of the U.S. Neutrality Act. To keep Brereton's mission secret from the U.S. press and Congress, as well as from Japan, the travelers had brought only civilian clothes and would use no titles of rank.

For Jim, being called "Mr. Davis" would be no shock; he had gone on active duty as a second lieutenant only in January. In flying school in Texas, cadets were called "Dodo" until they learned to fly; then they advanced to "Mister." But it was going to seem strange and disrespectful not to address the senior officers with their rank. Major General Brereton was the highest-ranking Army Air Corps officer ever assigned to Philippine duty; to Jim, a Major General was like a king.

Just an ordinary group of businessmen, flying down to Darwin in a four-engine bomber!

Fortunately for Jim, Brereton's junior aide, Lieutenant Edgar Wade Hampton, had been delayed in California — outranked and out-prioritized on the list for seats on the *Philippine Clipper* — thus Jim could occupy Hampton's space on this trip. As for actual seating, however, the bomber's vast interior offered surprisingly few spaces for sitting upright, even on one's parachute pack.

Rank hath no privileges on this bus, Jim thought. Quite a comedown for General Brereton — just after he'd crossed the Pacific in the elegant comfort of the *Clipper*.

"Not designed for 'PAX,' meaning 'passengers'!" Jim told Captain Allison

Ind, shouting over the noise. The Fortress had leveled off at 8,000 feet, and Jim had gone aft to see Ind, a non-flier who suffered greatly from airsickness.

"*Pax vobiscum*," Ind moaned. "This bomber's designed for keeping the *pax* — but *no* aircraft is designed for human beings."

Back here, there was an added noise, almost musical to Jim's ears at first, but he knew it could get monotonous: the continual clink of bottles. Cases of the Philippines' popular beer, San Miguel, had been stowed aboard as gifts for commanding officers of airfields suffering under Australia's wartime beer-rationing. General MacArthur was a major stockholder in the Ansor Corporation, owned by his friend Andres Soriano, which brewed San Miguel. Jim thought, *No matter how this trip turns out, old Mac's made some more pesos.*

He told Ind's prone form, "It could be worse. If this was wartime, you'd be lying between, and below, twin racks of five-hundred-pound bombs."

As if nothing could make Captain Ind's flight more unpleasant, he had insisted on occupying the narrow catwalk (only one foot wide at its tightest) that led to the dark bomb bay — leaving the forward section for the others. Now lying on his side, he looked utterly miserable.

Before takeoff, Jim had tried to persuade Ind to trade seats. Finally he had realized that this fastidious gentleman could not bear to let the others see him in the throes of his "wretched retching" into his paper cups.

Earlier, the modest Ind's shock had been evident when he inquired about toilet facilities and Jim showed him the relief tube, located behind the feeble dome light in the left bomb bay. "Not even a curtain around it?" Ind had protested.

A reserve officer, until recently an English professor at the University of Michigan at Ann Arbor, the scholarly Ind had arrived in Manila in May to serve as the Air Intelligence Officer of the Philippines. His influence was reponsible for Jim's presence on this historic flight.

In September, Ind had arranged for Jim — because of Jim's radio hobby and his familiarity with the islands of the Philippine Archipelago and many of their inhabitants — to travel secretly through the Southern Islands, to try to arrange for an embryo network of amateur radio operators. Captain Ind also knew that Australia's Commander Eric Feldt had established an efficient network of "Coastwatchers" in the Solomon Islands. He had persuaded someone in authority that Jim could glean knowledge from Commander Feldt, based in Townsville, that would be valuable in the Philippines.

Jim realized that his luck in having Army Brats for friends had caused, indirectly, his friendship with this un-military professor. It was because the beautiful, brown-eyed Louise and Jean Clagett had been Jim's childhood sweethearts that their dad had considered assigning him to be his junior aide and pilot. Even though Jim had told Clagett frankly that he hated the idea of being a general's aide, he took Jim along on his trips to Chungking in May and to Singapore in July.

Captain Ind also had been a member of that mission to Singapore and Java, led by the ailing Brigadier General Henry Clagett — Brereton's predecessor — to discuss Lend-Lease needs with the British and Dutch colonial officials. They had traveled in luxury from Manila to Singapore on the *Clipper's* fortnightly run — although Ind's queasy stomach had occasionally driven him from their white-linen table with its chef-prepared meals and into the comfortable berth the steward made up for him.

During that July tour, Allison Ind and Jim, frequently roommates, had become friends. Not only wisdom, but wit, Jim learned, dwelt beneath the Intelligence Officer's high forehead, topped with dark brown hair slicked back from a widow's peak; and humor glinted in the dark eyes behind silver-rimmed glasses. Except for a "spy fixation" that blocked the advances of some promising Asian beauties toward Jim, Ind's observant presence had added enjoyment to Jim's return to scenes of childhood visits in Malaya and Java.

Indeed, it was Captain Ind — as they sat alone, sipping *stengahs* at a pink-lamped table beside the outdoor dance pavilion at the Raffles Hotel — who had dared Jim to ask the alluring blonde in the revealing white evening dress for a dance.

Daphne was seated with a table of Australians — pilots and Nursing Sisters whose informal ways suited her own unconventional style — and she had danced with Jim until the orchestra packed up. That night had begun the most romantically exciting interlude of Jim's life. Although Daphne had a fiance named Robin, an officer of the Royal Navy aboard HMS *Prince of Wales*, he was far away in July.

Jim had been angry with Daphne when he left — furious, shocked, and frustrated by the way she had ruined his last night there — the one that she had promised would be "The Night." But after her note of apology, he began getting over it, and now all he could think about was how different — how perfect — it was going to be, *this* time.

Like most of the ManilAmerican boys he had grown up with, Jim had remained celibate into his twenties. Although he had experienced a sexual initiation as a boy, in a mountain *olag* (adolescent dormitory) of the Ifugao tribe, the Ifugao widow who was the resident instructor had been rough, rank, and impatient. That nauseating experience had made him determined to make his *real* "first time" as romantic as a Hollywood seduction. Daphne had promised him such — and she was a woman of experience. Singapore, unlike the straitlaced American community of Manila, bent on showing the Filipinos a good example, took a tolerant view of amorous peccadillos among the colonials, single or married. More than horse racing at the Turf Club or cricket on the bayside Padang, Daphne had told Jim, adultery was Singapore's favorite sport.

*Before this jaunt winds up in Singapore, and I wind up — I hope — in Daphne's bed, maybe I'll meet some Australian girls as pretty and well-stacked as those friendly Aussie Nursing Sisters in Singapore! Maybe I'll sweep one off her feet — a **nice** girl, who can't resist me — and I'll have myself a little whirlwind romance Down Under. . . . After all, it might be best to have some experience under my belt, before Daphne takes me on; I don't want her to laugh at me. Missionary position, or what? I've got a helluva lot to learn, and Australia might be just the place for me to learn it.*

Singapore had given him the best and the worst events of his life — almost simultaneously — he mused. *Daphne's thrilling response to my infatuation . . . and my accidental discovery, through Colonel LeClair's boozy clerk, of the top-secret, lousy, goddam, treasonous, Limey-caving pledge of my government: the fucking "Rainbow Plan"!* Remembering, Jim felt almost as nauseated as poor Ind looked.

Even more than airsickness had affected Captain Ind, however. Jim had noticed that the ex-professor had appeared worried for several days — ever since Brereton had assigned him the task of writing analyses of Australia's "social, economic, and military" conditions.

"A year's leave of absence would be necessary even to organize the material properly," the conscientious officer had told Jim. "Six months would be an extreme push. But the General wants me to have it ready immediately upon our return!"

Now Ind was forced to return to his cup, and Jim tactfully moved forward toward the flight deck, hunching over to keep his head from banging the metal ribs of the fuselage. He squeezed past the radio compartment, where Lefty Eads was curled up under an Army blanket beside the low-pressure oxygen tanks, sleeping through the thundering, rattling, creaking metallic cacophony. Lefty's pleasant, All-American features jiggled with the engines' vibration.

Lefty: Captain Harold E. Eads, Jr., a civil engineer, was a comparative "old-timer" of more than a year of Philippine duty, in contrast with the fresh-from-the-States officers in the plane's forward section. Lately, Lefty had been assisting Colonel Harold H. George (Jim's topmost candidate in The Dad Game), in planning the belated improvement of Philippine airfields, all composed of sod, mud, or dust in season. General MacArthur had chosen Colonel George to represent him on this Australia-Singapore circuit, but — to Jim's great disappointment — George was too deeply involved in getting the landing fields in shape, now that the funds were in hand. The dynamic Colonel (for whom Jim's mother had carried a secret torch since their World War friendship in France) had named Lefty as his representative to handle a taxing assignment: to figure the costs, in U.S. dollars *and* Australian pounds, of each of the construction projects that Brereton would suggest in Australia.

Poor Lefty — what a lousy job for a nice fella. Even worse than Captain Ind's "Encyclopedia Australiana."

Part 3 — Early Birds

> . . . *whoever, within the United States, knowingly begins or sets on foot or provides or prepares a means for or furnishes the money for, or takes part in, any military or naval expedition or enterprise to be carried on from thence against the territory or dominion of any foreign prince or state, or of any colony, district, or people with whom the United States is at peace, shall be fined no more than $3000. or imprisoned not more than three years or both.*
> — U.S. Neutrality Act, Section 960 of Title 18, U.S. code, enacted in 1794. Reaffirmed by Congress in 1935 when Italy invaded Ethiopia

Jim stepped over the trap door that led down to the section where Brereton's two staff members were riding. Captain Llewellyn was far forward in the bombardier's position, the bubble of clear Plexiglas in the plane's nose. Behind him, Major Caldwell sat at the navigator's table, with maps, charts, and cardboard circles for computing drift and ground speed, while the "bird dog" pointer of the radio compass dialed its constant, fruitless search for any radio beam intercepted by the loop antenna. A marvel to Jim, this navigator's radio compass was a "slave," performing identically to the main one on the Flight Deck used by the aircraft commander.

The jump-seat was still empty, so Jim pulled it out and sat behind "Mister" Eubank and his temporary copilot, "Mister" Brereton. Cruising speed, 250 mph. He could see out through the cockpit windows, but there was only a dawn-pink sky to view. On each side of the plane, nearly 50 feet of wing blocked out the sea below. He looked at the backs of the two senior officers and found himself reflexively playing The Dad Game.

He liked watching Eubank's hands. The stocky Oklahoma-born, Texas-reared pilot was reputed to be a scratch golfer, and it was easy to picture those thick, powerful-looking fingers entwined around the shaft of a club. Jim gave him five points for good golf.

But the poor man hasn't even had time to swing a mashie on the Stotsenburg course since he landed at Clark a week ago. Rank hath its drawbacks, and whoever wants it is welcome to it.

Wryly, Jim recalled his own last golf game, on Ferdinand Marcos' 24th birthday, 12 September. Ferdie had never played on the pretty little nine-hole course on Corregidor Island; so at his request — or insistence — Jim had agreed to be his host there, and had also invited Antonio Aquino. Both guests were new 3rd Lieutenants in the Philippine Army, which, in August, had been incorporated into the U.S. Army under General MacArthur.

Marcos recently had been acquitted of murder. Tony Aquino brought along his eight-year-old brother Benigno, nicknamed "Ninoy," already a good golfer.

Transported by the shuttle launch USS *Col. George F. E. Harrison* across Manila Bay and by the free "Toonerville Trolley" up to Topside, they arrived at the course adjacent to the velvet green parade ground, the Ciné theater, and The World's Longest Barracks. A fresh breeze blew in from the sparkling blue South China Sea, and it would have been a perfect day except for Ferdie's constant cheating.

Tanned, brown-haired "Gene" Eubank, 49, had a sparkle in his brown eyes and a broad grin that made it easy for Jim to believe the tales he had heard his friends' fathers tell of him. He remembered the exact words of one pilot, an "Early Bird," who had been stationed at Kelly Field, Texas, with Eubank and his friend Jimmy Doolittle. Around San Antonio, their colleague recounted, those two young lieutenants were infamous for "contour flying in minimum airspace, flying through hangars, doing vertical banks around the roof garden of the St. Anthony Hotel, or causing balloonists at Camp John Wise to hit the silk!"

Five points in The Dad Game for a hot pilot.

Later, Eubank had commanded the 2nd Bomb Group, flying the unpredictable old Keystone LB-5As at Langley Field, Virginia.

Jim loved to listen to the "hangar talk" of pilots, and now he relished the chance to overhear the cockpit conversation of these two "survivors." Like all members of the small fraternity of Army pilots, they had known each other for decades.

Now he learned that by coincidence the two had seen each other at Wake Island en route to the Philippines. Brereton, with Caldwell and Llewellyn, had taken off from San Francisco Bay on 21 October aboard Pan American's luxurious *Philippine Clipper;* after the stopover in Honolulu, they reached Midway Island on 25 October. Losing a "Dateline day," the *Clipper* reached Wake Island on 27 October and was joined there by a flight of three Philippines-bound B-17s led by Eubank, and by the first high winds and *Clipper*-rocking swells of "Brereton's typhoon."

Jim gathered from their conversation that Eubank had reported to General Brereton's room in Pan American's hotel, they had dined there together, and had spent the evening playing Liar's Dice with other waiting passengers. The typhoon then delayed the *Clipper's* departure until 31 October, when Brereton finally reached Guam; after two days there, the *Clipper* had been able to land in Manila Bay on the afternoon of 3 November. Eubank, who had led his trio of bombers south from Wake to Australia, landed at Clark Field the following day.

Watching the two men, Jim thought Eubank was like a kid at Christmas, as he showed the General the instrument panel and explained the wondrous functions represented thereon. They laughed as they reminisced about terrifying close calls while flying planes of wood and linen; Keystone bombers with a cruising speed of 90 miles per hour "with a good tail wind"; dead-stick landings in cow pastures; crack-ups; deafening Liberty engines; and the castor oil used as an airplane lubricant that was absorbed by their skin, causing diarrhea. Jim kept a book open on his lap (one his mother had insisted he bring, by a woman named Daisy Bates), and turned the pages occasionally so his eavesdropping would not seem obnoxiously evident.

Now Brereton said something that made Eubank laugh. Listening, Jim realized whom Eubank reminded him of — he looked like, sounded like, the beloved Oklahoma part-Cherokee cowboy humorist, Will Rogers.

And who wouldn't want to have Will Rogers for a father? If my part-Cherokee mother had married Will Rogers, I'd be at least a half-breed.

Ten points for Eubank's resemblance.

Jim stood up to stretch; this was the only place in the body of the plane where he could do so.

If this were wartime, I could be the Fire Control Officer. . . . And if I saw enemy planes on my right, I'd say — **calmly** *— on the interphone, "Bandits at three o'clock!" and the rest of the crew — there should be nine of us — would spring into action. Pilot and copilot would concentrate on completing the bombing mission, though hell should bar the way. Captain Ind would jump to one side of the dorsal bathtub and begin firing his fifty-caliber, with his butt bumping against the guy manning the twin Browning on the other side and no time for him to say "Excuse me." Lefty would perform the radio operator's*

Chapter 1 — Part 3 — Early Birds

combat job: firing the fifty-caliber from the radio compartment. The navigator would squeeze himself up through the hatch and maneuver himself along the catwalk to the bomb bay, reach up to the bombs hanging in the racks on either side, and pull out the firing pins of the bombs to be released. On the bomb run, the bombardier would peer into his secret-***secret-SECRET*** Norden bombsight, give directions to the pilot, and finally take full control of the plane over the target. If enemy fighters shot at us, or if we were hit by flak from the ground, and one of our gunners got wounded, the flight engineer would leap up from his jump seat and take over that Browning, firing pocketa-pocketa-pocketa. . . .

The new B-17Es would be better able to defend themselves than this D-model Fortress, Jim had to admit. Rumors described the E-series bomber as covered with blisters like a Tenderfoot Scout's feet after his first 30-mile hike. The Es even had a blister in the tail, where a tenth man, a "tail gunner," would serve.

Brereton, 51, dapper and youthful looking, with a round, shiny face, brown hair, magnetic, slightly protruding brown eyes and a quick, boyish grin, habitually spoke with a speed that reminded Jim of a machine gun. Now he yelled into Eubank's right ear:

"Speaking of primitive conditions — I could hardly believe there's *still* no landing field on Guam! Bob McMillan, the military governor, was in my 1911 class at the Naval Academy — had me to dinner all three nights the *Clipper* was stuck there. He said Congress finally gave 'em some dough for Guam, so they're starting to level a strip this month — but that sure didn't do your boys any good! How much mileage would you have saved if you could have landed at Guam and followed the *Clipper* route?"

"Two thousand . . . one hundred . . . and fifty-three miles, I figured. Multiply that by Rosie O'Donnell's nine bombers and my twenty-six ships, and you've burned a helluva lot of gas — plus the wear and tear on three hundred fifteen crew members. Actually, it was important to prove that it could be done, refueling at Port Moresby and Darwin, and I'm glad we did it. The awful, ancient charts just don't match up with the little islands; so our boys learned the importance of shooting the stars. Great training for the crews . . . but it might have been better to do it with just two or three Forts, rather than risking the entire Group. That's what I was thinking when we had to take our ships over the Jap-held islands in the eastern Carolines. We scheduled ourselves to overfly 'em in darkness at twenty six thousand feet, with no navigation lights — and complete radio silence! I was damned proud of those kids. If we were ever going to lose a straggler, that would have been the most likely place — and the worst."

"Yeah, sure would. McMillan, on Guam, is plenty leery of those islands we sweetly handed the Japs. Told me he's just seventy miles from a strongly fortified one — Saipan — and Guam's bare-ass naked, no defenses whatsoever. So he over-extended his authority as military governor and sent home *all* the American women and children — even civilians! He says the husbands hate his guts, but I think he's right."

Jim's squadron had buzzed a farewell to the USS *Henderson* as she steamed out of Manila Bay a couple of weeks earlier, on her homeward shuttle to the States. The old ship was riding high, lightly loaded to save room for the American women and children she would pick up at Guam.

The *Henderson,* now used as a transport by the Navy, held an honored place in Jim's affections — if not in the Navy's. From her decks in July 1921 as she stood off the Virginia capes, official observers from several nations had viewed the demonstration bombing of a war prize from the German Imperial fleet, the "unsinkable" battleship *Ostfriesland*. Seven Martin bombers, each carrying two 1,000-pound bombs, and directed by the outspoken champion of air power, Brigadier General William Landrum Mitchell, had left the battleship sunk by the stern in 21½ minutes. Mitchell claimed that his tests "had proved to the world that air power had revolutionized all schemes of national defense." The Japanese observers, expressing their admiration for the feat, had declared their intention to study this new concept.

Brereton continued, "I'm surprised High Commissioner Sayre apparently hasn't suggested that American civilian families should get the hell out of the Philippines —"

"Sayre's a diplomat. Doesn't want to alarm the Filipinos."

"Hell, it's *time* to alarm everybody! Not just the civilians, but the smug, ignorant foot-Army types. Sutherland won't give me permission to move the 19th Bomb Group down to Mindanao for safety. He uses the excuse that 'the war plan doesn't provide for any ground forces to defend Mindanao,' so the air force can't plan to base any aircraft there — only on Cebu and the *northern* islands. He can't see that if the bombers were five hundred miles south of Manila, they'd be out of range of the Jap planes on Formosa and wouldn't *need* Infantry troops to defend 'em! Besides, Clark will be crowded as hell when our new bomb squadron gets here, and the A-24s, by the end of this month."

Jim visualized the rich green paddy fields of the vast Pampanga Plain, from the Zambales mountains to the Sierra Madres, covered with gleaming new airplanes, wingtip to wingtip. The 7th Bombardment Squadron would soon bring 26 more Fortresses, and 52 Dauntless A-24 dive bombers were also on their way — awaited impatiently by the pilots and crews of the light bombardment group, who had already arrived in Manila.

Brereton continued, "Ever since I flew down to Mindanao — the minute I landed on the golf course of the pineapple plantation and saw that huge plateau — I've wanted to base our bombers there at Del Monte. Damn that smoothie Sutherland!"

Natalie Sutherland, beautiful and bright, with a crown of blonde curls and a store of mildly risqué jokes, was one of Jim's good friends. However, her handsome, aristocratic, and aloof father, Brigadier General Richard K. Sutherland — MacArthur's Chief of Staff — always gave Jim the impression that Sutherland suspected him of dishonorable designs on his only daughter.

Jess Villamor had told Jim that Sutherland was a more apt flying student than the popular Eisenhower; but evidently the experience of learning to fly had not enamored Sutherland of air power.

Like most Air Corps men, Jim resented the authority of the old ground-based Army. Mentally, he now applauded Brereton, who was known to be a disciple of General "Billy" Mitchell, the self-styled "crusader" for a separate air force. Eubank, too, was a Mitchell man, albeit a more diplomatic one; he'd been Mitchell's aide. Jim idolized Billy Mitchell and considered him a martyr, court-martialed, demoted, and banished to Texas for publicly charging the War and Navy Departments with "incompetency, criminal negligence, and almost treasonable administration of the national defense." Jim gave each of the officers in the cockpit ten points for Air Autonomy Advocacy.

Brereton continued, "And dammit, Gene — when we took off from Clark just now and I saw all your big silver birds shining in the moonlight, I thought they looked like sitting ducks. Scares the hell out of me. I told Rosie O'Donnell — if those bombers aren't *well* dispersed when we get back, I'm really going to chew ass."

"Lew, you know they have orders from me not to park off the airfield, and there isn't room *on* the field to decently disperse all the Forts. The whole of Pampanga province is just one giant wet rice field — we could never pull a 'Seventeen out of that knee-deep mud. Of course we've never been able to get a nickel to pay for drainage work around the perimeter."

"Hell, Clark Field just isn't ready for a first-class bomb squadron. I told 'em in Washington, it was crazy to send those Forts out here without some real anti-aircraft and decent fighter protection —"

Decent fighter protection! Jim thought. *General, the 20th Pursuit Squadron is all the protection you'll ever need. Give the man minus five points for chickenshit dispersal fussiness. He's as Jap-scared as an old lady.*

Eubank continued, "Hap Arnold's had a lot of people mad at him for sending the 'Seventeens out here. Everybody in the States, naturally, wanted to keep 'em there. And in Hawaii — they're really cussing us for 'stealing' their bombers."

"Yeah, they complained to me that Hickam Field's been downgraded to a refueling station for B-17s en route to Clark Field! I don't blame 'em for griping. They told me the Army has a total of only two hundred thirty-one planes — in all the islands of Hawaii — with the whole damned Pacific Fleet to protect."

"Poor Bill Farthing's getting into a lousy job. I feel sorry for him."

Colonel William E. Farthing had been ordered to take command of Hickam Field, Honolulu, in two weeks. His son, Bill Junior, as tall and dark-haired as Jim and a longtime friend, was now a cadet at West Point. Mrs. Farthing had invited Jim to spend Christmas with them at Hickam while Bill would be there on vacation, and Jim was planning to do so — unless he could join Daphne in Singapore for Christmas.

Although Daphne was freer to travel than Jim, he had not invited her to Manila because of his mother's "Limey allergy."

"Yeah," Brereton agreed, "Farthing's going to have both the Army and the Navy on his ass. But I feel sorrier for *me* in *my* job. Gene, I'm going below and try to get some shut-eye, if you'll try to keep this bus straight and level. I'll send Llewellyn up to play copilot."

"That's OK — I see Lieutenant Davis isn't busy. He can come up here for awhile."

Part 4 — Navigation Lesson

The German victories have inspired Japan's militarists as a "golden opportunity to carry their dreams of expansion into effect."
— U.S. Ambassador to Japan Joseph Grew, 12 September 1940

Mindoro, Panay, and Negros Islands, east of the plane's course above the Sulu Sea, had passed beneath the gold and crimson glory of a plane-surrounding tropical sunrise. Now the verdant Zamboanga Peninsula — the proboscis of Mindanao — lay to port, with Borneo's dark green mountains to starboard. Fortunately for Jim, when Eubank called him into the right-hand seat, the Sulu Archipelago was still visible below, like a scattering of rough-cut emeralds, and he was able to identify the main "pirate islands" by their shape and position.

"That's the ticket — know your terrain," Eubank said. "Flying in open cockpits in the States, you could never keep a map from blowing out; you had to know the rivers and the railroads, and fly by them. You knew how the look of the different states changed with the seasons — if you were looking down at wheat or cotton, or Texas bluebonnets. In the East, in the spring, if the hillsides were pink, you knew you were over Pennsylvania apple orchards. If you saw white, it was Virginia, with dogwood trees blooming."

Jim had never seen a dogwood tree: an ugly name, he thought. He had never seen the Celebes Sea, either; and now above that mysterious area he received his first lessons in Eubank-style navigation. Unlike most airplane pilots he had known, the Colonel actually enjoyed the arcane art.

As a boy, Jim had learned something of sailboat navigation when he lived at Lake Lanao on Mindanao Island, while his parents, with Dr. Frank Laubach, taught Muslim Moro adults to read. In return, the Moros — superb sailors, pirates, and smugglers for centuries — had taught Jim some of their ancient skills in reading the winds, stars, clouds, and swells. That was wonderful fun; but he had never seen any connection between the Moros' almost intuitive methods and the picky minutiae of flying-school navigation. Now, however, shooting the sun on the day-sextant, staring down through the drift meter, checking airspeed and altitude, spinning the cardboard E-6-B ground speed computer, he caught some of his mentor's enthusiasm and urgency. Eubank had to compensate for the same strong east winds that had swept some of the northbound Fortresses almost 100 miles off course.

Until we get into range of a radio, Jim thought, *he's really going to get this sophisticated ship and her sophisticated passengers to Darwin just the way a Moro would sail there in a* **vinta** *— by dead reckoning, with some important assists from these gadgets and a stopwatch. . . . But a sailboat can always wait for a breeze — if we run out of gas south of the Celebes, the last islands big enough for this behemoth to land on, we've* **had** *it.*

Jim had the honor of announcing, "It looks as if we should be over the Equator right now, Sir!"

He heard a few cheers, but none of the "shellbacks" (Eubank, Lefty, Ind, and Jim) who had crossed it before suggested inflicting an initiation ceremony on General Brereton and his two aides.

Eubank also showed Jim how, with the cowl flaps closed, he was stretching his fuel by feeding the leanest mixture possible, adjusting his settings to decrease the revolutions per minute and increase the manifold pressure, employing minimum applied Cruise Control, and taking advantage of the best winds, best altitude, and most efficient airspeed.

"Knowing how to wean an engine to the last drop saved some of my good friends during the damned Air Mail massacre," Eubank reminisced.

When Jim was 14, President Roosevelt — piqued over the increased demands of U.S. airlines — had abruptly canceled all domestic air mail contracts and assigned to the unprepared Army Air Corps the duty of carrying the air mail. Jim remembered the shock and sorrow in his friends' homes as the news came almost daily of crashes of their fathers' colleagues, flying in the open cockpits of inferior airplanes over unfamiliar routes at night in vicious February weather. In the first week, eight Army planes were wrecked, six pilots severely injured, and five killed. By the end of the third week, 10 deaths had resulted from more than 20 accidents. One of Jim's heroes, Captain Eddie Rickenbacker — a World War ace who had shot down 26 German planes — now president of a commercial carrier, Eastern Airlines, termed the switch "legalized murder." The toll continued to mount until June, when the airlines resumed the function.

Eubank's face looked weary. "It wasn't a war, so there's no monument to those men. Those of us who knew 'em are the only ones who remember their names now — and their families, of course. But to me they were heroes, just as much as if they'd been killed in a war. They did what the President ordered them to, even though a lot of those flights were clearly suicide missions. Imagine flying in the Rockies at night in a P-12, with no instrument but a turn-and-bank indicator — no directional gyro, not even an artificial horizon! If you ran into a sleet storm, that was it, that's all she wrote. For fuel economy, because of the Depression budget, our pilots hadn't been allowed to fly the twenty-five hours a month that's essential for proficiency. And the civilian airlines had radios that could receive from almost four hundred miles; but if you were lucky enough to draw an Army plane that had a radio, it only received from right below you — nothing more than thirty miles away."

"Yes, Sir."

"Well, at least, our buddies' lives weren't wasted. Their deaths aroused the American public, and they put pressure on their Congressmen to give the Army some decent planes and radios and equipment. Not *equal* to the commercial airlines, but a helluva lot better than the coffins we'd been flying."

"Yes, Sir."

Part 5 — Timor!

Without a declaration of war and without warning or justification . . . civilians, including vast numbers of women and children, are being ruthlessly murdered with bombs from the air. . . . If those things come to pass in other parts of the world, let no one imagine that America will escape, that Americans may expect mercy.
— President Franklin D. Roosevelt, October 1937

The monotony of long hours in brilliant tropical blue sky over unchanging dark blue ocean was punctuated by turbulence that increased in ferocity as the B-17 neared Darwin, located on the "equatorial disturbance" track. Thunderheads here might stretch higher than 40,000 feet — above the B-17D's limit of 36,000 — and Eubank flew around them, using up precious fuel, with the risk of getting off course and becoming disoriented. The ingenious Automatic Pilot was no help. And now, when they needed it most, the searching "bird dog" radio compass betrayed them: Lured by lightning, its pointer spun in wild confusion.

At times the plane's occupants were shaken about like dice in a bar-cup. Jim was impressed by — and thankful for — the steady strength of the four Wright engines and of the pilot. He learned that there was far more to do when flying through weather than to "cage the altitude indicator and fly with needle, ball, and airspeed," as he had been taught in flying school.

"A lot of pilots of my vintage," Eubank told him, "felt that using instruments was sort of a sissified way to fly. I disagree — especially since I notice that some of those manly fliers aren't around any more."

Eubank remained in the left seat all day, while each of the other men — except Captain Ind — had several chances to serve as copilot.

Jim's stints in the right-hand seat seemed to grow too short as he gained confidence, under Eubank's patient tutelage, and familiarity with the aircraft. But the bomber was so heavy on the controls and its responses were so sluggish, he knew he could never feel a real rapport with it.

*You can **admire** an elephant,* he thought, *but a polo pony is to love! I could probably fly a P-12 blind, coast to coast, like Ira Eaker. But this buxom baby, "She's too fat for me!" Straight and level is hard work, and the idea of making a hundred eighty-degree turn — or a **landing** — is intimidating.*

Flying over the Banda Sea, they could see in the distance on their left the dark green bases of New Guinea's mountains below a thick bank of cloud.

Cannibal country! And I'll be there by Saturday, Jim thought with anticipation.

Finally Eubank indicated, to starboard, what looked to Jim like a long thin dill pickle floating in the mustard glow of the descending sun over the Arafura Sea.

"That's Timor. Only five hundred miles left till Darwin."

Timor!

Five times, Jim had seen the movie *Mutiny on the Bounty*. He could perform a fair imitation of Charles Laughton as Captain Bligh — near-dead, haggard, obsessed — yelling in hoarse exultation, after 41 days and 3,618 miles of superb navigation in that 23-foot launch with his "loyal" men:

"It's *Timor,* lads!"

In Jim's mind, the island's name was always an exclamation.

Timor also had served as landfall for another flawed man and renowned navigator: Fred Noonan, chosen by Amelia Earhart to plot the course for her fatal round-the-Equator flight — when Jim was 17 and deeply in love with the beautiful, courageous pilot.

From here on, their B-17 would follow AE's sky-trail, from Darwin to New Guinea.

Sacred ground . . . sacred air . . . Earhart, air-heart, heart of air. . . .

Jim had felt cockpit-close to AE that June of 1937 in Manila, as she flew across Asia toward him, seemingly transmitting to him personally on 3105 kilocycles — by voice, not Morse. Devotedly, he had monitored — monsoon static permitting — her Kansas-crisp reports from KHAQQ, the voice of her silver Electra. From Akyab, Burma (her Stop #19), to Rangoon, Bangkok, Singapore; then south to Java and that long week of repairs at Bandung, and on: to Timor, Darwin, Lae, and . . . *where?*

Years before AE's flight, Timor, 512 miles northwest of Darwin, had served as the guidepost to Australia for air pioneers from England in open cockpits, during the golden days of record-breaking flights before war broke out in Europe. And Darwin itself, as the destination-dream of so many of Jim's heroes, had acquired in his mind an almost mythical aura. It was altogether fitting, he thought, that such a lodestone city should bear the name of a great discoverer, the globe-circling naturalist.

In 1919, before Jim was born, the brothers Ross and Keith Smith had been the first to fly from England to Darwin. It was Bert Hinkler, flying alone, nine years later, who had captured the imagination of eight-year-old Jimmy during Hinkler's flight across Europe and Asia, making less than 600 miles daily, reaching Darwin in 15 days.

Jim thought of Francis Chichester at age 28, unable to afford a parachute, flying "solo to Sydney" in January 1930 after only five months of flying lessons in England: locating that green pickle of an island; peering with myopic eyes from the windy cockpit of the little Gipsy Moth he called "Elijah," searching for the landing field at Atemboea.

There on Timor, Chichester learned that his rivals, Moir and Owen, having flown from England in their Vickers Vimy, had come through Timor ahead of him, beating him to Darwin. Now they would surely beat him to Sydney; and they did — but not easily. On his own arrival at Darwin, Chichester would discover that Moir and Owen had missed the landing field in the dark and made a crash landing in the lighthouse-keeper's potato patch.

That was only eleven years ago . . . and now look at this B-17's monstrous instrument panel!

Chichester had listed his instruments as "a speed indicator, oil gauge, level, altimeter, rev-counter, and compass." He preferred to fly using only rudder, for he said, "fiddling with the joy stick is the chief cause of fatigue, causing bad landings." He figured his wind-drift by means of lines painted on the wings: a drift-line for every 5 degrees, up to 30 degrees. With no radio and no real navigation aids, Chichester's safe arrival at Timor from England seemed to Jim a triumph of navigation equal to Captain Bligh's.

Amy Johnson, 27, also had flown solo from England — in the green Moth she called "Jason." Above this Sea of Timor, struggling through a heavy overcast with a faltering engine, she grimly had muttered nursery rhymes to hold down her fear. Called "the Lone Dove" by the press, Amy won Jim's heart by landing at Darwin (after 19½ days of flying) on his tenth birthday, 24 May 1930, although a few days later she disappointed him by crash-landing at Brisbane.

Jim was 14 when New Zealand's petite Jean Batten, 25, flew solo over Timor in a five-year-old Gipsy Moth, headed for her native island (and breaking Amy Johnson's record to Darwin by four days). Taking off from Sydney across the wild Tasman Sea, she reached Auckland in 10½ hours; there almost the entire population of both islands greeted her. Newsreels showed Jean at a celebration given by the local Maori people, who presented her with the Kiwi-feather cloak of a chief and named her *Hine-o-te-Rangi:* Daughter of the Sky.

Jean Batten was well qualified for her radio assignment later that year, when she spoke from Melbourne as "the voice of the Great Centennial Air Race." During those ten exciting days of October 1934, Jim ate all his meals beside his radios in his bedroom, unwilling to miss a word of Jean's bulletins or her descriptions of the flying conditions and terrain that she herself so recently had mastered. Of the 64 entries and 20 actual starters, 2 were killed; 11 planes, all flown by men, completed the Mildenhall-to-Melbourne course. Amy Johnson and her husband Jim Mollison, in a de Havilland Comet, had dropped out at Allahabad; and Jacqueline Cochran was grounded at Bucharest in a Granville. The winners, flying a DH Comet for 2 days and 23 hours, were C.W.A. Scott and Beryl Markham's close friend Tom Campbell Black. To Jim's delight, Americans Roscoe Turner and Clyde Pangborn, in an American Boeing, were judged "second in speed." Not all contestants made the 30 October deadline, however. Parer and Hemsworth landed their Fairey Fox in Darwin 8 February 1935.

* * * * *

At last the B-17's faithful bird-dog needle stopped its fruitless circling and pointed decisively to zero. Station KAZ, Port Darwin, lay exactly where Eubank had plotted it, and now he tracked southward following its transmission.

Later, in the tiny radio room, when they were close enough to hear KAZ's voice broadcast, Lefty told Jim, "When we land, we'll need an interpreter — I can hardly understand what the announcer's talking about!"

"It gets easier — I got pretty good at translating ''Strine' in Singapore last summer," Jim responded. "McDonald must have learned to communicate with the RAAF while he's been stranded in Darwin — and Pell can interpret for us, too."

Floyd Joaquin Pell of Ogden, Utah, had preceded the Brereton party, flying a Douglas B-18 down from Clark Field. Incongruously nicknamed "Slugger," Pell was a Captain, but a gentleman, nevertheless, Jim thought, and he bore his rank lightly.

Darwin Bay, south of Melville and Bathurst Islands, was about two miles wide at its entrance and formed a fine natural harbor where several small freighters were waiting their turn at the port's lone pier. The mid-afternoon sun burnished a reddish haze that obscured the low shoreline.

But where the hell's the city?

The Flying Fortress, lightly loaded as now, and with little fuel remaining, probably weighed only 13 or 14 tons — about half its operational weight, but still too heavy for Darwin's civil airport or the field at RAAF Station Darwin. After 14 hours of flying, Eubank would continue 45 miles south of the port to Batchelor Field, a raw red gash newly hacked out of the grassy plain. There was no control tower; the sole building was a wooden shack in a clump of dusty trees southeast of the runway.

Eubank's pre-landing checklist sounded interminable to Jim, who preferred the brevity of "GUMP" for his own P-40 landing reminders: Gas, Undercarriage, Mixture, Propeller.

The huge plane seemed to float over the strip as Eubank flared for his landing, and — with gear down and full flaps and windows open to create drag — touched down lightly, and brought it to a halt before he ran out of runway. Behind him, Jim mentally tromped on brakes until the bomber stopped in a cloud of red dust. "Over the fence and dirty," he heard Eubank say.

Immediately, the plane's metal skin began to crackle as it warmed to an egg-frying heat. As he dropped to the ground through the nose hatch, Jim encountered a mid-afternoon air temperature over 95 degrees, a lungful of powdery red dust, and squadrons of clinging, buzzing flies. His back was stiff from sitting so long; his legs felt rubbery, and he craved a shower.

Jim thought longingly of the cases of San Miguel they had brought for the Australian senior officers; it would be good and cold now.

This is a lousy opening act for our Mission in Mufti. I wish to hell **we** *could wear shorts!*

Frederick Scherger, Commanding Officer of the Royal Australian Air Force Station Darwin, welcomed the Americans cordially; his shoulder-boards bore the eight stripes of a Group Captain. He wore a pith helmet, short-sleeved khaki shirt open at the neck, and the type of wide-legged khaki shorts Jim had seen in Singapore, with knee socks. Similarly dressed was Brigadier D.V.J. Blake, the Commander of Darwin's Army garrison, except that his shoulder-boards had three small diamonds surmounted by a crown.

The officers from the three RAAF squadrons might have been selected by a Hollywood casting director for a flying movie, Jim thought: They all seemed to be his own height or taller, tanned, blond, blue-eyed, with friendly grins revealing flashing white teeth, and muscular legs extending from their baggy shorts.

Even more stunning were the young women — the first Jim had ever seen wearing military uniforms — tall, tanned blondes with glorious blue eyes and toothpaste smiles, modestly displaying lovely calves and ankles below tailored skirts.

Amazons! With gorgeous gams! What a challenge!

Even in such handsome company, Slugger Pell's good looks and athletic

Chapter 1 — Part 5 — Timor! 31

body stood out. Pell was the only American Jim knew who had ever been to Australia; he'd be a trusty guide for this was his second trip. The first time, he had made all the arrangements for the 19th Bombardment Group's mass landings en route to the Philippines. Barrels of high-octane gasoline for 35 thirsty B-17s, and beds, food, and liquids for the 315 fliers were scarce in isolated Port Moresby and Darwin; in the Australians' hospitality the "Yanks" unknowingly drank the garrison's entire beer ration.

Now, on even shorter notice, Pell had arranged for the Brereton party's greetings, meetings, housing, and runway space at six Australian air bases.

Beside Slugger stood an American Captain who had to be McDonald; his expression bespoke the mingled relief and apology of a pilot whose Commanding Officer has arrived with replacements for two damaged triple-bladed propellers.

The groups dispersed quickly into several parked Hudson bombers (termed "Export A-29s" by the Americans) to fly back to Darwin. Jim flew with Pell, who told him that en route down from Clark Field in the B-18 he had refueled at Santa Barbara Field on Panay Island; Del Monte plantation on Mindanao; Tarakan, Balik Papan, and Sandakan in Borneo; and Koepang on Timor.

"Too bad you couldn't fly down in a *real* airplane," Jim said. "After seventeen hundred miles, we still had a coupla gallons of Clark Field gas left when we landed. But I'll admit, it sure feels good to stand up and stretch! I've got a serious case of jump-seat rump."

"I've got just the cure for that. Did you bring your racquet?"

Soon after Slugger had arrived in Manila in June 1940, he had taught Jim to play the fast-paced racquet game of squash at the Army-Navy YMCA gym in the Walled City. After Pell's previous "trail-blazing" trip Down Under, he had told Jim that the sports-loving Australians possessed an abundance of squash courts.

"Hell, yes — I'm wearing gym shorts under my flying suit. I do need to work out the kinks, but I don't need to work up a thirst — I've got a huge one already."

McDonald said, "The RAAF squadrons have been saving their beer ration for you 'Yank visitors' —"

"Greater love hath no Aussie," said Slugger, who did not drink.

"— It's dark and kind of bitter, but it grows on you," McDonald continued.

"Anything wet will taste OK, after I beat Slugger five games."

And tomorrow, I'll search for traces of Amelia.

CHAPTER 2

Part 1 — Desolate Darwin

Darwin seems to be the end of the world . . . the town itself is a series of wooden, hutlike houses; the stores have practically nothing to sell; there are bars with no beer; you can't buy a cigarette in the entire town. . . . The land is very flat and everywhere the trees are bent from the wind, and there are cur dogs with drooping tails. It is a depressing place. There is no entertainment. Literally nothing.

— Cecil Brown, *Suez to Singapore*, 1942

Darwin, Northern Territory
Wednesday, 12 November 1941

Today will be Darwin Ladies' Day for me, Jim anticipated, thinking of the stunning Amazonian airwomen he had met yesterday. But now, while the comely WAAAF telegraphers were on duty — and he was mercifully excused from the technical discussions with the RAAF officers — he hoped to see this corner of the continent through the eyes of the two most remarkable women he knew of who had passed this way.

To start, he would try to follow up a lead given to him at last night's Welcome-Yanks party. Fortunately, he had made his inquiries early in the evening; for after the RAAF had demonstrated how well they had learned "The Army Air Corps Song" from the Clark-bound 19th Bombardment

Group — and had taught the Brereton group some of their own rousing ballads — very little non-musical knowledge had been exchanged.

Why had Amelia Earhart remained in this backwater for an unscheduled extra day?

Now that Jim had glimpsed Darwin, the mystery deepened: Why would anyone choose to linger in this fly-bitten dump? Of course, he thought, AE must have enjoyed the unequaled warmth of an Australian welcome. But she already had received welcomes of equatorial warmth while traversing two-thirds of the globe, and she rarely had alighted for longer than overnight.

If any living person knew why, it might be retired RAAF Sergeant Werner Fredericks. He had worked on the Electra that June four years ago, alongside Sergeant Stan Rose, now departed. Fredericks still lived in Darwin, and Jim was excited at the possibility of meeting someone who actually had seen AE. No address necessary, "Just ask any bloke on the footpath," Jim had been told.

Although it was still too early to call on Fredericks, the day was already scorching hot when Jim opened the door of his room in the Hotel Darwin, Ltd. Each bedroom in the small, white-painted frame building opened on a narrow wraparound unscreened verandah. The hotel was subsidized by the Queensland and Northern Territory Aerial Services (QANTAS). Before he had taken a step across the low porch he was surrounded by a noisy squadron of black flies, which evidently had orders to attack his eyes as their primary targets, with his mouth, nose, and ears as alternates.

"Wanna royde, myte?"

Jim gladly climbed into the cab of the Army lorry; the driver willingly accepted a Lucky, and they both smoked lustily in an attempt to keep the flies at bay.

The driver estimated "probably about sixteen hundred white Aussie civilians — all of 'em cows," lived in Darwin.

Downtown Darwin consisted of a row of one-story unpainted wooden shops on each side of the main street. A sign identified P.H. Mendis, Pearl Merchant; but Jim was more intrigued by the adjacent Blue Bell Squash Shop. He had never seen a store devoted to equipment for that game and he wondered if Slugger Pell had checked out the stock.

He was surprised to see Mura's, a Japanese-owned "Foto Studio." The preponderance of Chinese shops would be normal anywhere else in Asia, but here in "White Australia" he had not expected to find such as Barney Chan's Oriental Cafe, PASTRY A SPECIALTY; Man Fong Lau & Co., EXPERT TAILORING; and on the corner, TOBACCONIST, PATENT MED., DRAPER & OUTFITTER, Sun Cheong Loong.

"Fucking robbers, all of 'em, except the Jolly Shop," the driver said.

THE JOLLY SHOP — SELLS EVERYTHING looked to Jim like a sad shop, resembling a weathered wooden storefront on a Western-movie set.

Compared with Darwin, Jim thought, the dreariest little towns of West Texas would appear as gardens of Eden.

For Caucasian dining, The Moonlight Cafe offered late suppers, the American Service Co. specialized in "Hamburghers," and Kyriakos' Tropical Delicatessen tempted with Cold Suppers — ZERO IN THE TROPICS!

"No worries," the driver said. "Every fucking forty years a cyclone destroyes this barstid humpy-town, and it has to be rebuilt from the ground up."

"Maybe they'll make it look better next time," Jim said. He was accustomed to the annual Philippine typhoons that left thousands homeless; but rebuilding a Filipino house was easy. Bamboo was free for the cutting, as were *nipa* palm for thatch, rattan strips to tie the frame together, and neighbors helping each other. And the result, he thought, was attractive and cool. Here, however, there were few trees large enough for lumber.

Nearer the harbor lay the administrative buildings, each with a sagging wooden verandah running the length of the front. However, as they were unscreened against the swarming flies, Jim figured that the porches were merely decorative.

The driver identified the courthouse. "Busier than it looks. The only thing Darwin's got plenty of, is crime. Bloody town's full of fucking thieves — no-hopers and smugglers, stealing from each other and from the Army. And the 'Abos'' favorite sport is to eat men from other tribes, or even their own. The chiefs of two tribes are both in the town jail now — 'Bullblow' and 'McGlah' they call themselves, both in for murder — and both of 'em swear that when they get out they'll eat each other's liver."

Next door to the courthouse sat a more spruced-up wooden building with the additional distinction of a thorny but flourishing lime tree in its dusty yard. "Nyvy headquarters," the driver told Jim. "They keep a bloody gunner on guard inside that window at night, to shoot any bloke tryin' to swipe a bloody lime."

He explained that the fruit was prized because the only way to concoct a potable drink from the infamous Philippine "synthetic gin," smuggled here by Filipino sailors, was to cut its kerosene flavor with lime juice.

In the distance beyond the bay, purple islands looked more attractive than any man-made parts of Darwin — until the driver pointed out an island used as a leper colony.

Jim looked quickly away. When he was 12, his babyhood wet-nurse *amah,* Saadra, had been sent to the Philippine leper island of Culion when white patches on her skin were confirmed as leprosy. He had sailed his boat alone, without permission, to see her, and he still had nightmares about the place and its ravaged inmates.

A worn wooden sign offered the rental of the auxiliary launch, *Violet,* by the day or hour.

"Do you ever explore the beaches?" Jim asked the lorry driver.

The man shook his head. "If the fucking flies don't eat you alive, the croc-o-fucking-diles will."

Darwin's lone dock, as Jim had observed from the air, extended into the bay for an unusually long stretch.

"That's because of the bloody *toyde,* myte," the driver explained, showing him the high-tide marks on the cliffs. The tidal flow rose and fell to a maximum of 28 feet, he said.

Everything's extreme in this country, Jim thought, getting out to look around. On an impulse, he offered the remainder of his pack of Luckies to the driver, who accepted them with a wide grin.

"Ta," he said.

The headland seemed like a giant diving board, a true jumping-off place, with the blue waters of the Sea of Timor before him, merging into the Arafura Sea on his right and the blue-green Indian Ocean on his left.

Only five ships lay in the harbor. Farther out, a tanker with a peacetime name, *British Motorist,* evidently waited for high tide to bring her in safely. A three-masted lugger, *Mavie,* was putting up sail, while a naval tug, *Wato,* nudged a barge called *Kelat.* The activity on the wharf involved two ships, one on either side. A motor vessel, *Neptuna,* was being offloaded at the same time as a freighter, *Barossa,* from whose holds wooden piles were being noisily winched to the dock.

Those logs probably get a top shipping priority, he thought — *higher than food or beer for the troops. Nothing can be built here without those underpinnings, and they sure can't do anything with these poor stunted local trees.*

Yesterday he had noticed that every structure at RAAF Station Darwin — all wooden, except the two metal hangars — was raised on piles topped with metal shields as termite barriers. Today he had observed the same precautions in the town.

He wondered if Australian termites were really, as the lorry driver had claimed, the most voracious in the world. Could they possibly be worse than the *anay* that the ManilAmericans called "white ants," which had silently eaten the mahogany floor of his home to a paper thinness, first discovered when a dinner guest's chair crunched through during dessert?

Why should good people like the Australians and the Filipinos have to put up with termites — while in lucky Japan wooden temples stand un-chewed for hundreds of years? Maybe we could make the troublesome Japs stay in their own back yard if we threatened to send a B-17 over Kyoto with its bomb bays loaded with termites.

A few Aboriginals were working on the dock, wearing only loincloths. They were well-muscled, dark, and surprisingly large; Jim had expected them to be pygmies, like the Aboriginal tribesmen he knew in the Philippine mountains. Their eyes were deep-set, under jutting brows that resembled photographs of the mysterious stone heads of Easter Island.

God knows they need that overhanging protection from this blinding sunlight. . . . Am I seeing an example in Darwin of Darwinian adaptation? Did their skulls grow that way to shade their eyes?

An Aboriginal woman shuffled up to him on bare feet; she wore a filthy cotton dress on a dirty, grossly fat body. Tapping two dark fingers on her lips, she asked silently for a cigarette. He opened a new pack and gave her one, then obeyed her motion of striking a match and lighted it for her.

He felt as disappointed as he had been as a child traveling eastward from California the first time on a train. AmerIndians, as fat, unkempt, and stinking as this woman, had gathered under the open windows when the train stopped at dusty platforms in Arizona. They held up crude flat figures of painted clay: "Indian dolls" with black hair emerging in a tuft from a hole in the top of each head — for sale to the travelers. Reared on his mother's tales that glorified the Cherokee, Jim was bitterly disillusioned, until she convinced him that it was only contact with the white man that had brought the people to this sorry state. On the reservation, Leda assured him, there still dwelt noble red men.

Jim walked to the ramp where the QANTAS Empire Airways four-engine flying boat *Camilla,* of the Singapore run, was moored.

How ridiculous it was, he thought, that no civil airline linked this continent with the Philippines — or with the States — though Pan Am had a regular *Clipper* run to New Zealand. Australia wouldn't give landing rights to any American airline, because QANTAS wasn't allowed to land its flying boats in Hawaii.

Is that because giant, global Pan American Airways fears competition from dinky little Queensland and Northern Territories Aerial Services?

He was struck by a tempting thought: *Wouldn't it be swell to fly to Singapore in the luxury of an Empire flying boat — the gleaming* **Camilla** *or her sister — with comfortable seats, a crew of five to do all the work, and the stewards pampering the passengers as only British stewards can? Daphne could be at Kallang Aerodrome to greet me after a dramatic splashdown in Keppel Harbour. . . . No prissy English reserve in that girl; she would fling herself into my arms for rapturous hugs and long, warm, welcoming kisses.*

However — since no Flying Fortress had ever landed on Singapore — the prestige of being on the historic first flight would ease the discomfort of flying the 2,080 miles from Darwin to RAAF Seletar Aerodrome in B-17 No. 40-3097.

Even the arrogant, ever-so-blasé Limeys will have to be impressed; though they'd never say anything more enthusiastic than "Bit of all right, that kite."

You're as prejudiced as Leda! Jim scolded himself.

Exposed since his childhood to his mother's Irish hatred of the English, Jim had been struggling since summer to view them more fairly. He had never really known many of the breed until the July trip, and meeting Daphne that first evening at the Raffles had begun a prejudice-shedding experience. Although some of the staff officers he had observed in General Percival's and Chief Air Marshal Brooke-Popham's headquarters seemed to him like models for the caricature of Colonel Blimp, he also had met many Englishmen — and women — who were warm, honorable, intelligent, good sports, possessed of a subtle, dead-pan humor that delighted him.

*Leda would be pleased to see me marry a girl of any nationality but that one, goddammit. She could accept an Asian, Eurasian, Amerasian, Jewish, European, or African daughter-in-law — **anything** but a blue-eyed Englishwoman.*

When she had learned that Brigadier General Henry Clagett had ordered Jim to accompany him to the English bastion of Singapore, his mother had been so furious that Jim thought she would wreck his chance of making the trip. She had invited General Clagett to dinner, knowing his longtime appreciation of the culinary artistry of Wing, the family's cook. Like all of Clagett's old friends, Leda called the portly, booming-voiced general by his incongruous West Point nickname, "Sue," and at the table she had launched into a diatribe:

"Don't you know *why* 'the sun never sets on the goddam British Empire'? Because Providence can't trust those bastards in the dark! It kills me to see you stumbling into the lion's den — poor, trusting, American dupes, playing into the hands of the lousy Limeys. Listen, Sue, are you going to sell my son — and your son-in-law, and all the other American pilots and soldiers here — down the river, to those conniving devils who claim one-fourth of the globe as their own? Hells bells, is American blood going to be shed to preserve the stinking British Empire?"

Evidently General Clagett's enjoyment of Nine-Spice Chicken — followed by Wing's hand-cranked mango ice cream, Leda's best brandy, and Alexander's mellow Tabacalera cigars — together with his long friendship for Jim's parents, were sufficient to keep his famous temper calmed.

"DON'T WORRY ABOUT US!" he assured Leda in the voice that seemed better suited to reducing top sergeants to jelly than to engaging in secret diplomacy. "That's why I'm taking Jim along — so he can report to YOU when we get back! If he sees me offering to sell the store to the British, he'll stop me — won't you, Jim?"

* * * * *

Geography is Destiny, Jim mused, feeling quite profound. *If Darwin wasn't* located on the farthest northwest tip of this continent, there wouldn't be **anything** here — and there almost isn't, anyway. Yeah, it has one of the world's finest harbors, but a harbor needs a hospitable hinterland to back it up.

Now Jim realized what a challenge Slugger Pell had faced when he had arranged for the stopovers here of the 35 B-17s and their crews en route from the U.S. to Clark Field. The modest Darwin Hotel where Brereton's party was staying could not cope with that influx, and the RAAF officers and men had turned over their own barracks to the Americans. The hospitable Australians had probably slept in tents, along with the damned flies, Jim surmised.

In an odd way, Darwin in its isolation reminded him of Chungking: Although both were parts of a continent, each seemed to him like an *island* a thousand miles from civilization. Both were perched on high promontories above moving water; but downriver from Chungking, the Great River, the Yangtze, was held by the enemy. As the Burma Road was the only lifeline of blockaded Chungking, the sea was Darwin's; for the town was supplied entirely by ship.

Every can of beans, every gallon of "petrol," every cigarette must travel here by freighter for 3,000 miles, from the productive cities in the southeast.

No wonder they don't paint their houses, he realized; *in the space occupied by one gallon of paint you could pack six bottles of that dark, strong XXXX beer from Brisbane!*

Jim was accustomed to the months of delay in getting U.S. products to the Philippines by sea — but at least Manila produced its own delicious San Miguel beer. Fruits and vegetables grew abundantly in the islands, whereas nothing seemed to grow here at "The Top End."

Adelaide, *the* west coast city, lay 2,230 miles to the south; farther than Singapore or Manila: each about 2,080 miles north.

Hell, they should import San Miguel from Manila, and save their own shipping space for other stuff — and then Darwin wouldn't need to ration beer. I'll bet it wouldn't take them long to acquire a taste for it.

Due to its location, Darwin was now a military "boom town," where thousands of members of the Australian Imperial Force (AIF) restlessly waited for sailing orders. The strength of the garrison was reported officially as "forty thousand to fifty thousand," and Jim, who had never been surrounded by so many white men, thought fifty thousand seemed a low estimate. However, Captain Ind, ever the questioning Intelligence Officer, had suggested to him privately that in view of Australia's sparse population of seven million — "about the size of New York City's" — perhaps the Darwin numbers were inflated to impress Japan.

Jim had learned from the Australians in Singapore and Malaya that their military presence represented a mere fraction of the Diggers who were away from home. More than 120,000 volunteers were serving alongside British troops — most of them in heavy combat — in the Middle East and North Africa. Their absence had raised Jim's hopes of finding a nation of lonely, sex-starved, beautiful young Australian women who would be eager for brief, intense affairs with an attractive Yank pilot during each stop on his trip. The women in military service stationed here — Nursing Sisters, Navy women, Army women, and airwomen — were fully as glorious as his fantasies: so tall, so blonde, so tanned, blue-eyed, long-eyelashed, and bosomy, that he was constantly reminded of the Nazi propaganda film, *Mädchen in Uniform*. They were friendly, too. But the men-to-women ratio was all wrong: about 5,000 to 1, it seemed to him.

Australia had been at war for more than two years now, having declared war simultaneously with England when Germany invaded Poland. Although this nation had a military draft for home defense, "conscripts" were exempt from overseas duty. All these AIF men were volunteers, poised here in case a surprise Japanese attack on Singapore or the Netherlands East Indies should create a need for emergency reinforcements.

These were the world's highest paid soldiers, Captain Ind had told Jim, receiving the equivalent of U.S. $62 monthly in the lowest ranks. American buck privates, as Jim well knew, recently had had their pay doubled from $21 to $42. The German boots that had trampled Europe were worn by soldiers paid $21.60 — opposed now in Africa by British troops on a stipend of $12.20. The Japanese infantryman who had conquered vast areas of China and now threatened the colonial empires of the Far East was paid 37 cents a month.

"And the poor Chinese Nationalist soldiers get robbed of their pittance by their rotten officers," Jim had told Ind. "They have to loot the countryside to keep from starving."

In Shanghai in 1932, after the Japanese attack on the city, 12-year-old Jimmy had seen Chinese peasant boys his own size, refugees from devastated Chapei, forcefully "recruited" into Chiang, Kai-shek's army despite their screams and struggles. However, Jim knew better than to tell Captain Ind about the Red soldiers of the People's Army whom he had seen in Yenan. Much as he like and trusted Allison Ind, Jim knew that he would be suspected of Communist leanings if he told the Captain about that volunteer army of the people and for the people, who actually did not rob peasants but instead helped them with their planting. All good Americans were supposed to view Chiang as a saint and Mao as a devil.

Damn my Geminian ambivalence! But if Leda hadn't taken me with her to Yenan to see her pal Edgar Snow and interview Mao and his movie-star wife in their yao fang, cave house, I never would have felt that heady spirit of idealism — and then it would be easy for me to condemn those Long March survivors as just a bunch of lousy Communists.

Well, these well-paid AIF Tarzans sure aren't blowing all their pay on tailor-

made uniforms. . . .

Bare to the waist and bronzed to Filipino skin shades by the fierce sun, most of the AIF men he saw wore only shorts of khaki or white cotton, sandals, and assorted headgear: pith helmets, red baseball caps, or broad-brimmed bush hats to shade their eyes. He had not seen such an array of muscular manhood since Leni Riefenstahl's propaganda film of the Berlin Olympic Games. Six-footers were so common, it seemed as if that might be the requisite minimum height. Many were taller than he, and men of 6'6" were far from rare.

Sweating, he envied them their casual attire. In the Philippines, ranking Army officers still imposed "parade ground" uniform regulations. Although woolen leggings finally had been phased out for tropical wear, every Army man was required to wear a necktie with his uniform in public. Air Corps officers were no longer required to wear jodhpurs and high boots, but Army rules still demanded that neckties must be worn while flying: a rule born to be broken immediately upon takeoff.

Few of these soldiers had ever seen Americans before, and as Jim strolled through the garrison town, he could scarcely take two steps without being greeted, "G'dday, Yank!" and asked friendly questions. Several said, "Tough cheddar for you — comin' into 'Strylia by this back door!" In Singapore, the rich, rounded vowels of the few Australians had sounded to him like a couple of bass fiddles in a concert of massed flutey English voices; but here, where everyone spoke "'Strine," the effect was pleasantly overwhelming to his ears, like the sound of the surf.

He wanted to see the famous airport. But first, to his surprise, he walked into a meager Chinatown adjacent to the port area: two streets of unpainted wooden shacks and squalid shop-houses, their rusted metal roofs radiating heat.

Is "White Australia" only a myth? he wondered.

Although it was a far cry from Manila's affluent, gaudy Chinese district, the sounds and smells would be the familiar ones he had enjoyed on childhood walks with Wing in Manila, and had found the same in San Francisco as in Shanghai and Chungking. Like all Chinatowns, it would be enlivened by jostling bustle, minor-key tonal chatter, laughter, and the sight of calligraphic signs and laundry hanging like banners from horizontal bamboo window-poles. All Chinatowns were alike — tiny scraps of the original colorful fabric, and he was at home in any of them.

But this scene was incomplete: no women, young or old; no flocks of round-faced, bright-eyed children. This was like a place in a fairy tale, a town under an evil spell, where only wizened old men shuffled through the dust.

Only the tawdry tourist-souvenir shops were the same, and the hand laundries — CLEAN CLOTHES DELIV. TO YR SHIP — and tailor shops — 1 PR SHORTS IN 3 HRS. MAKE SUIT WHILE YR SHIP WAITS.

Chapter 2 — Part 1 — Desolate Darwin   41

Shorts!

"November is May in Australia," he had been told, and he had packed only one pair of shorts. Until yesterday, no one had warned him that Darwin claims the hottest mean annual temperatures in the world.

Slugger Pell had changed a ten-dollar bill into "shillings and florins" for each of the travelers. Now in Yee Long's tailor shop Jim got measured for a pair of three-hour khaki shorts. Unfortunately, old Yee did not speak Cantonese, so Jim tried to explain in sign language that he would prefer to have the shorts' legs slightly more fitted than the ballooning Australian style.

Stricken with a roaring thirst, Jim headed back toward the Caucasian shops, where surely Kyriakos's Tropical Delicatessen would have *something* cold to drink. He stopped at The Jolly Shop to look for some Aboriginal artifacts: paintings, musical instruments, weapons, or a boomerang, to take home for David. He found none, but in his search he came across some dusty brown bottles on a shelf with the patent medicines. He picked one up and brushed off its coat of dust. Yes, the label was the familiar gold foil, with the familiar name SAN MIGUEL in black with the capital S and M in red — but the rest of the label read: TONIC FOR NURSING MOTHERS. Made in Manila by the ANSOR Corporation.

For a few pennies, he bought a bottle, opened it, and tasted the amber liquid, as Mr. Jolly stared. It was the genuine beer, delicious as ever, though warm enough now for Australian tastes.

"Did you ever try this?" he asked Mr. Jolly.

"And get my tits full of milk? Not bloody likely, myte!"

"But this is *beer*. Here, have a taste."

"Beer can't be imported to Australia. The Brewers' Union won't allow it." With pursed lips, the proprietor took a tiny, suspicious sip, then put his head back and chug-a-lugged the rest. He laughed and wiped his mouth on his sleeve. "I'll give you a free replacement, myte. Damned clever of you Yanks to sneak it in here, calling it 'tonic'! So bloody clever, the Mums had it all to themselves. I think I'll order a hundred cases straightaway. Who owns this San Miggle — Yanks or Filipinos?"

"Mostly Filipinos — but one big stockholder is an American Army officer, richer than most, named MacArthur."

"That explains it. Those bloody Scots know how to turn a pretty penny."

* * * * *

Darwin's famous Ross Smith Aerodrome, where AE had landed, lay three miles from the little square-shaped town. As he walked toward it, the white sky seemed to burn his eyeballs, right through his Ray-Ban sunglasses. Shadows were stark black against harsh glare.

Strange, he mused: *We're only a few hundred miles southeast of Bali — where the golden light is an artist's dream. Everything's tough down here, even the sunshine.*

He was grateful when a dark blue RAAF bus, en route to the flying field, stopped to give him a ride. He paid a mock fare by giving the driver a cigarette, and sat down behind him.

The dusty little airfield probably hadn't changed much, Jim and the driver agreed, since the first England-to-Australia flight in 1919, when the Smith brothers landed their Vickers Vimy here after their 28-day journey.

"Lord — what nerve that took!" Jim marveled. "They *deserved* their knighthood. But rightfully, the field should have been named 'Sir Ross Smith *and* Sir Keith Smith Aerodrome.'"

"Too royte, myte! Give the bloody brother credit too!"

"When I was ten," Jim recalled, "after Chichester's solo fight, Kingsford-Smith flew his Southern Cross Junior alone from England in less than ten days."

"Too royte, old Smithy did — and then the flyin' sheilas began landin' here."

Leda, a pilot herself, hated the word "aviatrix," beloved by the press; Jim wondered how his mother would like being called a "flyin' sheila."

". . . Then the whole bloody world started comin' through Darwin, in that big Centennial Air Ryce. *Those* blokes put dirty little Darwin on the charts of international pilots. Now all the air mail for this entire continent, from all over the world, comes in through this bloody little aerodrome."

Although Amy Johnson and Jean Batten had prevented Amelia from being the first woman to land here, she always maintained that she felt no rivalry with her sister pilots. AE's goals, she said, were to prove that women could fly; to prove that flying was safe; and to promote the concept of "world friendship through flying."

But no woman pilot, Jim mused, *before or since, ever landed here with such a plane as AE's Lockheed Electra 10E.*

The big silver low-wing monoplane, 38 feet long with a 55-foot wingspan, had been designed for ten passengers. The seats had been replaced by six extra fuel tanks that gave Electra a capacity of 1,151 gallons and a range of about 4,000 miles. Those tanks so crammed the fuselage that AE and Noonan could neither see nor hear each other, but passed notes on the end of a bamboo pole.

The bus stopped at the civilian flight line to let Jim off. It would be back in 30 minutes, giving him more than enough time to examine the parked aircraft: a Fairey Battle and a couple of Moth Minors. He had hoped for some more exotic leftovers from the glory days: DH Comets, Miles Hawks and Falcons, Airspeed Couriers, Puss Moths, Desoutters, DH89 Rapides, Fairey Foxes, Airspeed Viceroys, Pander Postjagers, Lambert Monocoupes, or Klemm

Chapter 2 — Part 1 — Desolate Darwin 43

Eagles. . . . Of all those planes that had attempted to reach Darwin, even the successful ones had left no trace; no memorials, no plaques marked their historic passage across this dusty airstrip. It was as if the open-cockpit crates and the gleaming Electra had never been here at all.

* * * * *

— What the hell did you expect? Tire-tracks and tail-skid gouges enshrined in concrete, like the stars' footprints at Grauman's Chinese Theater in Hollywood?

Part 2 — On Amelia's Trail

The High Contracting Parties solemnly declare in the names of their respective peoples that they condemn recourse to war for the solution of international controversies, and renounce it as an instrument of national policy in their relations with one another.
— Article 1, Paris Pact ("Kellogg-Briand Pact").
Signed 27 August 1928 by 15 nations' representatives, including those of Germany, Japan, Britain, and the U.S. Later 48 other nations added their names.

Darwin
Wednesday, 12 November 1941

"Let's sit on the verandah, myte, and have a smoke-oh," Sergeant Werner Fredericks, a jovial, beefy, blue-eyed man, welcomed Jim. Behind him the starry flag of Australia drooped from the lintel of his unpainted door. They sat facing the wide, dusty, eye-searing, treeless street.

Mrs. Fredericks, thin and quick, brought mugs of dark tea. "Here's your billy," she said, and disappeared. The tea was so hot and strong that Jim had a hard time drinking it, but the buzzing flies that lighted on the rim seemed thirsty enough to immerse themselves in it.

Like the two lorry drivers, Fredericks frankly enjoyed sharing Jim's Lucky Strikes; Jim was beginning to wish he had brought many more 70-cent cartons from the Clark Post Exchange to give away.

The RAAF mechanic had remained in Darwin after his retirement because, he said, it was "three times as large and twice as nice" as his home town, Cobargo. He served now without pay as one of 50,000 veterans in the Volunteer Defence Corps, ready to defend their home districts if need arose. His wife wanted to stay here because their son was a crewmember of a transport that often put in at Darwin. Originally, the son had worked as a "pearler."

"— Not a bloody diver; not many Aussies dive. Our blokes sail the luggers that the divers — Chinese, Filipinos, Koepangers, Papuans — work from. But this year, due to the bloody war, the government put a ban on pearling till it's over."

Fredericks waved his cigarette in a wide gesture toward the bay. "You Yanks have your 'Pearl Harbour' — we've got a dinkum *Pearl Coast,* from Broome to Cairns. More than a thousand miles of the richest pearl-shell fields in the bloody world, that's what God gave us in place of good soil and decent weather. Northwest Australia's got mother-o'-pearl and father-o'-pearl and Gold Lip pearl shells nine inches across."

Acres of nacre!

"Pearling's our only industry here — but the bastard Japs wrecked it for us. Came down like sharks from Palau Island with their bloody huge pearling fleet. Never have to go ashore; they have their mother ship with 'em — the bloody *Nanyo Maru*. We call her 'Nanny Maru.' They scooped up so many million pounds of trochus shell, the bottom fell out of the New York button market, and now no honest Aussie can earn a living on this coast. All the while, the Japs were taking soundings of our shoreline, and the masts of their luggers were stuffed with wireless equipment. Those little blokes play by 'Rafferty Rules' — no rules at all! We've got to whip their backsides, before they get any bolder, and I'm betting Singapore will be the place. My son's troopship, the *Zealandia,* is gettin' up steam right now, to take men of the 8th Aussie Division up there to General Bennett."

Jim had met bluff, outspoken, egg-bald Gordon Bennett in Singapore and thought him a far more dynamic leader than the English Commander, General Percival. "Bennett will be glad to get those troops," he said.

"Well, Gordie will have to wait till the *Zealandia*'s crew ends its strike — second one this year. The first was in January, while they were docked here in Darwin; so my old lady was in seventh heaven with her baby boy home every day."

"Striking for higher pay for hazardous duty?"

"No, not this time. Mostly, they were wingeing about the lousy cook and the same thing served too often: same cold cuts of meat, not enough tongue or franks, tough beefsteak, no tinned fruit for variety, only local tropical fruits.

And there was washing troubles, not enough fresh water or soap or towels — and the dockers were coming aboard to use the ship's lavatories."

"Well, I guess things always get tough in wartime!"

"But the war's over *there*, myte — not here yet. And we must never let our workers down, even if the bastard Japs attack us here."

"Don't worry, Sarge. They'd never get past Singapore and the Philippines and the Dutch islands —"

"I hope you're right, Leftenant. 'Cause if they do, our Mother Country won't lift a bloody hand to help us — *can't* help us — after all the battles we've fought for her, over in the fuckin' Middle East. . . . The more I think about it, Singapore can bloody well take care of itself. I'd like to see Gordie Bennett bring all our blokes home — aboard *Zealandia!* — to guard Australia."

"Guard against invasion? Or sabotage?"

"We've got no worries about sabotage, not like your Philippines with thousands of Japs living there. Thank God, there's only a handful of the bloody yellow bastards in all Australia — and no more will ever be let in."

No more Chinese could enter now, either, he replied to Jim's question. Those few in the Chinatowns of Darwin and other northern towns were a remnant of some 50,000 men who had been allowed to come to work in the gold fields during the Queensland gold rush of the 1870s.

"And work they did! Like dogs. Ate no more than a handful of rice a day, and soon they were selling tins of food to our blokes, and lending money at interest. Thank God, our union leaders saw what was happening, before it was too late. When the coolies' contracts were up, our government repatriated almost all of 'em. Luckily, not many of their women were here to start families. Ten thousand Chinks lived here in Darwin at the peak time, and even by 1880 there were about five thousand Chinese here, to seven hundred whites. . . . We've got to keep Australia for us Aussies — we can't allow the Asiatics to take over."

Allsame "Yellow Peril" sentiments as the Filipinos and the Californians, Jim thought. Chinese immigration to the Philippines was prohibited; in the States it had been severely restricted since 1904, and further limited in 1924 by the Oriental Exclusion Act.

"Our White Australia policy's actually paying a compliment to those little buggers, 'cause we know they work so damned hard, and they're so shrewd — if we hadn't locked the door, we'd be working for *them* now. And they multiply like the bloody wild rabbits! Our cities would soon be as crowded and filthy and stinking and corrupt as any native quarter in an Asiatic city. And our union leaders want to protect us from the fuckin' twenty-five percent unemployment you Yanks have — they know that us white blokes would be the ones standing at the arse end of the jobless queue."

OK. That's enough polite small talk. Why did Amelia linger in Darwin?

On 28 June 1937 the watching world learned that she had safely made the flight to Darwin from Koepang, on the southern tip of slender little Timor. She had not departed the following day for New Guinea as planned; instead she had been "delayed at Port Darwin, Australia, due to an irregularity in health certificates."

There was never any further explanation why the two Americans — whose pre-flight immunizations had passed the scrutiny of health officials across South America, Africa, southern Asia, and most recently the English and Dutch colonies of Singapore and Java — had fallen afoul of Darwin's medical establishment on their sole stopover in Australia. AE had only two more landings to make, this side of home: Lae, New Guinea, and Howland Island, which was uninhabited except for vast numbers of "gooney birds." Jim had wondered: Were the Australian officials concerned lest AE might acquire a strange disease on those islands — or bring one?

The only other news of AE's stop in Darwin had been that during their layover on 29 June she and Fred Noonan had sent their parachutes home from here — and that RAAF Sergeant Stan Rose had worked on the plane's radios. The next day, the last of June, Amelia had flown her big Electra across the top of Australia and the bottom of New Guinea to Lae, on the southeast coast.

Responding to Jim's question, "Yes, of course," Fredericks remembered the tall young American pilot. "A fair dinkum lady. I still remember her plane's number, 'NR 16020.' And her nav', that Noonan — he was a lively bloke, as tall and black-headed and skinny as you —"

Jim had seen Noonan once, on a historic day. Noonan, 42, had looked ten feet tall to Jim, 15, who was in the wildly cheering throng that welcomed the maiden flight of Pan American's *China Clipper,* when Captain Ed Musick splashed down the four-engine Martin flying boat in Manila Bay on November 29, 1935, 60 hours after taking off from Alameda, California. Musick's choice of Noonan to chart the unprecedented flight, with stops at Honolulu, Midway, Wake Island, and Guam, was the highest honor an aerial navigator could receive.

"— With a good Irish thirst," Fredericks continued. "He'd picked up some dinkum whiskey in Singapore, and drank a bottle by himself while I was working on their plane. That evening, I helped him polish off another bottle to lighten his load. But that was the first night. He didn't drink the next night, before they took off for Papua; said he never drank when he had to work next day."

During his 20 years' experience in surface ships and planes, Fred Noonan had become known as a navigator and a drinker; finally, his drinking had caused Pan American to dismiss him. On his honeymoon, he had been in a car accident blamed on alcohol, shortly before AE hired him to go around the world with her. But his experience in route-finding over the Pacific was probably unequaled. People said that his recent marriage had reformed him; that he had promised not to drink during the flight, and that AE wanted to give him this opportunity because her father also had been afflicted with a weakness for alcohol. Evidently she wanted to prove that drinkers can be worthy of trust when given responsibility. Jim, whose mother had an "Irish thirst," did not want to hear about Noonan, but about Noonan's fearless pilot.

Yes, the watching world had been informed that Amelia Earhart and Noonan had shipped their parachutes back to the States from Darwin, because chutes would be useless on the long overwater flights and their weight could be better replaced by gasoline. But surely, in friendly Darwin, someone would have offered to handle that mailing chore? Two parachutes weren't really worth a two-day layover, Jim suggested.

"Too royte, they weren't. I offered to pack 'em and put 'em on the ship myself. Any bloke in Darwin woulda been glad to do it for the lydy." Fredericks drew deeply on his Lucky.

Silently Jim wondered how long it was before those two parachutes, loaded on a freighter at the long dock, ever reached Noonan's bride and AE's husband. . . . AE's chute was probably a Switlik, the type she customarily wore. . . . Months after the search was abandoned, the two bulky bundles would have been delivered, poignant messages saying "Don't forget us."

Jim always had always resented AE's marriage to the wealthy George Palmer Putnam, the publishing company heir whose nickname was "GP," pronounced "Jeep." Leda, who had been inspired by AE's example to take flying lessons (and as a qualified pilot had become the first Philippine member of AE's sisterhood of pilots, the Ninety-Nines), railed that "Publicity Putnam" was commercializing AE, "selling her like one of his damned books!" Leda had been furious when Jimmy paid a dollar at Heacock's for a handkerchief for her birthday that bore the stylized initials "AE" in one corner.

"Just look at that lens-louse!" Leda would remark when GP appeared in the newsreels, standing beside his wife in her open cockpit, frequently with one hand on his hip and the other resting proprietarily on AE's shoulder. In Jim's collection of AE photographs, he could easily distinguish those taken "before GP," with her un-selfconscious windblown curly hair and the open, Midwestern "Lady Lindy" grin. Even her beautiful wide blue eyes seemed to change, he thought, though they were still direct and magnetic. Her glamorous post-marriage poses resembled Hollywood publicity stills — after GP had schooled her to smile with her lips closed, so that the endearing little-boy gap between her front teeth would not show. Jim hated him for that.

He had been angry with his father, too, for questioning how Purdue University could afford, in the 1936 depths of the U.S. Depression, to give its famous faculty member the Electra — a $100,000 "flying laboratory." At a time when few young persons could afford college tuition, Alexander said, surely Purdue would not divert such a sum unless the university was offering an equal amount for scholarships. True, the Electra, with its 55-foot wingspan, was indeed a far cry from the little red-and-gold Lockheed Vega 5B in which — just four days short of Jim's twelfth birthday — "Lady Lindy" Earhart had made the first solo transatlantic flight by a woman. (Charles Lindbergh had made his Atlantic solo crossing in the week of Jimmy's *seventh* birthday.) Still, Jim resented Alexander's intimation that the U.S. government secretly might have shared part of the Electra's cost with Purdue, in the expectation that the flight might involve aerial observations of prohibited fortifications on islands held by Japan. He refused to think that his hero, President Roosevelt, would risk putting Amelia's patriotism to such a dangerous test.

Fredericks had finished his cigarette and accepted another. "Too royte, it was more than the medics or parachutes that caused the layover. The lydy was having engine troubles — one of 'em was still a bit 'crook,' running rough. So, while Sergeant Rose tuned and tested her rydio-telephone equipment, I did the same for her engines. With your Mr. William Miller checking on our progress all the while —"

"Who's he?"

"Somebody from your U.S. Civilian Aeronautics Authority. His formal title was Chief of Aeronautical Surveys of the South Pacific Ocean, but he was a likeable bloke, anyway. A pilot himself; served in your Navy, he told me. He was here at Ross Smith Aerodrome to greet the lady the minute she landed — stuck to her like a bush-fly the whole time she was here. Seemed to approve of the way Rose and me did our jobs, though."

"Well, of course those Wasp Juniors had a lot of hours on 'em by then."

Fredericks shook his head. "No, these engines were new. She left the five hundred fifty-horsepower Wasps in Java. These two were brand-new Pratt & Whitney *Senior* Wasps — the military version — that she'd had installed in Bandung. Gave her far better power. Cruising speed, two hundred. Top speed, at least two hundred twenty miles an hour."

Jim stared at him, astounded.

If this is true, all my calculations about AE's flying time were wrong. ***Everybody's*** *estimates were wrong as hell. We were told she was proceeding toward Howland Island at about one hundred eleven miles per hour, and it would take her about eighteen hours to fly those two thousand five hundred fifty-six miles from Lae to Howland. . . . But in eighteen hours, at two hundred or more miles an hour, she could really have been all over the map.*

Unbelieving, he questioned, "New U.S. engines — in Bandung?"

Bandung, Java, was one of his favorite cities; cool, clean, modern, it was the Dutch colonials' answer to tropical humidity — like Simla to the British and Baguio to the Americans. He had been there three times: first as a child, and next as an assistant to David Fairchild, the Florida botanist and plant collector.

The Fairchild group had been in Java when Holland was struck by the *"prang"* (war). As Hitler bombed their homeland, the East Indies Dutch had impressed Jim with their staunch determination to go it alone, and to resist the heavy pressures from Japan. And only four months ago, he had been back in Bandung with General Clagett. While the senior American officers discussed needed U.S. aid with Dutch officials, Jim had been assigned to tour the noisy new factories producing war materiel. . . .

But back in 1937, when AE was there, before the **prang** *— how could she have found her new U.S.-made engines for her Electra in that little resort town?*

Fredericks asked, "Didn't you know she'd stayed six days in Bandung?"

"Well sure. That was her twenty-third stop. The news reports said that an American airplane engine expert — F.O. Furman — and several mechanics worked on the Electra's engines and navigation instruments for three days there. Then Amelia flew down to Surabaya, but the Electra still wasn't running right, so she went back to Bandung, and Furman and his crew worked on it two more days —"

"It takes time to break in new engines, myte. Can't do it in one day."

Jim knew the importance of "slow-timing." Twelve hours was the minimum, flown in periods of not more than four hours each. He tried to test Fredericks' statement against the news announcements made at the time. "— Then, on 27 June, she finally flew to Timor — in five hours, they said. But there was never a word about getting *new* engines installed —"

"There was never a word about why Furman just *happened* to be in Bandung, either, was there? Well, now you know why."

"Not really. I mean, it makes sense for her to have more power, with the worst part of her trip ahead of her. I'm glad she did — even if it didn't do her any good. But why in the hell wasn't the public informed?"

Sergeant Fredericks sighed. "Well, son — if she could fly farther and faster than anybody figured, that might give her time to do some looking around at the other islands before she was expected at Howland. Royte?"

"Too right — I guess."

Part 3 — Wirraway Ride

Off we go, into the wild blue yonder,
Climbing high, into the sun.
Here they come, zooming to meet our thunder,
At 'em boys, give 'er the gun!
Down we dive, spouting our flame from under,
Off with one hell of a roar!
We live in fame, or go down in flame,
For nothing can stop the Army Air Corps!
  — Official song of the U.S. Air Force
   by Robert Crawford, © Carl Fischer, Inc.

RAAF Station Darwin, NT
Wednesday afternoon, 12 November 1941

    The best things about this Wirraway, Jim decided, were its good visibility through the long Plexiglas "greenhouse" — and its name. He had guessed correctly that the Australians had given their first "home-built" plane a name from one of the Aboriginal languages. He had assumed that "Wirraway" was an imitation of the sound of the plane's engine. (An "onomatopoetic" word, as Leda taught the Filipino students in her English classes, using examples familiar to them, such as *gecko*, the house lizard, and *manok*, the chicken.) His assumption was wrong.

RAAF Flight Lieutenant Wes Popkins, who had invited Jim up for this sightseeing ride, told him that *wirraway* meant *challenge*.

But unfortunately, Jim thought, *the challenge is all in the name. A Wirraway is too much like the AT-6 "Texan" that only challenged me when I moved up to advanced flying training at Kelly Field — and then not for long.*

Jim had first seen Wirraways in Singapore in July. He remembered the jubilation of the Australians in No. 21 Squadron at Sembawang, when their Wirraways were replaced by more modern American-made Brewster Buffaloes.

Australian engineers who had visited the U.S. in 1936 to study American methods of building aircraft had sensibly decided to use an uncomplicated airframe for initial home production. They chose a version of the Harvard trainer, North American Aircraft Corporation's NA-33, with a basic Pratt and Whitney single-row Wasp radial engine. One man could fly a Wirraway alone for its 500-mile range, Popkins told Jim, who did not doubt it. The plane could — eventually — reach an altitude of 23,000 feet.

Starting from scratch in 1937, Australia was now exporting a significant number of Wirraways to British forces in Singapore, India, the Near East, and South Africa. Jim saluted the achievement. Equipped for war with two fixed machine-guns fired through the propeller and a rear gun — all three of .303 caliber — and a bomb rack for two 250-pound bombs, the Wirraway was variously termed a fighter-bomber, fighter-interceptor, scout-fighter, and an army-cooperation plane.

But it's still a trainer. Its top speed, at eighty-six hundred feet, is only two hundred twenty miles an hour, and its max rate of climb is less than two thousand feet per minute.

Flight Lieutenant Popkins belonged to No. 12 Squadron; this was one of the squadron's 18 Wirraways. As they took off from the airstrip at RAAF Station Darwin, Jim saw on the ground the total bomber force of 14 U.S.-made Hudson (A-29) twin-engine medium bombers, bearing the RAAF's red and blue roundels on wings and fuselage. Eight belonged to No. 2 Squadron and six were from No. 13 Squadron. Armed with seven .303-mm guns, they carried a crew of four or five; their maximum speed was only 222 mph, but when used for reconnaissance without a bomb load, they had a range of 1,400 miles and a service ceiling of 24,500 feet. He also had seen Hudsons flown by Australians in Singapore and Malaya; both of the RAAF General Reconnaissance Squadrons, No. 1 and No. 8, were equipped with them.

Looking down at the RAAF airfield, Jim could understand why Batchelor had been preferable for the B-17s.

"Howja like flyin' a Kitty, myte?" Last night it had seemed as if every RAAF pilot at the party in the officers' mess wanted to ask Jim that, and it took some getting accustomed to; he had never thought of his P-40 by any of the

Curtiss Hawk names. (Strange birds: a P-40B was a "Tomahawk"!)

Still, in Singapore he had begun to like the British way of using names for aircraft types, instead of numbers and letters. More personal, he thought; and a plane — at least a pursuit plane — was a personality. "Kittyhawk" really sounded more *alive* than "P-40." And, certainly, "Catalina" was more musical and evocative than "PBY" — until they shortened it to "Cat."

Befitting a nation at war, the RAAF could call a fighter plane a fighter plane — even a Wirraway. The U.S. Army Air Forces, however, still attempted to lull U.S. pacifists by designating Jim's plane as a "pursuit," and he envied the RAAF its bolder terminology. Who *wouldn't* rather be a fighter pilot than a pursuit pilot, he thought.

As Jim had hoped, as soon as a couple of the men at the party found out that in July he had visited the Malayan airfields where their RAAF "mates" were based, many of them had clustered around to ask him about friends and flying-school classmates there. He was thankful for his good memory, as he recalled names of members of the three Australian squadrons: most memorably, Squadron No. 1, the RAAF's proud and raffish first-born, formed in the 1920s. He had been relieved to learn that the two reconnaissance squadrons, No. 1 and No. 8, exchanged locations every six months, because Kota Bharu, where he had spent a day as the guest of Group Captain Davis, Commander of No. 1, was the worst location, with the worst facilities, he had ever seen. Far up on the peninsula's east coast at the Thai border, too near the Japanese now based on the southern tip of Viet Nam, it had all the charm of a rumbling volcano.

He had marveled at the nonchalance and good humor of that squadron, flying their long search missions up and down the rugged coast and out over the South China Sea from that swampy raw jungle strip, eating such terrible food that when he had surreptitiously put his plate under the table, the squadron dog had refused it.

He had admired them all: Wing Commander O'Brien, Group Captains Noble and Davis, the pilots, air crews, and ground crews. The names of some of the Flight Lieutenants were invoked by their Darwin "mates" with flying-school anecdotes and much laughter: Lockwood, Douglas, Diamond, Ramshaw, Emerton, were names from Kota Bharu that were lodged in Jim's memory along with their sweaty, tanned, laughing Aussie faces.

Now that he had seen Darwin and Batchelor Field and had eaten the mess hall's canned food, he could comprehend that stoic acceptance of sub-standard facilities in Malaya. Those men were tough and rugged because they came from a tough and rugged country. They were "Spartan" — a bad word to Jim's father, whose sympathies were all with the democratic Athenians in the Peloponnesian wars.

But I don't mean that Australia's government resembles Sparta's in harshness; just the opposite! The people are so free, they don't let their harsh country, or any hardships, dominate them.

* * * * *

Popkins circled over Darwin, still at low altitude, but high enough for Jim to see Van Diemen's Gulf to the northeast, sheltered by natural seawalls that the pilot identified as the Coburg Peninsula and Melville and Bathurst Islands. Only a few miles from Darwin, Jim's beach-loving eye spotted a clear green creek with silver sand at its mouth, bordered by coconut palms and pandanus shrubs. He pointed to it, wondering why it wasn't crammed with off-duty AIF men cooling off; it would be an easy hike from their barracks.

"Rapid Creek." Popkins' voice on the intercom radio identified it. "Tough cheddar for us — the sharks claim the sea, and the crocs have got the beach."

Forty-five miles south of the RAAF field the Wirraway touched down briefly at Batchelor, where "Tough-luck Mac" — Captain William E. McDonald — was still trying to get his B-17 off the isolated airstrip and on its way to the Philippines. Sweating RAAF mechanics, lacking the proper tools and working in the open, assailed by sun and flies, swearing the most colorful profanity Jim had ever heard, were attempting to manhandle the huge new triple-bladed propellers into position on McDonald's bomber with his help.

Actually, Mac's damned lucky. He's still alive.

En route from New Guinea to Darwin, two of McDonald's four engines had failed. He had waited here while his squadron-mates flew on to Clark Field; then waited another week while Clark mechanics designed and built a rack inside a B-17 that would carry a spare engine down to him. Jim had seen that ingenious arrangement, before Bill Bohnaker, with Carey O'Bryan as copilot, had delivered the engine to McDonald. (That errand had made them the first to fly a B-17 south from Clark to Darwin; yesterday's flight was the second.) After it was laboriously installed, McDonald, with three good engines whipping up the red dust, had waved a triumphant goodbye to Batchelor — only to feel the ground give way beneath his wheels as the bomber crunched through the thin volcanic-ash crust, nosed in to "bite the dust," and bent two propellers like cheap spoons.

No wonder he's so nervous about getting out of here with the new pair.

In the intense heat, stung by bush flies, Jim was eager to get airborne again. He was already thirsty, but Batchelor's water, piped above ground from a nearby volcano, was too hot for hand-washing, much less for drinking.

Maybe they could use steam from the volcano to run a generator that would provide some electricity for night landing lights. At age 12, he had read that Guglielmo Marconi, the pioneer of wireless telegraphy, was interested in harnessing the power of Mount Etna. Jim had written to the one-eyed inventor, inquiring about the possibility of creating power for the Philippines from

Chapter 2 — Part 3 — Wirraway Ride

some of the active volcanoes, and a pleasant correspondence had evolved. Touching on many subjects (including a mutual belief in telepathy), they had exchanged letters about twice a year. Leda had opposed the pen-pal contact because of Marconi's links to his Fascist government, and when Jim was 16 and Italy invaded Ethiopia, she threatened to intercept any future letters and destroy them. He had called her "Mrs. Mussolini," and defied her by secretly sending, via *Clipper* Mail, his reply to Marconi's most recent letter (on the subject of microwaves and their relation to television). Marconi had died the following year, apparently without answering that letter. At least, Leda swore that she had never carried out her threat, and Jim had never known her to lie.

The RAAF mechanics had built a little fire to brew their "billy," which they hunkered down to drink in the shade of the Fortress' big wing. Surely, Jim thought, turning down a proffered mug of the dark, smoky drink, the water's hot enough from the pipe to make tea.

Sitting in the front seat, Jim felt like a student pilot again; it was easy to imagine that his Kelly Field instructor, Captain Chet Sluder, was in the seat behind him instead of Popkins. And — just like an AT-6 — on the ground the Wirraway's large view-blocking radial engine forced the pilot to taxi in S-turns in order to see what was in front of him. Even a P-40, with its nose high and its tail low, required the same kind of caution on takeoff, although its sleek in-line engine lacked the bulk of the one before Jim now: wreathed in cylinders that popped while a mechanic pulled the propeller through.

Airborne, the Wirraway's canopy provided fine visibility, especially for Jim. With its slow speed, he thought, it would be great for sightseeing — if there were anything to see. From the air, Darwin's isolation was starkly clear. Narrow-gauge railroad tracks ran south through roadless red desert for about 300 miles to the tiny hamlet of Birdum — and ended there. Beyond Birdum, he had been told, lay the "Never-never" and the "twelve-hour country," where a white man without water could not last beyond one revolution of the clock.

The ragged seacoast was a visual relief, with blessed blue "water, water, everywhere" — *but not a drop for this poor parched land,* Jim observed.

It was not true, however, that rain never came to the northwest, he had learned. It would come fiercely, and soon. Indeed, much of Brereton's urgency stemmed from Scherger's warning that after "The Wet" arrived, mud resembling tomato soup would make it all but impossible to improve the landing field at Batchelor.

This coast lacked a mountain range to ameliorate the climate. The sparse, bent trees told of the constant, cruel wind that blew from the hot interior and kept out the ocean's moisture until the year's end. But soon the wind would turn, and all at once Darwin would get 58 inches of its annual 60 inches of rainfall.

About 40 miles south of Port Darwin, Popkins banked and circled above the weird, mysterious "Termitaria." To Jim, it seemed like a desert burial ground of sun-worshiping giants, with gray tombstones perfectly aligned on a north-south axis.

"Some of the mounds are taller than twelve feet," Popkins said on the intercom.

More than twice my height!

Jim stared down, awed and appalled at an achievement demanding such discipline and purposefulness, created by millions of ravenous blind creatures.

What a plot device for a Sax Rohmer story starring the villainous Dr. Fu Manchu....

... Dr. Fu wants to clear the Whitefellows from this continent and establish his own nefarious Yellow Kingdom here, so he devises a code that instructs termites to eat Caucasian flesh instead of wood. They swarm to the settlements, where he has immobilized the Aussies by a hypnotic spell. End of White Australia. But wait — meat is more filling than cellulose, and the insects become sated. So, every night while Fu Manchu can't observe them, they entomb a pair of rigid hypnotized Aussies (one standing on the other's shoulders) in each of these tall mounds, to reserve them for later snacks. (Being blind, the termites work well at night.) Inside the mounds, the Aussies wake up, organize a breakout, capture Dr. Fu, and force him to revise his instructions and direct his insect slaves to devour each other. First, however, the termites are ordered to munch on their Manchu master....

"Rudimentary," Brereton had termed Batchelor's airstrip; Jim had thought the General was being uncharacteristically diplomatic, considering the lack of a control tower or any facilities other than a wooden hut in the cluster of dusty trees — *gum* trees, as unattractive as their name, members of the eucalyptus family.

However, after Popkins showed him the field called Katherine, about 200 miles southeast of Darwin, Batchelor looked far better. And when he saw Keats airfield, 130 miles southwest of Darwin, Batchelor's superiority was undeniable.

"Wouldja like to fly her awhile?" Popkins asked. Jim was delighted, doubly savoring the joy of a stick under his hand after yesterday's acquaintance with the heavy yoke of the Flying Fortress.

Popkins indicated that he wanted Jim to bank right and fly westward; but after a few minutes over the Indian Ocean, he shook his head and gave hand signals for a 180-degree turn back to the shore, then back down the coast again. "I was hoping to show you a 'beaut' convoy," he said. "Our famous Perth-class cruiser, the *Sydney*, departed the Navy base down at Fremantle yesterday, escorting probably five, six, or seven chartered ships north to the Sunda Strait."

"That would be a pretty sight."

"Too royte. But she's already taken 'em out to deep water. Too dangerous to hug this west coast — too many coral reefs and fuckin' Jerry or Jap mines. Up at the Sunda, she'll turn 'em over to a British escort and get 'em safely to Singapore. *Sydney's* our 'glory ship' — over in the Med, she sank a bloody batch of Eye-tye warships, including the world's fastest cruiser, the *Bartolomeo Colleoni*. That bastard could go over forty knots — till *Sydney* sent her under! Picked up more than five hundred survivors — first time a cruiser ever sank a cruiser with her guns, in this war, anyway. She carries a Walrus on a catapult —"

The Walrus and the Carpenter! Boy, I'd like to see that.

"She's a lucky ship, too — around Bardia, Crete, Calabria, Taranto, all that lot, she took all the hell the Eye-tyes could throw at her from sea and air, but their only hit was a harmless one on a funnel. It took another Aussie ship to keep *Sydney* in port for nearly a fortnight just now — no foreign fleet could have done it!"

"How did that happen?"

"A bastard troopship named *Zealandia* did it. Picked up a bunch of Army blokes at Sydney-side a month ago —" Popkins hesitated, evidently recalling the omnipresent poster warning: LOOSE LIPS SINK SHIPS, and wondering if this Yank was trustworthy.

"Sounds like the 8th Division, going to General Bennett in Singapore," Jim flaunted his insider's knowledge acquired from Sergeant Fredericks.

"Too royte, myte! Well, after they arrived at Fremantle to join the *Sydney* convoy, *Zealandia's* crew went out on strike."

"Bad food?"

"No — not this time. They demanded assurance that their pay would continue at the same rate, if they fell into enemy hands and were taken prisoner. So the whole convoy waited, day after day. Finally, our spanking new Labour government bashed its own principles and told *Zealandia* to get her arse into the convoy or have her charter canceled and be commandeered as a bare boat. So the *Sydney* finally got her little ducks in a row and sailed yesterday — thirteen days late —"

"Well, it won't take long to make Sunda Strait."

"Too royte, it shouldn't; *Sydney* can make thirty-two knots. She'd be there in no time, but that bastard *Zealandia* will make the convoy crawl. While they were out on strike at Fremantle, some of her firemen got drunk on watch and let the bloody fires get so low the boiler-stays sprang leaks. Now they can only get up enough steam to make eleven fucking knots."

Jim had hoped for a glimpse of Broome, which was mentioned in the book by Daisy Bates that his mother had insisted he must read; but as Broome lay about 700 miles down the coast from Darwin, it was out of the question.

For a long time he skirted the jagged coast southwestward, seeing no trace of human occupation. Finally, Popkins pointed out the distant promontory of Dampier Land, named for the raffish Englishman who Jim thought should be the subject of a movie, with Errol Flynn playing the piratical adventurer-explorer: a seagoing version of Flynn's *Robin Hood*.

"Broome's on the far side of Dampier," Popkins said. "And the town's not worth seeing, anyway, just a miniature Darwin. Without the pearling fleet, Broome'll soon be a ghost port," he predicted.

Before the world-wide Depression, Broome's pearls had brought the coastal town more than 100,000 pounds yearly. Two of the most famous pearls were found off Broome: the Southern Cross Pearl — actually four pearls naturally grown together in the form of a cross, bought by English Catholics for 10,000 pounds to give to the Pope — and the Star of the West, "worth a king's ransom."

Jim had hoped to see where the eccentric Irish lady, Daisy Bates, had first encountered the Aborigines, and Broome had been her starting point. From Broome's Roebuck Bay in 1900 she had boarded a ship with an Italian priest to visit the pitiful Trappist mission at Beagle Bay.

At the mission she had learned from the Aboriginal women of their new victimization, caused in all innocence by the unworldly priests. In their zeal to civilize and Christianize "the blackfellows," the priests had gladly performed marriages between Aboriginal women and nominally Catholic "Manilamen" — Filipino divers from pearling ships. Ignorant of Aboriginal customs, the priests had not realized that a wife was a property shared by her mate with his brothers. Thus, when a *lubra,* an Aboriginal woman, became the spouse of a sailor, she was in effect "married" to all his shipmates. Thenceforth, they lined up to demand their conjugal rights — after paying a fee to her husband — as long as their ship remained in the harbor.

Thanks to Daisy Bates' intercession, the mock marriages were discontinued; but her own life would never be the same. Adopting the land and its inhabitants (as those other intrepid Victorians, Lady Stanhope and Mary Kingsley, had done in Africa), for the next 35 years she had shared the rigorous life of naked nomadic tribes throughout the most barren parts of Australia. Five years ago, at the age of 76, she had withdrawn to Adelaide to write her memoir: a plea for understanding of these Stone Age human beings. "We owe them something," she insisted.

Jim easily could empathize with Mrs. Bates. Looking down at the barren, martian landscape, he marveled at the Aborigines' ability to survive for thousands of years in areas where a white man could not live 12 hours.

Since childhood, Jim had formed treasured friendships with members of Aboriginal tribes in the Philippine *bundoks* (mountains). During his teen years, he had served as a summer assistant to two eminent anthropologists working in different areas, and he had lived with reformed headhunters and with pygmy Negritos. Although he had not gone so far as Dr. Otley Beyer, whose teeth had been filed into points for a brotherhood rite, Jim had endured a puberty rite. While he was working for R. F. Barton, a hard-drinking Irishman who spent years interviewing members of the Ifugao tribe, Jim had agreed to assist Barton's research by sleeping in the village *olag,* the youths' dormitory. Ifugao widows shared the dark, barnlike *olag* with the adolescents, and served informally as instructors; it was at the rough hands of one of these that Jim had received his daunting sexual initiation.

In only two facets of their culture did Daisy Bates ever attempt to preach or to teach the Aborigines; she saw her duty only to learn from them, nurse them, and ease their lot as they passed into what she foresaw as their rapidly approaching extinction. From approximately 300,000, when the first prison ships brought the *Waigela* (Whitefellows) from England in 1788, their numbers had dwindled to an estimated 54,000 full-blooded Aborigines by the time of Jim's visit. Their mystical attachment to their harsh land, their mythic art, and their ancient rituals attached to certain landmarks, resembled those Jim knew of in connection with AmerIndian tribes in the U.S., such as the Anasazi, who had been forced to leave their home territory and had become extinct.

Daisy Bates's only vestiges of civilized comfort were an 8- by 10-foot tent and a 40-gallon portable water tank; but like other intrepid Victorian women, she kept up appearances in the proper fashion set by her Queen. She never left her tent in the morning until she was dressed in a white blouse with a stiff high collar and a ribbon tie, a long dark skirt beneath a long duster, sensible shoes, and black stockings — wearing a broad-brimmed hat with a fly-net, and carrying a large black parasol, with her hands sheathed in white cotton gloves. She had a dozen pairs of the gloves, which she cautiously boiled after each wearing because she was constantly nursing the tribespeople, who had the world's highest rate of trachoma and skin cancer.

Accepted as *Kabbarli* (Grandmother) by tribes all over Australia, she learned eventually to speak 188 of the Aboriginal languages. She was permitted to view secret ceremonies and blood-drinking circumcision rites that the tribe's own women would be killed for glimpsing.

Aboriginal women, Mrs. Bates reported, were treated with less respect than the camp dogs; yet her sole urgings toward reform were not directed to the men, but to the women themselves. She did not criticize the practice of eating human flesh, for that custom was universal, she maintained. However, she did remonstrate with the women for eating their newborn infants. In some dwindling tribes, she found that for years no newborn had escaped its mother's "terrible craving for baby meat." Although the women knew her feelings and wanted to please her, often a woman would hide from "Grandmother" when her labor began and would reappear with empty womb and empty arms.

Aboriginal men were not known to devour their own babies; they satisfied their carnivorous appetites with the flesh of kangaroos, wallabies, emu, snakes, lizards, male enemies, wives, and other men's children. Daisy Bates assisted at the burial of Dowie, a chief who had eaten four babies before he was nine years old and later ate each of his five wives.

Although the men evidently did not intend to eat their own infants, paternity was so nebulous that it could have happened in error. A father's identity was revealed to a woman in a dream: If she dreamed that a man was her child's father, that was accepted as fact. No man could claim a child as his own, however, unless he had appeared in the mother's dream.

The Aborigines' second troubling maternal aberration was also beyond Daisy Bates's power to control. Its results had more impact on White Australia than the first. For 40,000 years, every aspect of tribal life had been rigidly governed by tradition; but the coming of the Whitefellows tore the fabric, and Mrs. Bates saw an alarming breakdown of morals. Without needing the formality of missionary "marriages," male newcomers to Australia, of all races, took advantage of the docile brown women, and Mrs. Bates sounded the alarm about the resulting mixed-breed children. The women would not eat these infants, who they said had a bad smell; the tribes scorned them and so did White Australia. Approximately 23,000 "half-castes" were living, most of them in squalid limbo, at the time of Jim's visit.

Although he searched the arid red earth with his binoculars, the only place where Jim saw large numbers of Aborigines was the place that Daisy Bates accused of ruining their lives. Alongside the narrow railroad track to Birdum, their shelters of bark or gum-tree branches resembled an extended hobo camp. Here, they had learned, the traveling Whitefellows would throw food to them; and as the rails had extended throughout the continent, they drew the Aborigines like iron filings to magnets. Many of the Aborigines, once the finest physical specimens on earth, had degenerated into obese beggars.

Jim's mother had expressed only two regrets about Daisy Bates, whom she otherwise admired as "a spunky Irish biddy." One: that in adopting the Aborigines, she had abandoned her Australian husband and also her son, after he reached his teens. Two: Leda, who had embraced the modern science of nutrition, deplored Mrs. Bates's expenditure of two fortunes (from the sale of her Australian properties) to buy special food for the various tribes she lived with. All her money had gone to purchase three staples: white flour, tea, and sugar.

"They were better off eating witchetty grubs!" Leda complained.

Chapter 3

Part 1 — To Townsville

There is a dreamer dreaming us.
— Australian Aboriginal statement of belief

En route Townsville, Queensland
Thursday, 13 November 1941

"Darwin's permanent inhabitants," Captain Ind told Jim, "are prime proof of the Darwinian theory. None but the fittest could survive there."

The Fortress had just lifted off Batchelor Field's red runway and Ind was not yet airsick, although he had his cup in hand. He had come forward to be sociable while he was able, he said; but he would not accept the proffered jumpseat from Jim.

"Darwin's a tough place," Jim agreed. "With some pretty tough customers."

Jim's only regret in leaving Darwin was that Slugger Pell was not coming east on the Fortress; he would remain behind temporarily with the B-18. Slugger and Jim had played five games of squash both evenings at RAAF Station Darwin, and Jim was sorry not to continue the competition throughout the trip. Their games must wait until Brereton's group reached Brisbane. Pell would meet them there with the B-18 to fly them to Melbourne, because Melbourne's airfield could not handle the Flying Fortress' weight.

Jim mentioned to Ind, "Whoever decided that Captain Pell would be a good man to pave the way here was a genius."

Standing behind him, swaying slightly, Ind replied, "Modesty does not permit me to take a bow — nor does my landlubberly stomach."

Jim could think of no one who could have been a better representative of the U.S. Air Corps — for the RAAF's very first acquaintance — than Slugger. Jim had seen how they loved him at RAAF Darwin; he was their kind of "bonzer bloke," even though he didn't drink. Four years out of West Point, Pell seemed as independent, as casually immune to regimentation, spit-and-polish, and chickenshit as any Australian. His patriotism, humor, and sportsmanship matched theirs, and they had embraced him as their own.

Today's destination was Townsville, 1,161 miles to the east, the nearest sizeable settlement. Taking off from Batchelor, climbing out of the red cloud, hearing the bomber's huge wheels thump into their wells, Jim reflexively had waited for the release, the lightness that he loved in a small plane, though he knew a B-17 could never give that feeling.

*But maybe I'll find another kind of freedom — an absence of **inhibitions** — in this unconventional land. . . . My own inhibitions and hers: the unknown "She," the lovely "sheila" who's waiting for me. She'll be a "nice girl," only free from the damned stricture of marriage-before-bed that afflicts all the American girls and Filipinas I know in Manila. And San Antonio, "Mother-in-law of the Army"! I was lucky to get out of there before I promised a wedding ring to Paulette. . . .*

*. . . Surely Townsville **can't** be as dreary as Darwin. And if the Townsvillian civilians are like the uninhibited, "uniformed" Australians I've met, there's fun in store. Anyway, the RAAF men and women at Garbutt Field — I mean Aerodrome — are sure to be good company, good beer-drinkers, good laughers, even if the scenery's as bleak as here.*

. . . We might not even meet any civilians till we reach Melbourne and the government big shots. Dealing with these independent Aussie types on their home territory, I thought the only way to make progress would be in Slugger's easygoing style — so unlike Brereton's! I'd expected that when our tough, cocky, feisty, little General descended on the tough, cocky, feisty, big Australians, with his rapid-fire, radical recommendations for their immediate establishment of facilities for U.S. planes, sparks would fly. But so far — on our first stop — he seems to be doing OK.

This morning Brereton was in a good mood, pleased with his marathon discussions with Brigadier D.V.J. Blake, 54, Commander of Darwin's AIF garrison, and Group Captain Frederick Scherger, 37, Commanding Officer of RAAF Station Darwin. In the copilot's seat, Brereton was telling Eubank of his success.

Seated behind the two senior officers, Jim listened while Brereton praised Scherger as "energetic, efficient, and" — Brereton's highest accolade —

"very *impatient*" to begin the improvement of Batchelor, "to prepare the field for the bombers due any day from the States. It's the old problem of trying to beat the rains," he reminded Eubank, "four months of steady rain, on its way right now. And the situation is damned delicate, with me almost three thousand miles from Melbourne and not yet having reported to the chief of the air staff. Thank God, Scherger's blessed with sufficient initiative to agree to continue the work, even without orders."

Group Captain Scherger obviously was trusting that Brereton's plans would be approved in Melbourne, where he would meet finally with Air Chief Marshal Burnett and Prime Minister Curtin.

"Well, you're operating on trust, too," Eubank said. "Actually you're flying blinder than Scherger is." He reminded Brereton that the Australian government had given MacArthur blanket authority last month to establish ferry routes, training bases, maintenance facilities, munitions storage, and communications in Australian territory.

"But *you* don't know what the hell Congress will give you in the way of funds. Judging by our experience over the past twenty-five years, it won't be anywhere near enough."

"My God, Gene, don't I know it! Even though MacArthur gave me 'unlimited authority to allocate funds and initiate action,' if he doesn't back me up on the promises I'm making to these people, I could be in one helluva pickle."

So could Scherger, Jim thought. *Ye gods — this country's just installed its third government in seven weeks! Suppose they get war-weary, and elect a Pacifist Prime Minister who's scared that having U.S. bombers here will make the place a target for the Japs?*

"MacArthur'll back you, Lew. He wants these air bases," Eubank reassured the General.

"Well, he sure seemed glad to see me. I don't think he was just play-acting. I called on him in his penthouse right after I landed. He'd been resting — he was wearing his old West Point bathrobe —"

Unseen behind the pair, Jim grinned. Every visitor who ever saw MacArthur in his Manila Hotel apartment mentioned that bathrobe. Jim wondered if the General had any other clothes to relax in. And was it really the same robe he had when he graduated in 1903?

"— I gave him the sealed letter from George Marshall — he ripped it open, and when he'd finished it, he threw his arms around me in a bear-hug. A couple of days later, when he ordered me to make this survey, I caught on. I still can hardly believe such a change in the thinking in Washington, but I swear, I feel damned certain that Marshall gave him *carte blanche* to strengthen this entire area."

"Probably. That means the White House wants it done. The President knows damn well that Japan's getting ready for war. . . . But there's more to Washington than the White House. The view from Capitol Hill's a helluva lot more limited — and unfortunately, those nearsighted fellas hold the pursestrings."

I'll bet General Marshall's letter told MacArthur about the goddam Rainbow Plan that super-salesman Churchill sold President Roosevelt! That would explain why we'll be going on up to Singapore from here — so Brereton can see the set-up there and get to know Brooke-Popham and Percival, before they drag us into defending their corner of Forever England. . . .

Brereton was praising the Australian commanders again. Jim had even learned their home towns: Brigadier Blake came from Harris Park, New South Wales, and Group Captain Scherger was from Ararat, Victoria. Although he could point to their home states on a map, the location of their towns was beyond Jim.

He had enjoyed asking the young RAAF people where they came from; the names were so distinctly either exotic Blackfellow, like "Mooloolaba," which he liked, or plain vanilla Whitefellow, such as "High Popham," which he dismissed as too too *veddy transplanted Limey*. (Or "Pommie," as the Australians called the English.) Of course, he had known the same contrast in the States: the Aboriginal AmerIndian place names versus the East Coast homesick-colonists' English copies; but the U.S. admixture of French, Dutch, Spanish, and German names seemed to him to create a Technicolor effect, while Australian place names were a study in black and white (or Blackfellow and Whitefellow).

But how is it possible for Australians to develop such a national personality so soon, in such a newly-settled country? Unlike the English, they surely didn't get homogenized — or stratified — by going to the same schools. But they're all so buoyant, so humorous and friendly. What do they do with their sourpusses and curmudgeons?

With a population the size of Tokyo's, sprinkled over an area the size of the U.S.-minus-Alaska, how did they even keep the same language, the same accents?

Radio deserved much of the credit, Jim decided; it tied them together, so that even the isolated sheep ranches had voice contact — unlike the 7,000 islands of the Philippines, with their many different languages.

In Singapore, Jim and the other American officers had been shocked by the stubborn manner of General Gordon Bennett, Commander of the Australian brigades, when he argued with his superior, the English General Percival about the value of "irregular-warfare training," which Percival forbade. Now Jim understood where that independence came from. Any one of the officers or enlisted men he had met in Darwin seemed fully capable of telling his Commander to go to hell. And yet, the Australians' record in four wars for

England — Sudan, Boer, the "Great War" of 1914, and this one — had been outstanding.

Daly Waters lay just over 300 miles southeast of Darwin. No navigator was needed to find the place; Eubank followed the narrow railroad track that linked the tiny look-alike settlements: Batchelor, Katherine, and Birdum, where the toy railroad ended. That cluster south of Birdum had to be Daly Waters, because south of Daly Waters there was nothing.

As the bomber circled over the barren area, Jim wondered if a "Yank airfield" there would be as disruptive for the Aborigines as the railroad had been. He hoped not; perhaps, unlike the railroad, an airfield could provide good employment for some of them. Surely, Daly Waters — apparently waterless — could only be improved. From the air it looked to him like a "Hooverville" in the U.S., where jobless, homeless Americans huddled in makeshift shelters. About 25 shacks, their dusty metal roofs shimmering in the pitiless sun, stood around the Pearce Hotel and General Store. The red-clay airstrip had been first used in 1933, Lefty's notes said; and it was still as "rudimentary" as those of Katherine, Keats, and Birdum.

To the north of today's route, beyond a mass of tumbled hills, lay the huge Aboriginal Preserve of Arnhem Land; it occupied most of the eastern portion of the broad peninsula whose northwest corner Darwin perched on. Jim was glad that the tribes at least had been allowed to retain an area with water on two sides: the Arafura Sea and the western shore of the huge Gulf of Carpentaria. Arnhem Land, Captain Ind had said, was thought by some scholars to be the remnant of a land bridge that the Aborigines had traversed from southern Asia 40,000 years ago. That explanation left a mystery, however: Why had no tigers, elephants, or other large mammals also used the bridge?

Cloncurry was located about 550 miles southeast of Daly Waters. Eubank had asked Jim to serve as navigator, and Jim was so concerned lest he lose the plane in the trackless Northern Territory that he kept glancing to his left, to be sure that the blue squared-off Gulf of Carpentaria was still visible.

Lefty Eads had piled his paperwork on one end of the navigator's table, trying to get the records of the Darwin discussions in order, and wrestling with the complications of figuring estimates in metric measurements as well as feet and yards, while also changing U.S. dollars into Australian pounds. Sharing the little table, Lefty sat facing the plane's nose, so he could write with his left hand. Already, Lefty wondered aloud how he could manage to get all his calculations on paper for the upcoming estimates of Townsville's facilities, before leaving on Saturday for New Guinea.

General Brereton had ordered Lefty to enumerate for each subsequent stop, as he had done at Darwin, "everything necessary in plant and equipment to provide us with a great air base" — with estimates of all costs. To complicate Lefty's job, the decision was not yet firm as to whether Townsville or

Rockhampton, farther south, would be preferable as the site of the "great air base" for the northeast coast. After the visit to New Guinea, they would survey Rockhampton, and Lefty would make comparative calculations.

Jim could see that his friend was double-checking all his figures constantly, sharply aware of his responsibility; but like Slugger Pell, Lefty had a core of calmness that Jim envied. Captain Ind called him "the un-twitchable Eads."

Jim teased, "Remember the name of that play, *Waiting for Lefty?* I never saw it, but my mother read it and said it was great. Well, just tell General B. that he'll be starring in a performance with that name."

Lefty laughed. "It may have been a hit in New York, but it would have a short run in these parts!" As he looked down at his notes, he chuckled again. "It isn't just the Australian pronunciation that trips me up; some of the familiar words have different meanings. What we call a *plan*, the Aussies call a *scheme*. Every time they refer to one of these 'American schemes,' I feel as if we're engaging in high skullduggery."

"Yeah," Jim agreed. "Have you met a WAG yet? That's a Wireless Air Gunner. I know what each of those words means — but don't ask me how he does it."

As he glanced over Lefty's notes, Jim could understand General Brereton's concern for his own skin. For Brereton's *Project 1,* Lefty estimated an expenditure of $18,000,000 for "the immediate establishment of air bases for a ferry route of U.S. bombers from Hawaii to the Philippines via New Britain, New Guinea, Townsville (or Rockhampton), and Darwin."

Starting right now, this proposed ferry route was going to be surveyed by Brereton and the others aboard Flying Fortress No. 40-3097; after Townsville, they would go on to Port Moresby, New Guinea, and Rabaul, New Britain. No one aboard the B-17, except Eubank, had ever seen any of the suggested locations, and even he had never landed at Townsville or Rabaul.

As part of *Project 1,* "short-legged" fighter aircraft no longer would be sent from the U.S. by sea in crates and assembled in Manila. Instead, the cargo ships would dock on Australia's east coast in Townsville and Brisbane, where the planes would be assembled and flown to Darwin and thence to the Philippines by way of Timor and Borneo. Flying them from Australia's east coast to Darwin would necessitate establishing intermediate refueling stops across this barren northern sector.

Apparently the only two sites that might be suitable for building refueling facilities were Daly Waters and Cloncurry. Brereton would inspect both today — from the air, as their landing strips could not support the B-17.

Jim was astounded at the breadth of Brereton's plans, and at his daring in committing millions of scarce U.S. dollars for projects that he alone would conceive — on the spot. Already, the General envisioned hundreds of U.S. planes flying on aerial highways that would fan out in three directions from

Darwin (yes, *Darwin,* future hub of the Pacific!) — northeastward toward Hawaii, north to Luzon, and northwest to the Netherlands East Indies. To provide ground support for these armadas, he had devised his triple plan.

Meanwhile, the scene below was no improvement on Darwin. The Northern Territory's half-million square miles appeared to comprise only a featureless red wasteland, sere and hostile.

As the sun rose higher, heating the land, the air grew increasingly bumpy, and Jim felt sorry for Captain Ind.

"The poor professor must be popping his last cookies," he remarked to Lefty, whose pencil kept bouncing off the little table.

To Jim's surprise, Ind crawled forward for a brief unhappy look down at the terrain. "I have to see it," he gasped between dry heaves, "so I can truthfully say I saw the Northern Territory." He described the scene as "a vast, flat, pale red waste, pockmarked with those stunted, starved trees. And this," he reminded Jim, "is merely the *edge* of the huge and terrifying desert of the interior. There, a forced landing would mean almost certain disaster, through inexorable thirst and starvation."

After Ind's remarks, Jim "rode the meter," checking for drift every few minutes instead of the customary 15. Surely not even one Whitefellow per square mile could live down there, he thought; but incredibly, the Aborigines did, in small, widely scattered groups. The only signs of Whitefellows' occupation were the hundreds of miles of fences, built to keep out the voracious, invasive rabbits — as futile as France's Maginot Line.

Finally Jim saw a dozen large, dark creatures bounding away from the engines' noise.

"Now I know I'm in Australia," he told Lefty. "My first herd of kangaroos."

"That's known as a 'mob,' buddy."

On the map he saw a landmark, called Mount Brockman by the Australians, which Ind had said was a sacred site for Aboriginal rituals and for the body-painted men's ceremonial dances called *corroborees.*

"What the Australians call 'mountains' look to me like hills," he told Lefty. "I haven't seen anything yet that a Filipino would call a real *bundok.*"

He was glad that Noonan's planning had spared Amelia Earhart this desolate scenery. From Darwin her Electra had flown northeast, over the Gulf of Carpentaria and the Coral Sea, around the tail of New Guinea to Lae, on the southeast coast. That way, they had covered the distance — a little over a thousand miles — in a day.

While we, Jim thought restlessly, *when we finally get to Townsville, will have to mess around there all day Friday — including bearding the fearsome Feldt in his den — and won't get to New Guinea till Saturday night. Damn, I wish we were going to Lae, instead of Port Moresby, so I could see where AE spent those final days. . . .*

It seemed fair to assume that much of the land below was the Alexandra Station, comprising 12,000 square miles, west of Cloncurry; but there was no way to identify it.

Now Jim could empathize with Francis Chichester in 1930: flying 100 feet above that desert at 80 mph, leaning out of his open cockpit to peer myopically through the red haze, searching for Camooweal — 170 miles west of Cloncurry — a town "all of tin . . . in the center of the boundless unvarying plains." Chichester had missed it, but he learned later that all the other England-to-Sydney pilots "got bushed there," also. Missing Camooweal doomed his chance to beat Hinkler's record and dashed his hope to make the Darwin-Sydney run in three days. He had made it in four, though, in the little biplane designed by Geoffrey de Havilland that Beryl Markham (who earned her living flying one in Africa) called the "indomitable" Gipsy Moth. *Allsame indomitable Chichester!*

Now the remnants of frontier shacks appeared below more frequently; this was former Gold Rush country. "Gold fields" as the Australians said, and Jim liked the Klondike, easy pickins, gold-dust-at-my-feet, sound of it; it seemed so much more appealing than the claustrophobic scene of the Benguet Consolidated and other dark, noisy gold mines in the Philippine mountains. But now, seeing the arid reality of those flat gold fields, he thought: *Even though the Philippine mine workers are overworked and underpaid — at least, after a day's sweaty work, they have their glorious, cool green* **bundoks** *to revive their souls.*

Eubank descended over Cloncurry without waiting for Jim's navigational advice. He banked and circled over the little tin-roofed settlement that had been wistfully named for a town beside another Cloncurry River. Its namesake in Ireland surely was a green village whose stream held fish, as well as water, Jim supposed, although here the river named on the map was only a dry watercourse on the barren ground.

The shadow of the bomber's huge wings stretched a wide moving black band across Cloncurry, and at the sound of the four engines, people ran out of their houses, waving a greeting with rags and towels. To the townspeople's evident delight, Eubank buzzed the street, flying so low that Jim could read the names of the sagging Leichard Hotel and the sadly collapsed Bio Cinema.

"Just like a little town in Texas or Oklahoma," Eubank said. "People get lonesome."

"Don't kid yourself," Brereton cracked. "They just want to take advantage of their moment in the shade!"

The typical dusty landing strip bore no sign to mark its important place in aerial history. Jim was disappointed not to see statues or some kind of memorial to the men who had pursued their compassionate dream and made it come true in this God-forsaken spot: John Flynn, the Irish preacher who envisioned the possibility; Alfred Traeger, the radio genius who made it feasible; and the dedicated, courageous physicians who first began their mercy flights from Cloncurry to the isolated families in the Northern Territory. Now in 1941, The Flying Doctor Service's network encompassed the entire continent.

Here in Cloncurry and back at Daly Waters — as well as at Townsville (or Rockhampton) and Brisbane — Brereton had told Scherger, he wanted the Australians to build what they termed aerodromes: with assembly plants, training centers, and repair depots. Jim tried to picture such massive construction in this great emptiness. These gold fields would become magnets again, but for how long? After the war scare was over and the U.S. withdrew to its own shores, would Cloncurry revert to a ghost town? How could it do otherwise? Lefty's notes reported that the land between here and Daly Waters knew intervals of five, six, or seven years when no rain fell.

"That's not bad," Jim told him. "In 1930, when Chichester was here, it hadn't rained in Camooweal for nine years." He began to glance at Lefty's notes again.

Project 2 was to develop those air bases, and such other fields as might be needed, to accommodate an American air force, probably to be composed initially of a heavy bombardment group, three bomber reconnaissance squadrons, three pursuit/fighter groups, and their accompanying services, for tactical operations and training.

Estimated cost to the United States, around $35,000,000.

Jim was indignant. "Thirty-five *million* smackeroos! Damn it, Lefty, if Nichols Field could have had the thirty-five *hundred* bucks that's been needed since the 1920s for the runway — my squadron could be based there now, enjoying the bright lights of Manila, instead of being stuck out in the *bundoks* at Clark —"

Eads just looked at him and shook his head. No one knew the problems of the swampy, sea-level Nichols Field runway better than he, except Colonel George. In the final week of July — after the Japanese moved into southern Viet Nam, and President Roosevelt cut off Japan's oil, iron, and rubber imports, barred Japanese shipping from the Panama Canal, and appointed MacArthur a major general — the War Department had authorized $10,000,000 for Philippine defenses. Lefty, in haste to drain the muddy old runway and build a second one, had told the pursuit squadron commanders that they must clear out. His project was still unfinished when General Brereton had tapped him for this "human calculator" assignment. Colonel George, an ace fighter pilot, not an engineer like Lefty, had added Nichols to his own long list of fields to improve.

Well, at least Brereton's big thinking isn't limited to Australia. He agrees with Colonel George's fantastic proposed dream-plan for the Philippines: four fighter groups, instead of our one-and-only 24th Pursuit Group; two heavy bomber groups, and one light bomber group! And Sutherland endorsed it, and MacArthur has told the War Department that it's what's needed for a decent defense — and to scare the Japs into abandoning their southward advance. . . . But I'm not dumb enough to think Congress would give the Philippines — **and** Australia — that much money, no matter how much President Roosevelt wants it done.

Even Jim, who did not share completely the President's commitment to save England, felt that the courageous Royal Air Force deserved to have airplanes. Last year, the U.S. Army Air Corps had "deferred acceptance" of 8,586 new U.S.-built aircraft and ferried them to England. Early this year, the Lend-Lease program, FDR's clever circumvention of the Neutrality Act, had found enough supporters in Congress to get authorization passed, for a sum the Australians referred to as "the seven thousand million dollars," to cover war materiel for England and China. When that bill was passed on 27 March, no one had thought of building airfields in Australia, Jim was certain.

What's going to be left for us? And how in hell is our Depression-battered country, that can't even pay its schoolteachers, going to come up with all this dough?

Remaining on Brereton's Wish List, *Project 3*, for which, understandably, funds were not yet earmarked, seemed wildly grandiose to Jim: to survey the possibilities for developing training bases and additional operating bases to accommodate approximately *four* bombardment groups and one bombardment training center, in addition to *four* fighter groups and one fighter training center.

The plan that excited Jim and filled him with hope and anticipation was *Project 4:* to survey a possible ferry route for P-40s assembled in Townsville or Rockhampton to fly northwestward from Darwin to Chennault's secret Volunteer Group in China — by way of *Timor, lads!*, and Java, and sweet Singapore. Jim wanted desperately to be a member of the team for that survey, which General MacArthur had included in Brereton's Australian mission; however, there was a chance that Brereton might decide to return to Manila before undertaking it. If he did, doubtless his junior aide, Lieutenant Wade Hampton, would have arrived in Manila and would replace Jim. Captain Ind's romantic heart was on Jim's side; he had been dropping helpful remarks to Brereton concerning Jim's familiarity with the Netherlands East Indies and the entire "Malay Barrier," and his long friendship with Chennault.

The thought of holding Daphne again made him breathe faster. Although when he left Singapore he had promised himself that he would never forgive her, he could not bear to remain estranged from her. This time, he knew, he could persuade her to give up the opium. Word had come from Hong Kong that Emily Hahn, the writer who had been addicted for years, had renounced the drug in order to produce a healthy baby by the man of her choice. "If she can do it, you can," Jim would tell Daphne; surely her competitive spirit would surmount that challenge.

Only about 400 miles to Townsville now — and the view was improving: Patches of grassland, larger clumps of trees, indicated a more merciful pattern of rainfall. Twisted, dusty-looking gum trees were still preponderant, but here they were almost a normal tree color, not the ghostly pallor of those left behind in the Northern Territory. This was Queensland state. Cloncurry was the railhead for narrow-gauge tracks that led east and then north to Townsville, making the navigator's job a snap, just in time for jovial Captain Llewellyn to take over. Back in the jump seat, Jim listened as Brereton expressed his concerns to Eubank.

Group Captain Scherger had received from Singapore the RAF's November Intelligence Summary, and it was an ominous one. Previously, the RAAF had estimated that Japan possessed 2,860 military aircraft, many of them in the Fleet Air Arm; but now the British sources stated the total as 4,500 first-line airplanes.

"And you know what we've got in the Far East Air Force to go up against those. Thirty-five of these heavies. Two squadrons of mediums: B-18s, plus some spares. And fighters: seventy-two P-40s and twenty-eight P-35s."

"Don't overlook the Philippine Air Force. Those fellas are hot pilots."

"Sure — but flying an obsolete P-26, not even Slim Lindbergh could last five minutes in a dogfight. . . . The worst thing is knowing that we can't expect much more from the States. In a way, they're worse off than we are, because they don't even have these Fortresses. Not one single complete heavy bomber group in the entire U.S.," he reminded Eubank.

Brereton continued, "I don't need to tell *you*, we're a third-rate air power. I got the grim numbers in Washington when I left. There are still only two officers in the goddam War Department who have any real sense of urgency about what Japan might do out here — Tom Betts and Rufe Bratton — and they pitied me. In the entire Air Forces combat commands, we have only sixty-four first pilots and ninety copilots qualified for four-engine bombers. We have ninety-seven first pilots and one hundred eight copilots qualified for two-engine medium bombers. And not one single, goddam qualified dive-bomber pilot!"

Amid the noise of the plane, Jim strained to hear Brereton state the most important number: "Only one hundred seventy-one pursuit pilots —"

One hundred and seventy fucking fighter pilots — and **me***!*

"— desperate shortage of qualified combat men in all categories. Barely one hundred navigators or bombardiers, fewer than two hundred fifty radio operators, only about two hundred seventy aerial engineers."

Eubank said, "Well, I don't need to remind you that when we got into the World War, the U.S. didn't have even fifty pilots, and had no front-line aircraft whatsoever. In June of 1917, the only U.S. air power in France was Billy Mitchell in a French Nieuport! And consider the shape these Australians were in, just two years ago — only three hundred officers in their entire Air Force, and three thousand 'other ranks,' on the day they declared war. And now, Scherger says, they have *seventy thousand* men — and some women — in RAAF uniforms, here and overseas, and in the training pipeline. A country can do a helluva lot in a hurry, when push comes to shove."

"Dammit, Gene — like us in 1917 — the RAAF had the luxury of not needing to defend their home country," Brereton snapped. "In 1917, we could afford to waste fourteen months before American aircraft production got going. But if the Germans had been as close to this continent in 1939 as Japan is to us in the Philippines right now, the Australians wouldn't have had those two years to get ready. They'd be saying '*Heil,* Hitler,' by this time."

Jim could not imagine the irreverent Australians rendering obeisance to any foreigner, even to Hitler's apparently unbeatable Storm Troopers.

Tomorrow he would face Commander Eric Feldt, the boss of the Coastwatchers, in the meeting that was the sole reason for Jim's presence on this mission.

Feldt. *Strictly Teutonic — and probably Teutonically strict. Tough as a Hollywood Nazi.*

Suppose he quizzes me about my knowledge of radios — finds out I've never had any formal instruction — haven't even graduated from high school — **Mein Gott in Himmel!** *Making my crystal set when I was a kid won't impress ole Eric — hell, all boys do that. What if he gives me a Morse code test? I haven't tapped a damned key since I got out of flying school; I could send/receive at forty words per minute then, but now I probably couldn't handle more than about five words a minute. . . . He'll probably tell Brereton I've given him a lousy opinion of U.S. officers, and why the hell did they waste his precious time on me?*

But I know how I'll impress him; I'll tell him about the fine civilian Coastwatchers I've recruited in the Philippines: Claud Fertig and "Spence" Spencer from the gold mines on Masbate, the Physical Ed teacher at Silliman University on Panay, Bob Crump at Surigao, McNeil Crawford at Del Monte, Father Haggerty and the Ozamiz family at Cagayan de Oro. And down at Zamboanga, Fritz Worcester, and Tommy Jurika. That's an All-Star cast!

— Stars in the Philippines, but they're nothing in Australia. Those names — the people or the places — won't mean any more to Commander Feldt than it would mean to you if he told you Joe Doakes was a Coastwatcher at Mirranpongapongunna.

At last the Many Peaks Range of hills outside Townsville broke the terrain's flat monotony, and soon Black Mountain ("solid iron," they had been warned) broke the flight's droning monotony by affecting the plane's magnetic compass. Now the coast, luscious green against the blue Coral Sea, soothed Jim's sun-weary eyes.

The runway at Garbutt Field was not long enough to land a B-17 on. "A damned short cigar-butt," Eubank wisecracked. However, with "everything open," he managed to drop and stop inside the fields of tall sugar cane that surrounded the strip, while Jim mentally burned out the brakes.

In the silence, Brereton barked, "Lefty, put this at the top of your Townsville list: a *five-thousand-foot runway for Garbutt!*"

Eubank said, "And Lefty — add that we'd prefer for it to have *some* reference to the prevailing wind from the Coral Sea."

Part 2 — Tropical Townsville

If the president can be made to see that the trouble will start with Japan, perhaps we'll have more planes in the Philippines and Hawaii. For years he's had the idea that a war in the Far East would be impractical, and that an attack upon us by Japan is inconceivable. The Japanese will not politely declare war. They are treacherous and will stop at nothing. Hawaii, for instance, is vulnerable from the sky. It is wide open to Japan. Yet we bring the Navy in at Pearl Harbor and lock it up every Saturday night so that the sailors can spend their week's pay to please the merchants and politicians who have arranged that routine because they think it is good for business. And Hawaii is swarming with Japanese spies. As I have said before, that's where the blow will be struck — on a fine, quiet Sunday morning.
 — Brigadier General William Landrum Mitchell, 1934

RAAF Station Garbutt
Thursday evening, 13 November 1941

Air Commodore F. W. F. Lukis, RAAF, was neither tall nor blond; a most unusual Australian, Jim thought. The compact brunet officer, resembling Brereton in size and coloring, greeted each of the Americans with a grin as boyish as Brereton's own and an equally firm handshake.

Chapter 3 — Part 2 — Tropical Townsville

"Nice looking machine you have there, *Mister* Brereton!"

Five American "civilians" emerging from a giant silver bomber will be more conspicuous here than we were in the Outback at Batchelor, Jim realized. *And unlike Darwin, Townsville looks like a real town — or at least a* **ville** *— where real civilians won't be fooled by these Yank misters in mufti. Hell, if we're going to travel incognito (or "in the Congo," as David says) we might as well play it all the way — like Chennault's secret fighter pilots, sailing from the States "disguised" as missionaries, cowboys, and acrobats!*

The Americans' borrowed civilian suitcases were stowed in a lorry driven by an attractive young woman who wore the uniform of the volunteer WAAAF (Women's Auxiliary Australian Air Force), olive drab slacks and jacket, and a sassy-looking visored cap.

What a fine innovation, Jim thought; *women really add the missing ingredient to military life.*

Townsville seemed a charming little seaport, much like many in the Philippines, and Jim felt at home at once. Although it was much farther from the Equator than Darwin, it received an adequate rainfall and thus was "tropical" as Jim used the word, meaning humid. Royal palms and Ceylonese pipul trees lined the Esplanade, where he admired spacious, well-built homes, almost in the category of mansions, much like the "Sugar Barons' Row" in cities of the southern Philippines.

Alas, poor Darwin, he thought that evening in the Officers' Mess, as he relished every bite of fresh food: nothing *"tinned."* His sense of being at home was completed by a menu of seafood, with luscious fruits whose appearance he knew well, although some of their names had acquired Australian accents. "Mud crabs" had a delicate flavor that belied their unappetizing name. A salad of papaya and avocado, called paw-paw and alligator pear, was pepped up with a lemon dressing, and the dessert was ice cream with a delicate flavor. Jim recognized the familiar taste — combining the blandness of banana with the tartness of pineapple — of the large, sweet fruit he called ceramin.

"Its Latin name is *monstera deliciosa,*" an officer remarked.

The pilot seated beside Jim snickered. "Sounds like an Aussie shootin' a line to his sheila," he murmured.

The young flying officers were jovial company, beer was plentiful, and the Maidens in Uniform combined the attributes of beauty and friendliness. Best of all, RAAF Station Garbutt was home to only one squadron, No. 24. The competition for the Maidens' attention was nothing like that in Darwin.

If I just didn't have to meet Commander Feldt tomorrow, I could really like this place.

No. 24 Squadron was a new type, called "composite," comprised of both bombers and fighter planes: 5 Hudsons, 11 Wirraways, 3 Moth Minors, and 1 Fairey Battle.

Jim had seen only one Hudson bomber at Garbutt. The other four were temporarily on detached duty with part of No. 24 Squadron at Rabaul, New Britain. "I'll be meeting those fellows next week," he told their squadron-mates.

He wondered how well the composite squadron "scheme" would work for Americans; would fighter pilots feel the same squadron spirit if bomber pilots shared their unit numeral? Although he liked all the B-17 pilots recently arrived at Clark Field, he didn't care much for the idea of integration.

The RAAF officers were united, at least, in their appreciation of the sudden U.S. decision, personified by Brereton, to join in strengthening Australia's air defense. They also hailed the tidings that "you Yanks are beefing up your strength in the Philippines."

". . . Too right. With your bloody Fortresses, you're now in a position to retaliate against any bastard Jap aggression, anywhere."

". . . Too right. You Yanks have the *ability* to stop 'em, if you've the bloody *will* to use it," another commented.

". . . Too right. Our security depends on Singapore and Manila, myte."

". . . Too right. Now that you blokes will flank the bloody Japs' Indochina airfields on the east, with a force as strong as Singapore's on the west — we can stop wingeing about that dagger pointed our way."

Jim conceded, "You've had reason to worry, with so many of your troops overseas."

"If the Japs make trouble, we'll bloody well call our blokes home, myte," declared the man beside him. "The Fat Boy would screech like a bloody cockatoo, but our Diggers would come back, believe me."

But even if they were all here at home, Jim thought, *there would be only seven million of you — counting every woman and child. And Scherger says Japan has* **six** *million men in uniform.*

Like brothers, the members of the Commonwealth family were free with their criticism of each other; but as Jim had noted in Singapore, the Australians did not appreciate hearing Americans make unflattering remarks about the English. After dinner, drinking the delicious beer they called "Barbed Wire" (because of the pattern made by the label's four X's), the young officers would express bitter feelings about "the bloody Pommie generals." They were wasting the tanks, artillery, and — especially — the aircraft that Australia was arduously producing and shipping to the various fronts. Aussies were being killed, they said, because they lacked the Australia-made equipment that was diverted to "other Empire forces."

Weary of war talk and of playing Two-Up, Jim wangled an introduction to an attractive young woman wearing the double horizontal stripes of a WAAAF Flight Officer on her shoulderboards. Jim thought her trim, navy blue dress uniform was extremely becoming to her direct blue eyes, reddish-gold hair, and tall, slim-hipped figure.

The Maidens wasted no time on ironing their shirts, he had noticed; the material was a heavy white cotton, worn rough-dry from the clothesline. He was unable to complete his customary appraisal: *Is she well-stacked?* The shirts were oversized, their roominess and full sleeves would make for easy working; but the result was almost as sexless as the quilted blue jackets worn by female Chinese coolies, he thought.

The bozo who decided on issuing those shirts to the girls was obviously scared to death that their mammary glands would disrupt the RAAF.

The "Hair Dictator" must be a real woman-hater, Jim decided. Scarcely any of the young women's "crowning glory" could be seen beneath the dark blue, soft-crowned visored caps that resembled pictures Jim had seen of Greek fishermen's caps. What little hair was visible was severely restricted in a mandatory style evidently designed for glamorless utility. Shaped like a skinny elongated sausage, the roll of hair extended around the back of the neck from behind one ear to the other. Jim decided it was the feminine version of the GI haircut.

"Penny" Parker had been christened Penelope, she told him; however, as soon as her copper-colored hair had appeared, that name had changed.

"Just as well," Jim said. "Penelope sounds highly intimidating. But I'd like to see some more of your hair. Are you girls ever allowed to — uh — let your hair down?"

"Only when we swim."

Penny was "keen on swimming," she said. She was from "a little seaside spot just a bit south of Townsville," which she called "Mack-EYE," although the name was spelled Mackay. Her parents raised sugar cane. Here at RAAF Station Garbutt, she worked in the Cipher office. Jim knew enough not to inquire any further about that duty, so he told her truthfully that he thought it was a great idea to have women in an air force.

"Oh, the RAAF fought it like bloody hell," she told him with an enchanting grin. "Only two things got our service born — a total shortage of male wireless telegraphists and our Mrs. Bell, the mother of the WAAAF."

Flight Officer M.T.L. Bell (female Australians had those triple initials, too, Jim noted) was a pilot in her own right, and a "ground engineer," Penny said proudly. Early in the war, Mrs. Bell had begun to urge the government to utilize the abilities of Australian women. Finally, this February, the severe shortage of male telegraphers had forced the RAAF to accept some women. (Morse code sending and receiving minimum: 20 words per minute.) Mrs. Bell had been appointed Acting Director of the new Women's Australian Auxiliary Air Force; she had refused, however, to accept a rank higher than that of Flight Officer.

"The 'gallant' men gave her a room with two tables, one chair, one enlistment form, a telephone, and nothing else. Then they told her, 'Get us two hundred fifty telegraphist sheilas at once, and don't bother us any more!' Luckily, her husband was Group Captain J.R. Bell — one of the *original* RAAF pilots — so she knew all the senior officers, and through friendships and fossicking, she managed to get an organization going."

In less than a year, the WAAAF had grown to nearly 700 airwomen and almost 50 officers — including Penny — paid at two-thirds of the amount a man of the same rank received. An enlisted airwoman received five shillings, eight pence per day.

"Far less than a U.S. dollar," Penny said; but hundreds of women were applying; new "musterings" had been added (specialties which included positions as clerks, drivers, cooks, mess stewards, and aircraft painters); and 320 new recruits had been accepted.

So the world's best-paid army doesn't share its wealth with the dames, Jim thought. "Well, some day you'll be a rich Air Marshal, and you can buy me a 'pot of brew,'" he told Penny.

"Oh, there's no military future for us women — we're only in the service for the duration."

"Duration of what?" Jim had never heard the phrase.

"Of the *war*, you nonk! They're only letting in the minimum number of women, for the minimum time."

"That's too bad, if you like military life."

"Love it. But this has done our blokes some good, anyhow. They've never thought women were good for anything except keeping house and raising brats. But now that the men are working beside us — and it's the same in the war plants — they can see that we have brains; and we're gaining more respect. After the war, we'll not go back to being stepped-on sheilas, you can bet."

"You sound like my mother. She says 'Rosie the Riveter,' working in a war plant in the States, isn't going to settle for being a housewife, ever again."

"Good on your mum!"

"She'd like you, Penny. And she has excellent taste."

"Well, that's better than a poke in the eye! Almost as good as winning 'the Golden Coffin' — our state lottery!"

The RAAF's evening chorus of "Waltzing Matilda" resounded from the game room. "I'm beginning to like that tune," Jim told her. "But even after the words were explained to me, they still don't make much sense."

"The tune's an old Scottish marching song, but we like the words as well — they're our own beloved bush language. Tough luck, there won't by any more like that one; Banjo Paterson, the bloke who wrote it, died this year. He was our best man for bush ballads. He didn't just write in 'Strine, though — he could write in straight bloody English, too. He was a war correspondent in

South Africa, China, your Philippine rebellion — and the Great War."

Jim seized his chance to impress her. "Sounds like my friend Cecil Brown. He's covered the European war — I mean, *your* war — from Rome, Yugoslavia, Turkey, Cairo —"

It worked. The blue eyes widened. "Cecil Brown, the wireless reporter? My word, we listen to his broadcast from Singapore every day! Do you really know him?"

"He's my *pal*." Jim could not resist adding, "It was Martha Gellhorn — Ernest Hemingway's bride — who introduced me to Cess Brown at the Raffles Hotel. Listen, Penny, how about let's get a ride to downtown Townsville, and you can show me your favorite pub, and — since you get only two-thirds pay — I'll buy you a 'barb-wire,' and we can talk about Cess Brown, and about you."

She shook her head. "Thanks, Jim. I'd really love to — but that's not possible."

"Why not?" Ghastly thought: "Are you engaged?"

Penny laughed, showing her fine white teeth. "Not bloody likely! Every time I start to get interested in a bloke, he gets shipped overseas. The trouble is that you're in Queensland State now, myte. And in Queensland, the law says, no woman — not even a Queen — shall be permitted to enter a pub."

"Ye gods! Talk about 'stepped-on-sheilas'! So Queen Victoria's ghost is still in charge — that's awful."

Of all women in history, Queen Victoria was Jim's least favorite. He had hated her ever since he first learned that she shared his birthday, and because of her, his *own* 24 May was known around the world as "Victoria Day"! He felt that her smug, stodgy, dumpy, prudish imperialist personality cast a shadow of doubt on his own lively Geminian horoscope. He so hated the idea of any star-cast similarity with her that he had come to prefer the Chinese reading of astrology, linking character traits to the year of birth, rather than to the day. But never had he resented her so much as this minute.

"Tough cheddar — but no worries," Penny said. "After the war, I'm going to look for work in Brisbane. Come to see me there, and I'll show you a lively city where we can drink pots of brew in plenty of pubs."

"That's a date," Jim answered. "I can stand to skip the pub-crawl, but isn't there someplace in Townsville where we can dance, or see a movie?"

"The pictures are over by now, and it's too near Lights Out to go dancing." She did sound regretful.

"I'll be here till Saturday morning. Couldn't I take you to dinner in town tomorrow night?"

"We don't say 'dinner,' we say 'tea.' But I'd like to show you the beach, after work tomorrow. We could take some tucker — I have a friend who works in the mess hall; she'll fix us a cut lunch — if you'd care to bring the beer."

"Sounds *swell* to me."

"And then, before dark, I'll show you the dancing wild birds. . . ."

Part 3 — Coastwatcher Commander

"Jangga meenya bomunggur."
(The smell of the white man is killing us.)
— Plaint of Australian Aborigines,
Daisy Bates, *The Passing of the Aborigines*, 1938

Townsville, Queensland, Australia
Friday, 14 November 1941

"The two essential qualifications of a Coastwatcher," Commander Eric A. Feldt told Jim, "are initiative and integrity." His gray-blue eyes examined Jim from beneath broad, dark brown eyebrows, as if he were searching for signs of these two qualities but finding neither.

Hell, I've flunked already, Jim thought, *without even a Morse code test.*

In his trim, dark blue uniform of the Royal Australian Navy, the slender officer was handsome, with a long aristocratic nose, a small, well-shaped mouth, and a firm, cleft chin. The tanned face beneath the gray hair appeared younger than Jim had expected, for he knew that Feldt had been forced out of the Royal Australian Navy by an economy cut in 1922 — the year that Jim was two years old.

*Steely eyes, iron-gray hair — hard as nails. He's not only old; he's **cold.***

"I suppose you would like to see one of our Teleradios?"

"Yes, Sir, I would — if it isn't too much trouble."

Does he think I'm a Jap spy?

"My assistant will demonstrate one, below decks. But first, I suppose I should try to explain to you our Coastwatching scheme. Its embryonic state developed in the Great War, because the islands to our northeast had been German colonies since the 1890s. With our twelve thousand miles of coastline unfortified, our Navy was understandably nervy about German ships prowling about — so we had a few men trying to keep an eye on them."

Feldt stood up and pulled back a curtain from a map of northern Australia, showing the bird-shape of New Guinea flying eastward above the coast. Briskly, he tapped the northernmost tip of Queensland: Cape York Peninsula, which pointed sharply toward the New Guinea-bird's belly.

"Only a hundred miles between us just there, you see." Feldt turned and his eyes bored into Jim as if to see whether Jim was capable of following him. He took a deep breath. "If a man's home is threatened, he can stand in the door with a shotgun. However, if he wishes to protect his property, his best bet is to build a strong fence. Here in Queensland, the sheep-ranchers have erected 'Dingo fences,' six feet high, more than three thousand miles long, to protect their flocks from the wild dogs that Kipling called 'Yellow Dog Dingo.'"

He looks as if he's wondering if this ignorant Yank ever heard of Kipling, Jim thought. *Shall I recite "The Widow at Windsor" for him?*

"— But a fence is no good if there's a single gap in it," Feldt continued.

"Too right, Sir."

Maybe the Aussie phrase will show him I'm an OK bloke. Nuh-oh. He didn't like it. He thinks I'm mocking his countrymen.

Feldt went on, "Therefore, we — and you-lot in the Philippines, for the same reason, an unguardable coastline — need men to observe continually the island passages and sound the warning if any threatening ships or aircraft are loitering about."

Commander Feldt turned his back on Jim. His pointer tapped rapidly down the Solomon Islands, the New Hebrides, the French island of New Caledonia, and beyond. Hovering above them, like a swarm of bees, hung the clusters of dark, tiny Japanese-held islands.

"We invaded these German islands after the Great War began in 1914. And, incidentally, we treated their colonists very gently, allowing them to remain on their plantations, while we bought their produce. In 1920, the League of Nations mandated them to us. Now we had our rudimentary 'fence.' But in an island chain — such as you have in the Philippines — every sea lane is an open gate. We established District officers on each island, to attempt to prevent the natives from eating each other. Those officers were also to serve as our eyes.

"Fortunately, my Naval College classmate, Commander R.B.M. Long, a brilliant man — a *leader*, not a boss — was appointed as the Royal Australian Navy's first full-time Director of Naval Intelligence. Aware that our island screen was a mass of gaps, and imbued with the idea that Japan would one day enter the war, he pressed for a Coastwatcher scheme and got it approved. His foresight made my work possible. In 1939, when Australia joined England in declaring war on Germany, I was called back into the Navy, and he assigned me to close those gaps.

"War is the only event which will persuade any Parliament to cut the pursestrings for military purposes. I was allowed sufficient funds to have the Teleradios manufactured. And — as the hostilities were not on our own doorstep — I had the rare wartime blessing of *time*. God knows, I needed it. I've been hard at it for two years, on the islands, and finally we've patched up the holes in our fence."

Feldt's pointer gently indicated various colored push-pins dotted over the islands. "These are our Coastwatcher stations. We now have a few more than a hundred observers. They're stationed from here" — he indicated Hollandia, at the border with Dutch New Guinea — "from the western border of our Papua, New Guinea, through the Bismarck Sea and the Solomons Sea, all the way down to Vila, in the New Hebrides, the southern pillar at the end of our twenty-five-hundred-mile fence."

More than a hundred Coastwatchers! I had to sweat to recruit a handful in the Philippines. But hell, I had no pay to offer them.

As if Feldt had read Jim's mind and reproached him, he continued, "Except for the District officers, our Coastwatchers are all civilian volunteers, serving without pay: planters, miners, missionaries. Each man has his Teleradio — and ten or so loyal natives to carry it, should it become necessary for him to break camp. Coastwatchers at the northwestern end of the chain send their reports to Tulagi; those at the other end, to Vila; and in turn, Tulagi and Vila report to my headquarters here. Now, Mr. Davis, I must attend to my duties. My assistant, Sub-Lieutenant Evans, will demonstrate a Teleradio below."

Descending to the dank basement, Jim was sweating, relieved to be out of range of Commander Feldt's icy glance, but filled with a sense of failure and shame. He felt belittled and humiliated: as if, completing a flight check in flying school at Kelly Field, he had been on final approach in an AT-6 when Captain Sluder, his instructor, yelled for him to put his wheels down. He wanted to be liked, and he was accustomed to having people like him, and he had never met an Australian who had not been "matey" from the first handshake. Feldt had not even shaken his hand.

— Your sole excuse for coming to Australia, Jim berated himself, *and you flubbed it! He despised you, and you didn't learn a damned thing.*

Arthur Reginald Evans gave Jim a warm handshake. He was probably in his late thirties, but he had a boyish manner that Jim found refreshing after the stiffness of the "upper deck" meeting. Evans was from Sydney, and Jim had learned from Penny that Sydney people had a low opinion of Queensland.

"What's a sophisticated Sydneysider doing, so far north?" Jim asked him.

"I was lucky," the thin, dark-haired officer said, in a mellow voice that suited his Welsh name. "I was in the AIF. I had a cobber, a buddy, who knew a bloke who was matey with Commander Feldt. He got word to the Commander that I was keen to transfer out of the Army and into the Navy so I could work with him on radios. The Commander arranged it, and I'd follow him anywhere — even to some place worse than Townsville. Even into the bush."

No accounting for tastes, Jim thought.

"Here's our standard Teleradio, Type 3-B-Z. It was developed for Commander Feldt by Amalgamated Wireless of Australia."

Jim's heart sank when he saw the size of the radio. He had hoped for a gadget like the wrist-radio worn by the comic strip detective Dick Tracy; but this object was larger than a footlocker.

"How the hell could anyone get that thing up a mountain?"

"It breaks down into the components," Evans explained. "I'll admit, the speaker, receiver, and transmitter each weigh more than seventy-five pounds — but not much over one hundred."

"But then you'd have to lug the batteries —"

"Too right. And the charging engine, and the benzine to keep that running."

"And I thought your boss was exaggerating when he said ten natives were needed to carry a Teleradio."

"Actually, he was. Sixteen is best, and twelve is the minimum. The sets are tough as hell, though, and they rarely go crook."

Jim stared at all the dials; they reminded him of the instrument panel of a B-17.

"You can send by telegraph key or by voice. Three hundred miles is 'quids in' — easy. Up to four hundred by voice, and as far as six hundred by key."

Six hundred miles, Jim thought, *Clark Field to Zamboanga. Not bad.*

"Commander Feldt invented what we call the 'X' frequency, for emergencies. We've fitted each Teleradio with a crystal, cut to give that special frequency, and it will be received at any hour on a loudspeaker reserved for that channel, kept switched on day and night at Rabaul and Port Moresby."

"We have a 'Guard' channel like that for planes, in the States."

"Did the Commander tell you how he tested the equipment in the bush?"

"Hell, no. He was strictly business."

Reg Evans grinned. "He does come over a bit stiff in the office. Maybe it's the Navy — like being on the bloody bridge? But he's actually a bonzer bloke."

Jim had known whole flotillas of naval officers, and they didn't carry the "bloody bridge" on shore! He knew the Commander of the U.S. Asiatic Fleet, Admiral Hart. Even the limey Admiral *Sir* Geoffrey Layton of the Royal Navy in Singapore was more cordial than Feldt had been.

"The Commander wouldn't assign anyone else to test the Teleradio under jungle conditions. I've seen all those cannibal islands from the water — I was the purser on an island steamer before the war. But I've never been in the bush out there, thank you. Last year, though, the Commander himself spent three months up on a mountain behind Port Moresby, with his native guides, sending practice messages back here to us. He knows those hellacious New Guinea jungles like his own hand — he lived out there for years. When the Navy called him back in 1939, he was on duty as Warden of the gold fields at Wau."

Everyone in the Far East who cared about flying knew of the daring New Guinea bush pilots in their trusty Junkers. In the 1920s and 1930s, until the gold bubble burst, they had carried in the mining equipment and carried out the gold from the otherwise inaccessible area around Wau in the forbidding Owen Stanley range.

"Commander Feldt's a pilot himself," Evans said. "Flew a light plane between those bastard peaks, many a time."

Damn! A pilot, and a radio nut. But a helluva hard nut to crack.

Evans, however, was a compatible radio nut, and he obviously enjoyed showing Commander Feldt's collection to Jim. The basement was a museum of radio history. One item that drew Jim's admiration was a 1926 model of the pedal-operated transceiver devised by Alfred Traeger of Adelaide. Portable, compact, durable, and easy for an amateur to use, sets like this one had become the voices of the isolated sheep stations. They had made the Flying Doctor Service a merciful reality.

Back on the street, waiting for a RAAF bus to Garbutt Aerodrome, Jim was still wincing from his own self-doubts.

Well, Second Lieutenant Big Shot, the truth is out. All your so-called Irish charm, Irish wit, and Irish luck were really Leda's — and they didn't rub off on you. You've never done anything on your own merit, and you never will. You're only in Australia because you roomed with Captain Ind during the Clagett Mission to Singapore and Java. The only reason General Clagett took you with him then — and later to China — was that he likes Leda, and you were always hanging around his quarters when you were a kid, crazy about Jean and Louise. . . . Captain Chennault only happened to know you because you and Pat made sand castles on Waikiki when you boys were toddlers. . . . And just because Chennault let you come to Chungking, you happened to meet the Time-Life team, Teddy White, Annalee and Mel Jacoby, and Shelley and Carl Mydans. . . . You never would have met Hemingway if Leda wasn't Janet Walker's golf partner, so you got invited to the Walkers' party. And if

Hemingway's bride hadn't been in Singapore, you wouldn't have met Cecil Brown and the other newsmen. . . . General MacArthur only speaks to you because he met his gorgeous former mistress, Peaches Rosario Cooper, at one of Leda's parties! By yourself, you're nuthin'. Today you had your first chance to make an impression without your mama, and you fell on your ass. You went to Feldt's office with a chip on your shoulder, and he knocked it off. He's probably writing a report right now, demanding never to be pestered again by lousy Yank jerks like you.

Part 4 — Penny

A member of the Embassy was told by my [Peruvian] colleague that from many quarters, including a Japanese one, he had learned that a surprise mass attack on Pearl Harbor was planned by the Japanese military forces, in case of "trouble" between Japan and the United States; that the attack would involve the use of all the Japanese military facilities. . . .
— Telegram from U.S. Ambassador Joseph Grew in Tokyo to Secretary of State Cordell Hull, 27 January 1941

Townsville, Queensland
Friday afternoon, 14 November 1941

    Penny's evident enjoyment of Jim's company salved the sting of Commander Feldt's apparent dislike. She looked as beautiful now in the tropical daylight as she had appeared last evening in the starlight, when Jim had walked with her to the steps of her barracks. She had let him hold her hand as they walked, but when he tried to kiss her goodnight she shook her head, laughing. "Not so fast with the smoodgin', Yank — Garbutt isn't Hollywood!"
    Today, as Penny walked beside him in Townsville, heads turned to look at them. She was 5'10", and he was aware that their good looks and contrasting coloring made them an outstanding couple, even in this nation of stunningly handsome people. The austerity of her uniform and cap seemed to set off her

glowing skin and vivid blue eyes.

*We'd be a knockout pair if I could wear **my** uniform,* he thought; although he knew that the white shorts made by Yee Long in Darwin were showing his long, tanned, and muscular legs to good advantage. The shorts fitted him well as long as he stood up, though the legs were too tight for comfortable sitting.

Jim felt like shooting an entire roll of his 35-millimeter film on snapshots of Penny, but first he must take some photographs for Leda. She wanted a picture of Elizabeth Kenny's home in Townsville, and Penny had offered to help him locate the place before they went to the beach.

Only a few months ago, the famous and controversial Australian nurse had departed for the U.S., to continue her life work of developing a treatment to alleviate the crippling effects of poliomyelitis. Her revolutionary approach, involving the use of hot packs, massage, and re-education of muscles, had been rejected by a Queensland Royal Commission of Doctors in favor of the traditional method of immobilizing the affected limbs in casts and splints. After the American Medical Association and the National Foundation for Infantile Paralysis had approved her treatment, Sister Kenny had accepted an invitation to use the facilities of the Minneapolis General Hospital and to teach at the University of Minnesota.

Outside the shabby, unmarked little building that had housed the clinic since 1933, Penny posed in mock imitation of haughty *Vogue* models while Jim's Leica clicked.

He said, "My mother's convinced that the doctors here opposed Sister Kenny just because she's a woman. But the medical profession always hates to accept new ideas from *anyone*."

"Probably a bit of both. But she made our doctors bloody furious with all her skiting — she was always trying to attract the attention of the press. She claimed that eighty percent of the patients treated by her method recovered without any paralysis, and only thirteen percent of the doctors' patients did; that wasn't true. But then, we Aussies do tend to look down on ideas that are born here. If she'd only been English or American, even being a woman, I think our doctors might have listened to her. . . . Anyhow, she won. It's the rule now in every hospital in Australia that if a patient with infantile paralysis asks for the Kenny treatment, it will be given."

As they walked past the Queen's Hotel and the big houses, the first handsome buildings Jim had seen in Australia, Penny asked, "Is it really true that President Roosevelt was crippled by infantile paralysis? He looks so fit, in the newsreels, always smiling and waving his cigarette holder."

"It's true, all right. He usually uses a wheelchair, but the news photographers never show it. Just his legs were affected, though. His brain's sharp as a razor, and that's all a president needs."

But while they waited beside the wharves for a bus to the beach, the question nagged him: *Why in the hell did that brilliant leader let himself get suckered into the goddam Rainbow Plan?*

* * * * *

"Fossicking" for seashells had always been one of Jim's favorite pastimes, and the Australian verb seemed to suit the action perfectly. As the pair walked on the hard, wet sand, letting the cool incoming ripples wash over their feet, he held Penny's hand; it was warm and pleasantly gritty with sand.

Exquisite shells rolled up on this coast that was protected from the Coral Sea by the Great Barrier Reef. At Mackay, on her home beach, Penny said, she had found a Gold Lip pearl shell and several Black Lip shells; also a delicate spiny pink Murex Pecten which she called the Venus Comb. She laughed when Jim told her that in the Muslim islands of the Netherlands East Indies the same shell was known as The Comb of Allah. She was a good laugher.

Although he spotted a number of intriguing shell shapes half-buried in the sand, Jim found that every time he glimpsed Penny's bare feet he forgot about fossicking. His eyes automatically traveled up her stunning, long tanned legs (she had that rare skin of the redhead who doesn't sunburn), over the curves of her sun-faded, blue wool bathing suit — as he had surmised, the oversized uniform shirt had camouflaged a rich endowment — up to her laughing face with its sea-blue eyes and golden freckles. Her glorious hair, freed from its military configuration, brushed her shoulders in the breeze off Cleveland Bay, glowing like a flame in the brilliant sunlight. He reacted so vigorously to her nearness that he was embarrassed; surely Penny would notice the bulge under his swimming trunks.

She was 25 — four years older than he — and delightfully straightforward, without the flirtatious coyness that he had known in many American girls and Filipinas. Still, he was caught off guard when she asked, "Are you a virgin, Jim?"

Ye gods, he berated himself, *I'm even ambivalent about **that**.* He scuffed a pink Star turban shell with his foot, inserted his big toe into it, then quickly kicked off the shell lest she think it an unseemly action. He thought fast: *What answer does she want?*

He had never imagined that a woman would ask him that question. In discussions with male acquaintances he usually — without lying — had been able to *imply* the answer that he thought would be well received, depending on what kind of masculinity that particular man evidently admired. His sole, painful, adolescent experience in the noisome Ifugao *olag* had been so far from the soaring ecstasy described in Thomas Wolfe's books that he had never truly considered it to have been the real thing. Certainly the earth had not moved, as it had done for Hemingway's Maria and Robert Jordan in the sleeping bag; instead, his stomach had heaved. Still, to be technically truthful, in the Biblical sense he had known a woman — that unwashed Ifugao widow, the volunteer instructress.

He had been less than truthful in May, desperately trying to live up to Ernest Hemingway's apparent acceptance of him as a man of the world. When the writer had bragged, "I've bedded every woman I ever wanted to, and some that I didn't; and I'll be damned if I'll ever pay for any such favors," Jim had responded, "Same here, Papa."

Yet later that same month, in Chungking, when Theodore White, the brilliant young writer for *Time*, had admitted that he was "too Jewish and too Boston" to consider having a sexual experience outside of marriage, and that the men he had known at Harvard also had been virgins, Jim had said, "Me, too, Teddy."

Leda had known it would happen to him in the *olag*, he was sure of that, for she knew that the ethnologist she nicknamed "Boozer Barton" was fascinated by the Ifugao solution to adolescent experimentation. When she had given permission for Jim, at 14, to take the summer job in the *bundoks*, assisting Professor Barton, she surely knew that Barton would let Jim sleep in the young people's dormitory.

Still, Jim was certain that Leda had *not* deliberately planned (as some of his friends suggested) to cause him to shun any further sexual adventuring. She could not have guessed how unpleasant it would be for him. As a feminist, a Flapper, a member of the "Lost Generation," she liked to argue in defense of Bertrand Russell's advocacy of Free Love. Perhaps the freedom of the *olag* symbolized her rebellion against the strictures of the Catholic Church — which she now termed "a guilt machine." Or perhaps she was combining her wistful idealization of her Cherokee heritage and similar "noble savage" customs, under the influence of her friend Margaret Mead, who believed that growing up was easier outside civilization.

Jim wondered how he could tell Penny, "My mother arranged for me to lose my virginity." But in evading the truth, trying to be "all things to all men," he was nothing more than a chameleon. Right now, the important thing was not to louse up his chances with Penny.

Is she looking for a man of experience like Papa — or does she like the innocent Teddy White kind? All the Australian men I've met only talked about flying, drinking, and sports — they never mentioned what kind of man the "sheilas" prefer!

The only Australian whose romantic life was flaunted before the world was Errol Flynn, whose flamboyant film roles paled in comparison with reports of his Hollywood bed-hopping. The phrase, "In like Flynn" had been coined in his dubious honor.

That's my clue, Jim thought; *that's what I want.*

Chapter 3 — Part 4 — Penny

He took a deep breath. "No, I'm not a virgin."
He longed to add the question, "Are you?," but that was not something to ask a girl.
"Neither am I," Penny said.
Calloo, callay! O frabjous day! Is this glorious girl propositioning me?
Jim's hopes soared. Penny's declaration removed the only obstacle to a thrilling, fulfilling, erotic scenario. It was against the code of all the young men who were his friends and acquaintances to consider deflowering any young lady other than one's bride.
All, that is, except Punch, who always said his favorite song was "Life is Just a Bowl of Cherries." Punch recently had returned to Manila as an Air Corps second lieutenant, looking like British film star Leslie Howard. Now he was stationed at Nichols Field — too near Mariluz's family home. As a boy, Punch had called Mariluz a "gook," but Jim had seen the way he ogled her grown-up beauty.
I'll black his eyes if he tries anything. . . .
The thought of Punch reminded Jim of the small blue envelope in his wallet. He was thankful to have it; his lucky star had arranged every detail for tonight with brilliant foresight. In the hope of going on to Singapore from Australia, he had kept in his wallet the four items Daphne had given him in that envelope, samples made of latex from her father's plantation on Penang Island. "Only the very finest rubber is used to manufacture 'french-letters,' " she had said. That was in August, when they had planned to hold their consummating tryst at Mount Pleasure, Penang's beach hotel, deserted by the former peacetime tourists to that pearl of islands. That was to be the night that would fulfill Jim's aching, consuming desire for Daphne: the idyll that was wafted away on the dreamy fumes of opium.

* * * * *

The wildlife sanctuary, a short bus ride out of Townsville, encompassed several thousand acres of swampland and a lagoon where spectacular pink and purple waterlilies bloomed. Penny, back in uniform but still smelling deliciously of the sea, said that 10,000 birds, mainly waterfowl, nested or migrated through there. "Three thousand of them are *brolgas*."
Another ugly name. I've always liked to watch birds — but dammit, right now they're just a tiresome interruption in my progress toward the really important business of the evening. Hell, I can see birds any time at home, but I sure don't know any girls in Manila like Penny.
Against his will, the dry-season mating dance of the red-masked brolgas soon captured his attention, and finally almost took his breath away. Probably a thousand of the exquisitely graceful silver-gray cranes intently performed

their stately ritual: their long legs *en masse* delicately taking intricate steps in perfect rhythm to music that they alone could hear. Their strong extended pinions, revealing a fringe of white, undulated like surf on a gray sea.

The brolga ballet reminded Jim at times of a minuet, a square dance, a formal *rigodon* of the Philippines; but this was infinitely more artistic in his eyes.

*If Tchaikowsky had ever seen brolgas dance, he would have forbidden any lumbering human **corps de ballet** to use his **Swan Lake** music.*

As the sun dropped behind them, Penny allowed him to put his arm around her waist. "The Abo's do dances in their corroborees that imitate the brolga patterns," she murmured.

He was not surprised; many Philippine folk dances are based on observations of local birds. He squeezed her tightly, tormented by the longing of his body, while his mind was swept by a bittersweet universal pity for creatures of his own gender.

Poor devils, he thought: *We're all helplessly throbbing to the same drums as brolgas in the dry season. The Aboriginal dances to attract his woman; so does the Ifugao in his courtship dance; President Quezon dances the tango at Malacañang Palace; bachelor officers in my squadron are jitterbugging tonight at Clark with girls who drove up from Manila. Fred Astaire dances "Cheek to Cheek" with Ginger Rogers. The brolgas are lucky; they only feel the mating urge once a year, but we're never free from it. . . .*

* * * * *

Castle Hill was less than a thousand feet in height, but they stopped short of the summit when Penny chose a level spot on the east face. At last, they sat on her government-issue blanket and ate roast lamb sandwiches. They drank the last bottles of warm Fourex beer and smoked Jim's Lucky Strikes while they looked down at the lights of Townsville.

Lucky is the word for me. My fourth day in Australia, and I've already struck gold.

The brilliant, unfamiliar stars appeared, silvering the Ross River and Cleveland Bay, all the way out to the Coral Sea.

Romance under the Southern Cross! Jim thought jubilantly, but then, it seemed sacrilegious to think of the Christian symbol in the context of his carnal passion. He excused himself: *Well, it doesn't really look at all like a cross to me; more like the crosspieces of a kite.*

When Penny stretched out on her back, he thought, *Now or never.* He stroked her soft, tumbled hair, transmuted to gold by the stars. She smelled deliciously briny, like a mermaid. He kissed her deeply and she responded with kisses that drove him wild. Jim's hands trembled as he unbuttoned her

Chapter 3 — Part 4 — Penny   93

rough-dry cotton shirt. He tried to use both hands to reach beneath her, as he struggled awkwardly to undo the hooks of her brassiere.
Oh, hell, I should have started this earlier, while she was sitting up.
She laughed. "Well, all right. Even though this is our first date, I do like you, Jim." She sat up, pulled off her shirt and brassiere, and lay back again. "You can have a quick peek and a feel, but I'm keeping my knickers on tonight."
"What?" His hands flew to her cool, firm breasts, sea-scented and excitingly sandy, luminous in the starlight. He felt her nipples rise to his touch, and he bent to kiss them. "Penny, I need you *now!* I've got to leave in the morning! Look, we're safe — there's nobody else around here, and I — I've got protection with me. You don't need to worry about anything. *Please!* You said you liked me —"
She breathed deeply and gripped his arms with her hands. "I do, Jim, I like you a bloody lot, I really do, and I'd like to rug up in this blanket with you right now. I know we could have a bonzer frolic together — some time. But not tonight. It's against my principles to give myself to a bloke on the first date."
Dammit, she is a mermaid.
"First date, hell! That's ridiculous. It's our *second* date. What about last night? Are you an iceberg — or a damned tease? Can't you see I'm crazy about you?"
She laughed. "Was that what you call a date in America? I never saw a scene in a picture show of a mess-hall date! In Australia, that's a bloody first *meeting*. Tonight is our first dinkum date."
What do you do when she says No? Am I too inept, too inexperienced, to attract her? Or just too young? Is she laughing at me?
Seduction always sounded so easy when Punch bragged to the boys in the Court of Roses about his conquests: "I just swear I love her, French-kiss her, start pearl-diving — and she's my slave!"
Penny, however, sat up and matter-of-factly put on her brassiere and began buttoning her shirt. "Is it the Hollywood influence that makes Yanks oversexed? An Aussie bloke's least and last thought of the day is women. First comes the pub with his mates, then he punts on the horses, then he goes to the beach . . . and *then* it's time to think of pitchin' woo with his sheila."
"Well, Americans put first things first. Do Australian sheilas *like* to be last on a man's list?"
She laughed. "No worries, Yank. We get along."
Jim looked into her eyes, trying to win her sympathy. "Listen, you sweet baby, this is our only chance. . . . Suppose I was in the RAAF, going off to war in Africa tomorrow? Would you still be so damned prissy?"
"If I'd just met you, too bloody right, I'd be prissy. I don't play by 'Rafferty Rules'! What's the use of having standards, if you make exceptions for every

charming bloke who comes along? No Aussie girl would go to bed with any man on the first date, except a tart. But you're *not* going to war — you're just going up to Papua. You said you'll be back here in a week or less. I'll still be here — and we'll be *old friends* then!" She laughed again.

"You promise you'll — uh — give me — give yourself to me when I come back?"

"I bloody well promise you. And I promise I'll think about you while you're gone, Jim, and I'll be glad to see you and frolic with you, on our second date — and our third one, too, if you can stay over! But straightaway, we've got to toddle down the hill and catch the bus back to Garbutt, before Lights Out catches me out of my bunk."

Jim groaned. *My second strikeout today. Damn her principles. Damn Commander Feldt. Goddam the cranes and Fred Astaire, and damn all the women we poor bastards do our fool mating dances for. How can I walk to the bus with these baseballs in my shorts? Damn you, Yee Long, you made the pants too tight.*

Chapter 4

Part 1 — To Papua, New Guinea

Some observers believe that if Kurusu fails and Japan then moves, it will be an all-out attack against both Britain and the United States, beginning with an attack on Manila, since it is recognized that it would be the poorest naval strategy to attempt to attack Borneo without the elimination of Manila.
— Cablegram to William S. Paley at CBS, New York from CBS newsman Cecil Brown in Singapore, 15 November 1941

Departing Townsville
Saturday, 15 November 1941

"Saturdye's a fair cow of a dye to leave our Lucky Land," Flight Officer T.W.L. "Griff" Griffin told Jim. They were waiting for Eubank to complete his walk-around inspection of the B-17 before their flight to Port Moresby. "If you gotta leave Austrylia, Sundye's the best. Whole bloody country shuts down on Sundye — a bloke can't even buy a brew, or tyke his sheila to the pictures."

Ruefully, Jim said, "I'm just beginning to find out what a puritanical country you have here."

Griffin, 23, "an amiable blond giant," in Captain Ind's phrase, was a staff assistant to Air Commodore Lukis, who had lent Griff to Brereton to aid with his prospective surveys of Port Moresby and Rabaul.

Brereton appeared to be in a good mood this morning. He expressed his relief that Lukis, the energetic AOC (Air Officer Commanding) of this entire vast Northeastern Area, had approved of the steps Brereton had taken at Darwin. Jim had heard the General tell Eubank that Lukis, 45, a native of Balinjup, Western Australia, had proved to be like Scherger at Darwin, "another very efficient and helpful man, clearly alive to the situation. And his keen sense of humor made my job easier."

Brereton continued to amaze Jim with his plans: *The man's nuts,* Jim thought now. In Darwin, where weather and isolation seemed to conspire against any progress, Brereton had envisioned vast air armadas that would fan out from the red dust of Batchelor airstrip and fly northwest to Java and Singapore, northeast to Mindanao and Luzon. Now, in this sleepy, tropical, sugar-cane port of Townsville, the man could picture RAAF Station Garbutt as the destination for U.S. bombers by the hundreds, island-hopping down from Hawaii, and crated fighter planes on shipboard to be offloaded here and assembled. From here, all this aircraft would be dispersed, flying down to splendid new aerodromes guarding the cities of the southeast coast, or trans-Australia to Darwin — that future hub! — and thence as far north as China.

Lefty Eads had not gone to bed last night. He had been "pencil-pushing," trying to estimate the requirements, dimensions, equipment, and costs for an assembly plant to be built at Townsville for fighter plane parts that would come by sea from the U.S. to this little deep-water port. He had also had to figure estimates for maintenance facilities that must be built at Garbutt. Now he volunteered to join "Professor" Ind in the discomfort of the bomb bay; he was tired enough to sleep anywhere, he said, and he looked it.

Allison Ind's smile revealed his pleasure that today's flight to Port Moresby would be a comparatively short one of only 600 miles. He was also relieved, he told Jim quietly, that his task of acquiring information for his massive report on Australia would "perforce, be interrupted — albeit briefly — by these forthcoming visits to islands of head-hunters and cannibals. I'm bringing sufficient film for many reels of motion pictures."

Head-hunters were no novelty to Jim; he knew several reformed ones in the Luzon *bundoks* who still prided themselves on their collections of trophy skulls. American influence in the Mountain Province had not quite eradicated the custom; heads had been taken in an inter-tribal dispute as recently as four years ago. But cannibalism was unknown in the Philippines.

Damn, he thought, *why didn't I borrow a movie camera from somebody?*

— Everyone's on the ball except you, Jim reproached himself. *You've loused up everything you should have accomplished here. You're filling Slugger's seat on the plane, but you sure as hell haven't earned it. After yesterday, you should be sent back to Clark in disgrace. Thousands of miles flown, a free tour of*

Australia at the expense of the American taxpayer, with more to follow — and you failed in the one thing you were assigned to do. You didn't learn a damned thing about how to organize a Coastwatcher radio net. You even forgot to ask Commander Feldt about what kind of "ciphers" he uses! Do you think you can ask him to send you that information on a postcard? You've let down Uncle Sam — and "Uncle Allison" Ind, who went out on a limb to persuade Brereton to let you tag along.

In fewer — and milder — words, Jim had confessed to Captain Ind the frustration he felt over his failure to learn anything from Commander Feldt that would be useful in the Philippines.

"Don't worry about it, son; I know you did your best," Allison Ind reassured him, as if Jim were one of Ind's students at Ann Arbor who had failed an English exam. "The Commander's formality is rather formidable, I agree — especially since all the other Australians have embraced us like their lifelong 'cobbers.' I was hoping . . . well, I saw a hint of a twinkle in his eyes; and the way his lips turn up at the corners told me there's a human being under that shell — but it's obviously a hard one to crack. Who knows — perhaps he's possessive about his brain-child and wants to keep the concept for Australia. I noted that there's been no mention of spreading it to New Zealand —"

"But it's *not* his brain-child!" Jim said. "Sending a signal to warn that an enemy's coming — aren't there Bible stories about that? The Romans had *geese* to do it! In the Philippines, every coast has old stone watchtowers, where lookouts were posted to warn if Moro ships were approaching — then signal fires would be lighted on the hills and the people would scram, before the slave-raiders landed. . . . The only thing that's new here is using radios. But Feldt seemed to think I'm too dumb, or too young — or both — to catch on."

Griffin sat in the Flight Engineer's jump-seat and Jim sat behind him on the floor, wrapping his long legs around the base of the seat until the bomber headed into the breeze from Cleveland Bay, grazed the tall sugar-cane stalks, and became airborne.

I hope we scare the damned brolgas shitless, he thought.

He stood up. Looking forward and down through the cockpit windows, he saw Townsville as a lonely little spot on the green rim of the continent. On his arrival, this northeast fringe had seemed well populated, but that was only in comparison to the Outback. Although there were small settlements along the coast — Townsville was about equidistant between Cairns, on the north, and Penny's town of Mackay on the south — the nearest city was Brisbane, about 800 miles south. In flying school he had made a cross-crountry flight to El Paso, which had seemed far removed from the outer world; but even El Paso was within 500 miles of other cities.

His spirits were still low after the rebuffs of the previous day. He wondered: *In this so-called "Lucky Land," has my own Irish luck left me? Or did I leave it in the Philippines? Will I be lucky at poker again after I get back . . . or am I doomed to a lifetime of "bad joss," as Wing would call it? Will I always be at odds with senior officers — and never get to first base with an attractive woman?*

Too, the war-talk of the RAAF officers at Garbutt had begun to affect him. During the brief stopover in Darwin, most of the informal chat with the pilots had focused on Japan's aggressive move southward in Viet Nam and the ensuing threat to Malaya, Singapore, and the Netherlands East Indies. Here in Townsville, however, he had begun to realize what England's war was costing Australia.

After two years and two months of sending "Diggers" overseas to fight in Benghazi, Greece, Crete, Syria, Tobruk, and El Alamein, a single-minded dedication to winning was almost palpable here. The air of purpose reminded Jim more of the Dutch in Java, whose homeland was Hitler's captive, than of the English in Singapore — where he had met many who seemed to have committed themselves only to "carry on" with boozy Curry Tiffin parties, races at the Turf Club, and dancing at the Sea View. Quinine was imported secondly for Malaya's malaria and first for Singapore's gin-and-tonics.

Griffin had heard Ind's remark about "head-hunters and cannibals." The "Fuzzy-wuzzies" had not yet abandoned those habits, he volunteered now. "And in at least one tribe, when a relative dies, the family eats his brains." The task of policing the isolated settlements of the world's largest island (after Greenland), with its fierce terrain, was more than any government could accomplish, he told Jim.

Like Caesar's Gaul, he continued, New Guinea was divided into three parts. The Guinea-bird's 1,500-mile-long body was carved, north to south, by the 141st Parallel. West of the line lay Netherlands New Guinea: the bird's breast and its head (which craned to the Equator and was called by the Dutch "Vogelkop" — Birdhead).

The northeast portion of the bird's back and tail, formerly the German colony of Kaiser Wilhelm Land, had been mandated to Australia by the League of Nations after the World War.

Great Britain had claimed the southeastern strip of the island since 1884, but in 1906 had handed it over to Australia, under the name of Papua.

"'Papua' means 'woolly hair' in Malay — you'll understand it when you see the Fuzzies. So — what England dished out on our Aussie plate was the bird's underbelly, its private parts, and the skinny tail. It's an albatross to us — a big expense, no revenue, and plenty of headaches trying to govern the natives. But we can't let the bastard Japs add it to their collection."

Griffin had brought a copy of yesterday's *North Queensland Register,* the first Australian newspaper Jim had read. He was shocked when he saw the latest *Overseas Casualties* list. He had never imagined such a grim summing-up: a sort of box score with no wins, only losses. Almost two columns were required to note the barest statistics: each Australian's name, his home town, and the cause of his removal from action — *killed in action, died of wounds, missing and believed dead, severely wounded, slightly wounded, prisoner of war.*

The names of the small towns (*Bundaberg . . . Canterbury . . . Cootamundra*) were foreign and he could not locate them on a mental map. Each one appeared in his mind's eye as a dusty, lonesome Outback settlement like Daly Waters or Cloncurry, where everyone had known since his birth the local lad who went off to war. But as he read each place-name paired with the name of the fallen Aussie (*Alcock . . . Allchin . . . Gurney*) who had called that dusty spot "home" (*perhaps he was tall . . . certainly young . . . probably matey and sports-loving . . . beer-drinking . . . a good laugher until this happened*) the cumulative weight of the human pain encapsulated in those lines of print became almost too poignant for Jim to read. Still — although it was impossible for him to hold the newspaper steady against the vibration of the bomber and it was difficult to focus on the columns — he forced himself to read every single name on the list, with the man's home town, his state, and his fate; that was the only tribute he could give them.

God bless you poor blokes, he thought.

Jesus, he wondered, *do their mothers have to look in the newspaper every day for their names? Surely the families must have received some notice before the names were listed in the paper.* But he did not ask Griff about it, for the broad-shouldered kid in the jump seat (from Strathfield, N.S.W.) resembled all those other Aussies too much. A sheet of paper bearing overseas orders in Griffin's name could send him next week to join his mates in the African desert.

And he'd be glad to go. All those men on the Casualty List — like all the hundred twenty thousand Aussies who've gone overseas — were volunteers, willing to die for England: their damned old imperialist bitch of a "Mother Country."

Suddenly the paper in his hand began to shake so that he could no longer read it, although the plane had leveled off in calm air. His hands were trembling with a palsy that he could not control. He was not ill, except with rage — stricken with the realization that he was as vulnerable as any Australian to being ordered into combat to preserve the British Empire. Under the terms of the secret Rainbow Plan 5, the only event required to pit Brereton's Far East Air Force against Japan was for Japan to attack any British possession — *even if the English fired the first shot.*

Nor was that even the most sickening revelation of that late August night in the U.S. Air Attache's office in Singapore. According to the smuggled copy of Rainbow 5, which the drunken Lieutenant Jackson had showed Jim, after the

U.S. made the mandatory hair-trigger response of declaring war for England, the military might of the United States would *not* be concentrated against Japan! Incredibly, the major American war effort would be directed toward Europe — *even if Germany had not harmed a single American.* Only after Hitler was subdued would all U.S. resources and manpower be available to fight Japan.

Some crazy Samurai in a canoe could take a pot-shot at a village on the Malay coast, and I'd be in the war tomorrow. Hell, I'd be glad to fight for my Philippines — I'd even be willing to fight for Australia if it was attacked. But my Mother Machree sure as shit didn't raise her boy to fight for the "slimy Limeys."

Jim was still seated on the floor behind the jump seat, with his knees drawn up to his chest because his stomach ached, when Griff twisted around and asked, "Did you hear Cecil Brown's broadcast yesterday?"

Jim shook his head. "I was — uh — otherwise engaged."

"Great news for our war effort. Brown described a new revision of your American Neutrality Act, passed by your Washington legislature by 18 votes. From now on, your merchant ships will be allowed to be armed and sent into belligerent zones."

Harm's Way, Jim thought — *another route for us to stumble into England's war.*

"If you ask us, myte, we'd be nothing but happy to see your bloody Neutrality Act get scrapped altogether, so we could openly buy warplanes and munitions from you-lot. Of course, Lend-Lease is bonzer, and God knows, it's been a lifesaver for England — but we'd like to get it all out in the open and be able to pye our own wye. If your bloody Congress would repeal that bastard, we could buy Harvard aircraft from you blokes, instead of from the Canadians, who need them for their own use."

Hell, we need some for ***our*** *own use,* Jim thought. *When President Roosevelt called for production of fifty thousand planes a year, I didn't realize how many of those would be going to the British, the Russians, the Java Dutch, the Swedes, the Thais — and of course, poor China. The President wasn't exaggerating when he called us "the arsenal of Democracy."*

"Is the story true," Griffin asked, "that this same beaut bird we're flyin' in, and its mytes, was first intended for England, under Lend-Lease?"

Jim nodded. "All thirty-five of the Fortresses were. But then Mr. Churchill decided to let us have them in the Philippines."

"Pretty bloody generous of Winnie, I'd sye — when you think of the damage they could be doin' right now, flyin' across the Channel to bomb Jerry's war plants. That would be a bonzer payback for The Blitz."

Not so goddam bloody generous, Jim thought. *Thirty-five fucking Forts are a measly trade-off for getting the U.S. into the war. Wily old Winnie could be damned sure that basing the B-17s in the Philippines would pay him back a million times their worth.*

Cecil Brown obviously didn't have any trouble getting that news about the Neutrality Act past his nemesis in Singapore — Mr. Duckworth, the chief censor. And I know that Cess was happy to announce it, because it puts us a step closer to getting into the war. After the awful German bombing and shelling he's reported on, he's been convinced that the U.S. should get into the fight, before England and Russia go under . . . he'd never let his listeners guess how he feels, though; he's scrupulous about telling the news without any bias. But I'm his pal — his "cobber" — and I know how he feels about a lot of things.

All Jim's luck in making friends with the journalists in Singapore had sprung out of his friendship with Hemingway, he realized now. On those boozy evenings in May — at the Manila Hotel, at Jai Alai, and in little Spanish bars in the Walled City — he had listened to Papa's lamentations because his bride, Martha Gellhorn, was not returning to the States with him on the *California Clipper*. Instead, "Marty," with a contract from *Collier's* magazine, had elected to go south from China (which she had hated, Papa told Jim) to write special reports from Singapore and Java.

Thus, in the lobby of the Raffles Hotel in July, Jim had known instantly who the tall, attractive young American woman was, when he heard her speaking in her "Bryn Mawr accent," as Papa had characterized it, sniffed her delicate aura of expensive French perfume, and noted her slim hips in a pair of tan slacks with Fifth Avenue styling.

If Jim had not met Daphne that first night, he had often thought, he probably would have fallen madly in love with Martha Gellhorn. Bright, pretty, and charming, she had befriended him in Singapore as warmly as her husband had done in Manila, although her personality and her conversations with Jim were different from Papa's in every way. She was as frank as the man she laughingly called "Poppa," omitting the Spanish inflection: but Jim felt that Martha, for one, was always truthful.

"I have to travel by myself," she told him, "because Poppa wants to possess me completely. He's still angry because I refuse to write under the name of Martha Hemingway. His mother and I are the only women who've ever refused to let him dominate us — and you know how he hates Grace. I don't want him to hate *me*, so I do a lot of traveling alone."

Jim told her, "Papa said my mother was like his — they both want to dominate men. So he hated Leda, too."

Through Martha Gellhorn, Jim had met Cecil Brown. The CBS newsman, as tall and lanky as Jim and as fair-haired as Martha herself, had accepted Jim as if he were a fellow journalist and included him in daily lunches, dinners, interviews, broadcasts, slumming, and sessions in the Raffles' famous bar. In turn, Cess had introduced him to all the other American "vultures," as the war correspondents called themselves, while they waited to see how far Japan's belligerent reach would extend.

Martin Agronsky and John Young were Brown's friendly rivals on NBC's radio news; all the others reported through the printed word. Frank Gervasi was *Collier's* regular Singapore reporter; Martha Gellhorn's special assignment for the magazine was temporary. Yates McDaniel represented the Associated Press, while the United Press correspondent, Harold Guard, was English by birth, a veteran of the British Navy's submarine service. Leland Stowe represented *The Chicago Daily News*.

The other U.S. big-city newspaper, *The New York Times*, was now served in Singapore by an old friend of Jim's and Leda's, Tillman Durdin. As a young music student on a cruise in 1930, "Til" had jumped ship to remain in Shanghai; later his wife Peggy had taught English at the Shanghai American School.

In 1937 Durdin had been appointed Far East correspondent for *The New York Times*, and he began reporting on the Japanese advance along the Yangtze to China's interior. Hankow was tottering, and Jim's mother — on sabbatical from teaching — persuaded her friend Avram von Hartendorp, editor of *The Philippine Magazine*, to send her to China to write an eyewitness report. Leda and Tillman (whom Leda affectionately called "the Egghead") had become friends while they covered the fall of Hankow. The handful of die-hard reporters, including Leda's friends Agnes Smedley and Frieda Utley, had hung on so long they became known as "the Hankow Last-ditchers." While the Tri-cities fell about them, Leda and Agnes Smedley, mesmerized by the magnetic Chou, En-lai and convinced by him that Communism was the answer to China's agonies, had argued with Frieda Utley and the sensitive, brilliant, idealistic Til Durdin.

As the Japanese onslaught increased its ferocity, Hartendorp had feared for Leda's safety. He had dispatched Jim to fetch her back to Manila — not an easy task for a 17-year-old.

Jim had seen Til Durdin again in May, in Chiang, Kai-shek's refugee capital on the Yangtze, Chungking. His pleasure in seeing his friend there had been dampened by Durdin's weariness and disillusion. "These have been such depressing years since the fall of Hankow, Jim. It's utterly hopeless here in Free China — the graft, the misery, the lack of will to fight anymore. I've become 'browned off,' as Ian Morrison would say. Even I have begun to feel that it couldn't be any worse under the Red Chinese — it must be better."

In Chungking, Durdin had taken Jim to have tea with a Vietnamese nationalist, Nguyen That Thanh, who had been exiled from his country for decades by its French masters. Jim's sympathies were with any form of revolt against France, whose colonial governance he considered even more reprehensible than England's; but it seemed almost laughable that the French felt so threatened by this scrawny little fellow that they had sentenced him *in absentia* to death by guillotine. Jim had thought it was a pity the Vietnamese couldn't find themselves a more *leaderly* leader than this gentleman with the wispy goat-beard, who had learned English while working as a *sous-chef* to Auguste Escoffier in London's Carlton Hotel. Recalling the incident now, he saw again those bright, compelling dark eyes, and felt that handshake like the grasp of an eagle's talon. In Chungking the man had adopted a new "revolutionary name," which meant The One Who Enlightens. "You may call me 'Uncle Ho,'" he had told Jim.

Ian Morrison was another friend from Chungking who, like Durdin, had since moved down to Singapore. Ian was the first Englishman Jim had ever really known, and to Jim's surprise he had grown to like Ian a great deal. Morrison had lived for years in Japan and China, and Jim had never seen him display the supercilious attitude toward "Asiatics" that Jim hated in other Britons. (Even lovely Daphne had it, but Jim knew that her upbringing was solely to blame.) One of the few things he had ever heard Ian criticize about the Japanese was their attempted automobile production: "The only commercial car they've ever produced in any quantity was a pseudo-Austin 7, called a 'Datsun' — a dreadful little tin can, always going out of order."

In Singapore in July, Morrison and his wife Marie were living in an elegant apartment on the top floor of the island's tallest building, the 13-story Cathay Building, with splendid views of the green island — a far cry from the mud-walled, mud-floored Press Hostel in Chungking. The gregarious Morrisons entertained well and constantly, and made Jim welcome.

At the Morrisons' he had met another Englishman he grew to like, Noel Barber — the chief foreign correspondent of *The London Daily Mail* — in addition to the correspondents from the English and Australian newspapers.

Jim had never told Leda about Morrison and Barber; how could he speak to her of friends with such giveaway names as *Ian* and *Noel*? She would feel that he had betrayed his Irish heritage and become a "Limey-lover." And although he was indeed wild about a lovely Limey, of course he had never mentioned Daphne. His mail, however, still came to the Court of Roses; certainly Leda must have noted the pale blue envelopes bearing postmarks of Daphne's social round of house parties, from Kuala Lumpur and the Sultanate of Johore to Victoria Peak in Hong Kong and the lavish fiefdom of "the White Rajah" Brooke of Borneo.

Daphne would be sailing for Borneo aboard the SS *Vyner Brooke* in December, to attend the Christmas festivities at the Brooke mansion in Sarawak. She had passed along an invitation to Jim from the Brookes to join them then — with one caveat: if by some chance Robin, Daphne's fiance in the Royal Navy, showed up at Christmas time, the invitation would go to Robin instead. Although it made Jim furious to play second fiddle, Daphne insisted that to jilt poor Robin now, while he was serving England aboard HMS *Prince of Wales,* would not be cricket. Later, when he was out of danger, she would tell him that she was in love with Jim.

* * * * *

The Fortress' course was due North on the familiar "mag compass," Zero on the newer gyro compass. Jim's spirits finally lifted when he got the chance to sit in the bombardier's compartment. Most of his seniors had tried it earlier, but eventually had fled from the sun and its dazzling glare on the water and its heat in the Plexiglas nose. Captain Ind took a quick look, termed the Coral Sea "cobalt blue," and retreated to his dark bomb bay, cup in hand.

Jim peered out the port side so intently and so long that his neck stiffened. This was the first time since leaving the Philippines that he'd had something new and beautiful to see. It made him realize how the new B-17Es — fairly pimpled with Plexiglas turrets — would offer good visibility for a number of crew members: overhead, on both sides, and even from the tail.

He was entranced, as more than 700 miles of the northernmost strand of "the largest living object on earth" snaked along below. "Cobalt" must be the deepest, *bluest* blue of all, he thought; not so dark as a star sapphire. Against that ineffable blueness, the reef-pools glowed, palest turquoise rimmed in white foam; and between the pools extended gardens of thousands of tints and shades of color, and verdant islands large and small. Below the airplane and above the reefs occasionally shimmered banners of lace — miles of it, white, gray, or ivory — formed of millions of flying birds.

Feldt and his "fences," Jim reflected: *He talked about the Queensland sheep ranchers and their thousands of miles of fences to keep out the wild dogs and wild rabbits; and of course he showed me on the map of the Solomon Sea his "island fence," to keep out the wild Japanese. But he never mentioned how the tiny coral polyps built for Queensland's east coast had formed a barrier unique in all the world in size, beauty, and naval blockading power. Eighty thousand square miles of it, undulating southward from nine degrees below the Equator, down almost to the Tropic of Capricorn! Its width, ranging from nine miles to ninety, makes it far more fearsome to any attacker than a Maginot Line, because so much of its menace is invisible.*

Captain Bligh was a great navigator, but a lousy leader, in the old sergeants' definition of a leader as a man who takes care of his troops first, himself second. But James Cook, who saved his men from the ravages of scurvy by provisioning barrels of sauerkraut, was not only a good leader, but a great navigator, too. And a cautious one, taking care to send a sounding-boat ahead of his ship during a thousand miles of northward sailing along this Queensland

Chapter 4 — Part 1 — To Papua, New Guinea 105

coast, wary of the formation he called "a Wall of Coral." Still, he came close to losing **Endeavour** on that beautiful, treacherous Reef: right down there below me, just north of the Sixteenth Parallel. If only he could have seen those underwater cliffs as I can see them from here, with my God's-eye view. . . .

If Cook hadn't jettisoned fifty tons of stuff so the tide could lift his hundred and six-foot refitted collier from what he termed "the very jaws of destruction," hadn't successfully "fothered" her coral-plugged wound, hadn't managed to nurse her into that river mouth down there — about two hundred seventy-five miles north of Townsville — to make repairs . . . how long would it have been before the outside world learned about the lush east coast of Australia? If he hadn't claimed this coast for England in 1770 and described Botany Bay so glowingly, could the Aborigines — after their forty thousand free-roaming years — have been spared the smell of the white man for another century or so? Where would England have sent her convicts, after the American colonies stopped taking them? Would the ten-year-old boy criminals have been incarcerated in Tasmania, anyway? And would the Tasmanians have been hunted into extinction — whether Cook had ever escaped from the Reef or not?

Some day, Jim promised himself, he would sail Captain Cook's course in reverse: southward along the coast of Queensland. He would bring diving equipment and an air pump, and a good companion to man the pump — probably David, or Brinton Hill. Wearing a diver's globular helmet and weighted suit, Jim would plod around Cook's jaws-of-destruction reef until he could locate — and touch, and photograph — at least one of the six cannon that Cook jettisoned, along with more essential stores, during his nightlong, daylong struggle to free *Endeavour*.

Surrendering the bombardier's-eye-view perch to Major Caldwell, Jim returned to stand behind Griffin and peer out the cockpit windows. With a world-weary cynicism born on Castle Hill, he told Griffin, "The Great Barrier Reef is like a woman — beautiful, but deceitful."

"Too royte, myte. Never trust a sheila or a reef you can't see. And the coral's not the only dynger. The sting of a butterfly cod's one of the worst pyns there is, and it doesn't go awye for bloody months. And if you step on a stonefish — God, stone the crows and call the undertyker!"

Jim nodded. Stonefish lived also in Philippine waters, and their poison meant sudden death.

Finally, another striking natural barrier lay dead ahead. Gray-black "clouds" on the horizon grew in size and substance to become three-dimensional masses of vivid green, separating the intense blues of sea and sky. After the flatness of Northern Australia, this mighty rump of the Guinea-bird's tail, the Owen Stanley Range — stretching for 600 miles, reaching into cumulus clouds at 15,000 feet — smote Jim's eyes with its majesty.

"Austrylia's an old continent; our mountains are worn down like an old nag's teeth," Griffin said. "But New Guinea really is 'new,' and still emergin'."

Jim heard Eubank tell Brereton, "Those mountains sure look a damned sight better from this side. This hop is a piece of cake. Simply no comparison with the flight down to Port Moresby from Wake. Two thousand one hundred and seventy-six miles . . . over the Carolines in the dark, as you know, so the Japs wouldn't get nervous. After we finally made landfall on the north side of the island's tail, we had to climb to fourteen thousand to get over 'them thar hills.' But as soon as we were over them, we had to get the hell down; we couldn't afford to overshoot Moresby, because we were flying on fumes by then. I had gas for about twenty minutes left, and of course I was worrying about the kids in the other planes. Flew along the coast till we spotted Port Moresby — damned easy to miss it — then inland seven miles, and by the grace of God, found the miserable airstrip. After we were all safely down, Ed Jacquet said he could have filled a cigarette lighter with all the gas in his tank."

Brereton said, "Maybe we can find a better place on the north coast to build a field, so our ferry pilots can land *before* they have to tackle those mountains. After all, Amelia Earhart landed her big machine, and took off, over there at Lae. Before we leave New Guinea, let's take a look at Lae."

Hell, yes, let's do that. Let's walk around where AE walked. Let's change the name of the town to "LAE" in her honor.

"Yep, we should do that," Eubank replied. "Air New Guinea's been running commercial flights from Lae for years, but I don't know whether there's five thousand feet of level ground there that isn't swampy. There's another settlement on that coast, near Lae — Salamaua — that I'd like to check out, too. Or maybe we'll find that Rabaul's the best spot for a base, after all."

Eubank became silent as he nosed the bomber down toward the ragged curve of the Gulf of Papua. At the Gulf's western edge, the green shoreline, cut by rivers, was blurred by feathery casuarina trees.

As if a colossal sea serpent had emerged from the Gulf of Papua and had swum southward until its head was now 1,250 miles down the coast, the narrowing tail of the Great Barrier Reef ended here, allowing ships access to the Gulf— with care. The final vestige of the Reef pointed toward the largest and southernmost of the river inlets; Griff said it was the mouth of the Fly. New Guinea's greatest river, 800 miles long, the Fly was the only cut-through — albeit a tortuous one — to the north side of the island.

"If a bloke leaves the river, he has to hack his way through bush so bloody thick, two or three miles in a dye is a fair ryte."

Griff told Jim about the pioneer Scottish missionary, James Chalmers, who had explored and converted in Papua for 23 years. In 1900, with his mission

Chapter 4 — Part 1 — To Papua, New Guinea   107

established beside the Fly, tribesmen had killed and eaten him.

"And the Fuzzies got fat when the *St. Paul* was shipwrecked off the coast in 1858, with more than three hundred Whitefellow passengers. They ayte all but two — quite an insult, wasn't that, if those two were scorned for not looking as tyesty as their mytes!"

Strangely, the eastern shore of the Gulf of Papua appeared to Jim like a brown scab on the intensely green island; it was as sere and dusty as a piece of northwest Australia. Griff said that something called a "rain shadow" created a miniature desert around Port Moresby, watered only by the fiercest monsoons. The area appeared almost uninhabited, except for a scatter of bright dots on a small tongue of land in a land-locked little bay. Like flakes of mica, the metal roofs that sheltered Port Moresby's non-indigenous inhabitants reflected the sun's glare. Jim saw a Papuan bamboo-and-thatch village on stilts over the water and a small wooden pier, but no landing field.

Airstrips existed, Griff assured him — three of them, named for their distance from the port. "Three Mile" lay northeast of the settlement; "Seven Mile" was inland, farther northeast; and "Ten Mile" farther inland, farther northeast, near the hills where the dark brown winding Loloki River emerged from its canyon. Three Mile and Ten Mile were merely emergency landing fields; but the monsoon rains soon would bring the annual emergency that would force land-planes to use Ten Mile.

Seven Mile boasted a 3,600-foot runway, which had served the successive flights of almost all of the 35 Fortresses bound for the Philippines (a few had landed at Rabaul, New Britain). Additionally, a U.S. B-24 Liberator bomber, en route to Moscow on a Lend-Lease mission, had landed at Seven Mile in October.

"That Lib pilot was still cussing when he got to Townsville," Griffin recalled. "He said Seven Mile's runwye should be extended to five thousand feet, at least."

"Slugger Pell told the officials that we needed five thousand, before we brought our bomb squadrons through here," Eubank said. Over the settlement of Port Moresby, a tiny spit of land, he set a heading of 045 degrees, briefly following a narrow road through dusty-looking gum trees until a dead-end valley appeared. It was so rocky and uneven that it reminded Jim of a pottery bowl made by a child from rough river clay, collapsing as it baked in the sun.

"I thought for sure they would've improved Seven Mile by now," Eubank said, "but it doesn't look any better than the last time I saw it."

Jim peered through the cockpit windows down at the uneven terrain, worsened by bare brown hillocks. *Seven Mile Aerodrome!* Clearly, it was impossible, even for Eubank, to ease the huge bomber into that inhospitable space. He sat down behind the jump-seat, locked his legs around it, and braced himself against it. He thought of the pilots of the 14th and 19th Bomb

Squadrons — some of them no older than he — who had brought their B-17s over those terrible mountains on their last drops of fuel, to land in that hole, all in total secrecy, with no acclaim from press or newsreels.

His respect for Eubank's skill soared even higher as they landed — uphill — across gullies so deep that twice the fuselage seemed to have plunged below ground level, while Jim felt as if he were inside a fast-dribbled basketball.

In the silence after Eubank cut the engines, Jim heard him say, in his wry cowboy tone, "Wal, I don't notice much improvement."

"Inexcusable!" Brereton snorted. "Intolerable!"

Griffin explained, "Hard to get the Fuzzy-Wuzzies to work on it. They don't value money. Seashells and feathers are as good as gold to them."

And boy, do they like to flaunt their wealth! Jim thought, as a welcoming committee of huge Papuans ran up to greet the travelers. Their kinky mats of hair formed turban-like bases for ornate headdresses of feathers, with white cockatoo and rosy bird-of-paradise predominating. Jim had never seen personal adornment on such a scale: tattoos, white paint or blue; necklaces of cowrie shells, discs of bailer shells, strings of teeth and seeds; earrings of boar's tusks; and nose-piercing cassowary bones adorned bare chocolate-colored bodies clad only in G-strings, penis gourds, or wraparound lava-lavas of bark cloth or "ass grass." They grinned, showing betel-stained teeth, and chorused, "G'ddye, myte!"

Heat struck like a hammer. Jim's flying suit was already wet with sweat, as were those of the others.

*Thank God the Dutch got the **hotter** equatorial end of the bird,* he thought.

Allison Ind recovered quickly from his airsickness. As Jim now recalled from their Bali travels, the gentlemanly professor, like a *National Geographic* cameraman, had a keen scientific eye for the symmetries of the unclad female bosom. Around the B-17 now jiggled hundreds of shiny brown breasts, ranging from teen-points like dark ice cream cones to magnificent pendulous, chocolate papayas. Ind had his movie camera ready. Previously he had cranked it dutifully to record the drab military facilities in Darwin and Townsville; now he radiated the air of an artist unchained.

"Such an ingenuous display!" he murmured to Jim. "Superbly developed. . . . Eye-blinking. . . . The tattooed embellishments — to my Western eyes — are not really necessary to improve Nature's generous handiwork. . . ."

Less exotically, although no less cordially, the Royal Australian Army and the RAAF were represented by Brigadier B. M. Morris and a youthful-looking pilot, Squadron Leader C. W. Pearce, wearing pith helmets and khaki shorts. So efficiently did they shepherd the senior Americans into two staff cars that Captain Ind, too polite to demur, was on his way before he could turn the crank of his camera. Wearing a pitiful expression, he held it up to the window, as if wishing he could hand it to Jim, before a veil of dust marked his departure.

Evidently there were not many other cars in Port Moresby; Jim, Lefty Eads, and Griffin rode in a lorry driven by an RAAF enlisted man.

Damn, Jim thought. *No WAAAF drivers — no WAAAF at all in New Guinea. But I guess it's just as well for the poor sheilas — they'd melt in this heat, and choke on all this dry-season dust.*

Part 2 — Miserable Moresby

As the toad has its eye, so Port Moresby has its sunsets.
— Commander Eric A. Feldt, RAN

Port Moresby, PNG
Sunday, 16 November 1941

After a sweltering night in the RAAF barracks, on a metal cot with only a blanket between his bare back and the wire crosspieces, Jim was wakened at dawn by the light of a bare electric bulb overhead. Looming over him was a six-foot Papuan, with a bone through his nose and a grass skirt around his belly, who thrust at him a steaming cup of dark tea and a biscuit.

"Time sun he come up. You-fella bilong belly cry. Bring him he come kai-kai. Scone bilong cow oil. You-fella eatum. Drinkum billy," the man told him, with such a solicitous betel-bloody grin that Jim forgave him for breaking into a dream of Daphne.

Or was it Penny?

In spite of her cruelty on Castle Hill, she was the best thing he'd seen in Australia. Sitting on the side of the cot, he munched his first scone. Although the scone had not been warmed, the air temperature had melted the Australian butter, making its Pidgin name, "cow oil," appropriate.

It's going to be swell fun to see Penny again — I know she'll keep her promise. . . . Maybe the Fortress, after all the dust it's been inhaling, will need to have a new engine flown down from Clark, and we can be stuck in T-ville for a good long time. . . .

He rubbed his back, feeling the imprint of the cot's metal strips. *No wonder the Aussie fly-boys are so tough,* he thought. *And I don't think their scratchy GI blankets are made of the goldenest fleece of the nation's wool crop, either.*

Before the sun came bursting over the mountains he wanted to get outside and stretch his muscles in the cool, wide-legged khaki shorts that he had borrowed from Griffin.

The senior "misters" would be conferring all day, he thought. *Thank God they didn't ask me to advise them! So here I am, with a whole free day to carouse in Port Moresby.*

As he walked toward the waterfront, something reminded him faintly of Intramuros, Manila's medieval walled city. Yet nothing could look more unlike the Spanish fortress-city, with its cathedrals and statues, than this collection of dreary metal-roofed shacks. And the Papuans with their large bare, dark bodies so wildly decorated, bore no resemblance to the small-statured, neatly dressed Filipinos who attended masses and university classes in Intramuros. Still, the impression deepened as he walked. Finally, a sluggish breeze from the harbor — still at least a mile away — woke his nostrils to the acrid stench of urine. That was it.

Whenever visitors from the States complained to him about the odor in some sections of Intramuros, he used to say defensively, "Now you know how a real medieval city smelled." *So,* he told himself, *now I know how a real Papuan village smells. Travel is so broadening.*

Darwin was a sophisticated metropolis, compared to Port Moresby. He was already thinking of it as "Port Less-by." Probably fewer than 3,000 inhabitants, he guessed; it was hard to tell, because the shacks were scattered inland from the spit of land that held the pier. The spit itself — Paga Point — barely three-quarters of a mile in width and extending westerly into the landlocked bay for about a mile and a half, was shaped like the ankle and shoe of a chubby child, with the toe pointing south and the pier at the heel. Within this limited area, comprising five unpaved streets and a few shore-to-shore cross streets, were confined the Australian administration's offices and the "business district": a seedy assortment of pubs, two hotels, and the inevitable Chinese shop — Joe Chan's.

Is there a village anywhere in Asia where an expatriate Chinese hasn't set up shop? And what happens to the "White Australia" policy on a black-majority island?

All five east-west streets of this "downtown" trailed off when they reached a small hill that formed the sole of the spit-shoe. After taking a dusty path to the hilltop, Jim could see — and smell — all of the little bay. Although the urine odor emanated most noisomely from the pier and from the log canoes around it, he could see that the harbor's narrow entrance restricted the outflow of the water itself. The bay's rounded shape indicated to him that it was probably formed of the tip of a very small volcano, with only one break in its crater wall. That single gap was so narrow that Jim mentally saluted Captain John Moresby for finding the channel to this port — which he later modestly named for his father — in 1873.

Even Jim's own Manila Bay, with a mouth 30 miles wide, did not get enough tidal flushing action from the rolling South China Sea to cleanse it of the city's effluent. The most efficient solution for Port Moresby, he thought, would be for the Americans to load up a B-17 with bombs and blast holes in the southeast rim of the bay, opening it to the Gulf of Papua. That would be good practice for a bombardier with the super-secret Norden bombsight, too: doing the kind of "pinpoint bombing" that the Fortresses had been created for.

Of course, those perforations would diminish the harbor's security from storms — but it sure would improve the sanitation. And it would work a helluva lot faster than trying to persuade the Papuans that it's not nice to pee in the Bay.

When he was ten years old and lived beside Lake Lanao in Mindanao, where his parents were assisting Dr. Frank ("Each One Teach One") Laubach to bring literacy to the Moro people, the shores of that paradisical crater lake were dotted with "sanitary toilets": gifts to the Moros from the American colonial government. However, despite much effort by the bureau of health "privy counselors" to explain the connection between some of the Moros' customary uses of the lake and the cholera epidemics that ravaged the community, the fatalistic Muslim Moros used the toilet sheds only for storing supplies or confining senile relatives. Just last month, when Jim had returned to the Lanao on a mission to learn whether the separatist-minded Moros would side with the Japanese in case of war, he had seen only the crumbling traces of the never-used privies.

Around the curve of the bay to his right, Hanuabada, the Papuan village, extended over the water. To his eyes, its bamboo-and-thatch dwellings, resembling familiar Moro settlements in Mindanao, looked far less intrusive than the white people's ramshackle wooden houses with their corrugated metal roofs. Cooler, too, he knew; in this dry air there would be evaporation of the harbor water beneath the open bamboo floors of the stilt-houses.

The double log canoes were new to him. With a bamboo frame connecting the two hulls, they resembled pictures of the *kattumarams* of South India. Good stability, Jim realized — and the family can recline on the "deck." They were called *lakatois,* he was told by a Papuan who was floating past the pier aboard one, accompanied by his three wives, in various stages of pregnancy, and a swarm of naked brown babies.

"Swarm" was not sufficient to describe the collection of mosquitoes whining around him; it seemed more like a galaxy. Although he had grown up in company with Asia's mosquitoes and strong odors, on this morning Port Moresby's share of both struck him as outstanding.

One ship was docked at the pier: a small supply ship of the Burns Philp trading company, the *Mac Dhui*. Husky, sweat-slick Papuans were hand-winching net bags of coconuts aboard. As the winch squealed, parrots screeched from the palm trees in reply.

Inside his head, untouched by the screams of the parrots or the winch, Jim heard Daphne's throaty voice, singing. Ever since August, he had been hearing her song every time he saw a coconut — and they were ubiquitous in the Philippines. On one typical Singapore Sunday, at the customary champagne brunch at Sea View between St. Andrew's and the races, Daphne, charmingly tipsy, had joined the orchestra to sing — by unanimous request — her own madcap send-up of an English music-hall ditty. Her version, with gestures and Cockney accent, began, "I've Got a Lovely Pair of Coconuts. . . ."

Later, the orchestra had wound up with "There'll Always Be an England," joined by every voice in the place.

Although the fetid air here at the shore felt steamy, dry-season dust lay on every surface. The tall, skinny palm trees would provide no relief from the oncoming sun; to Jim they looked like worn-out feather dusters made of frayed green parrot feathers. A hunchbacked white heron with a crooked neck, cruel black eyes, and a beak like a yellow dagger stood in mud beside a clump of mangroves, whose brown aerial roots matched his spindly legs. The hull of an old ship that obviously had barely missed Captain Moresby's passage and impaled itself on a reef, added the final melancholy note.

The only attractive, non-dusty objects in his view were a squadron of brilliant blue kingfishers that flashed overhead, and — in the water — a pair of old Seagull single-engine flying boats, a couple of old Empire flying boats, and the 12 pristine U.S.-built PBYs of RAAF Squadrons No. 11 and No. 20.

Why should they worry about the awful landing fields?

Air Commodore Pearce had told the visitors last night how enthusiastically the two squadrons were enjoying the PBYs, which they, of course, called Catalinas. The big flying boats had been flown down from Hawaii the previous month by QANTAS pilots.

"Naturally, we were keen to pick them up ourselves — but since you Yanks aren't in the war, it had to appear as a civilian transaction," Pearce said.

Jim loved the awkward-looking "P-boats"; he had flown in them often with Commander Frank Bridget of Manila's Patrol Wing Ten.

Damn it, he thought, *I've always gotten along well with "naviators" — naval pilots — and with Aussies. Why did I have to strike out with the one Australian naval pilot who was so important for me to get along with?*

He turned and strode down the hill, back through the spit-town. Then he would head for the lorry track; the seven barren miles to the airstrip would be more scenic for a hike than this God-forsaken, stinking "port," he thought. At the first cross street, he passed a small, well-kept yellow frame building with the name HOTEL MORESBY.

Too bad we couldn't stay there; it sure would beat being barbecue-grilled on the RAAF's bare metal cot.

At the next corner, crossing a street marked "Musgrave," he passed the Burns Philp office, and thought of Penny. She had walked with him along Townsville's attractive Esplanade to the waterfront, where the Scottish immigrant, James Burns, had built his wharves for sailing ships. Those wharves would do, Jim had thought, to handle the American freighters loaded with crates of U.S.-built fighter aircraft that Brereton wanted. Jim had seen Burns Philp vessels in the Javanese ports of Batavia and Surabaya — each one bearing a Scottish name and captained by a Scot straight out of a novel by Jim's favorite author, Joseph Conrad.

Penny told him that after Burns and his partner Robert Philp had spread their trading agencies throughout the South Seas, Burns established Burnside Homes near Parramatta, NSW, where children aged three to ten lived in "cottage homes" with a matron. "So remember," Penny said, "not all Scots are tight with their money."

. . . Remember? I remember ever damned word I've heard since I was born — and I remember your promise, Penny. . . .

"Time for a smoke-oh!" From across the street a thin, gray-bearded man called to him. He was sitting alone on the porch with his bare feet on the railing of a small, neat, white-painted building whose sign read, PAPUA HOTEL. "Got any Yank cigarettes, myte?"

Jim glanced at his hack watch; it was not yet seven. The sun was still behind the mountains. *Oh, hell, a smoke screen might discourage the mosquitoes for a few minutes.*

"Sure. I guess it *is* time."

He crossed the gravel street and took the wooden steps two at a time. "I wanted to ask someone about that wrecked ship in the harbor. Have you been here long enough to know the story?"

The man laughed. "Only heard it a few hundred times. I've been helping run this hotel for almost four years. Before I came here, I was the assistant manager of the Cecil Hotel, over at Lae, and before that, I was a Patrol Officer out in the bush with the Fuzzy-Wuzzies. I've heard every story in New Guinea, and don't believe half —"

LAE, *the man said!*

"Were you at the Cecil Hotel in 1937, when —"

"When the unlucky lady pilot stopped there? True, I was. She was unhappy about being delayed with the weather and her nav's radio trouble, so I helped them pass the time — little dreaming it would be their last day alive. I gave her a booklet of Pidgin words from the hotel gift shop, and I drove her and the man out to a Fuzzy-Wuzzy village. The people loved her, but they couldn't believe she was a 'mary' — a *woman* — with that short hair, wearing khaki trousers, and without any baby. . . ."

A couple of Lucky Strikes later, Jim asked Anthony Lightbody, "You're not Australian, are you?"

"True. Pommie expat'."

Jim had heard that tone in the voices of expatriate white men in Manila; it meant, *Mind your own damned business.*

A gong reverberated inside the hotel. "*Kai* time. Please be my guest for breakfast. I'm browned off with eating alone in the empty dining room."

Jim stayed, more for the man's conversation than for the meal, but the eggs were fresh, the scones hot from the oven, the pats of butter firm on their bed of ice, and the billy tea was so strong it made him feel like running all the way to Seven Mile. The Papua Hotel, Lightbody said, boasted the "top" dining room and the "top" pub in Port Moresby.

"We're *nambawan*, as the Fuzzies express primacy. That reminds me — I'll give you a copy of the Pidgin Glossary, just like the one I gave Miss Earhart. But I hope it brings you better luck than it brought her."

Richard Archbold had signed the hotel's guest book in 1936, during his second of three New Guinea expeditions. While he was exploring the Black River and making aerial maps, a violent storm had destroyed his Catalina, forcing him and his party to build rafts to get back to the coast with their specimens.

"I admire the bloke," Lightbody said. "He could have stayed in the States in comfort, living the life of a rich playboy, instead of risking his life in that Cat."

"He's one of my heroes," Jim told him. He did not mention his own acquaintance and travels with Anne Archbold, Richard's mother, the Standard Oil heiress, aboard her custom-built Chinese junk, *Cheng Ho*. Although Jim had been along only as an assistant to the botanist David Fairchild, he thought it would sound like bragging.

Some members of Richard Archbold's team had stayed at Port Moresby's alternative lodging, the Hotel Moresby. Competition between the Papua and the Moresby was keen since the war had reduced the always-small influx of visitors, Lightbody said. "I'd like to put in one of those new Milk Bars that are all the rage on the mainland, to draw a local clientele — but our milk boat from Townsville isn't dependable enough —"

Part 3 — Seven Mile

> *[Japan's] policies, developed in Korea, Manchuria, and lately in occupied China, show that she intends to bar the areas which she controls to American commerce and industry. The "Open Door" in China is as much a basic part of our foreign policy as the Monroe Doctrine. Japan has closed every door to us in every area she has won by conquest. . . .*
> — Hallet Abend, *Ramparts of the Pacific*, 1942

Port Moresby
Sunday, 16 November 1941

Walking northeast from the spit-town, Jim passed a stretch of shallow, sandy beach on his right. Lightbody had given its name as "Ela" on the sketch-map he had drawn on the tablecloth with a butterknife; he had warned Jim that black sea-urchins, painful to step on, hid in the rank sea-grasses.

The sun had risen like thunder, and even through his Ray-Ban sunglasses the glare was painful. The houses with their peeling white or yellow paint, their blinding sunstruck metal roofs, and the yellow dust of the roads so lacking in shade, bounced the brilliant light into his eyes.

Later, at a bend in the shoreline, the trail passed an open-air market at a place called Koki, lively with Papuans from a nearby stilt-village. He would have liked to buy a wooden carved and painted Papuan mask, such as those he had seen pictured in *The National Geographic*, but the market's wares were only edibles: yams, live pigs, fish, and a small tethered crocodile with its jaws bound shut, thrashing its tail in the dust. It was called a *puc-puc*, he learned.

Jim had quickly realized that the sun was too intense for him to maintain a steady dogtrot. Although his sweat dried quickly in the bake-oven air, dust formed a paste that adhered to his body like a second skin. Nature is kind to the Papuans, he thought, insulating their heads with that thick hair full of air-pockets. Pith helmets were not worn in the Philippines; he had always thought them a British affectation, like swagger sticks. Now, however, he decided to borrow one before starting on another hike in New Guinea. He settled for running five minutes, then walking for ten, taking a sip from his canteen after each run.

About two miles from the spit-town the lorry track began to climb steeply. This was Three Mile Hill, the site of the emergency landing field; and on viewing the airstrip he had to admit that there was indeed something worse than Seven Mile. He took the hill at a walk until he reached a Papuan village at the crest — Baroko — more than halfway to Seven Mile; then he began his descent.

The exotic New Guinea scenery that he had anticipated was all in the distance; the area behind Port Moresby for about 20 miles was as parched and barren as West Texas, although not so flat. At least it was better than looking at the dreary shacks of the town. An undulating sea of dry brown grass was broken by knobby little rocky hills and an occasional clump of the scrawny eucalypts called gum trees, with their scabrous deformed trunks and their dull leaves. Even when Port Moresby got its annual rains — 80 inches, all at once, Lightbody had said — the gum trees would *still* look dusty, he thought.

This, on an island renowned for its massive forests of camphor, sandalwood, and ebony, of Tarzan-quality vines, and more than a thousand varieties of orchids! He felt robbed, especially of the chance to see new birds. New Guinea was known as a paradise of birds, and Lightbody had told him that more than 30 varieties of birds-of-paradise lived in the island's forests.

What a gyp! More than seven hundred species of birds on this island, and my only feathered friends are noisy parrots and parakeets!

While he ran, his eyes kept his mind occupied with avoiding pitfalls in the rough and deep ruts of the lorry track. While he walked, however, there was little to distract him, and thoughts surfaced unbidden into his consciousness. As usual, his mind was divided, and as always, that made him angry with himself.

Was he weakening, abandoning his principles — or gaining a more mature outlook, he wondered. The possibility that this trip would wind up in Singapore had heated his longing for Daphne and simultaneously eroded the force of his shock at her opium addiction. His initial rejection now seemed like a puritanical over-reaction to her weakness. It was, after all, curable, as Emily Hahn had proved. And the same powerful yearning for Daphne that had softened his opposition to her habit was also altering his antagonism to Plan Rainbow 5.

If Japan — perhaps at Hitler's bidding — should suddenly unleash its Saigon-based bombers against Singapore, could Daphne escape to the safety of Penang Island in time?

In Chungking, standing beside Captain Chennault, Jim had watched from the roof of Huang Shen — the hillside mansion of Generalissimo and Madame Chiang, Kai-shek — a merciless Japanese night-bombing of the city. And on his 21st birthday there, crammed in a stinking mile-long cave-shelter with hundreds of Chinese, his head bent beneath the low-vaulted rock ceiling, holding Doris Lim's tender, trembling body while the air became so foul that all the candles went out, he had endured a daylight bombing raid, the worst experience of his life.

He could not bear to think of Daphne's being exposed to such horror; he would rather have the U.S. fight Japan. Although he did not like all the Britons he had met in Singapore, he had made many warm friends there. He thought of the British journalists, all drinking *stengahs* at Ian Morrison's apartment: Noel Barber of the *London Daily Mail* and his colleague, Lawrence Impie, the *Daily Mail's* Old China Hand; Kenneth Selby-Walker, former manager for Reuter's in China; and likable, ruddy-faced "Gal" of the *London Daily Express* — O'Dowd Gallagher, the South African.

Too, Jim had been captivated by more than the tartans and bagpipes of the bonny Scots of the Argyll and Sutherland Highlanders — especially tall Ernest Gordon and red-haired Mike Blackwood, spare-time sailors and full-time gentlemen. Despite Leda's training, he liked too many of the Brits to want to see their little colony battered like Chungking.

And now, Australia — rather, the Aussies — had further complicated his thinking. A week ago, news of a Japanese attack on Australia would not have roused him to a war fervor. While he had greatly enjoyed knowing the Australian Nursing Sisters and the fliers in Singapore and Kota Bharu, they had been linked in his mind with Malaya. Now that he really knew how desperately isolated their country was — not just on a map, but by the length of that interminable overwater B-17 flight — and how spunky the people were, would he want the U.S. to go to war for Australia?

Hell, yes, he answered himself as he ran and the dust stuck to his sweat. *They're all alone down here, and nobody else can help these dinkum blokes. I've met only* **one** *Aussie I didn't like; the rest are swell. Penny has her funny principles, but her heart's in the right place — and what a gorgeous pair of coconuts! I still hate the secrecy of Rainbow Five, but I'll go along with it.*

— That's damned big of you, Jim sneered to himself. *MacArthur and*

Chapter 4 — Part 3 — Seven Mile 119

Brereton and Eubank will be delighted to have you on their side. Not to mention the President. After all, you applauded his secrecy in supporting Chennault. Are you tending to think that the English deserve U.S. backing as much as the Chinese do?

Beside the lorry track, tents of Australian airmen were blanketed with its dust. Before him, the "topless towers" of the Owen Stanley Range were hidden in clouds. On their steep green sides, wisps of smoke marked slash-and-burn clearing activity. Whoever Owen Stanley was, Jim thought, he sure got himself one helluva fine monument. In comparison with those fierce heights, the Philippine *bundoks* seem almost tame.

We still have some fine un-named mountains, though. And some day I'll explore one, and name it Mount James Thomas Davis. Unlike Captain Moresby, I'd never name anything for my father. Old Alex can find his own damned mountain — but of course he never will.

At Seven Mile, Jim sat in the shade of a gum tree and leaned against its trunk. His borrowed shorts were as sweat-soaked as his T-shirt. He pulled the damp Pidgin Glossary out of his pocket and used it as a mosquito fan.

Colonel Eubank had parked B-17D No. 40-3097 at the east end of the field, with its tail to the mountains and its nose toward Moresby Bay. Now the Papuan gas crew were hand-pumping fuel into it from 50-gallon drums. Watching them beside the huge silver plane, he marveled again at Eubank's safe landing in these wretched gullies.

And he'll have to do it again tomorrow, when we come back from Rabaul. . . . That is, if we can ever get the Fortress out of here, to go to Rabaul.

He sipped from his canteen, saving half for his return hike. He was ready for a "smoke-oh." He had given Lightbody the remainder of the first pack of Lucky Strikes, but he had a second, unopened pack tucked into the top of his wet sock.

"G'ddye, myte!" The crew had stopped pumping and were coming over to greet him. Their thick crowns of hair looked as uniformly circular as airplane tires, he thought. "You-fella bilong tabac?" one asked.

Yeah, me-fella belong tabac. Me-fella slave to tabac.

He kept three cigarettes and gave the pack to the leader of the crew. Jim was curious to see how a cigarette could be smoked beneath a dangling nose-ring of bone, tusk, or shell. By sign language, he indicated *Don't smoke near the gas pump.* Both sides of the runway were lined with red drums of high-octane gasoline.

The leader agreed, "Two-fella sing out plenty boom-boom!" and they all laughed. Above their wraparound lava-lavas, their dark muscular bodies, greased with pig-fat, glittered with thousands of separate rivulets of sweat.

Deeper than the screeching of the parrots, he heard a single-engine plane;

then he saw it, like a ghost from his past, coming in from the sea. Its conformation was so much like the AT-6 Texan that he had learned to fly at Kelly Field, that it would have looked natural to see his instructor, Captain Sluder, at the throttle. But those red-and-blue bullseye roundels identified it as a Wirraway, and he recognized the insigne of Squadron No. 24 from RAAF Station Garbutt in Townsville. As the pilot "dragged the strip" — flying low to get a good look at the field's condition — Jim saw through the squares of the long canopy that the rear seat was empty.

"Good luck, buddy," he murmured, "you'll need it, to land on this lousy roller-coaster strip."

He noted that the plane carried an auxiliary gasoline tank, so it could have come from the mainland or Rabaul. A Wirraway's normal range of 510 miles was almost exactly the distance to Rabaul, where the Americans would be going tomorrow.

Lord, I hope I won't be so outranked that I'll have to ride in that **crate**, he thought.

"Him-fella liklik balus," said one of the Papuans, and the others seemed to agree. Jim consulted the glossary and learned that *balus* meant either "pigeon" or "airplane"; *liklik* meant "small."

East of the field, the Wirraway made a 180-degree turn, descended slowly, and dropped to the ground like a stone. The admirable full-stall landing arrested it at once, sparing it the wracking bounces of taxiing over the gullies. *Just the way I would have done it,* Jim thought; *Chet Sluder himself couldn't have done it better.*

Before the dust-cloud had settled, the pilot pushed back his canopy and climbed out, wearing the Australian bush-uniform of khaki shorts and open-neck khaki shirt. He carried a canteen and a pith helmet, with which he promptly covered his head.

Jim stood up and clapped, applauding the skillful touch-down. "Good job!" he called.

"G'ddye, myte!" As the slightly-built pilot came closer, he asked, "Lieutenant Davis, I presume?"

David Livingston, the great Scots missionary, when newsman Stanley found him in Africa, couldn't have been more astonished to hear his own name, Jim thought.

I've heard that Australian voice before . . . but it couldn't be the same one.

The pith helmet tilted; blue-gray eyes looked up into Jim's. They belonged to Commander Feldt — and yes — they twinkled. He grasped Jim's hand.

"Just the bloke I came to see. I decided I could explain our Coastwatch scheme better out here than in my office, so I borrowed a machine and flew up to talk to you. Didn't expect such luck as to see you the minute I landed. But first — would you care to give me a look inside that bonzer Flying Fortress of yours?"

Jim was too surprised to say more than, "You must have left Garbutt long before daylight."

"Cooler that way. Had a tail wind, and made it in under three hours. But a Wirraway's nothing to skite — to boast — about; the poor birds were obsolete before they were born."

Inside the bomber, Jim felt like a king as he demonstrated the cockpit and all its panoply of instruments to the admiring Commander; fortunately, Feldt did not ask him about anything whose name Jim had not learned.

"We fighter pilots are too independent for all that teamwork when we fly, aren't we?" Feldt said as they emerged.

Although Jim agreed, he still harbored resentment over the Commander's coldness of the previous day, and he did not answer.

The gas crew had finished with the B-17, but they clustered around to ask Feldt for tobacco. He handed each Papuan a piece of stick tobacco to chew, and the leader showed him the empty Lucky Strike package from Jim, worn now as a hair ornament. Chewing hard, the crew members moved their pump to service Feldt's Wirraway.

Walking past the huge American plane toward the foothills beyond, Feldt took a pipe from his pocket and filled it. Jim was relieved, because he was determined not to offer the man one of his last two Lucky Strikes.

As if the Commander had read his thoughts, he said, "You were generous in distributing your excellent Yank cigarettes to the gas crew. But one cig apiece is plenty. Please don't spoil 'em — that makes it tough on our blokes." He offered Jim an Australian Craven-A, and Jim accepted it as a sort of peace offering. It seemed to him not only small, but hard, and lacking in flavor or aroma.

Gesturing with his pipe, Feldt indicated a coconut plantation at the foot of the mountains. "Not far from there is the bushy spot where I camped for three months to test the Teleradio. There on the left sits Mount Victoria, over thirteen thousand feet high, and on the right is Mount Lamington, about six thousand feet. Victoria's dead, but Lamington rumbles, and may blow off some time. Between them is the start of the native track that tortuously winds, climbs, and slithers through the mountains to Kokoda. From there, an intrepid bushwalker could get down to Buna, on the north coast, by way of another rugged trail."

Jim said nothing. Feldt drew on his pipe. "It's the configuration of the mountains that makes this area such an ugly dry patch on an otherwise wet and beautiful island. By contrast, the mountains look soft and green. But some of that green is *kunai*, a sword grass that takes over the territory — after the natives burn off trees to create potash for temporary enrichment of a new planting of yams."

OK — if he wants to talk botany, I can do that. "We have the same thing in the Philippines: slash-and-burn farming for yams, called *kamotes,* followed by sword grass, called *kogon.*"

"It's the curse of Asia. The roots spread insidiously underground, and no human hands are strong enough to dig it out." He turned to Jim. "Are you ready to start back to Moresby?"

Jim was surprised that the Commander did not plan to wait for a lorry ride. Caked with dust and thinking of lunch, Jim had begun to consider riding back if a lorry appeared; but now he felt shamed out of it by the older man, and fell in beside Feldt.

"Kunai," Feldt continued, "is almost as bad as the Red Tape Plant."

"Beg yours?" Jim tried an Aussie expression.

"The Red Tape Plant's one of the wonders of biology. Flourishes indoors, in offices — the larger and older the office, the heavier the infestation. Its seed is proliferated in envelopes from an already infected office, and it grows apace, strangling and paralyzing. Like a tapeworm, each segment has full male and female organs of reproduction, so it propagates continuously."

Jim laughed. Getting out of the office sure made a change in the old fellow, he thought.

"— Fortunately for you," Feldt continued, "the American air force is a young service, where the Red Tape jungle can be cleared away in places."

"But our air force isn't free like the RAAF. We're still under the Army's thumb — where the Red Tape Plant *flourishes.*"

"And you'll have to stay there, and make the best of it, until the threat of war passes. That's been the lesson coming from our war in Europe: the imperative need for cooperation between the services. A shooting war with a foreign enemy leaves no room for internecine warfare. Now our branches are getting so matey, the RAAF is even helping us to develop a less bulky Teleradio."

"That's good news, Sir. Ten or more Papuans to carry each one equals quite a crowd."

"True. But a Teleradio would be useless without those strong black legs to provide instant removal. I had to keep my men with me the entire time I camped out, from August to November. If Port Moresby had been seized by an enemy landing force, I could have moved at once to my mountain lair and kept watch from there, reporting to Townsville on enemy movements."

"You think the Japs would *want* that dry patch?"

"Moresby's certainly not beaut, but it's the gateway to the Coral Sea and northeast Australia. And it's now backed up by a screen of good men — not a paper one. In September 1939, I set out to visit every man in the Islands who had a Teleradio. I traveled by ship, motorboat, canoe, bicycle, airplane, and *boot,* throughout Papua, the Solomons, the New Hebrides, New Britain, New Ireland, and their satellite specks of land."

"Maybe your Navy people could put some fake lights on the Great Barrier Reef, and lead the enemy ships to run aground?"

Feldt shook his head. "The Japs have better charts of our waters than the RAN has. We often catch their ships offshore, masquerading as pearl luggers — loaded with highly sophisticated sounding equipment. We have several of their crews in our mainland prisons right now."

"Good. Have you caught any mine-planters? Do you think the *Niagara* —"

In June, the sleek British passenger liner, veteran of many crossings between Vancouver and Auckland, had exploded within sight of New Zealand.

"We don't doubt that she was sunk by a mine," Feldt answered. "Probably Japanese, but possibly German. Incidentally, it isn't generally known, but in addition to the passengers who were lost, there was a large amount of gold aboard the *Niagara*. Perhaps twenty-five million pounds. She went down in waters shallow enough that after the war an effort will surely be made to salvage it."

"I'd like to come back and help with that. Not to keep any of the gold, but just to explore the wreck. My dad has figured out where some of the Spanish galleons went down in the Philippines, and my brother and I are going to try to locate one some day."

"Poor little New Zed is so underpopulated, with barely more than a million and half souls — and eighty thousand of her men fighting abroad. They've even begun conscripting married men. It's impossible for the Kiwis to guard their coasts properly."

Funny, Jim thought, *I'd been thinking **Australia's** too underpopulated to do that same thing.*

"The Japanese do skulk around, but it's been the bloody German raiders who've made their presence felt ever since the war began. We know of four, for certain, and it's only because of them that we were able to convince Churchill that he must let our cruiser *Sydney* come back to protect our shipping. But mine-warfare is such a sneaking, un-sporting affair that it makes every seafaring man feel nervy. We've found mines laid off Sydney, Melbourne, Hobart, and Adelaide, and there's little we can do to defend against them, save constant vigilance. They're a terror after dark, when any unusual noise aboard ship — even a sailor dropping his mug of billy — can cause everyone to dash for a life preserver. And it happened after dark, around nineteen hundred hours, almost precisely a year ago, that a mine destroyed your *City of Rayville*."

"An American ship? I never heard about that!"

"American as New York. Merchant ship of the Pioneer Line, just under six hundred tons, about four hundred feet in length. She was heading for Melbourne after loading dried fruit at Port Adelaide and twenty-five hundred tons of lead ingots — weighing fifty-six pounds each — at Wyalla. At the western end of the Bass Strait, about six miles off Cape Otway, she struck a mine of uncertain origin. Those ingots broke through the bulkheads into the bow, the engine broke off with a roar, and the forward part of the ship sank in five minutes. The aft end stayed afloat for forty-five minutes, and the men were able to get into their Carley floats — uh, lifeboats. Next morning, local fishermen came out and towed them into Apollo Bay. They'd been alerted by the lighthouse keeper, who saw the explosion."

"You mean the whole crew survived? What luck —"

"Of the thirty-seven men aboard, thirty-six survived. Unfortunately, in abandoning ship the Third Engineer died. Actually, the German raiders have not caused great loss of life in their attempts to cripple our shipping. At least they've had the decency, after they sank a ship by shelling or torpedoes, to pick up the bedraggled crew and passengers and dump them on the nearest island. But without our Coastwatchers, who get the word from the natives and then wireless to my office in Townsville to send a ship — some of those survivors would remain marooned out there as long as Robinson Crusoe."

"Sir — speaking of waiting — how long do you predict we'll have to wait till, as you said, the threat of war passes, so our air force *can* push for independence from the Army?"

"You're assuming that Japan is your only potential enemy, and I suppose you're right. Davis, you've caught me at a pivot-point in my thinking. During the past two years, while I was desperately trying to shut all the gates in our protective fence of islands, I felt that Japan might attack us — or Singapore — or *you* in the Philippines, at any moment. But now that our fence is more secure, and you-lot have your splendid Fortresses in place . . . while we mustn't let down our guard for an instant, I've privately concluded that Japan has missed her better opportunities and does not now intend to enter Germany's war."

"Sure hope you're right, Sir. But, while we're keeping our guard up — I forgot to ask you in Townsville what kind of code, uh, cipher, your Coastwatchers use?"

"Just that utterly simple old thing, 'Playfair,' known to every schoolboy; but it has the virtue that it needs no documents — other than a list of agreed-upon keywords — and no wheels or mechanical devices. Of course, it has the disadvantage of being low grade. However, I've devised a variation by which the bigrams are broken, making it a little more secure than the original."

"What if it's compromised? How could you send a new code to your hundred-and-some Coastwatchers out here?"

"Via Teleradio, we'll send a replacement phrase. Not the very words, of course, only the clue, which our people would know — as would the Islanders who've agreed to coastwatch."

"The Papuans?"

"Oh, no. They're still sending their messages by 'boo-boo' drums — in a code no white man can ever decipher. The European settlers are the ones we call 'Islanders.' A motley crew . . . doubtless you find the same types in the Philippines. Blokes who, in general, drink strong waters to excess, are coarse of speech, very likely to have skeletons in their closets. They'll bicker among themselves, but show a united front to outsiders — to whom they're kittle-cattle and difficult to deal with. Islanders are loners, who can live without the company of white men — or white women — but who get along well with the natives. That's essential to an Islander's survival, as it is to a Coastwatcher's, for the natives have a sixth sense about a bloke's trustworthiness."

What an improvement the bush makes in this man! Jim thought.

The Commander was far better looking than Jim remembered, with aristocratic features: a fine long nose (the nose of a leader, thought Jim, the possessor of a good-sized nose himself) and a cleft chin (Jim's chin bore the same indentation). The pith helmet hid Feldt's iron-gray hair, and beneath his heavy dark brows the eyes that had appeared steely gray-blue in his office were now as vividly sapphire as the New Guinea sky.

He left all his formality and taciturnity in Townsville, Jim thought, *along with his dark uniform, brass buttons, and spic-and-span white cap. Now's my chance to pump him for everything I might need . . . before he clams up again.*

"Sir, what about Japanese residents on the islands?"

Feldt grinned. "Even though about ninety-nine percent of the inhabitants out here are black, our 'White Australia' immigration policy includes the islands. That's kept us free of the potential Fifth Columns of large Jap colonies, such as those you have on Mindanao and Oahu, and on the West Coast of the States. The French short-sightedly allowed some Japs to settle on their islands — along with Indians — because they're such hard workers, which the natives are not. But we're fortunate that the French on New Caledonia are on our side; they've rejected the Vichy government. So if war comes, we won't have any trouble rounding up the Japs on Bougainville and any other French island, and interning them in Australia for the duration."

Emboldened by the Commander's changed attitude, Jim asked, "Aren't some of the Islanders Germans?"

"Of course. Some Italians, too; but we've already interned those of dubious loyalty. Probably most are Germans, because so many of these islands were colonized by Germany. We may have more Germanic names on our Coastwatcher roster than any other nationality — I've never counted them."

"But you don't think a person with a German name might be a potential Fifth Columnist, Commander Feldt?"

The upturned corners of the well-shaped mouth widened in a hearty laugh, Feldt's only reply.

Mustn't push my luck, Jim thought.

"Sir, what's the most important advice you give your Coastwatchers — based on your three months of playing that role?"

"My most important warning about living in the bush is something I'd learned many years earlier: Eat as well as you possibly can — or your health will suffer. Everyone in the tropics has malaria germs in his body; I'm sure your own blood's full of them like mine. But they only attack a weakened host. A period of malnutrition is an invitation for them to hold carnival in a bloke's bloodstream . . . while his wracked body sweats under a palm-thatched roof, far from help or comfort. And if it goes on, malaria can end in Blackwater Fever — the dark piss that usually signals the end of life. There's nothing sadder than to see one of your healthy mates become a malarial wreck, with his face turned that ghastly gray color."

*He's thinking about a friend he cared a lot about. This man **has** a heart; he's not all head. He's as dual, as split, as Papa Hemingway and I both are — and his two sides don't balance easily, either. But he might have bigger **cojones**, as Papa would say — and more real guts — than either Papa or me.*

Feldt changed the subject to one more to Jim's liking: Singapore. The Commander knew that MacArthur was sending Brereton to give the British and Dutch the firm assurance of U.S. assistance that had not been authorized at the time of General Clagett's summer mission — before Rainbow 5. Feldt evidently assumed — as Jim only hoped — that Brereton would take both Jim and Captain Ind to Singapore with him, in view of their previous acquaintance with the colonial officals.

"Davis, while you're in Singapore, I'd like you to knock up a friend of mine."

Holy cow! When Feldt melts, he melts. Some dame he knows wants to be impregnated by an American? Sort of a Lend-Lease Emily Hahn arrangement? Well, if she's over twenty-one, and not too ugly, I guess it would be OK to oblige. . . . Hands across the sea, and all that. . . . But I sure wouldn't want Daphne to find out about it.

"Any friend of yours, Sir, is a friend of mine," Jim managed.

"Fine. He's now assisting Colonel Jim Gavin."

Obviously, "to knock up" translates differently in the British Empire.

Feldt continued, "Did you happen to meet Gavin?"

Jim hesitated, wondering how to phrase his reply. Of course he remembered triple-initial Colonel J. M. L. Gavin. Surely Feldt must be aware that Gavin headed "No. 101 Special Training School," which he had set up to train small units for "irregular warfare." It was just the sort of clandestine operation Feldt would relish. And it was the very sort that was kept under close cover, not only from Japanese spies, but from General Percival and Governor Sir Shenton Thomas, who had made cuttingly clear their opposition to any such un-British activities. Through Colonel Warner LeClair, the U.S. Military Attache, Jim

Chapter 4 — Part 3 — Seven Mile 127

not only had met the dynamic Colonel Gavin, but had even visited his spartan headquarters. Surely it wasn't something that Americans should discuss; would Feldt be shocked to learn that Jim knew about the school?
Or is Feldt, in effect, "spying" for the Navy — checking on the Army's secret project? Hell, I've gotta trust this fellow.
"Yes, Sir, I met him," he replied. "He seemed to have a lot of energy and ideas."
"Gavin's got those, all right. And God knows, there's a shortage of energy and ideas in Singapore. Well, I *should* resent Gavin now, because he got a bloke to join him there — a splendid man I wanted so much to keep down here. Have you heard of Spencer Chapman?"
"The Arctic explorer? Sure, Sir."
"Far more than the Arctic — Spence has roamed every continent, now. Australia was the only one left, so he was glad to be posted out here last year, a thirty-three-year-old major in the British Army. Yes, he's a Pommie — and a Cambridge graduate, to boot — but you'd never guess it. Not a bit airy-fairy; he's as down to earth as any Aussie. After the war began, he'd been doing things like training ski troops in Switzerland; then after France fell, he trained small units in England for smash-and-grab raids on the Continent. He was here only a year — our bad luck — but he set up a bonzer training ground for irregular-warfare units, down at Wilson's Promontory. That's the southernmost point in Victoria State. Taught bushmanship, ambushing . . . all that sort of thing. He flew to Singapore in September. Here's what he says about the atmosphere there —"
Feldt reached into a pocket of his sweaty khaki shirt and opened a limp, folded paper. "Chapman says, 'In Australia the impression I gathered was that the outbreak of war with Japan was only a matter of months, but that Australia was in no way ready to defend herself. Here in Malaya my impression is just the opposite. One gathers that Japan is economically incapable of making war; but that if she did, the British and American fleets would prevent her reaching Malaya — and in any case, that the defense of the Peninsula, especially Singapore, is impregnable.' "
Jim laughed. "I'd say Major Chapman's impressions are right on target. I'd sure like to . . . uh . . . 'knock him up' when I get back to Singapore."
If I have time, he thought to himself — *while courting a certain well-stacked blonde.*
"He'll need a sympathetic ear. He's been bloody frustrated there, trying to get permission to train Malays, and the Chinese units, for jungle fighting."
"He might as well give up and come back here — he'll never get that. I happened to attend a meeting at Fort Canning last summer where your General Gordon Bennett spoke. He appealed to General Percival for permission to give his two Aussie brigades training in 'irregular warfare,' and

Percival slapped down the idea, cold. And as for arming the Malays and Chinese — the English will *never* agree to that."

Feldt shook his head. "What a waste of manpower. Naturally, they're afraid to trust the Malays with arms, after they've exploited Malaya and let in the Tamil Indians and the Chinese to take the paying jobs. Still, it would be wise to have a reserve force of trustworthy natives. And the clever Chinese — who have such good reason to hate the Japs — could be extremely useful."

"They're already organized, too. I met a smart English-speaking Chinese named Chin Peng, who's been working ever since 1937 to get all the Chinese associations in Singapore to work together in sending relief supplies to China. He calls his organization 'The Anti-Enemy Backing-Up Society.' "

Jim did not add that Colonel LeClair privately maintained that Chin Peng's support was for Mao and the Reds, and that "Anti-Enemy" actually meant "Anti-Chiang."

A Papuan family, heading for the mountains, was approaching on the trail; the man led the way, he wore a circular boar's tusk through his nose, and striped eagle feathers radiated from his black bush. Necklaces of cowrie shells, hornbill beaks, and dogs' teeth draped his dark chest, along with a sort of breastplate formed of small horizontal strips of bamboo, painted orange, which extended from neck to navel. He was followed by a bony razorback pig, ahead of five "marys" — wearing skirts of grass or bark cloth, and with shiny brown breasts jiggling — who carried infants born and unborn. Behind them stalked a domesticated cassowary with a piece of vine for a leash, a troop of painted, naked children, and some scrawny dogs of yellow dust color.

"G'ddye, myte! You-fella bilong tabac?"

Feldt gave each of the adults an Australian cigarette, and the Papuans responded with appreciative betel-red grins. During the exchange, one of the marys squatted on the trail and relieved herself of a strong, steaming stream of urine. Embarrassed, Jim paged through the Pidgin booklet for an apt remark, perhaps a compliment for the children. He learned that in the local Pidgin a child was termed a "pickaninny"; a girl-child was a "pickaninny mary"; and a puppy bitch was called a "pickaninny mary bilong dog."

The Papuans trudged on, calling out the standard Aussie farewell, "G'luck!"

Jim was surprised that all the Papuan women he had seen were smokers, as were the Aboriginal women in Darwin. Few women of his acquaintance smoked, except his mother and Daphne.

"That's one of the few things we've given them — a hunger for 'tabac,' " Feldt said. "At least, that fellow can afford to get trade tobacco for his marys — he's a rich man. Each of those little bamboo tubes hanging down his chest represents ten gold-lipped pearl oyster shells that he has at home. That's why the natives won't work for our money. A shilling means no more than tuppence

Chapter 4 — Part 3 — Seven Mile

to them — but a feather from a Salvadori bird-of-paradise can rent you a friend's mary for the night."

"Smart fellas. Why should they grub around, building an airstrip, just for white man's cash?"

The Papuans in the gas-pumping crew at Seven Mile, Feldt said, were Matai Bushmen, "the best workers," who had acquired a taste for trade goods. They were paid monthly: a bolt of calico, two sticks of trade tobacco, free room and "tucker," and "two bob — about thirty-five U.S. cents."

"Up in the goldfields," he went on, "Jim Taylor and the other Diggers got the landing strips for their Junkers this way; they'd invite all the neighboring tribes for a big 'sing-sing.' They'd lay-on some pigs and a big pile of yams, and provide a feast. The natives would dress up in their best paint and feathers and dance all night. Next day, there you'd have it — a patch big enough to land a Junkers on, all tamped down by those bare stamping feet."

Hearing about the legendary prospector-pilots from Feldt, the former warden of the Wau goldfields, refreshed Jim like finding a pitcher of cold beer on the lorry track. When Feldt spoke of "Sharkeye" Park, who had braved the dangers of terrain and hostile tribesmen to climb to Wau, and was rewarded by his rich discovery in 1921, Jim's own brown eyes brightened. This was like walking beside an intimate friend of Lindbergh's, he thought.

Feldt knew Cecil John Levien, whose Guinea Gold company had bought its own single-engine DH-37 biplane, after every Australian air carrier had refused to attempt to fly into the wild terrain and treacherous weather of the goldfields. Feldt knew "Pard" Mustar, who assembled that DH-37 and got it into regular service between Wau and Lae in 1927.

"Meanwhile, Ray Parer was starting his own aerial service, flying a DH-4 to the nearby Bulolo goldfield. . . ."

The Commander reminisced about quadruple-initial, quadruple-career A.A.N.D. Pentland, who had flown with the RAF in the Great War and shot down 23 Germans; later piloted planes to Wau and Bulolo; subsequently became a coffee planter at Goroka in the Highlands; and now served as an RAAF Squadron Leader.

Later, Feldt spoke with affection of the "pure" explorers — not goldhunters — pioneers, so recent in time. He knew the Leahy brothers, who eight years earlier had been the first white men to see the Wahgi Valley.

As the Commander described the dangerous, dedicated work of the District Officers in the remote areas, guided by the precept of Papua's longtime governor, Hugh Murray, "this land is for the Papuans," Jim began to feel that the Australians were trying here to atone for their fathers' treatment of the mainland Aborigines. By this philanthropic governance of their New Guinea wards, they were making an apology for the merciless annihilation of the Tasmanians.

Allsame Americans. We killed the indigenous AmerIndians when we occupied their homeland; but in our Pacific island colony, we kill the locals with kindness.

"All New Guinea natives were Stone Age men less than a hundred years ago," Feldt said. "And many still are — if not most. Contact with Europeans has hardly changed their lives at all. Knives and axes have replaced their stone tools, and cloth is replacing garments of bark or grass; but most villages look and sound much as they did in the remote, isolated past. Like you United Statesers, we have a big continent of our own, and we've been a colony, too. We're a different kind of imperial power from the British and the Dutch. Like your government in the Philippines, we don't yearn to keep any colonies. When you don't exploit them, they're too expensive to afford! We plan to give these people independence, just as soon as they can manage it."

"Well, give yourselves about five hundred years."

Feldt laughed. "We're thinking of fifty."

"*Impossible!*"

This was a topic Jim had heard discussed during his entire lifetime. Unique among colonial empires, the U.S. had promised to give complete independence to the Philippines in 1946. While his father maintained that Jeffersonian democracy was impossible to export, Leda insisted that nothing less than an Agrarian Revolution would free the Filipino peasants from bondage to the rich Filipino landowners. Jim — seeing both sides — felt that he was an expert on the subject.

"These Papuans," he told Commander Feldt, "are five hundred years behind the lowland Filipinos, who had a civilization and a written language before the Spaniards ever arrived. Then they were exposed to three hundred and fifty years of Spanish civilizing — and now they've had forty years of American government, deliberately giving them more and more experience in running their own country. We've taught them English, so they can communicate with the rest of the world — and with each other — and given them the highest literacy rate of any Asians, and the freest press in Asia. But after all that, they've just re-elected as their president a man with wildly extravagant personal tastes: a would-be dictator!"

"Yes, all the world knows what your Filipino Napoleon, President Quezon, said about government — that he'd prefer a government 'run like hell by Filipinos, to one run like heaven by Americans.' Evidently his countrymen agree. And the Papuans would undoubtedly prefer a government run like hell by Papuans rather than our best efforts to create a heaven here. And if they choose to elect a spendthrift dictator, shouldn't they have that privilege?"

"My dad says people aren't ready to govern themselves until they'll willingly stop their cars at Stop signs when nobody's looking."

"Wise bloke, your dad. Only a very few Papuans have ever seen a car —

Chapter 4 — Part 3 — Seven Mile

much less driven one, or brought one to a stop. And yes, we've left education in the hands of the missionaries; but our government's getting into that now. In a couple of generations, we'll have some native leaders trained, who can take over."

"In all their seven hundred languages? They'd have to issue government regulations in Pidgin! And — talk about Army-Navy tribal warfare — your Stone-Agers will be living on the warpath again. They'll go back to collecting their neighbors' heads, and eating 'Long Pig' once a week!"

"Vile habits. But we're teaching them better manners all the time."

"If you change them too fast, they'll despise their parents and their legends and rituals, and they won't know who they are," Jim echoed his mother's lament for the Cherokee tribe.

In silence they reached the RAAF barracks. Hot and angry, Jim promised himself a pith helmet for his next New Guinea hike. But for now, he had in mind a fresh pack of Luckies and an air-temperature shower in the spartan RAAF lavatory hut before lunch.

"One more thing, Lieutenant Davis," Feldt said.

Uh oh, here it comes, Jim thought. *Nobody tells an Australian how to do anything, and survives.*

"Sir?" Jim took a deep breath and braced himself for a barrage of blistering Digger profanity salted with Royal Australian Navy expletives.

"I must tell you this. A final requirement of your Civilian Coastwatcher is that he must not flinch at the knowledge that if war comes, he may be shot as a spy if he's apprehended."

Good Lord, Jim thought. *I've talked some swell fellows into volunteering to run a Philippine Coastwatch radio net. But — he says **if** war comes, and **if** they're caught. Those are two big "ifs," that really make his warning unnecessary.*

Relieved, Jim said, "Yes, Sir. Thank you, Sir."

With a hearty and sweaty handshake, Feldt turned back toward Seven Mile. "G'luck!"

Chapter 5

Part 1 — Over the Owen Stanleys

Many a lad will see his mother,
  and the husbands — wee ones and wives,
Just because the Fuzzy Wuzzies
  carried them to save their lives
From a mortar or machine-gun
  or a chance surprise attack,
To safety and care of doctors
  at the bottom of the Track.

May the mothers in Australia,
  when they offer up a prayer,
Mention these impromptu angels
  with the fuzzy-wuzzy hair.
    — Brisbane *Courier-Mail*, 31 October 1942

Seven Mile Aerodrome
Monday, 17 November 1941

   The six o'clock sunrise was still on the other side of the Owen Stanleys as the travelers assembled at Seven Mile. Eubank was making his walkaround inspection of No. 40-3097 with the aid of a flashlight (called a "shoot-lamp" by the Papuans).

Allison Ind had not slept well, disturbed by the "weird calls and howls" of the natives high up in the hills.

Brigadier Basil M. Morris laughed. "That's a sign that all's well, and they're having a peaceful sing-sing. It's when a sudden silence descends that we get uneasy." Morris, 53, the Australian Army Commander in Papua, was going to accompany the Americans to Rabaul, about 500 miles to the northeast.

Ind still looked unhappy. "That sing-sing sounded far from reassuring to me. And then I'd barely gone to sleep before the predawn arousal by that callous orderly and his infernal eye-smashing electric light! I'm still woozy-eyed. I plan to cat-nap on my cat-walk all the way to Rabaul. Wake me up if there's anything worth looking at."

With no facilities for night operations at Seven Mile or either of the other airstrips, takeoffs from New Guinea had to be made by daylight, with landings before the 6:00 p.m. darkness. Jim wondered what a pilot would do — where would you land, if darkness caught you in the air? And where could you make a forced landing if a storm gobbled up your gas? Today's flight was being made with the minimum of fuel for the round trip, to insure that the bomber would land lightly at Rabaul, where the seasonal rains already had begun to affect the runways.

This is a place for flying boats, not land planes, he thought again.

As the increasing light contrasted the hillocks and the deep hollows of the airstrip, it also revealed Brereton's frown. "Squadron Leader Pearce is very energetic and helpful," he told Brigadier Morris. "But airdrome construction is proceeding far too slowly. No sense of urgency is apparent, although the damned eighty-inch rains are *imminent*. Some of our Army bombers have been damaged here because of the condition of the runway."

He thinks an Army Brigadier has more pull than an RAAF Squadron Leader — and he's probably right, Jim thought.

Morris replied, "We've requested another stone-crushing machine to be shipped up from the mainland. We've only one crusher here, and every piece of rock it grinds out has been used to improve the road from Moresby to Seven Mile. Papuans aren't like the Chinese, willing to break up stone with mallets."

"But a road to an unusable airfield is *worthless!* It'd be better to use the rocks for the runway. If the vehicles can't navigate the damned road, let 'em walk. I don't know how much time we have left. The Japs have dropped all caution in their statements. Radio Tokyo quotes Premier Tojo and Foreign Minister Togo as shouting that Japan's aim is 'to force Britain and the United States from East Asia.' "

The morning air lay hot, dry, and motionless. "Wind direction's meaningless here, anyway," Eubank said. "The only way to get out of here is downhill." He taxied to the top of a rise, facing Port Moresby and the Gulf of Papua.

Inside the crackling metal skin of the Fortress the air was hot enough to bake potatoes, Jim thought. Brigadier Morris, in the jump-seat, wearing uniform shorts, began to unbutton his tieless, short-sleeved shirt. "Rabaul's the 'metropolis' of the Northeast Territory, and I don't get there as often as the fly-boys do," he told Jim, who was sitting on the deck behind him, his flying suit unzipped to the navel.

Gathering speed, the bomber bounced down the alley formed by the rows of fuel drums and the dusty Army tents. Its undercarriage dropped into a pit, and the port wing skimmed perilously close to a hump. Drunkenly, dangerously, the plane wallowed, jolted, jounced, and slammed the ground with impacts that threatened to tear it apart.

Jim wrapped his arms around the jump-seat and hung on with all his strength, waiting for the noise of a blown tire or — worse — the plowing shock of a lost wheel.

Blessedly, Eubank and the power of 4,800 horses pulled the Fortress up out of the dust and into the bumpy air above Port Moresby. High over the Gulf of Papua he made a 180-degree turn and began a wide spiraling climb toward the Owen Stanleys. Jim mentally saluted the Boeing engineers who had designed an undercarriage that could bear the unguessable stress of such pounding.

Through the top of the cockpit window Jim could see what looked like two giant cones of pink cotton candy, the peaks of Mounts Victoria and Lamington, swathed in clouds backlighted by the rising sun. Between their huge shoulders were crowded lesser mountains. Australian pilots flew through the Owen Stanleys at 8,400 feet, following "the Gap," a twisting 7,500-foot pass, but Eubank obviously was taking no easy short-cut in the dim light and morning mist. He was nosing his plane upward at 140 mph toward 15,000 feet for certain clearance.

Eubank had warned his passengers that the oxygen bottles would not be broken out, except in an emergency, because he would descend quickly, north of the mountains. Oxygen was in short supply in Manila, and although Colonel George and Lefty were getting an oxygen factory started, none was being produced yet.

Jim, like all the other pursuit pilots on Philippine duty, customarily flew higher than 10,000 feet without oxygen because of the shortage. Now the familiar "cheap drunk" feeling was beginning: He felt clever, careless, and especially carefree without the responsibility of flying the plane. He sprawled on the deck and peered out through the lower cockpit windows, thinking: *When Australians drink too much, they get "sparky." Sounds better than "drunk." Sparky is how you feel — drunk is how the other guy acts. . . .*

Chapter 5 — Part 1 — Over the Owen Stanleys

Brigadier Morris was from Victoria state, a town named Upper Beaconsfield. Jim found the name delightful. Morris soon showed evidence of mild hypoxia by becoming increasingly talkative, as he tried to show Jim the two "bush tracks," the foot-trails that climbed from the south coast into the Owen Stanleys.

The "Kokoda Track" began as an offshoot of the same lorry track that Jim had hiked on to Seven Mile. With his father's binoculars, it was easy at first to follow its pathway through the dry, knobby bald hillocks and on between the military formations of rubber plantations. He could glimpse its traces as it crossed a plateau called Sogeri and climbed to Imita Ridge; then it dropped out of sight in a canyon thick with jungle. It emerged to climb a steep rock face, called the Golden Stair for its rugged natural "steps" with risers to 18 inches in height.

"When a bloke gets to the top of the Golden Stair, the bushwalkers tell me, he's been on the track for at least twelve hours, and he's covered nine miles. And Kagi Ridge is still ahead of him — that's six thousand five hundred feet high. There he enters the rain forest, where the track gets difficult. He struggles on to the Yodda Valley and Kokoda — it's midway between the coasts, so he's come halfway. Eventually, the track drops off so steep and slippery that he can just sit down and slide into Buna. That's a mission settlement on the north coast; but it's so small that if he's not careful he'll slide on into Huon Gulf!"

One glance made obvious the necessity for the pioneering air supply to the goldfields; the terrain was a thrilling nightmare scene. During this year, Jim had flown over the awesome mountains of central China and of the Malayan Peninsula, as well as those of Mindanao and northern Luzon, but he had never seen anything more elementally striking than the tumbled masses of the Owen Stanleys, wrapped in green rain forests and white mists, cut by wild rivers in deep chasms. The B-17 was a toy airplane here. How could mere men attempt to cling to those god-sized slabs, to build their nests there?

Yet bare brown feet had made a trail that boot-wearing white men had followed to find gold. Northwest of the Kokoda Track, the "Bulldog Track" led to the goldfields. Morris showed Jim the mouth of the Lakekamu River, about 150 miles north of Port Moresby on the Gulf of Papua. The Bulldog Track, he said, followed the river north for a difficult 50 miles to the place called Bulldog; there the walker began another 50 rough miles into the Bulolo River valley, at an altitude of 3,000 feet, to reach the rich outcroppings of Wau, Bulolo, and Edie Creek. (Of the three famed goldfields, Edie Creek was Jim's favorite name; surely, he thought, the prospector who found that lucky creek was thinking about bedecking that certain Edith with gold nuggets.)

There at Wau, Eric Feldt had served as a Goldfield Warden for 17 years: from the year after Sharkeye Park discovered gold until Australia declared war in 1939 and called him back to a navy blue uniform.

What a change of scene! No wonder poor Feldt was so grouchy in his Townsville office, forced to wrestle with The Red Tape Plant instead of the raw, exciting basics of the goldfields.

The valleys of gold lay in such deep rain forest, Morris told Jim, "Even if we flew directly over the area we couldn't see the eight dredges working down there under the klinkii pines and hoop pines."

Lightbody, the hotel man, had served as a Patrol Officer in the mountains during the Gold Rush years. Both he and Feldt had known Errol Flynn, who first came from the mainland to work as a Patrol Officer in 1930, but caught gold fever and began prospecting around Wau. Both older men said that Flynn became known for quick fisticuffs before he departed for England in 1933 to try his luck in films. Concerning his luck as a prospector, the stories differed. Feldt said that Flynn had sold his stake for 2,000 pounds to pay his way to England. Lightbody, however, had seen a "treasure map" that a properly grizzled Californian said Flynn had given him in return for a Hollywood favor. The map purported to show where Flynn had hidden a quantity of gold in the jungle near Wau; but the old fellow's search had been futile.

Lightbody also had described for Jim the struggles of Pard Mustar to get the first Guinea Gold airplane, the DH-37, into the Wau valley.

First, Mustar had persuaded a friend in the penal service to use prisoner labor to build an airstrip at the port of Lae — the same field used by Amelia Earhart ten years later. Next, Mustar "bushwalked" up to Wau from the north coast, climbing the steep and slippery, fiendishly difficult mountain trail — the miners' only route — an eight-day ordeal for a distance barely more than 13 map-miles. At Wau, he got a clearing made for a landing field (with one end abutting a mountain and its "entry" end 300 feet lower); then he spent eight days hiking back to Lae.

Mustar's de Havilland biplane had arrived by ship in Rabaul, New Britain, disassembled. He got a boat-ride to Rabaul, assembled the single-engine DH-37, and flew it to Lae, 400 miles across the Solomon Sea. At last, in April 1927, Mustar was ready to make the first 13-mile flight from Lae up to Wau. On his first two attempts, he could not locate the airstrip he had built in the rain forest and was forced to return to Lae in humiliation. Finally, with a miner aboard who knew the terrain intimately, Mustar landed at Wau. The men of the fierce pygmy Kukukuku (pronounced "cooker-cooker") tribe, who had harassed and wounded white prospectors with bows and arrows, crawled one at a time under the de Havilland. Lying on their backs on the ground, they inspected the undercarriage of this *balus* (pigeon), to ascertain from its genitalia whether the bird was a mary, capable of producing others of its kind.

Guinea Gold's DH-37 was now Guinea Airways; and Mustar's 50-minute shuttle flights immediately became routine. The airplane had transformed the pursuit of gold from a back-pack operation to more than any prospector's wildest dreams.

Later, in 1927, Mustar went to Germany to buy one of Professor Hugo Junkers' W-34s — an awkward-looking, angular, all-metal plane with a single uncowled BMW radial engine that bore a propeller having four eight-foot blades — manufactured in Moscow because of limitations placed on Germany by the Treaty of Versailles. The plane cost 8,000 pounds, representing many nuggets of gold; but it could use a small landing area, and it was capable of lifting 2,000 pounds of supplies, equipment, or miners. After Guinea Airways bought a second W-34, the possibility of bringing in dredges, disassembled, was envisioned. In 1929 Mustar procured a Junkers G-31 "Iron-ass Annie," a corrugated metal plane that was the embryo of the famous Ju-52. The G-31 cost 30,000 pounds, but it could carry three tons. Ships brought sections of the gold dredges to Lae and the G-31 carried the parts to Wau; after assembly, each dredge weighed about 3,000 tons. More Junkers were added to carry in men, supplies, and horses — and to carry out the gold — until Wau became the world's busiest airport. For a few years, until the gold bubble burst, New Guinea's annual airlifted tonnage totaled more than the combined air freight of all other countries.

Jim was shivering from the chill of the altitude, although he had put on his leather A-2 jacket. After fumbling drunkenly with the zipper, he thought, what the hell, and left it unclosed.

"Rug up, myte!" Morris advised.

Jim peered at the sheepskin collar of Morris' fleece-lined jacket and told him, "You blokes sure know what to wear in the mountains."

"Sheepskin feels better than a poke in the eye with a burnt stick!" Morris replied. Jim thought that was the funniest thing he had ever heard, and they both roared with laughter.

Suddenly, random loud *thumps* added to the bomber's accustomed din, as the four propellers cast off shards of ice that struck the metal fuselage. At last the B-17 made its final ascent through the mist and leveled off at 15,000 feet.

To reassure Morris, Jim yelled, "Pretty soon, Colonel — I mean Mister Eubank — will be pointing old Number Forty's nose down toward the good old warm Solomon Sea!" Although Jim had never seen that sea, he was confident of its temperature.

The goldfields lay in the corner of the area of northeast New Guinea that had been claimed by Germany in 1884 and called Kaiser Wilhelm Land. After the World War, the League of Nations had mandated its governance to England, which had passed it on to Australia; thus it was known as the Mandated Territory.

Gold had made the north coast more prosperous, and had brought more Europeans than "poor little Moresby" could claim, Brigadier Morris went on.

"The joke was on the Germans — that they never discovered the gold while they had it. And yet, it was German-made Junkers — and Aussie pilots — that finally made the gold accessible!"

He and Jim had another good laugh over that irony, until Jim fuzzily recalled the more recent irony. Even in his tipsy condition, he knew better than to remind Morris of Crete, where ANZAC troops had been slaughtered in May by German paratroops. Now it came back to Jim, as his photographic memory continued faithful through the fog of hypoxia. The German invasion of the island had been launched by a sky-darkening fleet of more than 500 all-metal, trimotor Junkers Ju-52s. Jim remembered news photographs and his own shock at seeing the ungainly plane that had been a prewar workhorse in this sinister role — the sturdy, stable, reliable backbone of several European national airlines, including Germany's Lufthansa. The Ju-52 that Germans fondly nicknamed *alte Tante Ju,* like a beloved, hard-working, homely old aunt, had abandoned useful chores to become a machine of war. Hitler was rumored to have four identical Junkers for his personal use, with the same serial number painted on their corrugated metal fuselages, to keep his actual whereabouts a mystery.

New Guinea's Eastern Highlands, now visible below, held a medical mystery, Morris said. In 1932 a gold prospector had found an area, Okapa, where the tribespeople died of a disease they called *kuru.* Later, white people termed it The Laughing Disease, because the sufferers usually lapsed into a harmless, babbling insanity before they died. It struck adults of the Okapa tribe, but no one unrelated to the tribe had ever contracted it. Medical researchers had been unable to locate the source of the fatal illness or the means of transmission.

"Must have been someone they et," Jim said, laughing at his own joke.

Morris chuckled. "I'm all royte, but I think you have a slight case of kuru yourself, cobber."

Foggily, Jim thought of the "Microbe Hunters" in Paul De Kruif's book, the inspiration for his desire to become a physician-researcher. "Tell you what I'll do. . . . I'll come back here when I'm a doctor-detective, and I'll find out what's causing that stuff. Then I'll be famous, and you can say you knew me when!"

"Too royte, I'll dip me lid to you then!"

Jim tried to hold on to a wisp of thought: There was something else, some other medical sleuthing that he must complete before he could solve the kuru case. Oh, yes — he had promised his mother to find out what had caused her full-term infants, his sisters, to be born dead, after she had successfully borne two sons. That ended his laughter; now he felt close to tears.

* * * * *

Chapter 5 — Part 1 — Over the Owen Stanleys 139

With the Owen Stanleys safely crossed, Eubank was making a rapid descent to the north coast, while welcome warmth and oxygen re-entered the B-17. Still descending, with the brilliant blue Solomon Sea to starboard, the bomber followed the New Guinea shore northwest until the Huon Peninsula loomed ahead, backed by 13,500-foot Mount Bangeta.

Out of sight beyond Bangeta lay "Margaret Mead country," the great gray-green, greasy, septic Sepik River, where the anthropologist had lived and worked. She had been one of Leda's pen-pals ever since MM first published her studies of AmerIndians. Leda had written to her, disputing the bad influence that MM attributed to missionaries. She told MM that it was solely due to the urging of her own Catholic missionary teachers that Leda had applied for a scholarship to Smith College, becoming the first Cherokee descendant to graduate there. A fiery correspondence developed; MM thenceforth sent Leda copies of all her studies; and eventually Leda and Jim had visited MM and her husband Gregory Bateson in Bali.

Jim was sure that MM's rosy reports of ideal societies where adolescents were reared with no sexual inhibitions had influenced Leda to let Jim stay in the Ifugao *olag. Some day, I'll tell Mead how it worked in reverse for me — when the experience with that rough-and-ready widow/teacher inhibited me almost permanently.*

Finally down almost to the level of the shoreline's palm trees, the bomber skirted the dark blue Huon Gulf, banking left for better visibility, then circled over the area. Seeking a site for a major air base on the ferry route, the senior officers were evaluating the terrain of the Gulf's three small settlements. From the air, they looked like travel-poster pictures: curving beaches bordered by waving green palms that sheltered villages of bamboo and thatch, cradled between sea and sky, while outrigger canoes and puffy white cumulus clouds floated on the vivid equatorial blues.

Salamaua lay to the south of the Huon Peninsula, Finschhafen sat on the Peninsula's eastern tip, an obviously inviting location for one of Germany's early attempted colonial settlements — all of which had proved disastrous because of malaria, Brigadier Morris explained.

Tucked into the wide angle between Salamaua and Finschhafen was the village that had been selected to replace Rabaul as the capital of the Mandated Territory. Rabaul was subject to daily seismic tremors, and a disastrous volcanic eruption in May 1937 had forced the decision to move the seat of government from New Britain to New Guinea. However, nothing tangible had been accomplished as yet, Morris said.

"If you-lot decide to make Rabaul a fully equipped stop on your air ferry route from Hawaii, that'll keep the place alive. If not, the city will die on the vine, after it stops being the capital."

Still slightly tipsy and bored, Jim mentally rejected all three of the settlements below as sites for a future "major airdrome." Surely Rabaul must have more to offer than these. He could understand why Brereton and Eubank would want a good landing field on this side of the Owen Stanleys, for the sake of weary crews flying from Wake Island. And certainly this jungled beach was far more esthetically appealing than dusty Port Moresby. But still, the narrow coastal shelf, in the shadow of a helluva mountain (at 13,500, Bangeta must be more than 2½ miles tall, he figured woozily) looked like a lousy place to land even a Piper Cub.

Brereton's comments gave voice to Jim's opinion. "Even if bulldozers were available to level the ground, the terrain would make it impossible to extend the runways enough for heavy bombers."

Then suddenly Jim realized that the name Brigadier Morris was saying — this village that would become the new capital — a name that in Morris's ripe Aussie vowels sounded to Jim like "Loy," actually was the town of Lae!

Right *there*, the globe-circling Amelia had set down her big Electra on that 3,000-foot, jungle-bordered strip. It was her last recorded landing: Stop #26, Wednesday, 30 June 1937, with 22,000 miles of the earth's equatorial belt behind her, and only 7,000 Pacific miles remaining between her and Oakland, California, her starting point. She had flown here from Darwin that Wednesday, on a northeast heading, over water most of the way: Gulf of Carpentaria, Torres Strait, Gulf of Papua.

Jesus, how weary she must have been; how her blue eyes must have burned from the strain of searching for this tiny settlement!

Why didn't you spare yourself, and land at Port Moresby that day? A stupid question: because you had to shorten, as much as possible, the most difficult leg of your journey. From Lae to Howland Island would be two thousand five hundred fifty-six miles, over open water.

Fully awake now, he stared down at the little settlement, engraving on his brain the beach, the wharf, every tree, every shack, each gasoline drum beside the sod landing strip. There was the hangar marked GUINEA AIRWAYS, where she had parked her Electra.

Lightbody had prepared him for the shock of a fantastic coincidence: Guinea Airways possessed a ten-passenger Lockheed Electra, in outer appearance the twin of AE's. She had seen it at Lae, and it was still in service now. The local people of the Leiwomba tribe called each Electra a "biscuit box" for its shiny metal covering, like that of an English cookie tin, unlike the familiar dull corrugated metal of the Junkers. Jim had hoped to see that other Electra parked on the Guinea Airways apron where *hers* had stood, and to snap a picture of it; but it was not there today.

That two-story wooden building beside the beach must be the Hotel Cecil, where AE and Noonan had stayed, he reasoned. According to Lightbody, the hotel had been "completely rebuilt in 1932," so it was in good condition for

Amelia's visit five years later. Now, in 1941, it still looked clean and well kept, surrounded by brilliant flowers beneath tall palm trees.

A tropical downpour lasting 24 hours — a sample of Lae's annual 180 inches of rain — had grounded AE here, while static prevented the Electra's and Guinea Airways' radios from receiving the time signals transmitted by the U.S. Bureau of Standards or those from the U.S. Navy, vital for Noonan's celestial navigation.

Meanwhile, the Electra was meticulously inspected and its fuel tanks in wings and fuselage were topped off with more than 1,300 gallons of fuel.

Jim crossed his fingers, wishing that Eubank — who could easily land the B-17 on Lae's 3,000-foot strip — would decide to make a closer inspection now, so Jim could touch down on *Amelia's* runway. He yearned to see it through her blue eyes, as she jauntily waved goodbye to the small, mostly black, group at about 10:30 that morning — 2 July on this side of the Date Line, 1 July on Howland Island and in the States.

With both props churning the humid air, she would taxi off the Guinea Airways apron to head west on the sod strip, toward the town, to the end of the runway. Then she would wheel around to face the sea on her takeoff roll, faster and faster, finally lifting heavily off, probably just a few agonizing inches above the dark blue waters of the Huon Gulf.

If I could walk on that very soil where those flying feet had trod. . . .

Jim clenched his jaw; he hated the bastards who shot her down!

As Wing had expressed it, the lady pilot had "bad *joss*." AE's luck evidently had turned in Burma, when monsoon torrents had forced her to return to Akyab before she could make Rangoon. Again, between Bangkok and Singapore, she'd had to wrestle the Electra through that fierce tropical rainstorm. Next came the bad week in Java, of repairs and more repairs. . . . Or was the Electra getting a more powerful engine installed, as Sergeant Fredericks had told Jim in Darwin?

If only she'd done as Lindbergh did before his Atlantic solo, and consulted an astrologer! Those two heroes were so much alike in their all-American Midwestern qualities — even in their appearance. Both had confidence in their own ability and in their planes; but unlike Lindy, she had too much American disregard for cosmic forces. Singapore was full of Chinese masters of astrology who could have told her when the stars would be propitious for the remainder of her odyssey. . . .

At 17, Jim had secretly wept in his bedroom when his short-wave radio sputtered and spat out those ominous triple dots and dashes with her call letters on Sunday, the 4th of July in Manila. He had yelled to David, and within 20 minutes they heard her own Kansas voice that Jim had been tracking ever since her Stop #19, Akyab, Burma.

"S-O-S — KHAQQ   S-O-S — KHAQQ." Through the crackling interference, the weak signal was still unmistakably Amelia. He closed his capiz-shell bedroom windows to shut out some of the incongruous sounds of firecrackers, but the two boys had their ears tortured by static as they tried to pick up the faint clue of a position report.

Surely the *Itasca,* the Coast Guard cutter that had been stationed at Howland for her radio to home on — or USS *Ontario,* midway between Lae and Howland, or USS *Swan,* between Howland and Honolulu — had been able to read her transmissions clearly, the brothers reassured each other.

Jim had been dreading the distress call; he would not leave his radio to eat, and Wing brought his meals on a tray. Until those final desperate dot-dashes, all her messages had been by voice. She was transmitting on 3105 kilocycles; but the high-frequency direction finder that the Navy had set up on Howland was unable to cut her in. Jim bit his lip in agonized frustration as he heard *Itasca* repeatedly ask her to transmit on 500 kilocycles, so the cutter's low-frequency equipment could fix her position, but she obviously never heard the request.

"Cloudy weather cloudy. Overcast. About two hundred miles out."

"Please take bearing on us and report in half hour. About one hundred miles out. Position doubtful."

Doubtful? They *must* have been under a towering ceiling last night, Jim realized. His stomach began to ache.

"We must be on you but cannot see you but gas is running low. Have been unable to reach you by radio. We are flying at one thousand feet."

Howland Island rose only 20 feet out of the ocean. But the *Itasca* was rigged to emit plumes of smoke that would guide the Electra there.

"We are circling but cannot see island. Cannot hear you. Go ahead on seven-five-zero-zero kilocycles with long count. . . ."

Oh, **please** *God — let her get the homing signal!*

"Earhart calling *Itasca.* We received your signals but unable to get minimum. Please take bearings on us and answer on three-one-zero-five kilocycles."

"We are on the line of position one-five-seven dash three-three-seven. Will repeat this message on six-two-one-zero kilocycles. We are now running north and south."

Jim spun his dial, wondering: *What's that "one-five-seven dash three-three-seven"? A sun line, or a compass heading? What it means is that Noonan doesn't know where the hell they are.*

"Land in sight ahead!"

Those four thrilling words were the last in-flight message reported by any listener. Later Jim learned that besides himself and other short-wave listeners in the Philippines, apparently only the radio station on Nauru Island in the British-held Gilberts had picked up that transmission on 6210 kc; Nauru had reported it to the U.S. Navy. When he told non-radio-buffs about receiving that message, some disbelieved him, but ham operators with experience in transoceanic radio all had tales of similar inexplicable skips or bounces. Two amateurs in California had intercepted several of the same transmissions Jim had received.

The Electra's estimated flight time, Lae-to-Howland, was 18 hours, but Jim had heard AE attempting to communicate with *Itasca* for more than 20 hours. He feared that she had missed the tiny speck in the ocean and had flown on into the Japanese-held Marshall Islands, 600 or 700 miles northwest of Howland.

News broadcast that evening from KGMB Honolulu and KGEI San Francisco reported that *Itasca* had steamed out to search for the Electra, believed to be adrift somewhere between Howland and the Gilberts. A Navy PBY sent out from Honolulu, some 2,500 miles east of Howland, was forced to turn back, battered by hail and snow. The battleship *Colorado* was headed west from Pearl Harbor, and destroyers *Cushing, Drayton,* and *Lamson* would accompany the carrier *Lexington,* ordered from Santa Barbara, California, by President Roosevelt, to join the hunt for the big silver plane. AE's friend Paul Mantz, the expert pilot who had helped her to plan the flight, said that the empty extra fuel tanks in the wings and fuselage should keep the Electra afloat for several days. George Palmer Putnam and Fred Noonan's bride, Mary Bea Martinelli, were in Oakland "anxiously waiting" for news.

Because Jim had not given up hope, he was shocked and furious when the Navy called off its massive $4 million air-sea search on 19 July. The *Lexington* had reached the area 11 days after the Electra's disappearance, and the carrier's 60 planes flew grid patterns for six days over more than 150,000 square miles of water east and west of Howland. He had hoped that the *Lexington* would proceed northward into the Marshalls and launch her planes, equipped with cameras, to photograph every foot of the islands.

Let's show the world how the Japs have violated the non-fortification clause of their Mandate, he thought. *That's the least we could do for Amelia's memory. But it's sure as hell not enough.*

Later, he learned that Japan adamantly had refused to permit any naval or aerial search of the Marshalls. If President Roosevelt had ordered a search, in defiance of Japan's curt note, it would have appeared almost as a declaration of war. The leader of an isolation-minded, militarily weak nation was too astute a politician to take an action so risky at home and abroad, and his instincts were proved correct by an almost simultaneous new belligerence from Japan.

During that same week of Amelia's disappearance, on a date that would live in Chinese memory as 7/7/37, the Japanese army flexed its muscles at the Marco Polo Bridge, and then marched on Peking. The United States was as helpless as the League of Nations to send assistance to the Chinese capital, which fell within the month. During the ensuing siege of Shanghai, Japanese planes bombed the American Dollar Lines steamer *President Hoover* and the flagship of the Asiatic Fleet, USS *Augusta*. On 12 December their bombs sank the USS *Panay* while the gunboat was evacuating Americans from ravaged Nanking. One of Jim's heroes, the famous newreel photographer, Norman Alley, a passenger aboard the *Panay*, had filmed the attack and brought his reels to Manila to develop en route to the States. ManilAmericans who were invited to a private screening were incensed to see the bombs dropping on the clearly marked U.S. vessel; but those shots were cut before the newsreel was shown in any theaters.

"Why?" Jim asked, and his father told him, "President Roosevelt is not ready for a *casus belli*." The United States could only protest verbally and accept Japan's apologies.

Not only Americans, but Asians, Europeans, the entire civilized world (and some Papuans in the vicinity of Lae) had grieved with Jim for the courageous young Kansan.

Leda, however, had refused to cry. "Amelia always said she wanted to go quickly, in her plane. . . . The goddam men will say she should have stayed home with Publicity Putnam, and stuck with a teaching career. But she *was* teaching — as a master teacher, using herself as an example — and not just in one classroom. She taught men that women can fly, and she showed women how to reach for the stars."

* * * * *

Old Alex was right — for once — Jim admitted to himself now. *Leda and I were so mad at him, when AE was lost, for mildly suggesting that four million dollars was a lot for the navy of a country enduring a severe depression to spend. More than a dozen ships and scores of planes had examined more than two hundred sixty-two thousand square miles of ocean, he reminded us. Leda — usually so critical of Navy spending (versus domestic projects such as FDR's Bismarckian Social Security Act) — averred that the search for Amelia was a "highly legit" use of taxpayers' money. What Dad was hinting was that the government probably had a big stake in what AE was doing out there; but we didn't get it.*

And Alex reminded them, in his Mr. Milquetoast way, about the cost of building those three runways on Howland Island "for Mrs. Putnam's sole use. Wasn't that an uncommonly quixotic gesture for President Roosevelt? But how unfortunate that those runways will remain unused hereafter."

"Hey! — they'll be used, all right," Jim told him; "the Air Corps will use 'em!"

Alex shook his head. "I'm afraid not, son. Since Mrs. Putnam was unable to demonstrate that U.S. land planes could cross the Pacific, that dream has been snuffed out, just as definitely as the *Hindenburg* disaster has ended dirigible travel across the Atlantic. Whether or no the Japanese had anything to do with the lady's disappearance, the final result will be that the only nation flying land planes from Pacific islands will be Japan."

... *The old boy was right on target, that time. The Department of the Interior (traditionally begrudging military control) under "the curmudgeon," Secretary Harold Ickes, refused to appropriate any funds for maintenance of the runways. Howland Island was reclaimed by jungle and birds. And Lord — do we ever need it now!*

Its name should be changed to Earhart Island — and U.S. planes should land there regularly. That's a memorial AE would like.

Part 2 — New Britain

The military training of the natives, otherwise than for the purposes of internal police and the local defense of the territory, shall be prohibited. Furthermore, no military or naval bases shall be established, or fortifications erected in the territory.
— League of Nations Mandate, Article 4

Airborne over New Britain
Monday, 17 November 1941

With a final sweep over Finschhafen, Eubank crossed over turbulent Vitiaz Strait, which separates New Guinea from New Britain and links the Solomon Sea with the Bismarck Sea. On the tattered map, the larger island of the Bismarck Archipelago — New Britain — looked to Jim like a knobby green lizard: an Australian goanna, or a Komodo Dragon. The lizard was attempting to devour, head-first, a skinny green "snake" called New Ireland. Rabaul lay at the distant tip of the "dragon's" fang; only narrow St. George's Channel prevented the dragon's jaws from clamping on the 200-mile-long New Ireland snake.

Boy — wouldn't Leda relish the irony of those names!

The Whiteman range (another ironic name) that formed the spine of 350-mile-long New Britain was composed of volcanoes that rose as high as 8,000 feet. Their bases extended across the 50-mile breadth of the island, creating an irregular coastline, and their steep sides offered few horizontal areas for plantations or landing fields.

As the B-17 climbed, an Olympian view spread out below, with the Solomon Sea on Jim's right and the Bismarck Sea to the west of the island. He enjoyed it even more when Brigadier Morris commented that they were probably the first mortals ever to see that vivid, shimmering panorama from this vantage point, for the Australian pilots customarily flew at lower altitudes alongside the island.

The Solomon Sea, on Jim's right, seemed to change color constantly as the plane moved. To his oblique vision its vibrant greens and blues looked far more alluring than the familiar dark blue, empty Pacific. On its surface lay scattered, like shards of emerald, turquoise, and jade, islands whose names sounded musical and exotic as Morris named them: Bougainville, Choiseul, Santa Isabel, Tulagi, Guadalcanal — and *Vella Lavella!* That one sounded to Jim like a nonsense song waiting for him to write it. How could it miss, rhyming with *bella, bella?*

These jewels formed the "fence" that obsessed Commander Feldt. His Coastwatchers were in place on those verdant Solomon Islands, scanning the iridescent sea and the intensely blue sky for interlopers. Jim grinned inwardly as he realized that right now, excited Coastwatchers undoubtedly were keying their monstrous Teleradios, reporting the sighting of a Flying Fortress.

*They jolly well **better** warn Rabaul about us,* Jim thought, *or Feldt will have their ass!*

Another plane shared the blue sky. Eubank spotted its bright glint first, and pointed. Jim watched it grow as it closed the distance, obviously returning from Rabaul and heading for New Guinea.

Eureka! Electra! The hair on Jim's neck prickled as the silver Guinea Airways 10-passenger, twin-engine Lockheed dipped its wing in salute as it passed. Jim sat silent for a long time, feeling shivery from more than the altitude, thrilled by that ghostly apparition. It seemed to him like a message from AE, but he could not grasp its meaning. Was she saying that she was still alive? Or that she was dead, but her spirit could not rest; perhaps condemned to wander like the Flying Dutchman, until someone — perhaps Jim himself — solved the mystery of her fate?

He thought of Pard Mustar, the trailblazer for that Guinea Airways scheduled flight, flying his single-engine, self-assembled de Havilland to Lae over this 400 miles of steep mountains, scattered islands, and blue-green ocean for the first time. *If you go down on this route, abandon all hope.*

Commander Feldt had asked Eubank to test his "early warning scheme" by sneaking up on the city from the east, through a gap in the mountains, instead of flying in over the southern entrance of Rabaul's bay.

In those blue-green waters dwelt 20-foot sharks, Morris said. And from those peaceful-looking Solomon Islands the infamous "blackbirders" had captured young men to work as slaves on the plantations of Fiji and — yes — Queensland, until international opprobrium finally ended the raids. The inhabitants, however, also preyed on each other. Only a few years earlier, the explorer and circus-animal trainer Martin Johnson had taken his bride, Osa — wholesome and fresh-faced as a Midwestern college cheerleader — sailing through the Solomons in search of a cannibal ceremony to photograph.

Jim asked Brigadier Morris to point out Malekula, where Johnson had filmed that feast of Long Pig; but it was in the New Hebrides, too distant to see, even with Alex's binoculars.

"Johnson should have been making charts as he sailed — that would have been a damned sight more useful," Morris told him. "The bloody charts of all the Pacific islands are fair cows for actual navigation. Islands that don't exist have appeared on maps for centuries — while real islands aren't shown at all, or are miles off. We're luckier out here than in most areas, though — thanks to the bloody Germans. During their regime, they did some turn-of-the-century cartography. But even those charts aren't dependable, and we've been working on corrections for several years. It's the Japs who have the best charts now, we suspect."

Another "cannibal island" down there — New Caledonia — had posed a Fifth Column threat inside the Australians' sphere until ten months ago, Morris said. The tiny French colony had been governed by representatives of the Vichy regime, with a Vichy warship alongside, until September 1940, when a quiet citizen named Henri Sautot led a bloodless coup, with the quiet assistance of a few Australians and Britons. Thereupon New Caledonia, situated in the aptly named Loyalty Islands, had declared its allegiance to the Free French under the distant leadership-in-exile of General Charles de Gaulle.

To Jim, the name "Caledonia" had been a joke, part of a crazy song yelled by Spike Jones' noisy band:

"Cal'donia! Cal'donia! What makes your big head so HARD?"

Below the plane's port wing, the Bismarck Sea seemed to Jim small and confined, in comparison to the colorful sweep of the Solomon Sea. Enclosed in a ring of small volcanic-tip islands and only 500 miles wide at its east-west widest, it appeared to him like the water-filled crater of a huge submerged volcano. A portion of the long northern coast of New Guinea formed its southern boundary; the only other islands of any size were this lizard-shaped New Britain on the southeast and the snake-like New Ireland forming the northeast rim. Beyond the tiny Admiralty Islands lay the Equator — and beyond that, invisible in the dark Pacific, the mysterious, threatening, Japanese Mandates.

Until the World War, most of the islands Jim could see had been — like that northeast quadrant of New Guinea where Lae was situated — claimed by Germany as part of Kaiser Wilhelm Land. In 1920 they had been entrusted to Australia's care under a Class C Mandate of the League of Nations. Australia had been cautious, Morris said, about building new airdromes out here, or improving existing landing strips, because anything that resembled a military airfield would be considered a breach of the Mandate.

Well, the League sure can't complain about Seven Mile! No one could possibly see a resemblance to a military airfield there. Or to a civilian field, either.

American military men long had suspected that Japan was fortifying some of the more than 3,000 islands north of here, which she held under a similar Mandate. Those were her reward for siding with the Allies during the Great War, and they included the Carolines, Marianas, and Marshall Islands. Almost as soon as Japan took over the vast area in 1920, U.S. Naval Intelligence officers began to urge a policy of "courtesy calls" by Navy ships on various Japanese-held islands. The State Department had vetoed the suggestions, however, preferring to avoid any friction with Japan.

Because the U.S. had never joined the League, it had no voice in it, and although the League had the authority to monitor all mandated areas, it had no power to enforce inspections. Beginning in 1933, the Mandates Commission filed formal complaints because Japan refused to permit ships, planes, or persons from other nations to move freely in those areas. Japan's response was to withdraw from the League, while continuing to hold the islands.

Part 3 — To Rabaul

Within a fortnight of the beginning of hostilities the US would find herself bereft of . . . insular possessions in the Western Pacific.
— Hector C. Bywater
Sea-Power in the Pacific: A Study of the American-Japanese Naval Problem, 1921

Airborne over New Britain
Monday, 17 November 1941

Brigadier Morris identified one old volcano, over 7,500 feet high, as Mount Ulawum.

"Ulawum means The Father," he explained. "That little fellow beside him is The Son, and since Old Dad's latest blow-off that other little bastard has popped up. We're still about seventy miles from The Mother — just like a woman, she wants to be near the bright lights of the city. She's not half The Father's size, but she's bloody active, all royte."

Morris said that the Germans had called New Britain "New Pommerania," and New Ireland "New Mecklenburg."

All colonists must be homesick.

During Germany's harsh 30-year protectorate, Morris continued, the big ships that arrived loaded with European goods for the sustenance of the colonists had so awed the inhabitants that a religion of sorts had sprung up, and still flourished. "Whitefellows" called it "the Cargo Cult."

"The natives believe their gods had intended all that stuff for *them*, but the bloody white men intercepted it! So they keep on waiting for the gods to send a big 'sail-o' with *their* rich cargo — and in the meantime, why bother to work for peanuts?"

The natives of New Britain were called Melanesians, he said, "That means 'black,' and they're the blackest lot of all. In their language, *rabaul* is the word for mangroves. The mangrove roots catch the silt the rains bring down the mountains, and build the shoreline farther out, so I guess if it wasn't for the odd earthquake, the bloody mangroves would eventually fill up the harbor."

Rabaul smelled like Hell. Long before they reached the Gazelle Peninsula, which formed the dragon's head, sulphurous fumes and gritty ash flowed into the B-17, burning Jim's eyes and causing all the men to cough and swear. He had smelled that rotten-egg, hellfire-and-brimstone stink many times before, while climbing volcanoes; but it seemed far worse here, inside a plane. The clean air of the sky was for him an integral component of flying.

The Mother had erupted two months ago, Morris said. Now her perfectly formed breast seemed to display her temper only intermittently — moments of grumbling and smoker's cough were followed by bursts of apparent fury that hurled hot ashes and rocks into the air. "Reminds me of my own dear mother," Jim said.

General Brereton evidently saw the eruption as Nature's attempt to frustrate his already difficult mission. "Unbearable!" he barked, when the hot yellow wind pelted the Plexiglas nose cone with blinding debris. "How in hell can we inspect this place? This is intolerable!" He yelled to Brigadier Morris, "How often does this goddam bitch blow?"

Flippantly, Morris replied, "We hadn't had a real pop-off since Vulcan, across the bay, blew up four years ago. But quakes are routine — sometimes thousands of tremors in a day."

"And it took your people *this long* to decide to move the capital to Lae?"

"Listen, Lewie — New Guinea's not immune to quakes and shakes, either. And Huon Gulf can't compare with Simpson Harbour. This is one of the finest natural harbors in the Pacific. You could hide the entire U.S. bloody fleet here — and the Royal Australian fucking Navy, too — safe from any sea attack. As for Rabaul proper, we call it 'Germany's Revenge,' because the bastard Huns left us such a sturdy lot of buildings! We couldn't possibly winkle out enough money from Parliament to replace them on New Guinea."

Obviously angry, Brereton barked, "Jim! I'm going below. Take my place up here."

Jim scrambled out of his way as Brereton pushed past Morris and climbed down into the navigator's space. Jim knew that all seats below were filled; but Brereton frequently stretched out to rest on an Army blanket in the narrow curtained "tunnel" between the navigator's and the bombardier's sections.

Jim was delighted to sit on Eubank's right as copilot. Forty miles to the east, across St. George's Channel, he saw the 7,000-foot mountain that formed the head of serpentine New Ireland. A well-named island, he thought; its cover of rain forest makes it an emerald islet.

Noon. Miserably hot. A coat of ash had formed a yellow paste with Jim's sweat, and his teeth crunched on grit.

We took off from Seven Mile at o-six hundred. We'd better high-tail out of this smelly joint pretty damned soon, to be sure of landing at Port Moresby before dark. Captain Ind will be crushed if "sun him go sleep" before Ind gets to film the full-breasted marys at Moresby. And General Brereton will bust a gut if we're forced to spend the night here with the fucking Mother!

Rabaul actually boasted two airfields, an "upper" strip on a hill southwest of the city, and a "lower" one beside the bay. Several of the B-17s on the mass flight to Clark in October, too low on gas to attempt to reach Port Moresby, had landed on the upper field, Vunakanau. Three of the Fortresses — piloted by Major Birrel Walsh and Lieutenants Walt Ford and Sam Maddux — had broken through the volcanic-clay crust of that high runway. Australian ground crews had dug them out. Because of those mishaps (and to oblige Commander Feldt by sneaking in, to test the Coastwatcher network), Eubank would land on the bayside field, Lakunai.

As the B-17 turned west to approach the hidden city through a saddle between volcanoes, she began to buck. The plane was traveling light, with only enough fuel remaining for the return to Port Moresby. Jim's arms and legs tensed, mentally helping Eubank to wrestle the bomber through the sudden sickening helpless drops in altitude and loss of power caused by the intense heat from The Mother's crater. The volcano stood formidably on their left — one of six guardian volcanoes that ringed steep-sided Simpson Bay — and her blasts of sulphurous yellow smoke seemed to be aimed directly at the visitors.

"Buckle your lap belt, Sir!" Jim yelled over his shoulder to Brigadier Morris.

Most tropic island bays, and many lakes, appeared to Jim like craters; Blanche Bay actually was one. The beautiful bay, 11 miles long and more than 2 miles wide, was the caldera of an enormous ancient volcano. Only a narrow gap between two peaks at the south end had allowed the sea to enter.

Morris leaned forward to tell of a placid island across the bay near the southwest shore, a traditional spot for Melanesians of the Tolai tribe to gather for their sing-sings. An added attraction may have been that the surrounding water was hot enough to cook a pig, and boiled fish swirled continually around the island. In May 1937, during a convocation attended by hundreds of tribespeople, the ground began to slant beneath their dancing feet, quickly forming a cone that roared and vomited molten lava, killing more than 500

Tolai. After erupting for 27 hours, the former island had joined itself to the southwest wall of volcanoes and acquired the "Whitefellow" name of "Vulcan."

"Tough cheddar!" Morris yelled. "Nearly destroyed the finest city east of Australia."

Jim thought Vulcan looked remarkably small and innocent to have created such devastation, although it was still emitting puffs of steam. A hapless boat that had been sailing through the channel beside the island was still incongruously perched atop the bridge of land thrust up from the bay.

Wryly, the Brigadier said, "The volcanoes are Rabaul's best coastal defense. Well, we do have two bastard coastal guns — a four-incher and a six-incher — at Praed Point."

Simpson Harbour lay in the curve at the north end of Blanche Bay, where Captain Simpson in 1882 had named the harbor for himself. The bay, Morris said, Simpson named "not for his sheila, but his ship," HMS *Blanche*.

Inside this bowl the German colonists had built a small city, planned for permanence, on the narrow crescent of low shore north and east of Simpson Harbour ("Simpsonhaven" during their regime).

Jim admired the sturdy stone buildings and the two wide avenues shaded by a double row of huge mango trees. Even viewed through stinking yellow smoke, Rabaul was far more attractive than the ramshackle towns he had seen in northern Australia. True, Townsville had its mansions, but they were few. Rabaul struck him as emblematic of the German character: solid, conservative, putting down deep roots — while volcanoes smoldered underneath.

Manila might have looked like Rabaul, he realized: all stolid practicality, but without the charm of Daniel Burnham's artistic planning that had made Manila "the most beautiful city in the Orient."

Germany had not hidden her hunger to add the Philippines to her Pacific possessions as a second "Kaiser Wilhelm Land." After Commodore Dewey's victory over Spain in 1898, German — and British — warships had lurked outside Manila Bay like sharks.

If the U.S. hadn't stayed in the islands, the Filipinos' freedom from Spain would soon have been replaced by a new bondage to another foreign empire. Jim wondered which one would have snapped up the prize.

England had sacked Manila in 1762, followed by a three-year occupation during hostilities with Spain. Although Jim had no respect for England's colonial policies, he thought that life under a second English rule would have been more bearable for the Filipinos than it had been under Spain.

Under Germany, they would have suffered most of all. They were lucky we stayed. No other country ever did so much for a colony and then gave it independence, like the U.S. is doing.

As recently as 1930, Henry Cabot Lodge had called for the U.S. to get out of the Philippines and sell the islands to Germany. He saw them as a weak link in the Pacific line of defense, and in view of the "slight possibility of a major war in the Far East," the loss of American lives "for a possession of questionable value to their country is not a pleasant one," he wrote in *Harper's*.

If we'd sold the Philippines to Germany, it wouldn't be only the Filipinos who were out of luck. Singapore, Hong Kong, Australia, and New Zealand would be overrun and enslaved, as Europe is now. . . . But what about the "Yellow Sharks"? Can the Philippines stay free, after we turn the islands loose in 1946?

* * * * *

It was nearly time, Jim knew, for a *real* copilot to start the pre-landing check. He prepared to relinquish the copilot's seat to one of Brereton's aides, the bomber pilots; but Eubank shook his head. "Stay right where you are, and start on the checklist."

Pleased and flattered, Jim reached to his right to retrieve the knee-board and checklist. After he would read each heading loudly and clearly, Eubank would repeat the key word and either take action or indicate what Jim should do.

A week ago, Jim thought, the idea of serving as copilot on a B-17 during a landing would have terrified him.

By now I've learned enough about the instruments — and the blessed checklist — to be able to do it well. But while I'm guarding the throttles and monitoring the engine instruments — still a task for four eyes — I mustn't get preoccupied with cockpit duties. I should scan the sky for planes, unlikely as that seems, or — far more likely — for birds. And check the terrain below. After we get down into this cup, over the water and out of the volcanic turbulence, landing will be a snap. But sneaking in past The Mother is hell.

Relishing the authority of a copilot, Jim again reminded Brigadier Morris to keep his lap belt buckled. In the absence of a Flight Engineer, he asked Lefty over the microphone to insure that all "crew members" were in their proper places for landing. He also gave Lefty the job of the Radio Operator: to be sure the trailing antenna was retracted.

Below the plane to starboard, four large green fields in a square caught Jim's eye. Morris leaned forward and yelled that they were the Aussies' playing fields for baseball, "footy," Cricket, and Old Cricket.

"Gunners will check their guns and make sure they are in proper position for landing." *At least I can skip that one. . . .*

Jim made sure that all switches of the automatic pilot were turned OFF, booster pumps ON, mixture controls in AUTO-RICH position, and intercoolers OFF.

Now the plane was above Simpson Bay, and he glimpsed the two black protuberances known as The Beehives, near the bay's entrance — volcano tips that had emerged overnight after an earthquake about 70 years earlier.

He ascertained that the carburetor filters were in the ON position; Eubank had already opened them to keep The Mother's volcanic debris out of the induction system.

After Eubank reduced speed below 180 mph, he said, "Gear down," and Jim put the landing gear switch in the DOWN position. Eubank looked out his left-hand window and reported, "Down left." Jim checked on his side and said, "Down right." As the huge extended wheel slowly revolved, demonstrating that the brakes were OFF, he looked for cracked rims or evidence of leaks from hydraulic lines. The tires looked fine, despite Seven Mile's rough treatment.

Lefty crawled back toward the tail. "Tailwheel down," he reported through his microphone. Jim returned the landing gear switch to neutral; the warning light was green.

Lakunai Airdrome lay on the southeast shore, about four miles south of the town, at the foot of the three too-familiar volcanoes: Mother, 2,160 feet high, with her newest "baby," Rabalankai, only 800 feet high, and South Daughter, 1,620 feet.

"That one and North Daughter, behind the harbor, are going to be fair cows like their Mum!" Morris predicted.

Jim looked below him and decided he was lucky, on his first landing as copilot, to have the best runway they'd seen — level and smooth.

Even better than Garbutt, hemmed in with all that sugar-cane garbage. And Lakunai looks as if it might even be a fraction longer than three thousand feet: what luxury! Of course, Colonel Eubank could easily land this monster on two thousand — with my expert assistance.

"Hydraulic pressure," he called out. Eubank checked the pressure gauges, got a normal reading of 800 pounds, checked hydraulic pump, toggle switch, and cowl flap controls. The hydraulic system was in good order, and Jim was relieved; he would not be required to stand by ready to work the hand pump.

Sulphur Creek, a long narrow inlet, formed a fine landmark just north of Lakunai airfield. Fortunately, visibility over the landing strip was good, thanks to a south wind that carried the plume of ashes back across the saddle. The smooth, level runway ended almost at the bay's edge and ran southeast until it formed an angle with a wide road leading south from the city.

"RPMs."

Flying parallel to the runway on the plane's upwind leg, at an altitude of 1,000 feet, Eubank told Jim to increase revolutions per minute to 2,200, because of the plane's freedom from weight of fuel or bombs.

Lakunai's runway and taxiways were nearly empty, with plenty of room for the B-17. The only planes here were two of the Hudson bombers from

Townsville's No. 24 Squadron; the other two were at the upper field, Vunakanau. For almost a year, a detachment from No. 24 had been stationed at Rabaul, designated an advanced operational base, with its main assignment to coordinate seaplane reconnaissance for hostile ships. One of the Hudsons would take Brigadier Morris back to Port Moresby later in the week.

"Turbos," Jim read. Eubank decreased manifold pressure to 23 inches and signaled him to turn the turbo controls full ON and to readjust manifold pressure. With the turbos in that position, Jim was nervous about exceeding the allowable limit for manifold pressure, and kept checking the red warning lines on the four gauges that monitored the engines.

"Flaps."

The inland end of the landing strip was too close to the volcanoes to allow Eubank the luxury of starting his base leg two miles out. He had room only to turn left, and left again; the steep glide would require full flaps sooner than usual. After airspeed had dropped below 140 mph, Jim lowered the wing flaps one-third, and after Eubank rolled out of the turn on final approach, at 120 mph, Jim placed them in the full DOWN position.

As the bomber changed to gliding attitude, Eubank reminded Jim of a symphony conductor as he smoothly reduced power, blending the plane's needs with its change to an attitude of gliding. He retarded the throttle all the way and signaled Jim to move the propeller controls to full HIGH RPM.

We did it! Greased it in! Brought the big bird down in perfect style!

Typically bronzed Diggers, typically bare, except for baggy shorts and wide-brimmed hats, stood along the side of Lakunai's landing strip watching. As Eubank gently touched down, Jim saw their wide grins, and their welcoming hands clapping. The bomber rolled easily toward the water's edge, on the smoothest surface yet — not sod, but a substance that resembled a clay tennis court. As always, Jim mentally stepped on the brakes, but he knew that applying brakes before the full weight of the Fortress had settled could cause the big tires to blow out, or even damage the landing gear.

With the two inboard engines cut, the outboards idling, Eubank turned off the runway and taxied slowly toward a cleared area.

Suddenly, the B-17 seemed to hesitate, like a horse that loses its footing. It struggled to go on, then heavily fell forward, as a horse falls, helpless to save its rider.

Something like a baseball bat struck Jim in the stomach, knocking the wind out of him: His lap belt had kept him from being hurled against the instrument panel or the unbreakable Plexiglas windshield, but it seemed to be cutting him in half.

Oh, God, I've wrecked the Fort; what the hell did I do wrong?

In that terrible instant, Jim's entire future passed before his eyes like a speeded-up Charlie Chaplin film; but there were no laughs. Scenes of a court-martial, loss of rank, ejection from the Army, loss of pilot's license, strangers pointing fingers, and a lifetime of disgrace raced through his mind to the accompaniment of mocking laughter. He had no future among his own kind; he would remain out here as an expatriate Islander, with a huge aluminum skeleton in his closet.

Eubank had cut the outboard throttles. The shocking silence was broken by a bellow from below.

I've killed the General.

Part 4 — Rotten-Egg Rabaul

Please know that I am quite aware of the hazards. . . . Women must try to do things as men have tried. When they fail, their failure must be but a challenge to others.

— Amelia Earhart

Lakunai Airfield, Rabaul
Monday, 17 November 1941

Jim's head was bowed, his face in his hands, his breathing rapid, his mouth so dry he could not speak.

Eubank twisted around in his seat and looked back and up — *up* — at Brigadier Morris in the jump seat. "You OK, Sir?"

Oh, Lord. An international incident. End of friendly Aussie-American relations.

Morris was doubled over, his face red, but obviously his lap belt had saved him from real harm, and he grunted affirmatively, "Uh huh."

Over his microphone Eubank directed, "Lefty, check on everyone and report to me."

"Yes, Sir." Lefty sounded as cool as if it had been a normal landing.

Jim thought of Captain Ind, airsick on his dark catwalk, possibly crushed by cases of San Miguel.

There's nothing soft in this plane. Everyone's surrounded by bare metal surfaces capable of inflicting grave injury — or death. And every bruise is my goddam fault.

Eubank quietly told him, "Feels like we're damn near flat on our belly. Come on, Jim, let's see how bad it is."

How do you say: Sir, I'm sorry I wrecked your beautiful bird? I'll donate two hundred fifty thousand dollars for a new one, out of my pay check.

To exit through the forward section was out of the question; the four heavy engines dangled so perilously close to the ground that any extra weight might stand the bomber completely on its nose.

Oh, shit — we're stranded in this stink-hole — till Clark can send another 'Seventeen to get us out!

Silently, stooping, he followed Colonel Eubank and the furious, but mercifully unhurt, General Brereton aft to the dark bomb bay. They waited for Captain Ind to scramble outside ahead of them, blinking in the hot white sun, clutching his movie camera. The force of the accident had hurled him off his catwalk, thrown off his eyeglasses, tousled his normally sleek dark hair, and spilled his "throw-up cup," to his distress. Jim was so relieved to see Ind able to walk, he felt like hugging him.

Exiting on the starboard side from the waist door, they were immediately greeted by the entire contingent of the small detachment. Flying Officer W. H. Robinson was in command of this advanced operational base.

The air was so hot and acrid with smoke that for an awful instant Jim thought the Fortress was burning. Gratefully, he realized that the flying ash emanated from The Mother.

Was the landing gear hopelessly crumpled? It was impossible to tell yet; the huge wheels were sunk deep in volcanic ash which had been glazed over with a brittle crust too thin to support the bomber's weight.

SO IT WASN'T MY FAULT! THANK YOU, GOD, AND HALLELUJAH!

Still, he felt gut-wrenched to see the great plane in such an ignominious crouch. More than a mere airplane, the B-17 was a symbol of U.S. strength: the warning to Japan to keep peace in the Pacific.

The Australians offered condolences in their own way, with concern laced with cheek. Although they well knew the "secret" rank of the American senior officers — and the importance of this mission to Australia and to the future of Rabaul — obsequiousness was not in them.

"Tough luck, Yanks — Up to your arses in ashes!"

"Crook, is she? Well, crack hearty, you be right pretty soon."

"Guess you didn't see the *Safe Limit* runway markings?"

Eubank, in his flight suit spotted with ashes and sweat, merely shook his head, his lips in a tight straight line.

Brereton retorted, "Hell, no — we didn't bring a microscope! Damn near destroyed our plane, and everybody aboard!"

Officials in Rabaul had "laid on" a festive lunch at Government House, but Brereton snapped, "Just tell 'em to send us some sandwiches — and ice water!"

If there's a piece of ice in Rabaul — which I doubt — it would be warm water by the time it got here.

Already the enlisted Diggers were shoveling the ash away from the undercarriage, "like bloody wombats," Jim heard one of them say; but their helpful, sweaty exertions appeared sadly futile to him.

Brigadier Morris was upset that the Governor and other civil and military officials were not on hand to greet the Americans. Evidently the Coastwatchers had assumed that the Fortress would land on the high runway at Vunakanau, as a B-17 had never landed here at Lakunai before — so the Teleradios had not alerted Robinson. The "sneak approach" through the saddle on the east had been the surprise that Feldt had hoped for. Presumably, the high officials were now assembled across the bay at Vunakanau, but no one could be certain. There was no telephone line between the two airfields, and Vunakanau was out of sight behind Vulcan.

Eubank said, "Come on, Jim," and zipped his flight suit open over his sweating chest. Jim gladly followed his example. As he walked beside the aircraft Commander all the way around the "beached whale," he learned what a heartfelt walkaround inspection entails. Taller than the Colonel, he could see and touch the rivets in surfaces above Eubank's reach.

He could hardly bear to glance at Eubank's usually humorous face as the older man carefully, lovingly, sorrowfully examined each section of the plane for outward indications of stress damage. To protect their fingertips from burning when they touched the stove-hot metal, they moistened them on their tongues and then heard them sizzle as the moisture evaporated. Jim felt sure he would run out of saliva before he could make the complete circuit; he had to reach so far back in his gullet to find moisture that he nearly gagged. He wondered if the hairs on his bare chest were getting singed by the aluminum.

From the waist door they proceeded forward. The Diggers had already uncovered a large portion of the undercarriage. The right landing gear, as it emerged, looked normal: the main wheel's tire intact, rim flanges not cracked, safety switch operable. Hydraulic line, struts, joint clearance, were all miraculously OK. Inside the wheel nacelle, control cables, pulleys, and electrical wiring had the requisite tautness; and no oil leaks were visible. Number 3 and 4 turbo wheels moved freely; no cracks between buckets. No cracks in the engine exhaust systems. No signs of oil leaks in the nacelle or on the engine. All 12 propeller blades OK.

Every few minutes, adding to Jim's continued apprehension of doom, reverberations from The Mother's coughs made the ground tremble under his feet, while her ashes inside his flight suit chafed his skin like sandpaper.

Chapter 5 — Part 4 — Rotten-Egg Rabaul

The radio loop on top of the cockpit, normally more than 15 feet above the ground, had been effectively chopped down to the range of a basketball hoop. Passing under the right wing, they found it canted forward at such an angle that Eubank could not reach the trailing edge, so Jim checked the flap and aileron surfaces.

Not all the smoke and heat were coming from The Mother. Some of the Diggers had built a small fire, on which they were brewing their strong billy tea. Thirsty though Jim was, he could not accept a proffered mug of the scalding black liquid.

Jim's hopes began to rise as everything on the port side checked out satisfactorily. By the time they reached the pointed tail beneath the sharply upthrust tailfin with its red and white stripes, he felt like whistling; but his mouth was too dry.

These birds are just too big, he thought. *They're supposed to measure sixty-seven feet and eleven inches long, but I swear, I think the heat's expanded it to sixty-eight feet! A helluva tough ship, but too goddam big. If you louse up when you're flying a fighter plane, you only kill yourself and the plane — not eight other blokes.*

When finally they had completed the walkaround, Eubank grinned his Will Rogers grin and announced to their RAAF hosts, "Well, I can't recommend it as a steady diet for landing gear, but apparently she's in good order. Go ahead — *yank her out!*"

While Eubank and Brereton were conferring with Flying Officer Robinson and other pilots of No. 24 Squadron who were drinking their billy while they hunkered down in the shade of a wing, Jim went over to the side of the runway where Captain Ind, still slightly pale and uncharacteristically disheveled, stood cranking his movie camera. He looked to Jim like a newsreel cameraman, filming the scene of a tragedy: a noble airplane brought to her knees, as a pair of noisy Caterpillar tractors bore down on the B-17.

Jim gratefully accepted an Aussie's proffered refreshment, a quart bottle of Koala beer, a sweet, warm, uncarbonated strawberry-flavored soft drink, and drank it in long gulps, but Ind took only a couple of sips from his bottle and set it on the ground.

"Don't get dehydrated," Jim warned the Michigander. Jim felt sure that modesty was at the root of the Captain's abstinence. Ind still was embarrassed about using the plane's relief tube, which he called "that piece of aerial plumbing right out in front of everybody."

"These Diggers truly exemplify the spirit we've observed all during this trip," Ind remarked admiringly. "It's an attitude that says, 'Let's all put our shoulders to the wheel and get this job done, so we can have a smoke-oh and some beer!'"

"Too right," Jim said. "Bonzer blokes."

"As a matter of fact, they seem so extremely businesslike with this airplane extraction process that — well, you know, we Intelligence types are overly prone to suspicion. I asked one of the RAAF personnel if we're the first visitors to 'let down' for a landing in such an abrupt manner, on this airfield. He said, 'Too right you're not! These bloody giants don't visit Rabaul en route from Wake to Port Moresby unless they have to — but when they do, it's best to have a bloody shovel, and a bloody tractor or two, bloody well ready!' "

Jim laughed. He had never heard Ind say an "American" curse word, but the gentle ex-professor seemed to enjoy repeating the expletive so commonly used in Australia that it surely had lost the shock-power it still held for the English in Singapore.

Singapore! Shockable, scandalous, sinful, gin-swilling, sophisticated, smelly, smug little fishing-village fortress — I'm on my way back! And this time I'm going to conquer you. . . .

"I guess profanity is in the ear of the listener," he told Ind, feeling profound.

"I trust that no ears but yours can hear me, what with the bloody noise of those bloody tractors. Concurrently with the shock of that landing, I'm also shocked at the obvious lack of anything to defend this important harbor from an attack by air. If our bombers can get here from Wake Island, it stands to reason that Japanese planes can swoop down easily from the far-closer Carolines or Marshalls. Rabaul could be throttled completely from those strategic islands that we so generously granted to Japan — and which Japan has been so effectively consolidating during our years of scrupulous, ingenuous, treaty observance."

"Yeah — the Aussies are playing fair with their Mandate. They sure haven't done anything to make this landing strip suitable for bombers!"

"Meanwhile, the Japanese are cheating, fortifying *their* islands, but we have no way of proving it. . . . General Clagett — like every Air Corps officer I've met in my brief experience in the Army — has enormous respect for 'the martyr of air power,' General Billy Mitchell. From what the General tells me, if only the Mandates Commission had known of the warnings that Mitchell gave, way back in 1912 — that Japan was planning a Pacific island war that posed grave danger to the Philippines — perhaps they wouldn't have been so generous in handing over all that territory to Japan."

"Too bad the Senate killed President Wilson's plan to get the U.S. into the League of Nations."

"Oh, Jim, you have it backwards; it was Wilson's rigidity that made any agreement impossible. But I know where you got that idea, and I have the greatest admiration for your charming mother. She's a splendid teacher of English; but when it comes to history, your father is the objective historian."

Embarrassed, Jim mentioned Billy Mitchell's five-month honeymoon spent touring the Pacific, including his efforts to scout around the Japanese Mandates. "Did you ever read his 1925 report?"

"Surely you jest, Jim. Of course I haven't seen it. Why would the War Department favor me, merely because I'm the sole Air Intelligence officer of the Philippines? That report has been sealed in a 'classified' file ever since General Mitchell handed it in. It's only because he had so many friends — and talked so freely to them, and to the press — that anyone knows that the fabled twenty-five-page report ever existed. In it, I understand from General Clagett, Mitchell forecast an aerial attack on our military installations in Honolulu."

"Yeah, on a Sunday morning. That's the way I heard it, too."

Ind loves spy stories. But actually, I've been able to hear a whole lot more of the word-of-mouth true ones than he has, because I've been hanging around with military brats for twenty-one years, while he just got called up a year or so ago. Nice as he is, as a Reserve he can't ever gain the buddy-buddy intimacy of the officers who served together in the World War. But the best spy story I know about the Mandated Islands is one I promised I'd never tell.

Sometimes — late at night, over drinks — the fathers of Jimmy's friends spoke with each other in low voices after they thought their sons and their sons' guests were asleep. The fathers knew what was in the sealed files, because they knew the men who had been involved.

Jim recalled one night, in the quarters of a Marine officer at Cavite on Manila Bay, when he and his friend had sat on the mahogany stairs in the dark and listened, hardly breathing. The nape of Jim's neck prickled as the two Marines downstairs in the *sala* reminisced about their friend "Pete" Ellis. Lieutenant Colonel Earl Hancock Ellis, USMC, in 1921 had presented a report, "Advanced Base Operations in Micronesia," in which he declared his belief that Japan's military clique was planning to create, on the newly-bestowed Mandates, bases from which to wage a Pacific island war that would encompass attacks on Hawaii and even the U.S. mainland.

Two years later, Ellis's superiors told him, in effect, "Prove it." Because German nationals were permitted to travel freely in the islands, Ellis had assumed the guise of a German trader and had scouted the Marshall Islands. He had continued on into the western Carolines, where he died mysteriously at Koror. When Japanese authorities informed the U.S. government of his death and cremation, permission was asked and granted for a U.S. Navy Chief Pharmacist to travel to Koror — on a Japanese vessel — and bring back Ellis's ashes. Afterwards, when the pharmacist debarked in Japan, he was a victim of irreversible amnesia and it was impossible for him to describe any aspect of his journey.

The two Marine officers Jim had eavesdropped on (in his own mind, he was "spying") evidently were convinced that Ellis had been poisoned when his mission was exposed, and that the pharmacist's amnesia was drug-induced.

After the two boys had tiptoed upstairs and tucked themselves in under their mosquito nets, Jim's friend whispered, "My dad would kill both of us if we ever told anyone about that." Jim, never doubting that the officer would indeed do so, had promised, "Scout's honor, I swear I never will."

Captain Ind's chances of learning that particular spy story were slight, for now in 1941, Ellis's 30,000-word 1921 report was still classified.

This trip had made Jim realize just how effectively Australia and New Zealand were separated from the U.S. mainland — just as the Philippines were — by something like a vast minefield, formed of those 3,000 Mandated Islands.

Jim thought about Amelia and the massive effort to find her. *If we need to be rescued from Rabaul, no one will ever read about it in the newspapers.*

"Sir, do you think President Roosevelt knows what General Brereton is doing in Australia?"

"Of course he does, son."

"What would happen if a paper — like the *Chicago Tribune* — found out about it, and accused the President of violating the Neutrality Act?"

"He'd just have to deny any knowledge of it; perhaps call General Brereton a 'loose cannon,' acting without authority."

"My mother would never believe the President would lie. He's like a saint to her."

"Do you feel that way about him?"

"Well, I used to. I guess I don't believe in saints so much anymore." He wanted to add: *Since I learned about FDR's goddam Rainbow Plan, I've lost all my illusions.* But he could not mention that forbidden knowledge to anyone.

I get the impression that Ind himself doesn't know about Rainbow yet. But surely Brereton and Eubank must know.

Almost three hours into the operation of digging out the Flying Fortress, Brereton removed his cigar from his mouth and announced, "Thanks to Colonel Eubank's skilled piloting, it appears there's no serious damage."

Everyone applauded and whistled. Jim gulped down the last drops of his second quart of Koala beer.

Towing lines from the tractors had been attached to the rings on the main gear. Eubank and Brereton climbed up through the nose hatch. Jim and the other Americans were joined by about 25 sturdy Diggers and local Melanesian men on each side, to push forward on the undercarriage and on every other strong surface. Fortunately, most of the thin-skinned areas were too high to be touched and damaged.

All the Diggers and blacks were as tall as Jim, or even taller, so they had to crouch, as he did, to get a hand-hold to push on. As Jim strained with all his strength, sweaty hands slipped off the hot metal, men swore and fell in the ash-pit, the roaring Caterpillars labored, spewing ash dust on the men. The four engines thundered; as Jim felt their mighty vibration he wondered if Eubank was pushing the manifold pressure beyond the red line. *That man can make a plane do things it doesn't know it can do,* he thought.

Slowly . . . the huge plane inched forward, climbed out of its crater, rolled to the *Safe Limit* section of the runway, and waited impatiently for Jim and the others to scramble up through the fuselage hatch.

As they rose over Simpson Bay and out through the 11-mile-wide entrance, choking again in The Mother's fumes, Jim, exhausted, tried to stay awake to view the spectacular vistas on either side.

He heard Brereton, in the right-hand seat of the cockpit, say curtly over his microphone, "Lefty, cancel your survey for Rabaul. 'Rubble' would be a better name — and at the rate those volcanoes are working, that's what it soon will be. That stinking dump will *not* be made a ferry stop."

Tough cheddar, Mangrove City — your chance to make history just blew away on a cloud of your Mother's smoke!

Brereton had been so incensed over the near-accident that he had told Lefty not to present Flying Officer Robinson with the case of San Miguel that had been intended for him, as the man in charge of the detachment at Lakunai. Captain Ind, however, had enjoyed talking with the England-born Robinson, and he had made a plea on behalf of the Sergeant.

"Sir, he's a fine 'Shropshire lad,' doing his best out here — and he has no materials available with which to strengthen the runway."

General Brereton had relented.

God knows the poor blokes deserved it, after being out here for almost eleven months, Jim thought. After a few hours in Rabaul, he felt thirsty enough to chug-a-lug the entire case of beer himself.

Mercifully, they would be spared the frigid climb over the Owen Stanleys, notorious for building up thick clouds each afternoon. Instead, Eubank would take the long way around, making an "end run" across Milne Bay, the split between the final two feathers in the Guinea-bird's tail.

Jim heard Brereton tell Eubank, "Damned if I feel like going to that bloody Dining-In shindig tonight. Can't we get out of it?"

Jim wanted to shout, "I second the motion!" For the first time in his 21 years, he did not feel like partying. Although he had enjoyed the Dining-In occasions in Singapore, that dressed-up formal tradition seemed out of place in a backwater like Port Moresby.

*Hell, we'll swelter in our white suit-jackets — and **neckties**,* he thought. *All I want is a shower and a beer and a bed — even that bed-of-nails RAAF cot.*

"Lewie," Eubank replied, "they've been saving their beer ration for us. And tomorrow we go back to Australia."

Well, that's something to celebrate, anyway, Jim thought just before he fell asleep: *leaving miserable Moresby, never to return — and holding Penny's beautiful body in my arms tomorrow night. I'll gladly drink a couple of toasts to that prospect.*

Chapter 6

A Dining-In

No cares have I to grieve me,
No pretty little girls to deceive me.
I'm happy as a king, believe me,
As we go rolling, rolling home.
Rolling home, rolling home,
By the light of the silvery moo-oo-oon,
Happy is the day when the airman gets his pay,
As we go rolling, rolling home.
   — Royal Air Force song, "I've Got Sixpence"

RAAF Clubhouse, Port Moresby
Monday night, 17 November 1941

    The evening turned out far better — and far worse — than Jim had anticipated. Returning from Rabaul, Eubank had "poured on the coal," making the end run south of New Guinea's tail in good time. Back at Seven Mile, the B-17's rugged undercarriage again proved its mettle by enduring the pitch-and-toss landing. The late afternoon sun was just warming up for its spectacular show over the distant Indian Ocean, and there was sufficient light for Allison Ind to film the buxom marys assembled to greet the plane.
    This he did, to his evident pleasure and theirs. They smiled broadly as they filed past his lens in an impromptu parade with their babies on their hips, their

gleaming brown breasts swaying and displaying their tattoos. To Jim, however, something was missing; the camera was strangely silent. Then he saw that Ind was circling his closed fist in the air beside it.

"Where's your crank?"

"Quiet, son. . . . It must have slipped from its clip, unobserved, at Lakunai Airdrome. But I couldn't disappoint these willing, dusky ladies by letting them know that their innocent display of nature's bountiful endowments is not being recorded permanently. What the maidenly eye cannot see, the maidenly heart cannot grieve."

Jim saluted. "Sir, chivalry's not dead, as long as you're alive!"

After a shower of unheated-but-warm water in the lavatory hut and a brief siesta on the bed-of-nails metal cot, Jim was ready for some of the dark, delicious XXXX beer from Queensland. The welcome word came down that jackets and neckties would be classed as "improper attire."

In the Officers' Mess hut, the Dining-In started with an Australian version of formality: toasts to the King and Queen and to President Roosevelt, a brief hail-and-farewell speech from Squadron Leader Pearce and a hands-across-the-sea reply from Brereton.

Dinner consisted of the usual "tinned tucker," augmented by a mystery stew which turned out to be crocodile. Jim had sampled the pale rubbery meat in Mindanao and had not yet acquired a taste for it, but his good appetite and plenty of beer to wash it down took care of that. The table decoration was a 50-pound jackfruit, the largest Jim had ever seen. The cut halves, seeded and laid lengthwise on the bare wooden table, resembled green-hulled canoes for pygmies, cushioned inside with pulp like rich yellow satin. For dessert, everyone marched around the table singing, spoon in hand, and dug into the jackfruit in passing. This began to get messy; the floor became perilously slippery, and soon the Flight Lieutenant who served as master of ceremonies proclaimed a "Major Bones' Amateur Hour," a takeoff on the U.S. radio show of Major Bowes, to begin forthwith in the RAAF Clubhouse.

The long, low RAAF Clubhouse, with its walls and peaked ceiling of raw, unadorned wood, looked to Jim just like a boys' camp "rec hall"; but the songs were rowdier, and the Clubhouse had an "Oasis" along one end. No Yanks could buy beer tonight — RAAF Squadrons No. 11 and No. 20 were "shouting" (treating).

Because the hall lacked a stage, performers were to stand on the Oasis/bar, while the master of ceremonies, "Major Bones," stood by with a washbasin "gong" to silence each unimpressive contestant. The visiting Americans were required to perform first.

Allison Ind stepped up on a chair beside the bar, but popular demand compelled him to step onto the bar itself. His fervent recitation of "Casey at the Bat" was well received by their sports-loving hosts.

Chapter 6 — A Dining-In

Eubank was next to ascend the Oasis. He told a hillbilly story in a broad Texas accent with a relaxed, twangy delivery that intensified his resemblance to Will Rogers and convulsed the audience. The Australians kept applauding and demanding encores, until finally he pleaded that he had exhausted his repertoire.

No one would ever guess what that man's been through today, Jim thought, proud to be on the same team with Eubank, who surely would prove to be "the star performer of the evening," in Brereton's words.

General Brereton had just made that comment to Jim when Dr. Edward Thomas Brennan, the huge jovial Public Health administrator of Papua, said, "Up you go, myte," and placing his big hands under Brereton's armpits, boosted the General to the bar-top.

Jim stared, expecting lightning to strike; but Brereton only grinned his irresistible boyish grin and launched into a bawdy English song from the World War about Piccadilly Lilly and her enterprising relatives. It drew such laughter that Jim decided his own contribution would not need to be a Sunday-school piece.

Well primed by now with the strong Fourex beer, Jim had been longing for his clarinet. He knew that his variations on Glenn Miller's "String of Pearls" would have been a crowd-pleaser; but the only musical instrument in the Clubhouse was a wind-up phonograph. He sang "Please Don't Burn the Outhouse Down," a sort of American version of "Piccadilly Lilly," concerning a family down on its luck by trying to get ahead. As he launched into the first line, he realized that "outhouse" might be an unknown word to Australians; but they joined heartily in the chorus, substituting "shit-house," and gave him a table-thumping response with calls of "Good on you, myte!"

Later, one of the Aussies proposed a toast to "Joe DeMygio! The pypers call him a 'Yankee Clipper,' so he must be one of you-lot. They sye he's managed to hit the byseball in fifty-six consecutive gymes in two months of this past winter season, and any bloke who can do that must be a dinkum Yank!" Jim was touched by this tribute to his hero's batting streak.

Then he thought of Hank Greenberg. How many hits might Hank have made, if he hadn't been so patriotic and missed the season? Although Greenberg, the consistent hitter for the Detroit Tigers, was 30 years old and not required to register for the draft, he had done so, and his number had been called. The day after his two home runs on 6 May had given the Tigers a victory over DiMaggio and the Yankees, Greenberg reported for duty at Fort Custer, Michigan.

When a beer-toast to "The mighty Casey at the wicket!" led to the singing of "For He's a Jolly Good Fellow," Jim took the entire Royal Australian Air Force to his heart. Of course he would gladly give his life to help them defend Australia . . . and even New Guinea. Even Miserable Moresby!

A mass songfest evolved, and he was pleasantly surprised to find how many songs the two groups knew in common: picnic-type, sentimental, and merrily obscene bar-songs. Singapore parties with the RAF and the Scots served his memory well now. When Eubank and Brereton sang the World War ballads — "Tipperary," "Pack Up Your Troubles," and "Mademoiselle from Armentieres," the young RAAF officers joined in lustily. Like Jim, they had learned from listening to older fliers, allies in that war. The visitors taught their hosts a few American favorites, and the Aussies, in turn, sang the RAF's "Gremlin Song" and rendered some bush ballads: about tying a kangaroo down, a wild colonial boy who scorned to live in slavery, and the rousing one concerning the sheep-stealing hobo who drowns himself in the billabong.

New Guinea had inspired its own bush ballad, which began, "I love to see mary pee."

At one point, Flight Lieutenant Mac Lexington, sitting beside Jim remarked, "Bloody shyme about the bloody beer austerity." Jim agreed heartily.

"Keeps a party so bloody *dry*. Before the war, we'd have poured so much beer on the floor by now, we'd be up to our arses in it!"

Jim laughed. He felt like giving each of the Aussies a goodbye hug; he hated to leave them in this rotten place; he wanted to take them with him tomorrow, back to their beloved "Lucky Land." *Now,* he thought, *I really know what Mateship means.*

His new mates were singing a tune with an almost martial beat that somehow projected a haunting sadness. The lyrics told of a girl who waited every night under a lamp post by a barracks gate. Her name did not sound Australian — "Lili Marlene."

"That's from you-lot," said Lexington. "Our blokes overseas learned it from that bloody Yank tart." He sounded angry enough to fight.

"I don't get it. It's sure not an American song. What's the story?"

He soon regretted asking, as the jolly evening turned black. At first, he fought against believing what his table-mates now told him: His fellow-American, a woman, was despised by the Australians — and by the British — for her poisonous broadcasts from Berlin of Nazi propaganda, beamed to the Commonwealth troops in North Africa. Her name was Mildred Gillars, and on her program, "The Club of Nations," she played American records, favorites of the Diggers and the Pommies, as well as this "Lili Marlene," popular with German troops in the Afrika Corps.

In mock-syrupy tones, the RAAF officers quoted for Jim her daily opening words: "Hello, gang. Throw down those little old guns and toddle off home. There's no getting the Germans down!"

"We call her Axis Sally. She bears down hard on our blokes, because she knows they're fourteen thousand miles from home. She teases 'em, saying

Chapter 6 — A Dining-In

'You-lot had better hurry back Down Under, before you lose your sheilas. Don't you know your wife's now *down under* a bastard from the Home Guard, right in your own bed? Come on, Cobbers, it's so easy to surrender — just hold up your hands and say *kamerad,* and the Germans will take you out of that filthy desert, and you'll soon be on your way home.'"

Jim felt physically ill. He had been ashamed of his countrymen before: ashamed to learn of American soldiers' water-torture of Filipino prisoners during the "insurrection," ashamed of the American authorities at Brent School whose racial policy had caused him to quit school in protest, ashamed of Punch who had caused the young pregnant Filipina's suicide — but this American woman in Berlin was something unnatural, like Quisling in Norway, working for the enemy.

Was Axis Sally a "traitor"?

When Lindbergh was called one for asserting that Germany was unbeatably strong, Jim defended him by arguing that since the U.S. was not at war, public statements could not be classed as treason.

Evidently his Australian table-mates saw the pain he was feeling. They made warm efforts to convince him that they did not blame him, or any other Yanks, for Mildred Gillars' broadcasts, and then they insisted that he join them in some more rowdy songs.

Still, he felt relieved when Brereton announced that the Americans — much against their will — must get some sleep, in view of their early takeoff for Brisbane.

Brisbane? He means Townsville. The General must be drunker — more "sparky" — than he looks.

Walking to the barracks beside Jim, under the huge golden stars, Allison Ind looked up at the brilliant Southern Cross. "When Jesus was on earth, he could see that constellation. From Jerusalem, it was visible on the horizon at the time of his crucifixion. And Dante speaks of it in his *Divine Comedy*. But as it continues to move southward, eventually Australians and New Zealanders will only be able to see it on their flags."

"Then *we'll* be able to use it for navigation, some day."

"I hope our jolly sing-sing didn't make the natives apprehensive."

"I doubt it. Probably just makes 'em think maybe Whitefellows are human, too," Jim replied.

"Well, I hope they'll be quieter tonight. I'm dreading that thirteen-hundred-mile flight tomorrow."

"But Townsville's not half that far!"

"General Brereton's decided to skip Townsville and go straight to Brisbane."

Damn the luck! I won't see Penny till we head home from Melbourne.

In the spartan barracks the open windows let in the lusty young voices from the Clubhouse, still singing:

> *Fuck 'em all! Fuck 'em all!*
> *The young and the short and the tall,*
> *Fuck all the blondies and all the brunettes,*
> *Each airman is happy to take what he gets.*
> *So we're giving the eye to them all:*
> *To those who attract and appall,*
> *Each Sally and Susie,*
> *You can't be too choosy —*
> *So cheer up, my lads,*
> *Fuck 'em all!*

Chapter 7

Part 1 — To Brisbane

The kangaroo can jump incredible.
He has to jump because he's edible.
I could not eat a kangaroo.
But many fine Australians do.
Those with cookbooks as well as boomerangs
Prefer him in tasty kangaroo-meringues.
 — Ogden Nash, Verse to Saint-Saens's,
 "Carnival of the Animals"

Above the Coral Sea
Tuesday, 18 November 1941

How many men have been lucky enough to see both ends of the twelve-hundred-mile-long Great Barrier Reef? Jim wondered, as its southern extremity, the spectacular triangle of the Swain High — 100 miles to a side — flowed below the B-17. *Certainly, damned few Americans have!*

Although he surely could not claim to have surveyed all of its 80,000 square miles of 3,000 atolls, islands, and cays, he had viewed hundreds of them in their myriad forms. Looking through the crystal lens of the shallow waters, he had marveled over dozens of shades of coral. Winged seeds of casuarina trees, and floating coconuts, had taken root on golden-sand islands, and their leaves swayed dark green over the pale green water. Over the centuries those tiny sea creatures had wrought a giant sea-chain, forming a Coral Archipelago of infinite variety.

Today he knew the names of the aerial armadas which rose in such numbers that the shadows they cast on the sea were far larger than that of the Fortress. He recognized the flight patterns of the terns and the petrels, grossly nicknamed, he thought, "muttonbirds" for their flavor.

Swain Reef formed a green signpost pointing south toward Capricorn Channel, off Australia's east coast. Capricorn Channel was a signpost to a marker that existed only on maps and in men's minds.

Although he had never seen a copy of Henry Miller's *Tropic of Capricorn*, the mere knowledge that the book was banned in the U.S. gave Jim an anticipatory itchy feeling about traveling south of that latitude right now. He was leaving his old familiar Torrid Zone — perhaps to find a new and more torrid one, he hoped. That thought mitigated his disappointment in having to postpone his return to Townsville and Penny.

He was thankful that General Brereton had given his final approval to the choice of Townsville as a major depot, over Rockhampton, farther south on the Tropic of Cancer. Perhaps the Fitzroy River's huge rocks, which gave the town its name, had posed questions about the terrain's suitability for a landing field. Or Townsville's deep bay might have tipped the scales in its favor. Jim only knew that his chances of seeing Penny again would have been nil at Rockhampton.

Rockhampton, like Penny's home town of Mackay, was sugar-cane country. Two things Penny had told him had astounded him: first, that in Australia the grueling work of cane-cutting was done by white men. Of course it was; there were no other hands to do it, but Jim still could not picture such a thing. She also had told him that many of the cane plantations had been developed by Italian immigrants, but were now being taken over by "British Aussies." Probably 70,000 Italians had settled in Northern Queensland, and many of those considered "of dubious loyalty" were being loaded on trains to be interned away from the coast.

Jim had been shocked. "How can their loyalty be disproved?"

"Well, if they were born in Italy — that's an enemy country — they have to be investigated."

"But how can they live? How can they grow any food, if they're taken inland where it never rains?"

"Oh, they're good at grapes, and grapes don't need much rain. The Eyeties can make wine."

"But Australians don't drink wine. Who'll buy it?"

"They can sell it to each other."

* * * * *

Over the milky jade-green Coral Sea, he played the role of radioman and was successful in tuning in on New Zealand's government radio station, 3YA, broadcasting "gramophone records" of haunting Maori songs. He regretted that there would be no chance on this trip to view New Zealand's renowned scenic beauty, or to try the sport fishing that Wild West author Zane Grey had revealed to the world. Most of all, he would have enjoyed flying southeast from Australia across the Tasman Sea to Auckland, along the path first traced by the great Australian pilots Kingsford-Smith and Ulm in 1928 — the same year they had made the first trans-Pacific flight.

Francis Chichester, after making his fortune in New Zealand, had flown alone in 1930 on the world's first long-distance seaplane flight over those 1,400 miles from New Zealand to Australia.

New Zealand had no national airline to cause the rivalry that was still keeping Pan American Airways out of Australia, and the isolated island nation had welcomed overtures from PAA. Pan American's world-famed *Clipper* pilot, Captain Edwin C. Musick, made a survey flight of the proposed route in March 1937, and Jim remembered the newsreels of that jubilant welcome. The entire population of both islands seemed to be on hand to greet Musick when he set down PAA's Sikorsky S-42B in Auckland Harbour.

Jim had empathized fully with the New Zealanders' exuberant ovation, for at age 15, he had cheered with the throngs beside Manila Bay when Musick splashed down there after the first flight of PAA's *China Clipper* on 29 November 1935. On that day, symbolized by more than 110,000 Air Mail letters delivered, Manila had moved from the world's shipping lanes to the air lanes. Musick had taken off from Alameda, California, on 22 November, exactly 100 years after the first clipper ship had sailed into San Francisco Bay. He had stopped overnight at Honolulu, Midway and Wake Islands, and Guam, thus shrinking the 8,000-mile Pacific crossing from a two-week steamer trip to 59 hours and 48 minutes of flying time.

New Zealand had not been so fortunate. During Christmas week of 1937, the *Samoan Clipper* made the first scheduled flight from Honolulu to Auckland. In January 1938, en route New Zealand on the second regular flight, Ed Musick and the *Samoan Clipper* went into the sea after leaving Pago-Pago, for reasons never determined. PAA employees all over the world paid respects to their great pilot with a simultaneous, unpublicized five minutes of silence.

With the S-42B gone, New Zealand's "air bridge" was also lost and service suspended. Barely a year ago, in the fall of 1940, Pan American had resumed passenger and mail service to Auckland from Honolulu.

Sir Charles Kingsford-Smith eventually had crossed the Tasman Sea six times in his *Southern Cross*. Once in 1935, in spite of illness, he insisted on flying Jubilee-postmark mail from Australia to New Zealand. His Sydney-born copilot, Patrick Gordon Taylor, proved his mettle when one engine threatened to "go crook" due to an oil leak. *Six times,* Taylor belly-crawled out on a wing with oil to replenish the engine. For saving "the Old *Cross"* and its crew, he later received the George Cross.

Taylor attributed his charmed life in the air to the "lucky" brown leather flying helmet he had worn in the Royal Flying Corps in 1917, when he shot down a German plane over France. It became so stained and scarred that his friends chided him for wearing it when he landed to face the welcoming American crowds in Hawaii and Oakland in 1934, having flown from Brisbane with Kingsford-Smith in the Lockheed Altair *Lady Southern Cross.* Later, he had done movie flying for the Kingsford-Smith story *Smithy;* but Jim thought Taylor's 35 years of pioneer flying deserved a film of his own. Jim pictured himself playing the role of Taylor in the wing-crawling scene: dark hair whipping into his eyes; hands clutching the sides of the wing; a shot of the raging sea below — a sudden downdraft — his hands slip — and the audience gasps. . . .

Movie hunger! Until now, since childhood Jim had never spent an entire week without seeing a movie.

Maybe it's just as well we're going to have a taste of city life, and let New Zealand's scenery wait till my next trip. In New Guinea I saw enough of nature — in the raw or semi-clad — to last me for a while. Now I'm ready for a sophisticated city, full of movie palaces, bright lights, cold drinks, good food.

Hot showers! Hot jazz! Hot lips! Hot-eyed red-hot mamas who can't keep their hot hands off a Hot Pilot! Tall, blonde, friendly "sheilas": smooth dancers, good drinkers, good laughers, with those marvelous sheila-legs. . . .

* * * * *

Officially, this Brisbane landing had two justifications: General Brereton wanted to establish a major repair depot somewhere, and the Brisbane bulge on the map appeared to be a good location. Still, the Americans had learned from the Northern Territory that Australian terrain could not be judged by its appearance on a map. Rivers, for example, had proved to be dry gullies, invisible from an airplane.

Another plus for Brisbane: Its Amberley Airdrome possessed the only runway south of Townsville that was long enough for the Fortress to land on. In order to fly to Melbourne for talks with the highest Australian authorities, the group would trans-plane here and divide into two sections. Slugger Pell, the indefatigable liaison man, would be waiting at Amberley with a B-18 and another plane that could land safely at Melbourne. Actually, no one was certain that Amberley itself could take this bomber's weight, because No.

Chapter 7 — Part 1 — To Brisbane 177

40-3097 would be the first B-17 ever to land there.

We're making history, Jim thought — *and now we're following the flight path of Kingsford-Smith!*

In the week of Jim's eighth birthday, on 31 May 1928, the Australian World War ace (eight German planes downed), with his Australian copilot, Flight Lieutenant C. P. T. Ulm, had departed from Oakland, California, in the *Southern Cross:* destination — Brisbane. Their boldness was measured against the disastrous results a few months earlier of the Oakland-Honolulu air race sponsored by James B. Dole, who had offered $17,500 to each of the first two pilots who could fly from Oakland to Honolulu. Ten persons had been killed in connection with the race and the subsequent rescue missions.

To Jim, the participation of several Americans in the Australians' trans-Pacific attempt was a source of pride. The Fokker F. VII had been lent to them by an American rancher, G. Allan Hancock; its three Wright Whirlwind J5A engines and extra fuel tanks were installed by Boeing in Seattle; and the navigator, Harry W. Lyon, Jr., and radio operator, James W. Warner, were both Americans.

Together the four men safely flew the 2,400 miles to Honolulu; then on, through a night of tropical storms, to land on the cricket grounds of Albert Park at Suva, Fiji, for a record nonstop overwater distance of 3,144 miles. After taking off from the cricket field's 300-yard strip for the relatively short flight to Brisbane, 1,780 miles, fierce winds and rains battered them; their induction compass "went crook," and their magnetic compasses became unreliable, allowing the Fokker to veer 110 miles off course. However, when the morning light revealed Australia's coastline, "Smithy" had no difficulty locating Brisbane, his birthplace. A huge, cheering crowd greeted the *Southern Cross* after its 7,347-mile flight: elapsed flying time — 3 days, 11 hours, 11 minutes.

Copilot Charles Philippe Thomas Ulm, rejected by the RAF, had fought for England on the ground at Gallipoli, as so many other Australians had; and like so many other Australians there, had been wounded — three times. He had kept the name "Charles" for his *nom de guerre,* calling himself "Charles Jackson." Jim had never been able to learn what type of secret work had required Ulm to disguise his identity; but he enjoyed speculating.

Sadly, their luck had abandoned the pair later, Jim recalled. Six years ago, a few months after the Jubilee mail flight with Taylor, Kingsford-Smith was flying *Lady Southern Cross* from England to Australia when he and the *Lady* disappeared over Burma.

The sea that they had defied finally claimed Ulm near Honolulu in December 1934, ending his attempted trans-Pacific flight in *Stella Australis*.

And now the American Charles — "Lucky Lindy" — had fallen into misfortune, too: his baby boy kidnapped and murdered, his patriotism questioned.

* * * * *

In the distance Jim saw the Glass House Mountains (where no one ever throws stones, he surmised). Their charming name was quickly matched by Mount Glorious and little Mount Coot-tha, and those in turn subsided to low hills splashed yellow with masses of a flowering tree or shrub. Neat fruit orchards and farms merged into green suburbs from which long boulevards, brilliantly outlined with blooming plants, led into a handsome, low, wide-spreading city, backed by a park as large as all downtown, with a golf course gracing one corner. Impressive buildings dominated by a tall clock-tower almost filled a peninsula that was tipped by another tree-filled park, the size of a dozen city blocks. That central-city peninsula nestled in one of several horseshoe bends of a river. A real *river*, broad and generously winding, the Brisbane River appeared to Jim to be dawdling its way into Moreton Bay as if loath to leave a land where its water was prized far more than gold.

How Kingsford-Smith must have rejoiced when he saw this beautiful city beneath his **Southern Cross**, Jim thought. *He probably homed on that prominent old clock-tower. Now I understand why so many Aussies have told me, "Too bad you Yanks came in by the back door!" After Desolate Darwin, Tropical Townsville, Pitiful Port Moresby, and Rotten-smelling Rabaul, here at last is a fine metropolis, worthy of being the capital of this enormous state of Queensland.*

Brisbane's commercial airport, Archerfield, lay eight miles from the city. RAAF No. 23 Squadron was based there now, a composite squadron with three Hudsons and twelve of the ubiquitous Wirraways.

Closer to the city was the flying boat base with the delightful name of Pinkenba. But Jim was shocked to see obsolete Curtiss Seagull amphibians still in service at Pinkenba. When he was two years old, walking with his *amah*, Saadra, on Parañaque beach near his home, he had loved to see the mahogany hulls and khaki fabric wings of Seagulls flown by the Philippine Army Air Corps, taking off and landing there on Manila Bay.

Amberley Aerodrome, about 60 miles southwest of Brisbane, spread alongside a little town called Ipswich. That so-English name seemed incongruous to Jim, for the land was fecund with tropical fruits: neat plantations of banana and custard-apple trees, fields of pineapples, and dark green mango trees. At the heart of each plantation sat a rambling frame house, looking comfortable, unpretentious, and inviting, raised on sturdy posts and wrapped with a wide verandah draped with bright-flowered vines.

The field was comfortably large, and its dark runways, composed of tarmacadam (nicknamed "tarmac") appeared reassuringly solid. Neatly lined up were more parked airplanes than Jim had seen in all of Australia. In addition to the uniformed figures down there, a number of civilians seemed to be waving a welcome. He could imagine how Kingsford-Smith felt when he made his final approach, that chilly morning of 9 June 1928, after history's first trans-Pacific crossing. Surely his weary, weatherbeaten, craggy face must have cracked in a huge grin.

Hail, conquering heroes of the skies! But we've flown only thirteen hundred miles today from Port Moresby — in perfect weather, unlike Kingsford-Smith's nightmare final leg from Fiji. Those people must have come here for something more important than us. The days of "CHEERING THRONGS GREET PLANE" headlines that thrilled me as a kid are all over. Now planes are so scientifically designed, so full of accurate instruments, and so common everywhere — even in New Guinea! — that they're almost like cars and buses. The only excitement left is bad weather. The record-smashing, the gamble, the romance of those golden days of aviation are gone forever, dammit.

Part 2 — "Beaut" Brisbane

A Reef such as is here spoke of is scarcely known in Europe, it is a wall of Coral Rock rising all most perpendicular out of the unfathomable Ocean . . . the large waves of the vast Ocean meeting with so sudden a resistance make a most terrible surf breaking mountain high especially in our case when the general trade wind blowes directly upon it.
— James Cook in his Journal, 1770

Brisbane, Queensland
Tuesday afternoon, 18 November 1941

It was good to see Slugger Pell again, standing beside the hard crushed-rock-and-tar runway. He told Jim, "These Aussie civilians have been here since daybreak, waiting to see the 'Seventeen land. They were terribly disappointed when I arrived in the old B-18, so I'm glad you made it! Loads of gorgeous girls have been coming up to shake my hand and tell me I'm the first Yank they've ever seen except a few rich tourist snobs from a cruise ship. And when *you* got off the plane — all the girls around me were asking if you were married, and how long you'd be in Brisbane!"

"They'd better watch out. I feel as if I've been in the jungle for months, with nothing but men around. Helluva way to live."

The 54 parked airplanes were Avro Anson British-built, twin-engine trainers, belonging to No. 3 Service Flying Training School based at Amber-

Chapter 7 — Part 2 — "Beaut" Brisbane

ley. Gilly Douglas, one of the instructors who greeted the Americans, told them, "As of January this year, we were graduating four hundred new pilots every month, from all our flying schools put together. But by last month, we had upped the total number who got their wings to fourteen hundred, and we plan to continue to graduate that many every month."

The instructor sounded proud — deservedly so, Jim thought. When Jim had entered Primary flying school at Randolph Field in 1939, fewer than 300 pilots were graduated annually from Kelly Field (then the U.S. Army's only Advanced flight school), after the 12-month course. Now the course had been cut to seven and a half months; the Randolph-Kelly annual quota had been expanded to 7,000 pilots; and with new flying schools being established all over the U.S., a total of 30,000 pilots were being awarded their silver wings every year.

. . . *Considering the vast disparity in population,* Jim thought, *I dips me lid to the Royal Aussie flying instructors.*

General Brereton, chewing his cigar, appeared favorably impressed with the airdrome as a site for his proposed repair depot. He was angry, however, about the crowd of civilian greeters — concerned that the news of his secret mission might reach Japan — although Slugger already had elicited a promise of silence from the editors of the *Courier-Mail* and the evening *Telegraph.*

"They won't print anything about this visit," Slugger murmured to Jim, "but I think every paper in Australia has reported the leak of a secret memo from General Marshall, about our B-17s at Clark Field — that they're the strongest concentration of heavy bombers in the world, and they could defend the Philippines without any help from the Navy. If Japan attacked, he said, the Forts could burn Japan's 'paper cities' to the ground."

"But they couldn't fly that far — and back — without refueling!"

"I guess General Marshall hopes the Japs don't know the Forts' range."

The air felt cool and dry after New Guinea, not desert-dry like Darwin; pleasantly humid, but not so steamy as Townsville. *Now, when the Aussies tell me "November is like May in Australia," I can finally believe them.*

Half the group would go on to Melbourne tomorrow with Pell in the B-18 he had flown down from Clark Field. The others, including Jim, would fly there in a Hudson with an RAAF pilot from No. 23 Squadron at Archerfield.

Not much choice between those twin-engine birds: both noisy, hot, and not exactly designed with passenger comfort in mind. Damn, I'd hoped for something more exotic — maybe a twin-engine British Dragon-Rapide; now, there's a name with sex appeal!

The long ride into Brisbane on an Army bus was well compensated by the pleasant scenery. Jim sat in front, right behind the young uniformed driver. Friendly, broad-shouldered, and pretty, she seemed delighted to answer his questions and to volunteer information — apparently not merely as her duty assignment, but from innate hospitality. Her evident pride in her country and her city of "Brisbun" did not, however, lead her to claim perfection for them.

The cascades of yellow blossoms tinting the hills were "golden wattles," she said, "our national flower." The farmhouses were built high off the ground, not in fear of floods but to hold off termites. "Without the metal plates on the posts, the bloody bugs would gobble up your house while you slept!"

Jim felt at home with the brilliant tropical flowers. The vines on the verandahs were bougainvillea; hedges were formed of hibiscus; and poinsettias grew as tall as he. Among the flame-flowered royal poinciana trees that lined the highway, he noticed a tree some distance ahead whose green branches were laden with large pink and white flowers.

"It's a galah tree," she answered his query. "Look sharp at it as we pass by."

The tree was on the left and Australian drivers, like those in the Philippines, drove on the left. As Jim looked past her attractive profile, the "blossoms" tumbled out and flew away, screeching harsh cries.

She was a good laugher. Galahs, she giggled, were pink-breasted white cockatoos. "They're such silly birds, we call a silly person a 'galah.'"

Australia had more than 600 species of birds, she said. "And every Aussie's a dinkum bird-lover. Maybe that's because our continent broke off from Asia before we got any big mammals to love."

The majority of birds he saw now were fruit-eaters and new to Jim; but the fearless black-and-white magpies he had first seen in Darwin were here also, doing the same kind of crazy, fighter-pilot aerobatics.

Those seem like good omens, fighter pilots and pink-breasted sillies. . . .

Every state in Australia, she said, contained "jillions more birds than people." She had grown up on a farm at Mooloolaba, 90 miles north of Brisbane. Queensland was home to 20 million sheep and to just under 1 million persons, of whom 300,000 lived in Brisbane. The winding Brisbane River had been discovered by three escaped convicts. Later, a prison colony had been established on the site of the present city, opened to free settlers only 99 years ago. Queensland's area was "larger than France, Ireland, Italy —"

She ticked off the names on her fingertips while she steered with her elbows. With a copilot's reflex, Jim reached over her broad shoulder and took hold of the wheel, although the highway was broad and straight, and there was no other vehicle to be seen.

"— Great Britain, Portugal, and Spain — all put together!" she concluded.

Allison Ind, seated beside Jim, had been writing in his pocket notebook while he kindly let Jim monopolize the conversation. Now he obviously could not resist the chance to acquire some specific information for his massive survey. He had already noted the area of each state; Queensland contained 670,500 square miles.

"So that gives those fewer-than-seven-hundred-thousand Queenslanders in

Chapter 7 — Part 2 — "Beaut" Brisbane

the countryside almost one square mile apiece," he remarked.

"Yes, Sir. But it's worse in the Northern Territory and Western Australia — two miles or more for each of those poor blokes to rattle around in. It's our biggest problem, underpopulation — fewer than the city of Tokyo! Our seven million are scattered thin, in a country almost as big as the States — where you-lot have more than a hundred million!"

More than *130* million, Jim corrected her mentally. He had often heard his mother bewail the increase above the turn-of-the-century million mark. If it reaches 150 million, Leda predicted, the AmerIndians — who traditionally limited the size of *their* families — would surely be robbed of their remaining lands. Jim and David used to tease Leda, "As soon as all the starving Irish had arrived, they wanted to pull up the drawbridge."

Ind said, "But our desert area doesn't compare in size with yours. The United States can grow more food than Australia possibly could."

"Oh, we don't intend to run a baby race with you Yanks — nor yet with the bloody Japs and their 'propagate and multiply' scheme!"

In January, Japan had embarked on a 20-year population plan declared essential "to provide leadership for Asia." The government would encourage couples to marry at an earlier age, with the national norm an average three years younger by 1950. Abortion and all forms of birth control would be illegal. Setting a goal of a five-child family, by 1960 a nation of 100 million Japanese was envisioned for the mountainous island empire of 142,300 square miles, excluding the Mandated Islands.

In the Philippines, however, with 115,000 square miles and a longer growing season than Japan's, the Filipinos had been unable to grow enough rice to feed their 18 million, and annually imported rice from Indochina.

The driver continued, "Our labor unions want to limit immigration, so there'll always be a job for every Aussie. Ever since the Depression began, we've been the only country not suffering unemployment, and they want to keep it that way. Sure, with the war production, and so many of our blokes overseas, we could use some more hands now — but after the war's over, they wouldn't want to go home, and they'd be fighting us for jobs."

Ind asked, "Are you referring to Orientals?"

"Too right, myte. If we let down the bars for six months, you can be bloody certain that sixty thousand Asiatics would come pouring in. And at the ryte they multiply, in a couple of generations our cities would be as teeming and filthy as Calcutta or Shanghai or Tokyo — while we whites would be pushed into the sea! We've been overrun with the bloody *rabbits,* and we learned our lesson. Our goal is to get our numbers up to twenty million, by bringing in two hundred thousand new settlers from Great Britain every year.

"But with the bloody German sea raiders sinking passenger ships, it's got too dangerous for emigrants from the British Isles to make the journey —

much as they'd surely like to. Just before the war, England took in almost ten thousand Jewish children from Germany, and now, God knows, they'd be far safer here, if they could come."

Jim thought of the *St. Louis* and its human cargo of more than 900 Jewish refugees whom no nation in the Americas would accept, who had been forced to return to Nazi-threatened Europe after 40 days of sailing 10,000 miles. He thought of the newcomers to Manila who were adding so much to the city's cultural life — refugees including Mona Lisa Steiner, the artist/botanist; Trudl Dubsky, the ballerina; and lovely Hanna Kaunitz.

"Some Jews are still managing to escape from Germany and get to Shanghai and Manila," he told her. "I'll bet a lot of them would be willing to risk the boat trip down to here — and they'd be good citizens, smart and hard-working."

"Yes, and they're white — and intellectual, too. But that's the trouble — they're *city* people, and we've too many city people now. Jews couldn't stand the isolated life on a sheep station, with no concerts or theaters. . . . Now I'm going to make a couple of quick detours to show you-lot Brisbane's best sights. Bloody shame you have to go down to Melbun tomorrow, and miss seeing our beaches! We have five bonzer racecourses, too. A beaut little zoo up on Mount Coot-tha. And our museum in Bowen Park has a Coral Pool with samples from the G. B. Reef, and also the aeroplane from Hinkler's sixteen-day solo flight from London —"

The clock-tower Jim had seen from the air was visible for miles from the bus; it stood 320 feet high, she said, and marked the heart of the city. Now its base appeared: the classically handsome, many-columned City Hall, surmounting two-acre Albert Square.

At ANZAC Square, their driver-guide stopped the car beside the War Memorial, an open circle of columns capped by a heavy crown of stone and bronze. *Grecian, simple and impressive,* Jim thought. They did not get out, but she described the interior, with inscriptions, "naming the battles where Aussies and Kiwis fought in the Great War. And in the center, the Flame of Remembrance always burns. Underneath, in two crypts, are the records of the soldiers from Queensland who served."

How will they match this, when the war they're fighting now for England is over? There's no room downtown for another memorial this size. They can't double up on this one — the names of the battlefields aren't the same.

Their charming guide's final treat lifted his spirits; she drove down George Street, turned on Alice, and suddenly they were riding under a brilliant orange-red canopy of blooming poinciana "flame trees," beside a green hill lapped on three sides by the broad sun-silvered river. The Botanic Gardens and the aviary and animal area could be toured only on foot, but the glimpse was tempting. Jim felt like asking the driver if she would like to assemble a

Chapter 7 — Part 2 — "Beaut" Brisbane

picnic supper and meet him there before the Gardens closed at sunset. Surely in egalitarian Australia it would be OK for an officer to have a date with a enlisted female "rating" (*or is she an "other ranks" female?*). Besides, he was supposed to be disguised as a civilian. Regretfully, he decided General Brereton might not approve.

* * * * *

Lennon's Hotel would rank as first class even in Manila, Jim decided; and after New Guinea it seemed a paradise: clean and modern, with real mattresses and crisp linen sheets. The elevators were the first self-operated ones he had seen; he supposed that the wartime manpower shortage had forced the Elevator Operators' Union to abandon those jobs. Mrs. Shaughnessy, the warm and hospitable manager, seemed to have everything under perfect control except her own luxuriant flyaway hair — and the new chef. She was close to tears as she told the Americans that the Italian-born chef, who had made Lennon's dining room famous, had been "nabbed" recently by the authorities and sent to an internment camp. His former assistant, a dinkum Aussie, now presided over the kitchen.

White linen tablecloths in the dining room were set with silver, crystal, and fresh flowers. Jim ordered "grilled barramundi," because he liked the sound of it.

"It's a fillet of giant perch — at home in either fresh or salt water," the grandmotherly waitress told him.

"How big is a giant perch?"

"Stand up," she ordered. He laughed and did so, thinking, this is the kind of service you get in an egalitarian country.

"The bastard's about as long as you are, Yank — around six feet. Thinner, though; only about a hundred and thirty pounds. Any more questions?"

The rookie chef turned out the best meal since Manila. Jim's barramundi was delicious, and all the vegetables were fresh; nothing from a "tin." After a generous wedge of pie made from locally grown cherries and topped with vanilla ice cream, Jim was ready for a stroll and a movie. The gray-haired waitress named the "picture theaters" on Queen Street — "the street that goes to Victoria Bridge" — His Majesty's, the Majestic, the Regent, and the Wintergarden. On Albert Street were the Metro, the St. James, and the air-conditioned Tivoli.

This is my kind of city, Jim thought.

Slugger was the only other member of the group who felt like going to a movie. "But first, I want you to hear the good little dance band downstairs. Let's go down and have a chocolate ice-cream soda. There's a good Milk Bar — that's what the Aussies call a soda fountain."

"I'll listen, but I couldn't drink anything but a short Barb-Wire. What irony — after Fourex beer has kept me alive for about three thousand thirsty miles, now that I'm finally in the shadow of its brewery I'm too full of dinner to do it justice."

As soon as they walked into the room, the short-skirted leader of the all-girl orchestra welcomed them, "Hello, Yanks!" and the players segued into "California, Here I Come," followed by a medley of not-quite-new American popular tunes. Jim felt like a Hollywood star.

They sat at a table beside the dance floor and ordered draft beer and a milkshake. Slugger did not smoke; "Cuts your wind," he and the other Air Corps pilot-athletes said. Now he said, "Let's play squash as soon as we get to Melbourne."

We've got to get in all the games we can, before June, Jim realized. In less than seven months, Pell's routine two-year Philippine tour would be up.

Since Jim's childhood, his friends who were Army Brats and Navy Juniors had entered his life in two-year spans of time and then were gone. Now his friends themselves, not their fathers, got the orders that sent them away too soon. In his boyhood, those sobbing farewells at Pier Seven — when the old Army transport *Grant* or *Republic* pulled away, and the deep cacophony of whistles died, and the 31st Infantry Band stopped playing Sousa marches and packed up the instruments — had been so painful that he had schooled himself to take friendships more lightly. But he had not yet perfected his discipline for separation.

Although Slugger was a fierce competitor in all sports, his nature was more philosophical than pugnacious. His tough-guy nickname had seemed to Jim an overdose of West Point humor (elsewhere termed "sophomoric," but at the Military Academy, he supposed, it was probably "yearling" humor) — especially after Jim grew to know his friend's deeper, compassionate side.

Nicknames, some of the reverse type, evidently were popular with Australians. Last night in the Officers' Mess, the young RAAF fliers had been doing some justified "skiting" (bragging) about their two top-ranking Aces. "Bluey" Truscott, a redhead, had downed 15 Germans over the English Channel, and "Killer" Caldwell had shot down 20 Germans and Italians over North Africa. They also spoke of a notoriously slow cricket player known as "Slasher." After that, Jim had decided that "Slugger" was not too bad a nickname. And anyway, considering Pell's thick brown hair and high forehead, his handsome, slender face with its long patrician nose, barely cleft chin, and serene blue eyes, Jim realized that if he used his real name — Floyd — he would inevitably be tagged with the gangster's sobriquet, "Pretty Boy Floyd."

Slugger **seems** *so easygoing, while quietly doing a thorough job of everything he undertakes,* Jim thought. *He must have had to push like hell* sometimes, to get the stockpiles of high-octane gasoline in place — even in New Guinea and Darwin — in time, and in sufficient quantities for the thirty-five thirsty B-17s. He just makes everything look easy — even his slam-bang squash serve.

Like Jim, in his teens Slugger had advanced from the rank of Star Scout to Eagle Scout. However, Jim had been disgusted to learn that in the quiet Mormon community of Ogden, Utah, vandals had interfered with Slugger's merit badge requirements. As one of the tests in Pioneering, he, like Jim, had built the required bridge of tree limbs lashed together that would support 200 pounds; but Slugger's bridge had been destroyed — then rebuilt by him — three times, before the Scout examiner was able to approve it.

Jim had told him, "I would have gone after those rats and knocked their blocks off!"

Slugger merely laughed and said, "If I'd made a search for them, I wouldn't have had time to rebuild my bridge. Then they would have defeated me. Besides, they might have been Japanese farm-workers' kids. Those boys weren't allowed to join our 'white' Scout troops — even though they'd been born right there in Utah — so I didn't blame them for being mad at us."

Jim had observed that Pell, like other Westerners who had attended school with Japanese-Americans, never spoke of "dumb Japs." Only the Americans from towns in the East and the South, who perhaps had never seen an Oriental (other than a Chinese laundryman) outside of Charlie Chan and Mr. Moto movies, scorned the intelligence of Asians. The ManilAmericans knew better. Asians could be baffling, maddening — yes, even inscrutable — but stupid they were not.

Pell's West Point classmates also termed Slugger "a dual personality." That pleased Jim, who was always acutely aware of his own dichotomy.

* * * * *

But Slugger's two sides seemed to meld together into a single gold coin: each unique, both compatible.

Jim was delightfully surprised when two tall and attractive, albeit giggly, young women came over from a nearby table. They had been in the crowd at Amberley Aerodrome since sun-up to see "the big American aeroplane" land, and didn't Mr. Pell remember meeting them there this morning?

Of course he did, said Slugger, always the gentleman; how could he forget such lovely ladies? He introduced Jim, as the girls supplied their own names: Gail and Fiona. They had come to Lennon's with their younger brothers, they said, hoping to meet the Yanks. One glance at their definitely brotherly, blushing, grinning, freckled escorts convinced Jim they were "nice girls," not "tarts."

The young women sat down; each said, "I'll have a Barb-Wire, ta (thanks)," and giggled. Jim noted that each had a swimmer's tan, was "well stacked," and possessed the tribal attributes of handsome legs, fair hair, and blue eyes.

"We want to learn to dance the Shag," said Gail, who had done most of the talking. "Will you blokes teach us?"

Jim said, "We'd be delighted. Nothing to it — just a double hop on each foot. You're talking to the Maestro of Shag, my little cockatoo. Mind if I call you Galah?"

"Go ahead. My word, but you Yanks are polite!"

Slugger told Fiona, "I'll teach you the Salt Lake City Shag — the best in the West."

"Oh, we went down to see that ship, and the *Northampton*, but we didn't meet any sailors, so we didn't learn their dances."

Slugger laughed and shook his head. "I'm not talking about the ship — sailors only know how to dance the hornpipe! Salt Lake City's the name of the biggest town in my home state of Utah."

"What a funny name for a town!" Fiona giggled.

Gail put in, "It was better in March, when the *seven* ships came in, and all those bonzer Yank sailors marched in the parade through downtown. We screamed and threw confetti and streamers and *pelted* them with flowers!"

In August, the heavy cruisers *Northampton* and *Salt Lake City* had made a brief, unheralded stop at Brisbane, ostensibly for "oil and supplies." As Manila's Subic Bay routinely had serviced all U.S. Navy vessels in the Far East, ManilAmericans surmised that the unusual visit Down Under actually was prompted by President Roosevelt's desire to emphasize to Japan the new U.S. support of Australia. His intention had been spelled out more boldly in March. Just after Congress had passed the President's unprecedented Lend-Lease Act, he had ordered seven naval vessels, with their 2,100 men, to make courtesy calls at Brisbane and Sydney. Jim had seen the newsreel footage of their arrival and tumultuous welcome by crowds of 250,000 in Brisbane and 500,000 in Sydney. Three years ago, Jim had watched as three U.S. cruisers — *Trenton, Milwaukee,* and *Memphis* — steamed into Manila Bay after a wide sweep south and west to join in the ceremonies honoring Australia's 150th anniversary and the opening of Singapore's great Naval Base. They were the first U.S. Navy ships seen in Australia since 1925.

Pell, a natural athlete like Jim, was a superb dancer, fluid, relaxed, and inventive. When the all-girl band swung into the old familiar Big Apple (long since outdated in Manila), Jim told him, "Shine!" The few Australian couples, along with Jim and the two girls, cleared the floor and formed a circle around him while Pell performed solo an improvised routine of jive-steps. The girls followed Jim in clapping in rhythm and shouting encouragement to Slugger,

and soon the other spectators joined in:
"Go, Man, go!"
"Truck on down!"
"Swing it, Gate!" (Or "Swing it, Myte!")

To Jim's delight, after his own turn to Shine, accompanied with encouraging calls of "Give 'er a go, Rubberlegs!" he received as much applause as Slugger had. Mentally, he doffed his cap modestly, like Joe DiMaggio in the newsreels after making a home run.

Soon Gail and Fiona, convulsed with embarrassed laughter, had learned Truckin', Peckin', and the Suzy-Q. When the band packed up, the two seemed close to tears that the Yank pilots must depart for "Melbun" in the morning, and they promised to write.

Gail was a good dancer and a good laugher, but a shy good-night kisser.

Chapter 8

Part 1 — South to Melbourne

> . . . *the strange, as it were,* **invisible** *beauty of Australia, which seems to lurk just beyond the range of our white vision. You feel you can't* **see** *— as if your eyes hadn't the vision in them to correspond with the outside landscape.*
> — D. H. Lawrence, *Kangaroo*

Airborne over New South Wales
Wednesday, 19 November 1941

Even this old Hudson shouldn't take more than three hours to put us over Sydney, Jim estimated — only about 470 air miles south of Brisbane. Having no crew duties on the flight, he found the ride unexciting, with the blue Pacific flowing on forever below the port wing, and the coast of New South Wales on his right, looking exactly like the Queensland coast it replaced.

Thank God, Colonel Eubank gives me chores to do on **his** *plane. Otherwise — if I had to ride in the Fortress as a passenger — I'd go nuts right now: thinking about how we've got to fly this same damned entire course in reverse before we can take off from Dynamite Darwin for Singapore — and Daphne. I'd go through hell for that girl, and I* **will***, too — skirting these same goddam three thousand miles of monotonous coastline of this overgrown island. The only thing different will be that on the return trip the sea will be to starboard and the land will be to port.*

Chapter 8 — Part 1 — South to Melbourne

If a bird could possibly fly directly across the continent from Melbourne to Darwin, he figured, the distance would be cut to about 2,000 miles.

But not even our marvelous four-engine, mechanical bird would dare to fly directly northwest like that. If we went in, a search party — with luck — might find our mummified bodies in maybe twenty years. Better to go down at sea than be fried alive on the Simpson Desert, or lost in the Macdonnell Ranges.

The little railroad trains below looked engagingly picturesque. As they tootled up and down the narrow coastal tracks, they appeared to Jim like HO-gauge models from a Lionel catalogue. South of Brisbane, the border between the states of Queensland and New South Wales had appeared as evident to him as if the east-west line were painted on the ground; the railroad sheds told the story.

In Townsville, Penny had explained why Melbourne beer did not travel north into Queensland. "Irish blarney's partly to blame. Also the idea that every Aussie state's an independent kingdom. It's a good example of why we need a stronger federal government in Canberra. Now that Labour's in power, we may get it."

About a hundred years ago, Penny said, the British Colonial Office had advised the colonies to adopt a uniform railroad gauge of 4'8½". Later, however, an Irish engineer persuaded the government of New South Wales to use the Irish gauge of 5'3". Victoria and South Australia went along with that choice — but the following year New South Wales decided to revert to "the Pommie gauge." Victoria already had laid some "Irish" track and South Australia had ordered rolling stock for the wider gauge; they refused to change. In another display of independence, Queensland and Western Australia decided on a 3'6" gauge.

"That's why we don't get Melbourne beer in Townsville," Penny told him. "A case of Foster's stubbies sent up here by rail would need to be re-loaded to cross New South Wales, and re-loaded again to enter Queensland. The unions like it, though — there are always plenty of jobs at the borders."

*But can those toy tracks carry anything really **heavy**? Well, it's lucky that most of the rainfall and population are on the seacoasts, so supplies can come in by ship.*

* * * * *

The smoking stacks of Newcastle's blast furnaces waved a gray signal that showed Jim a double message: *You are nearing Sydney, and you have left pastoral Australia. Now you're back in the twentieth century — like it or lump it.* His response was also divided.

Although he resented the ugliness of the steel mills that marred the green coastline, he was proud that Americans had designed them; and he was glad for this isolated country to have the facilities to build its own twin-engine Beaufort torpedo bombers. He had read in this morning's *Courier-Mail* that Australia recently had produced its thousandth Bren gun carrier. And surely the home-made Wirraways were better than nothing.

Newcastle's facilities had helped Australia's neighbors, the East Indies Dutch, Jim had learned in August when he had toured the new defense factories in Java. With their homeland fallen to the Nazis, the Indies Army had no source of rifle ammunition that matched the caliber of their weapons. They had shipped all their rifle barrels down to Newcastle, to be re-bored to use ammunition purchased from England. One of the promises General Clagett had made on that Lend-Lease survey was that he would try to expedite the promised shipment of 50,000 U.S. rifles to Java, although he reminded the Dutch officers that American and Filipino infantrymen were forced to drill with mock rifles of wood or bamboo.

Part 2 — Sydneyside

> *No amount of money will buy time. Even the most generous preparations do not open up the years that have passed and enable us to lay the foundations of a great industry and a great aerial army.*
>
> — Dr. C. D. Walcott
> U.S. National Advisory Committee for Aeronautics, 1919

Airborne over New South Wales
Wednesday, 19 November 1941

    Jim knew Sydney Harbour Bridge from the newsreels showing its opening, three years ago. It was hailed as the world's largest steel arch bridge, though not the longest, with a span of 1,650 feet. Including the approaches, it extended for two miles, carrying "eight lanes of roadway, two electric train tracks, and two footpaths," the guidebook said. But now, from his God's-eye view the great steel-gridded arch seemed dwarfed by the magnificence of its location.
    What a glorious spot for a city! He gazed down on blue bays following bays, golden beaches following beaches — lavish gifts of Nature for this nation of athletes.
    One of those beaches must be Manly, "named in admiration for the splendid bodies of the Aborigines seen there in 1788," his pocket guidebook said. A

hundred years later at Manly, a South Sea islander, Tommy Tanna, gave Australians a new sport when he shot the breakers while standing upright on a flat board.

Jim wondered if White Australia had sent Tanna back to his own island after his sport was adopted. Or was he perhaps allowed to roam the perimeter of the continent, searching for the Holy Grail of surfers — the perfect two-mile wave?

The beaches looked strangely bare, with only a few clusters of frolickers on the sands, and in the blue water the shark nets had few swimmers to protect. The bays held only fishing vessels, coastal steamers, and Navy ships; the scene lacked the lively sails of pleasure crafts.

Inland, green golf links, racecourses, and parks merged toward the backdrop of the Blue Mountains; but not many people were out to enjoy them. Only a few cars and a number of buses and horse-drawn wagons moved on the broad streets. Sydneysiders, he realized, in their handsome, widespread city, in the midst of all that natural splendor, were working on war.

What a damned shame that Aussies — by nature a happy-go-lucky lot, like Americans and Filipinos — have to submerge their inborn playfulness, and slave and die for their Mother Country's bloody (yes, truly bloody) war.

"You should see it on a week-end!" the pilot yelled. "War or no war, Aussies will never give up their play-time! Isn't that what we're fightin' for?"

Jim's guidebook gave the population as 1,300,000 inhabitants: as many Aussies as the entire state of Queensland with a second Brisbane added; "second in size only to London among the 'white' cities of the British Empire." The guidebook had not prepared him for this stunning sight of Sydney, after the thousands of empty miles.

He spotted the airport named for Kingsford-Smith at Mascot, eight miles south of the city. Sacred ground — where Francis Chichester had landed his *Elijah* in 1930 during a red dust storm, after flying alone 14,561 miles since leaving London. Jim yearned to land there, and thought wryly of the irony that Brereton's mission required the Americans to land on some of Australia's worst airfields, but to overfly this "civilized" one.

Surely *that* bay, south of the city, must be Botany Bay, where Captain James Cook made his first landing on this verdant east coast 171 years ago: a fateful day for England's prisoners. Later Cook named the bay for the profusion of previously unknown plants discovered on its shore by Sir Joseph Banks, the naturalist aboard *Endeavour*.

But why not name it Banks Bay, after the bloke who did the work? Granted, "Botany Bay" *had a better rhythm — except perhaps to Sir Joseph's ear.*

It was easy to locate the naval base at Garden Island, with its long graving docks — still unfinished, still far smaller than Singapore's. The bartender at Lennon's had told Jim that by 1944, when the project would be completed, the

Chapter 8 — Part 2 — Sydneyside 195

docks could service capital ships of 45,000 tons. Now — like Surabaya in Java and Subic and Cavite in the Philippines — 10,000-ton ships were the largest that Garden Island could handle.

The bartender had told Jim what to look for, and he spotted them easily: a war-worn Australian destroyer damaged by German dive bombers in the Mediterranean, and the cruiser *Perth*. *Perth* had "won her fuckin' funnel stripes in the Battle of Cape Matapan," the bartender had said. While she was evacuating 1,200 ANZACs and Tommies from doomed Crete, a German bomb had struck the galley, killing the galley crew and some of the evacuees, "but luckily, the steam from broken pipes put out the fire. *Perth's* a dinkum Aussie ship, a charmed ship," he had told Jim: luckier than HMS *Kelly*, sunk from under her Pommie commander, Mountbatten, during that frantic rescue effort at the time of Jim's 21st birthday.

Jim tried not to think about the scene in *Perth's* galley as the scalding steam poured out of the pipes. He had never seen a war-damaged ship, and he hated the raw, bent edges of torn metal, the blackened areas, the machine-gun stitches that marred the decks and the funnel, bearing its proud battle stripe. It was almost as bad a sight as a cracked-up airplane.

Crete held a double resonance for him. When he and David were small, their father would tell them a bedtime story each night: always a legend of Greece or Rome. The next day they would act out the story in their play. Among their favorites were the tale of Romulus and Remus, the exploits of Hercules, and the aerial escape of Daedalus and Icarus from Crete.

Sometimes Alexander began with a description of the palace and its treasures, while the boys urged him to get on with the story. After King Minos of Crete had commissioned Daedalus to design the labyrinth which successfully contained the maiden-devouring Minotaur, the progeny of Minos's wife and a bull, the king had turned against the skillful artisan. Imprisoned in a tower with his son, Daedalus devised bird-wings, securing the feathers with wax. The wings worked, and father and son soared out over the 1,900-room palace at Knossos toward safety in Sicily. But Icarus — history's first overbold pilot — flew too close to the sun, melted the wax, lost his wings, and plunged into the blue Aegean Sea.

"That was the saddest thing that could happen to a father," Alexander had concluded. "Daedalus hung up his wings and never flew again."

"Heck," Jim had argued, "flying's more important than one dumb kid!"

Now the legend of Daedalus was being kept alive by a small group of men who had flown in the World War and subsequently remained on active duty as Army Air Corps pilots. They called themselves "Daedalians," in honor of the first pilot; their pledge was to place "service to the nation above personal safety," while demonstrating the importance of air power. The roster of the Order of Daedalians listed many of Jim's heroes, and both Eubank and

Brereton were charter members.

On Crete in May of this year the legend had been twisted. British Empire troops were trapped, wingless, while gliders, flying as silently as Daedalus, dropped armed parachutists who shed blood to a Minotaur's taste. Attempted escape by sea was punished with bombs from the air.

Part 3 — Over the Capital

*They go to an island to take special charge,
Much warmer than Britain, and ten times as large;
No custom-house duty, no freightage to pay,
And tax-free they'll live when at Botany Bay.*
            — Whitehall Evening Post, England, 21 November 1786

Airborne over New South Wales
Wednesday, 19 November 1941

Alexander, a graduate of Yale University's School of Architecture, had mentioned to Jim his interest in Canberra — 150 air miles south of Sydney — and in Walter Burley Griffin, the American architect who had won the international contest in 1912 to design Australia's Federal Capital. The guidebook described Griffin as a "small, shy, modest non-smoker and vegetarian."

The bloke sounds like a soul-mate of my dad's, Jim thought, *except for Alex's after-dinner cigar and a dab of fish or chicken.*

Like Alex, Griffin sure was no businessman — busting his ass to design an entire city, with his wife's help, for a measly prize of thirty-five hundred dollars. And after seven frustrating years of wrestling against The Red Tape Plant, Griffin gave up in despair. That sounds like something Alex might do: give up his dream instead of fighting for it.

Canberra (Canb'ra) took its name from the local Kamberra Aborigines, a branch of the Ngarrugu totem group who had lived in the area until the Whitefellows arrived. The name (fortunately, Jim thought), had won out over others proposed: "Eucalypta," "Shakespeare," and "Wheatwoolgold."

Surprisingly, the Capital Territory was not on the coast, but 80 miles inland, at the end of a fine wide highway that came southwest from Sydney. To Jim, accustomed to the narrow, teeming streets of Asia, this land approach to the capital city was eerie in its emptiness. In its entire length — probably close to 200 miles — he counted only a dozen cars, most of them Austins, with two buses and a few horse-drawn vehicles.

Viewed from above, the city-not-yet-a-town reminded Jim of a half-completed stage set abandoned by theater carpenters. The RAAF pilot circled the Hudson over the deserted-looking place, banking to give his American passengers a good view, and audaciously buzzed the white marble buildings.

Only three facets of Burley's design (winner over 136 others) were clearly evident to Jim. First, the pristine streets of the white city would radiate from central plazas, on the order of L'Enfant's plan for Washington, D.C. The other elements seemed most meaningful for Australia: Hundreds of young trees had been planted. Third, the beginnings of a dam across a small river indicated an intention to form a lake beside a long, low, white civic building with many windows and tall arched doorways.

Jim felt as if he were discovering a lost city in a wilderness, mysteriously abandoned, like an Angkor Wat or a Mayan metropolis that had never known life. Canberra was still a dream city — a dream interrupted first by the Depression and now by England's war.

He hoped the dream of Burley Griffin and the Australians would become a splendid reality. He liked the spirit behind it — especially since he had seen Darwin and, from the air, towns such as Cloncurry and Daly Waters. Just as the American West's ugly cattle towns, gold miners' shanty towns, and fish cannery towns had been transformed into proud cities like Dallas, San Francisco, and Seattle, so Canberra seemed to represent a coming-of-age statement by Australians. Canberra would say: *Now that we've been here for one hundred fifty years, we have raised our eyes from our goldfields and our sheep stations, to see the unique beauty of our continent. Here stands the pledge of our commitment that henceforth we will create only buildings that are worthy of this land and its dynamic people.*

In the Philippines, Commonwealth President Manuel Quezon had become obsessed with a plan to replace bayside Manila with a new capital city farther inland. He wanted a seat of government built acccording to a grand plan, "a second Washington, D.C." Quezon often had spoken before the U.S. Congress in his quest for Philippine independence.

Unfortunately, Quezon had not held an international architectural design

Chapter 8 — Part 3 — Over the Capital

competition — or even a national one — and although he spoke often to Alexander about "getting some of your ideas," he had never done so. The new capital was perhaps even further from completion than Canberra, although Quezon — renowned as a lavish spender — had sorely strained his nation's treasury for its construction. Dr. Claude Buss, an adviser to U.S. High Commissioner Francis Sayre, had told Alexander that Quezon had dangerously slashed the Philippine Army's budget for funds to build his monument: Quezon City.

Oh, hell, Jim thought — *old Alex would have appreciated a snapshot of the way Burley's Chicago vision is getting translated into 'Strine. Even a blurry photo from a vibrating Hudson. Did I deliberately forget to take one? Well, Alex will just have to come down here and see for himself.*

— You stinking bastard, Jim accused himself, *you know damned well that no ships or commercial planes are plying between Manila and Australia. The only way Dad could get here would be via Singapore and the Dutch East Indies. And with both of them on war status, it would be nearly impossible for an American civilian to book passage — even if Alex could afford such a trip, which of course he cannot.*

Jim managed to ignore his inner voice by searching the land below for old evidence of a plane in trouble, but he saw no sheared-off trees or scarred ground, even with Alex's binoculars. It was hard to believe that ten years had passed without a clue to the disappearance of the *Southern Cloud*, a commercial plane of Kingsford-Smith's company that had vanished on this comparatively well-populated stretch between Sydney and Melbourne.

Today's RAAF pilot told Jim that the mystery had "ruined Smithy's airline — and Aussie aviation, too."

Part 4 — Misty Melbourne

> . . . *civilized man has never had a greater opportunity to find his home in the middle of a natural paradise than that offered him in the Australian city.*
> — Walter Burley Griffin

Melbourne, Victoria
Wednesday, 19 November 1941

From Canberra to Melbourne, just over 300 miles, would take the Hudson about an hour and a half with luck and a tail wind, Jim had figured.

He was right, and they landed in daylight — but a different kind of daylight. Although his eyes had tired of the harsh Australian sun, he missed it now, as though the lights in a room suddenly had been dimmed. Down here at the southern tip of Victoria, the southernmost state, the air was chilly, the sky was gray, and the city itself seemed gray — much as Jim supposed London might look.

Here in Melbourne, Americans were not entirely unknown Men-from-Mars, thanks to Colonel Van S. Merle-Smith, the U.S. Military Attache, and his small staff of American officers. When Jim first met the Colonel, upon landing, his hyphenated name and cool, aristocratic bearing seemed rather "Pommified," putting Jim off. However, Jim was impressed with the efficiency of the planning already in place for this visit: an *immediate* conference for

Chapter 8 — Part 4 — Misty Melbourne   201

Brereton with the Chief of the Australian Air Staff, Air Chief Marshal Sir Charles Burnett; a meeting for Allison Ind in the morning with a professor who would know almost everything Ind needed for his survey — and a dinner party at Merle-Smith's home tonight. There, he promised Jim, some "lovely local 'sheilas' can meet you."

* * * * *

Merle-Smith's home
Wednesday evening, 19 November 1941

"Too bad you missed the Cup," Jim's dinner partner said. She was about his age, and she wore a WAAF uniform.

"Believe me," he told her truthfully, "I've been gnashing my teeth about our bad timing. The only time in my life I'll probably ever get down here — and in November, too. Why couldn't we have made it by the famous First Tuesday?"

Of course he knew why. When the 80th Melbourne Cup Race was run on 4 November, Brereton, Eubank, the Flying Fortresses, and Prime Minister Curtin had all been unavailable.

"You wouldn't believe how lively Melbourne is at Cup Time. All the rest of the year, it's stuffy and sedate, and the sidewalks roll up at dark — but we make up for it during Cup Week. It's a carnival!"

"I remember the newsreels — the crowd all chanting '*Phar Lap!*' when he won the Cup." The great Australian gelding, big in body and in heart, had captured Jim's imagination that November of 1930, when Phar Lap had run the two mile race in 3 minutes and 27¾ seconds.

She nodded. "We called him *The Red Terror.* When I was small, I saw him *in person,* ridden by Jim Pike at Geelong, about sixty miles from here. . . . When Phar Lap died in California, I was eleven — just the age when girls are crackers about horses — so of course I cried buckets. But all the adults were crying, too. Aussies were wild over him, more than any Hollywood star."

"I was twelve. Too old for a boy to cry, but I did." He had never told that to anyone before. But he did not dare ask her if she thought Phar Lap's sudden, mysterious death in 1932 had been caused by American gangsters who would not tolerate a horse who won every race. His own theory was that some untraceable poison had been used, but he hoped Australians didn't think it.

She lightened the conversation by offering to go with him on Saturday on the tram to Flemington Racecourse, the site of the Cup races.

"Ajax, our new wonder horse, is due to run then. He'll draw a crowd of punters — bettors — so we'd best go early. Of course, it won't be like the hundred thousand who cram in there for the Cup."

"I'd really like that — if I can get the day off. And I wouldn't miss the hundred thousand others, if you'll go with me." He meant it; he liked her. She was not the blonde Aussie Amazon of his fantasies, but was rather small, with a figure trim-but-not-*too*-trim, brown hair worn in a soft bun, and large, rather wistful brown eyes.

And she likes me, too; I can read her eyes — the soft brown kind that should never play poker, because they can't hide feelings. Her lashes are like Louise Clagett's — long, black, and so thick you can see them in profile across the room — they just won't stop. This is the greatest country for growing eyelashes on the sheilas. It must be Nature's way of protecting them from the blinding sunlight, like the jutting brow of the Aborigines.

Her name was Albion; her friends called her "Albi." Jim resisted the temptation to crack a joke about "perfidious Albion"; he felt sure that she had been exposed to that poetic reference all her life. Colonel Merle-Smith, whose office she worked in, had introduced her as *Mrs.* Birdsall, and she wore a gold wedding band. However, her husband was not present tonight, Jim had deduced by the process of elimination.

"We've been talking to each other too much," she whispered. "We should turn to our other partner."

Jim tried, but the lady on his left was giving her profound attention to Sir Keith Murdoch, whom Jim had met earlier in the evening.

Sir Keith, the Director-General of Information, was also the managing director of a group of Melbourne newspapers. Jim guessed that it must chafe Sir Keith to refrain from printing news of the Americans' secret visit. Murdoch, 55, had warmed to Jim during cocktail conversation, when Jim's retentive memory produced the names of the Australian correspondents he had met at the Raffles bar in Singapore: Tom Fairhall of the *Sydney Telegraph,* Colin Fraser of the *Melbourne Sun-Pictorial,* Harry Standish of the *Sydney Morning Herald,* Ray Maley of the Australian Associated Press, Bill Knox, writing from Johore for the *Sydney Mirror,* Ian Fitchett, the official Australian observer, and Douglas Willkie, filing for Murdoch's own papers, the *Melbourne Herald* and the *Weekly Times.*

Murdoch also was interested in photographs of Aussies overseas, for his *Sun News Pictorial.* He mentioned the Australian photographers in Singapore, who had warmly invited Jim to go along on their "shoots" at the Digger camps and the RAAF airfields, all the way up to the miserable jungle strip at Kota Bharu in Malaya. Jim had high praise for the newsreel cameramen, Frank Bagnoll and Jim Collins, the still photographer Cliff Bottomley, and everyone's favorite, the official photographer for Murdoch's Australian Ministry of Information, the delightful Hedley Metcalf.

"A correspondent can have a greater influence than most people realize," Sir Keith told Jim. "I was a war correspondent myself at Gallipoli in 1915, and my reporting has been credited with causing our withdrawal from that untenable situation."

Jim was shocked, thinking of the effort to be objective that was made by most of the American foreign correspondents of his acquaintance. Of course, in Chungking the *Time* and *Life* reporters and photographers were hobbled by their certainty that Henry Luce, back in New York, would never print anything that reflected badly on his anointed — Chiang, Kai-shek. But Jim had watched Cecil Brown broadcasting from Singapore for CBS, and Brown never gave the slightest hint of his personal conviction that the U.S. should enter the war against Germany.

Murdoch had continued, "My son Rupert's only ten, but he has printer's ink in his veins, and he's keen to be a war correspondent. But if you Yanks will only give us a hand and get into the scrap, we could get this bloody war over before Rupert's old enough to go."

Jim never knew what to say when Australians implied that Americans should stop being bystanders and join them in fighting Germany. *What does Murdoch think I can do about it? Declare war? Or would he like a statement from me that he could print, quoting, "unnamed American sources"?*

These were the best mutton chops Jim had yet eaten, about two inches think. He had never tasted mutton before Townsville, but by now he felt like an expert. He gave up on the lady to his left, hopelessly monopolized by Murdoch, and concentrated on trying to hear what Albion was discussing with Slugger Pell. He and Pell had a hot rivalry in squash, but they had never vied for the same girl. He hoped Albion would not fall for Pell's undeniable charm and good looks, although Jim felt that he could compete fairly in those categories. Where Slugger had an unfair advantage was in the *savoir faire* acquired at West Point — with none of the arrogance — and his maturity. Slugger would be 28 next month, and everyone knew that girls preferred older men.

Much as Jim liked Slugger, he did not want the prospective "day at the races" to include him, either.

I'm even glad there isn't room here for dancing. If she danced with him I'd be out of luck.

But what he overheard was almost as threatening as dancing. Albion was saying that she, like all of Melbourne, was "crackers about *football*" — a sport never played in the Philippines. Jim's interest in football was limited to the annual Army-Navy game, and then it was the ferocity of the emotions it revealed between the two bitterly jealous Services that engaged him, far more than the game itself.

We'll be back in Manila in time for that big bash, he thought.

Everyone was wondering how General Brereton, as a graduate of the Naval Academy, would react when Army scored. By tradition, as the game was rebroadcast in Manila's bayside Army-Navy Club, an officer would write each new development on a blackboard, and the Club would erupt with cheers. If popular Horace Greeley was back from Chungking, he would again be the scorekeeper. Greeley, an Air Corps pilot, had been a cheerleader at West Point and would perform flips when Army made a touchdown. If Horace was still in China, his 1937 classmate (also Slugger Pell's classmate), Colin Kelly, a B-17 pilot, would do the honors.

Albion was telling Pell about Melbourne's own football hero, Keith "Bluey" Truscott, now a war hero as a Spitfire pilot in England. Jim waited for Slugger to tell her about his own prowess at football. Jim knew he had led his high school team from Ogden, Utah, to Honolulu to play McKinley and Kamehameha. His West Point classmates said that Slugger had played halfback and fullback equally well and was a brilliant open-field runner. According to them, Slugger had earned immortality along with his letter "A" in a great winning game over Navy in 1935, as a varsity halfback in his third year. But now Pell was only asking Albion about Bluey's technique and about the differences between American and Australian football.

Hell, I could have faked a football conversation like that. With that slender poetic face of Slugger's, if he doesn't tell her, she'll never guess that he really played as well as the beloved Bluey. I'll be damned if I'll tell her; friendship has its limits. But maybe it doesn't really matter — I think she's falling for his personality.

Jim's competitive spirit was as aroused as if this were a squash match with Slugger. At the first chance to break in, he told Albion, "I'm hoping to play some tennis at your famous courts — Kooyong and Albert Park, where Quist and Bromwich played."

Her eyes sparkled. "So you're keen on tennis? So am I. Are you very good?"

He played his trump card, "Well, I had a pretty good teacher — Dwight Davis."

"That must be your father, Lieutenant Davis. I'm sure he —"

"No — my father's no good at sports. I mean the Davis Cup Davis."

He could see that she was impressed. During Dwight Davis' term as Governor-General of the Philippines, his handsome and popular children — a son and two pretty daughters — had frequently invited Jim to play doubles with them. Although they were in their teens and he was only 11 by the time they left Manila, he was already tall for his age. He had readily absorbed the tennis tips offered by their jovial blond father, the donor of the heavily ornamented sterling silver bowl for winners of amateur international tennis team competition.

Two years ago, Australia had won its first Davis Cup by the efforts of 5'6" dark-haired Adrian Quist and blond John Bromwich. World-famed as a doubles team, they singly had defeated the American Bobby Riggs in Merion, Pennsylvania. Previously, Quist had been kept from the Wimbledon championship by American Donald Budge. In the 1938 Davis Cup competition, Budge had defeated both Quist and Bromwich, but subsequently he had become a professional.

"The U.S. would still have the Davis Cup if Don Budge had kept his amateur standing," Jim teased Albion.

"Look out, Yank — we can take it again, as soon as the war's won and the games are played again! Quist and Bromwich are both in the Army now — not overseas, because they both have asthma badly — but they'll be playing, and winning again, I assure you!"

She was cute when her face was animated, Jim thought, but Slugger had her attention again, with a comparison of tennis and squash.

Their host also was blessed with charm — and an understated wit, Jim conceded. Allison Ind had said that "Van" Merle-Smith came from a prominent New York family; perhaps his cool, deliberate manner indicated a bred-in-the-bone emotional control that would be useful in an emergency. Jim decided that someone in Personnel in the War Department had chosen well — for once — when Merle-Smith was assigned to represent the "Yank Army" to the Australians.

Major General Lewis Hyde Brereton, up there at the head of the table in his white sharkskin suit, also had held diplomatic assignments. Leda had told Jim: "Lousy Lewie — that scrappy, snappy, tactless bantam rooster, was our U.S. Air Attache to France, Spain, and poor little Belgium after the war! It's a goddam miracle he didn't start another one!" All during this trip, observing Brereton's brusqueness with the Australian officers, Jim had tried to picture the impetuous flier in that delicate diplomatic role of Air Attache.

Allison Ind, the kindest of men, once remarked that Brereton was as direct as a machine gun, and operated with much the same rapidity. "He prefers to make his mistakes on the run. He knows he'll make them — but his mistakes will be those of commission, not omission. He has a tremendous job, and no time in which to do it."

Well, Jim decided, maybe the War Department did miscast Brereton as a diplomat in postwar Europe — but they've put him in the right slot now. It's *time* for machine-gun speed, and to hell with diplomatic toe-dancing.

As Jim was watching, something Merle-Smith said obviously delighted Brereton, and his round, shiny face was transformed by a wide, quick, hard, eye-crinkling grin, displaying white, perfect teeth. Behind the rimless glasses, his dark arched brows lifted, and his brown eyes sparkled like a boy's.

Like a kid whose baseball just broke the neighbor's window — a kid who knows that no parent could punish a boy with such a grin. Who needs diplomacy, if your face can light up like that?

The Personnel types in the War Department also had shown unusual acuity, Jim thought, in assigning Lieutenant Robert H. O'Daniel to the consulate staff here in Melbourne, in this nation of so many sons o' the ould Irish sod. O'Daniel was sitting across the table from Jim, and his warmth, wit, and humor radiated almost tangibly to include Jim, who hoped to see more of him. Although his looks were not striking — it was the kind of blue-eyed, brown-haired, rosy Irish face one saw on every street — the young Army officer had a magnetism that made Jim wonder why Albion was not in love with him. He had watched them together during the pre-dinner drinks, and he was sure that they were only friendly co-workers. *Well,* he thought, *if she can resist Bob O'Daniel's sex appeal, maybe she can resist Slugger Pell's.*

After dinner, his hopes for cornering Albion to have a private talk were dashed when he saw her thank their host and start to make a quick exit. He caught up with her at the door as she began to put on her blue wool overcoat. He took it out of her hands and folded it over his arm. Fortunately, Pell was trapped by Murdoch at the moment. "Please don't be a party pooper, Albi. It's still early."

"I wish I could stay, but I live five miles out, with my aunt — and she worries if I'm late."

"OK, if you insist. But at least I'll walk you to your car."

She laughed. "If I had a car — which I haven't — the rationing formula allows each car only enough gasoline to drive twenty miles each week."

"Twenty miles! Eighty miles a *month* — in your huge Australian distances?" Now Jim understood why the highways were empty. This was a side of wartime living that he had not seen in Singapore or Java, with their rich natural supplies of petroleum.

"But Melbun's a good tram town, luckily."

"Then I'll walk you to your tram — and hope it's running late."

Outside, he offered his arm and she took it. After a few minutes in the chilly, raw night he was thankful for the warmth of her small body beside him. The top of her head came to his chin, so she was the same height as Mariluz. And like Mariluz, she was comfortable to be with, not trying to fill every silence with conversation. As a secretary in the U.S. Military Attache's office, she had learned to understand Americanese, and when she spoke, she modified her native 'Strine so that American ears could relax.

The walk to Elizabeth Street was short, but the tram was agreeably late. She lived with her Aunt Alice in the northeast suburb of Essendon, "but not so far out as Essendon Airport."

Jim laughed. "You can say 'Aerodrome,' if you want to. I'm getting used to it. I'll probably get home and catch myself saying I'm stationed at 'Clark Aerodrome.' I've also learned that Aussies don't hesitate to ask visiting Yanks personal questions — so I'll beat you to it, and ask you why you're living with

Aunt Alice."

She was a widow — at 20. She had married her high school sweetheart right after their graduation. Dennis had volunteered right after the war began, and he had been killed soon after he reached Libya, she told Jim.

He admired her evident lack of self-pity. Dinkum Aussie, he thought. He had never had a date with a widow; he had always thought of them as old women. Now he suddenly realized: That takes care of the virginity problem!

— *You lecherous rat, you're as bad as Punch*, Jim accused himself, then reconsidered.

Like hell I am. Punch's favorite sport, he says, is deflowering virgins; I think that's brutal. But it's different with divorcees, and experienced women like Daphne — and, sure, widows. A little roll in the clover wouldn't rob them of anything; in fact, they might be grateful. . . .

Yes, Albion liked movies (she didn't even call them "the pictures") and she would be glad to stay in town after work tomorrow, to have a drink and dinner with him and see a movie.

"They'll be ancient to you, though. They have to come from California by ship, to Singapore or Batavia, then on another ship around our northwest and east coasts."

"I don't mind. A movie's like an intelligent girl — on closer acquaintance, there's always more to discover. Even a bad movie's fun to see a second time; then you can find more flaws to laugh at."

With a mournful-sounding whistle the tram approached, adding its steam to the foggy night, and halted beside them with a squeal of brakes.

Jim overcame his impulse to kiss her.

Down boy, don't scare this sweet chick, he told himself; *slow and steady wins the race. There are more important things in store.* He took her hand and squeezed it as the tram doors hissed open.

"Your hands are freezing!" She sounded genuinely concerned and called over her shoulder, "I'll bet you didn't bring any warm clothes to rug-up in —"

"Nobody warned us — but my heart's warm!" Embarrassed to fall back on that old cliché, he yelled, "*Warmer* since I met you!" as the tram door slammed shut behind her.

Chapter 9

Part 1 — Buckley's or Nothing

> ... An' if sometimes our conduck
> isn't all your fancy paints,
> Why, single men in barricks
> don't grow into plaster saints. ...
> — Rudyard Kipling, "Tommy"

Victoria Barracks, Melbourne, Victoria
Thursday, 20 November 1941

Of all the many ways that Queen Victoria was commemorated in Australia, Jim thought, the attachment of her ubiquitous name to *barracks* — the most masculine of shelters — seemed the most incongruous.

Despite the name, however, he admitted that Victoria Barracks, where the Americans were domiciled, had been well chosen to keep their mission inconspicuous, while welcoming them in a setting of great beauty. The barracks lay south of the city, below a wide curve of the River Yarra, in an area of gentle green hills adorned with a few mansions and government buildings. This place of parks and public gardens was reached by St. Kilda Road, a broad avenue bordered by triple rows of trees.

The room Jim shared with Slugger Pell offered splendid views, but was so chilly that they wore their brown leather A-2 flying jackets zipped up to their necks. Unfortunately, the Americans' masquerade as civilians would not permit them to wear their government-issue jackets outside the barracks.

In the mess hall, they joined Allison Ind and his roommate, Lefty Eads, for breakfast of steak, eggs, and tea. Jim sympathized with Ind's lamentations over having left all his civilian wool clothing — as well as his "warm wife and children" — in Michigan. Ind also expressed his dread of the long cold tram ride he must endure en route to the University of Melbourne, on the other side of the city. "It's ridiculous to be freezing our backsides in a nation of wool growers! Who'll go shopping with me to buy a sweater or a sheepskin — or both?"

The others grabbed at the suggestion. Jim agreed that it would be possible, back in the Philippines, to sell barely-worn garments of "genuine Australian wool" to officers returning to the States . . . as soon as the Freeze was lifted and personnel began to rotate in normal fashion.

On Princes Bridge, the yellow-and-green tram clicked over the muddy Yarra, giving the American passengers a wide, misty view of a gray city under an overcast sky.

"Beautiful — but bleak," Allison Ind said, hugging himself to keep warm. "South of the Thirty-seventh Parallel, peacetime population, about seven hundred thousand, diminished now by some of the six hundred thousand Australians serving overseas."

Not even Pell, in making all the arrangements for Brereton's mission, had ever traveled south of Brisbane before. He had not known of Melbourne's chill springtime, or he would have warned the others. Nor did he know where to shop; but yesterday they had noted attractive shops on Collins Street (where Pell, the non-drinker, also admired the many Milk Bars), and other clothing stores near the elegant Menzies Hotel on Bourke Street.

They left the tram at Bourke and Swanston and window-shopped at Myers, at Foy and Gibson, and at Buckley and Nunn. All the windows were equally tempting.

At Buckley and Nunn ("Our Ninetieth Year"), Captain Ind said, "I'm too cold to look any farther. My quest endeth here."

And there it did. The grandmotherly saleslady shook her head sadly. "Warm jumpers? Sorry Yanks, but without a ticket, you haven't a Buckley."

"Beg pardon?"

"That's our little joke. There are just two choices, Buckley's and *none*. All clothing is *rationed*. We're fighting a war, you know."

Jim thought, *Yes, lady, we know. We've suffered the agonies of thirst alongside your dear Diggers, with the damned beer rationing; but this is too much.*

"Bloody shyme," she said as they departed. She assured them that soon Melbourne would be enjoying a month or more of temperatures ranging between 95 and 100 degrees Fahrenheit. "We had a record one hundred seventeen degrees a couple of Januarys ago."

Part 2 — *Rainbow* Revealed

> *In Australia we do not ask workers to accept unjust conditions in industry, for justice is the very thing for which we are waging war.*
> — Prime Minister John Curtin, 1941

Factory outside Melbourne
Thursday afternoon, 20 November 1941

This is where I came in. It's time to leave this endless newsreel, Jim kept thinking.

He had been assigned to tour Melbourne's war production factories, just as he had done in Java in August. A meaningless, useless task, it required only smiles, nods, occasional questions, and words of admiration upon hearing the proud statistics.

Still, it wasn't exactly like Java. In Bandung, Java's prewar mountain resort, the factories were warm, the brown Javanese workers were silent, and his massive, friendly Royal Netherlands Army "conducting officers" spoke good English with Dutch accents. While Melbourne's cavernous facilities sucked the heat out of his body, the cordiality of the all-white workers was warm indeed, and his massive, friendly Australian guides spoke a form of English with a unique accent, in a monotone that was sometimes lost in the clamor of the machinery.

Here, fortunately, Jim had a companionable American "translator" and transportation arranger in the person of Lieutenant Bob O'Daniel. Although O'Daniel obviously had viewed these clangorous assembly lines before, for he understood the processes and remembered the names of the union leaders who guided the tours, he appeared to enjoy the exercise.

The Commonwealth Aircraft Corporation's acres of factories and hangars had been "a sandy waste" only three years earlier, when a dozen young Australian men had been sent to the States to learn how to make airplanes, Jim was informed. They had returned with the plans that were subsequently modified to produce the Wirraways, now being built here by 5,500 men and women, in numbers that were a military secret but sufficient to permit exporting them. As evidence, a test pilot was checking out a new one on the adjacent flying field.

Jim tried to think of something nice to say about a Wirraway to a young woman who was stenciling numbers on a fuselage.

"I had a ride in one in Darwin. Good visibility."

. . . Once you get off the ground, so that monstrous radial engine stops blocking your view.

She gave him a radiant smile, and as they trudged on down the line O'Daniel told Jim, "Well done."

The torrent of statistics seemed to Jim as unending as in Java. "Thank God, I've got a good memory," he told O'Daniel, who evidently was blessed with the same retentive ability.

Starting from scratch two years ago, the Aircraft Production Commission was now producing twin-engine Beaufort torpedo bombers. Far more complicated than the little Wirraway, a Beaufort was comprised of 30,000 parts, Jim was told; every one of those was fabricated in Australia, in 400 widely scattered factories throughout the South. The bomber, with a crew of four, had a range of 1,060 miles when carrying the maximum load of 2,000 pounds of bombs or 2,127 pounds of torpedoes. Its service ceiling was 25,000 feet; maximum speed 259 mph at 8,500 feet. Its armament consisted of nine .303-inch guns.

During a "smoke-oh" break the noise stopped and the workers gathered in clusters to light up and chat. Jim passed around his pack of Lucky Strikes to O'Daniel and the trade-union representative who was showing them through the Beaufort assembly area, as well as to several trade-union representatives who joined them.

O'Daniel said that Australian industry had not been so much *converted to* war production as *created for* it.

Sincerely, Jim told the Australians, "Your speed in getting all this going in such a short time gives me a lot of respect for your unions. You seem to have done it without giving up any of the workers' privileges."

Bob O'Daniel laughed. "Oh, these Aussie unions are the world's most vigilant guardians of workers' rights. And with the new Prime Minister a Labour man — he started as a lumberjack, out in West Australia, and became the leader of that union — there sure won't be any 'wartime overtime' required, I betcha."

"Too right, myte," their guide agreed. "And no bloody restrictions on strikes, either."

Their tour completed, as the two Americans walked to the train stop O'Daniel said, "We're lucky to get out before the aircraft workers' exodus begins, or we wouldn't get a seat on the train."

"But it's still early!"

"Well, they're patriotic as hell, but they still hang up their tools thirty minutes before the official end of the workday, so they can have plenty of time with their mates at the races or the beach or the pub — wartime or no wartime!"

He told Jim a story that had just come down from Sydney, passed along (or invented) by Australians who had the ability to laugh at themselves. It concerned a Japanese freighter in Sydney Harbour a week ago. Her cargo of cotton textiles had been off-loaded, and on her departure, a Japanese officer called out from the deck to the longshoremen, "We'll be back!" One of the wharf-workers yelled up to him, "And we'll be waiting for you!" But the Japanese had the last word: "Oh, no you won't. We'll come on a week-end, and you'll be at the races!"

Jim mused, *Those trade-union types wouldn't be so matey with us Manila visitors if they knew Brereton had put the Philippine Air Depot on two shifts, for a sixteen-hour workday, as soon as he arrived. They'd be as mad about that as the Civil Service Commission was.*

As well as "the roaring Gael," my mother. Boy, wouldn't Leda get a kick out of the strength of these Aussie unions!

Since she had left the Catholic Church, Leda had given her devotion to a new Trinity that she believed would solve all the problems of humanity: Education, Birth Control, and International Trade Unions. She often expressed her regret that as a schoolteacher in the Philippines, she'd had no chance to join a union.

"If I'd had a union behind me, I wouldn't have been suspended all those times, for 'inciting desires for Philippine independence' in my students, and for singing the praises of Margaret Sanger and Birth Control to my high school classes!"

He told O'Daniel, "My mother loves to tell us how her grandfather Hogan, arriving in steerage from Ireland, was greeted at the dock by a Catholic priest and a union organizer. Later, when he worked in the coal mines of Oklahoma, he rose to be the leader of his local. She brags about the strikes he led for safer working conditions in the mines, in spite of retaliation from the bosses, and

Chapter 9 — Part 2 — Rainbow *Revealed* 213

even death threats."

"Sounds like my own Irish forebears, only they went to work in the Massachusetts textile mills — they were called 'lint-heads.'"

Although Leda had felt betrayed when trade unionists of Germany, France, and England had fought each other in the World War, she believed now that if Japan's workers were unionized, the Trade War with the U.S. never would have developed.

"Too bad Merle-Smith's office doesn't observe union hours," Jim said. "I have a date with Albion, but I'm going to kill some time at the museum while I wait for her."

"Albi's very conscientious about her job — and there's an extra load on her this week, with the Brereton blitz. I'd like to come with you — to the museum, not on your date — but I can't resist this rare chance to get home early and see my doll-baby in daylight."

O'Daniel's wife had just produced their first child, last week; that explained why she hadn't attended Merle-Smith's dinner party, and why O'Daniel said he felt only "brotherly love" for Albion. His previous station had been Singapore. He said he was thankful to get his pregnant wife off that threatened island and down here to safety.

Although no one else was waiting for the train now, O'Daniel spoke in a low, conspiratorial tone as they strolled up and down the platform, smoking Jim's Lucky Strikes. When Jim learned that Bob O'Daniel had worked in the office of Colonel Warner LeClair, the American Army representative in Singapore, he surmised that Bob was probably in Army Intelligence. Bob and his wife had left Singapore in June.

"I just missed you there," Jim told him. "I was there in July, as a junior aide to General Clagett."

"Ah — the Clagett mission from Manila. Getting wish-lists from Percival and Brooke-Popham of their needs from Lend-Lease —"

"Too right. Then we went on down to Java, to find out how much the Dutch wanted, and in August I was back in Singapore. I worked for Colonel LeClair for two weeks — so I knew your replacement, Jack Jackson."

Aboard the train to Melbourne, Jim explained that when General Clagett was stricken with a malaria flare-up at the Oranje Hotel in Surabaya, the Dutch physician, Dr. Van Helsing, had ordered the portly General to return to Manila by ship at once. Colonel Lester Maitland, next in rank, had assumed command of the mission, assisted only by Jim and Captain Ind until more help arrived from Manila. Colonel Francis Brink (father of Jim's petite friend Leilani) flew to Java with two other officers to continue the talks with slim, aristocratic Governor-General van Starkenborgh Stachouwer, dynamic General Berenshot, Dr. Van Mook, and other Dutch officials. At the conclusion, all the senior officers decided to fly back to Manila on KNILM, the Dutch airline, without returning to Singapore. Jim was dispatched to retrieve the excess luggage the party had left at the Raffles Hotel and their secret reports written in Singapore, which had been left there in Colonel LeClair's office safe.

Jim sat silently amid the rattles of the train, reliving that fortnight in memory. Colonel Maitland had given Jim vocal orders to remain in Singapore for two delirious weeks. Jim would forever be grateful to Maitland (already his hero, as the first pilot to fly from California to Hawaii), and he would always wonder if Maitland had given him that assignment so that Jim could be with Daphne again. Only two incidents had marred that idyllic time: the night of opium on Penang Island, and Lieutenant Jackson's drunken revelation about Plan Rainbow 5.

Now, to Jim's astonishment, O'Daniel began to provide background music that fitted Jim's thoughts. Had he read Jim's mind? He was whistling the tune of Judy Garland's song in *The Wizard of Oz* — "Over the Rainbow."

He's trying to find out if I learned about the goddam Plan when I was in LeClair's office!

Jim responded, "That was a great movie. I saw it *five times*. But when I saw it in Singapore with Lieutenant Jackson, he talked so much it was ruined for me."

"That's too bad." O'Daniel's poker face revealed nothing.

Jim continued, "Jackson drinks too much, then blabs too much. He shouldn't be in that office."

"Thanks. We've wondered about him. Colonel Merle-Smith will arrange for him to return to the States immediately. Aside from that, did you enjoy the movie?"

He wants to know my opinion of Rainbow?

"Well . . . uh . . . no. I thought it gave the Wizard too much power over a citizen of Kansas."

O'Daniel nodded. "Not only the Wizard, but the Munchkins, too. Way too much power."

"Munchkins? I didn't get that connection. Jackson didn't tell me about them."

"Munch, munch. *Rijstaffel* eaters."

That Dutch word for "rice table" flashed a sickening picture into Jim's mind. In the paneled dining room of the luxurious Hotel des Indes in Batavia, 24 copper-colored Javanese waiters had circled around a banquet table set to honor the Americans. At every place was a dinner plate thickly mounded with steaming rice. Each waiter carried a large, heavy serving platter of beef or pork or chicken or seafood, each in its unique spicy sauce. This was only a "twenty-four-boy *rijstaffel*," the host apologized; in deference to Holland's present suffering under the Nazis, the number of bearers and viands had been reduced from the traditional 60. Jim had watched in disgust as the sweating,

Chapter 9 — Part 2 — Rainbow Revealed   215

red-faced Dutchmen had dug into those mountains of food.

He told O'Daniel, "I get it. Actually, I liked everything about those Munchkins except their monstrous appetites."

"You might not be so fond of them if they get scared and drag all the 'citizens of Kansas' into defending them. They're getting pretty nervous."

Hell, the Indies Dutch have been nervous ever since they bravely followed Roosevelt in cutting off sales of oil to Japan, in July. And they have a right to be nervous — their oil is what the Japs have gotta have.

Aloud, Jim said, "Jackson didn't tell me that the Munchkins had power over the citizens of Kansas. You mean if Tojo — I mean Toto — bites a Munchkin, Dorothy has to help the Munchkins punish him?"

"No bite is necessary. Only a move by the dog that appears threatening to the Munchkins. The Good Fairy of the West promised the Munchkins in August that all they need to do is to say, 'It's time to punish that dog.' Then Dorothy and the Wizard and you and I and the citizens of Kansas will have to pick up our sticks and beat hell out of him."

"But if the dog doesn't threaten Kansas, I don't think Auntie Em and Uncle What's-His-Name will want to take off after him, just for the sake of the Munchkins."

Bob O'Daniel shook his head. Grimly, in a very low voice, he said, "I'd advise you to try to get your parents back to the States before the Munchkins call for help. Because there are no tornado cellars on Wake, Guam, or the Philippines."

Both were silent while Jim absorbed the shocking new information that the Dutch, as well as the British, could involve the U.S. in a war with Japan under Plan Rainbow. Jim had no desire to defend Holland's East Indies colonies.

Bob's mention of Wake Island, Guam, and the Philippines fitted the earliest Rainbow Plan, calling for those U.S. possessions to be sacrificed while all effort would be pitted against Germany. Jackson had termed that defensive strategy "the April version" of Rainbow — which the U.S. had not approved. Jim was optimistic that the present intensive buildup in the Philippines meant that under Rainbow 5, the War Department had decided not to abandon the archipelago.

*If we go to war because the Singapore Britons or the Indies Dutch feel threatened — we can wear a halo, as the Brits and Aussies do about declaring war in 1939 for Poland's sake. They **chose** to fight for justice, they like to say — they weren't forced to defend their own territories from an attack. But how many Americans want a halo that badly?*

Finally, with a firm handshake, Bob O'Daniel told him, "Next stop is Swanston Street, where you get off."

Part 3 — Dreamtime

We belong to the ground, it is our power and we must stay close to it or maybe we will get lost. If you do not stay close to the ground you don't know who you are any more, maybe Balanda (white man) or maybe Yolngu (Aboriginal), who knows?
— Narritjin Maymuru, bark painting artist

Melbourne, Victoria
Thursday afternoon, 20 November 1941

On Flinders Street Jim left the train and boarded the green-and-yellow tram northbound on handsome, busy Swanston Street. As he admired the many attractive young women leaving the government offices, the title of that Nazi propaganda film *Mädchen in Uniform* again came back to mind.

And the girls in civilian dresses look snappy, too, even though they have to buy their own outfits, and Albion said the top wage for women is about two pounds, ten shillings a week — about eight bucks American.

He was learning to recognize which uniform designated a WRAN (Royal Navy), an AWAS or a WRAAC (both Army), or an AWAL, although he had forgotten what an AWAL was. He had been confused about WAAAFs and WRAAFs ever since Darwin, but he knew both were with the Air Force. *And you can always tell a WENL,* he thought; *but don't try to tell her much.* WENLs were the broad-shouldered Amazonian drivers of the military vehicles that shared Melbourne's streets with omnibuses, taxis powered by cumbersome, air-fouling charcoal canisters, and the rare Austin. Jim had heard remarks that linked the WENL to "beauty duty," implying that the best-looking of them invariably drove the official cars of the highest-ranking officers; but he also had glimpsed exquisite faces at the wheels of lumbering lorries.

The gray uniforms of the AANS, the Army Nursing Service, always reminded him of Daphne's merry friends, the Nursing Sisters in Singapore — the first Australian women he had ever known. Here they wore red coats, and here he saw them in groups with Therapist/Masseuses from the Veterans' Hospitals, whose dress uniforms bore red epaulets.

*So few civilians . . . and so few **men**, he noted once again. . . . The only ones visible seem to be the CITs, the non-volunteers, exempt from overseas service; or members of the Home Defence Guard, too old or too unfit for other duty.*

War is hell, leaving all these gorgeous dames without dates! In Manila we have just the reverse: a city full of handsome, red-blooded American men at the peak of their virility, and a severe shortage of eligible women. We need a Lend-Lease agreement tacked onto Brereton's list of projects: several thousand of our blokes, in exchange for a like number of sheilas-in-uniform!

He got off at Little Lonsdale Street, where the National Museum, National Art Gallery, and Public Library filled an entire block with their impressive, neo-classical buildings, set well back from the street on grassy terraces. Twenty broad-shouldered Aussie men or WENLs could walk abreast up the marble walk without touching shoulders, he estimated.

Time allowed him only a quick walk-through of the Library — the largest he had ever been in — and he regretted not being able to browse in any of its 600,000 volumes. He had planned a similar speedy glimpse of the National Gallery, but there he was stopped frequently by the glowing masterpieces of artists whose paintings he had never seen except in reproductions: Corot . . . Rembrandt . . . Tiepolo . . . Van Eyck. A winter scene held him for a long look; although he had never heard of the artist, he recognized the talent of Puvis de Chavannes.

In the Hall of Australian Ethnology, he found clues to the other Australia he had yearned to know, and he marveled at the mysterious, myth-laden art of the Aborigines: the *old*, "Old Masters."

Every decorated surface represented an ancient legend or a secret ritual: a code in color, he thought. Geometric designs were incised in a 15-foot length of bamboo, a ceremonial musical instrument, the two-toned *didgeridu*, and filled-in with color; similar didgeridus were as short as five feet. Stories of the Dreamtime heroes, the Creators, in their animal and human forms, were carved in the soft wood of hoop pine, kauri, and baobab.

He studied a painting on bark which displayed a barramundi fish externally, while simultaneously showing all its bones and inner organs with complete accuracy.

"We call these X-ray paintings," the elderly curator explained. "The Aborigines believe that the barramundi was the Creator of Rivers in the Dreamtime."

The pigments, the man told Jim, were red and yellow ochres, white pipe clay, and black manganese, dug from distant pits used for thousands of years, and carried to certain ceremonial sites, and laboriously ground to powder. Fixatives varied according to what was available: juices squeezed from stems of wild tree orchids, emu fat, or yolks of the sea-turtle's eggs.

Jim was fascinated by a series of black and white photographs by C. P. Mountford of Aboriginal art seen on rocks and in caves. His neck prickled as he studied a photograph of a cave wall marked with incised concentric circles and a man's left hand outlined in a spit-spray of white paint. In a cave in Arizona he had seen the art of the Anasazi Indians, employing symbols that in his memory were identical to these. He promised himself that some day he would take photographs, using color film and flashbulbs, in the caves here and in Arizona, for accurate comparison.

With envy he read an account of a great Corroboree held near Melbourne in 1843, when 700 Aborigines had assembled from their campsites to dance, sing, and perform their rituals and ceremonies.

If they do that every hundred years, I'll come back in two years to see it.

He was the only visitor in the Hall of Ethnology, and the white-haired curator seemed to appreciate Jim's interest.

"You can buy old artifacts like these for pennies, in any dusty junk shop, because most Australians aren't interested in them. The Aborigines don't realize that this is art — it's just a part of their life, and they're all artists. Those few of us Whitefellows who care, feel a sort of desperation because so much of this has become a lost art. The Aborigines living now don't know how to make some of these things; they say they were made by their ancestors in the Dreamtime."

The Dreamtime creation myth was about as accurate, the curator said wryly, as the guesses made by scientists. "Although the Aborigines aren't seafarers now, they must have come here by boat — forty thousand or more years ago — because Australia was already an island continent when they arrived. If there had been a land bridge, the higher mammals of South Asia would have come with them."

Not all of the widely scattered clans had been totally isolated from outsiders during those thousands of years, he said. Those Aboriginal groups whose "spirit country" lay on the northeast coast had long maintained friendly relations with seafarers from the New Guinea area; possibly their ancestors had originated from those Pacific islands. Similarly, the northwest coastal inhabitants had maintained a thousand-year acquaintance with fishermen from Java who came for trepang/sea slugs. It was from the Javanese that the Aborigines had acquired the term *balanda* for white people. Jim knew the unflattering term, used by the inhabitants of the Netherlands East Indies to refer to their Dutch colonial masters; it meant "red neck" in Javanese.

Damnation! If those Munchkin Balandas get scared, we'll have to save their colonies for them — so they can keep on milking profits from their conquered Spice Islands.

"We know so little of the rich spiritual life of these First Australians," the curator sighed, "and some of the symbols used by artists right here in Victoria will remain forever unknown."

"Don't any of their old men remember?"

The Australian shook his head. "When Whitefellows farm or build on their land, the Aborigines lose their inspiration for their art, and without their art they die. They've been extinct in this State of Victoria since about 1850."

Extinct? **Seven years** *after those seven hundred artist/dancers met here to celebrate their last Corroboree!* Jim felt half sick. He had to leave quickly before he said something angry to this sad old man who had devoted his life to trying to preserve these remnants of the Aboriginal culture.

Jim wanted to get outside and walk — or run. But he had promised Albion that he would look at an exhibit at the west end of the McCoy Hall of Zoology. She would not tell him what to look for. "You'll know it when you see it," she had said.

As he strode down the corridor, past glass cases displaying hundreds of reptiles, the thought struck him: the Anasazi AmerIndians, along with uncounted other North American tribes, had long been extinct. His anger about the Aborigines fizzled away like air let out of a balloon, but it did not evaporate; it congealed in a heavy weight of shared guilt and regret.

Far down the hall, he recognized the familiar form he had seen only in pictures, and his heart lifted with a thrill. Splendid, fabled, red-gold Phar Lap!

In Phar Lap's first and only race in North America, he had won the $50,000 Agua Caliente Handicap in 1932, just before his sudden, mysterious death. Sorrowing ANZACS had brought back the body of "the Big Fellow," and it had been mounted well.

The magnificent gelding had been bred in New Zealand and trained in Australia, Jim learned now. Phar Lap had run the two-mile course for The Melbourne Cup three times:

1929 Finished 3rd. Weights of 7.6
1930 Finished 1st. Weights of 9.12. Time, 3 min., 27¾ secs.
1931 Finished 8th. Weights of 10.10.

Phar Lap's size overwhelmed Jim — 9.12 tall; too large for a racehorse: a super-horse. The first crime, Jim thought, was castrating him, so that he could not sire colts who would carry on his champion bloodlines.

This is another Shrine of Remembrance. These Aussies sure don't want to forget their heroes. . . . It was Phar Lap's perfection that led to his death, at the hands of Americans with crucifixion minds who couldn't tolerate such a superior creation. But it wasn't only his superb conformation that made the ANZACS — and the world — love this Big Fellow so deeply. All the qualities we admire in a horse were magnified in him: loyalty, affection, intelligence — and that dinkum Aussie spirit of give-'er-a-go-mate, even when he was unfairly burdened with saddle-weights beyond any precedent.

Jim longed to stroke those glossy chestnut flanks; but the soulless brown glass eyes disturbed him. He realized that the glowing body that retained the look of life would feel cold to his hand.

What the hell's the use of a Shrine of Remembrance? Dead is dead.

Part 4 — "Franksgiving" Dinner

> *Their [the Australian Aborigines'] doom is to be exterminated, and the sooner their doom is accomplished — so that there be no cruelty — the better it will be for civilization.*
> — Anthony Trollope

Melbourne, Victoria
Thursday evening, 20 November 1941

    Albion had agreed to meet Jim at the Menzies Hotel at 509 Bourke Street, an easy ride by tram from the museum. The lobby, staid, sedate, and expansive, reminded him of the pillared lobby of the Peninsula Hotel in Hong Kong; except that the women here were more youthful and beautiful — and their crisp uniforms looked to him more stylish and becoming than the lumpy tweeds and frumpy hats whose wearers chatted over the Peninsula's tea tables. The few civilian men here, however, were dressed far more casually than the Englishmen in China.
    Another difference that Jim noted with pleasure was that in the Menzies' lobby real cocktails and highballs — not tea — were served on the waitresses' trays. He had felt frozen since the factory tours, and the marble museum and tram ride in the clammy evening air had not helped. He ordered whiskey and water (as in Singapore, "whiskey" meant scotch, although he really preferred rye, unobtainable in the outposts of the Empire). He saw martinis on a tray,

evidence of Dutch gin from Java.

Maybe I can ply Albion with martinis tonight — and who knows what might happen? . . . Not much chance, though; she hardly drank anything last night. Well, hell, nobody with any brains gets soused at the boss' dinner party.

Thinking of the Peninsula Hotel brought unwelcome thoughts of Punch: *back in Manila now, the bastard — probably trying to seduce my sweet sisterly Mariluz.*

It was in Hong Kong in 1932 that Punch's rotten mother picked up that English rotter and started to spend every night with him at the Peninsula — leaving Punch locked in the room of the "Hotel Cheapo" where all of us visiting ManilAmericans were staying. Of course Leda took pity on Punch, and invited him to join our family on the trip up the Yangtze to Chungking! And of course his nympho mother was delighted to get rid of her brat; but he almost ruined the trip for David and me.

Albion's smile when she saw him made up for the day's dreary, noisy, chilly factory tours. She was carrying a bulky package wrapped in newspapers. When he stood up to greet her, she handed it to him. "Sorry I'm late! Would you like to go to a cozy pub around the corner? I feel the eyes of too many gossipy wowsers examining us here."

"Sure. This is the weakest drink I ever tasted."

Maybe she's had a hard day, too; maybe she's really planning to tie one on tonight. Well, if she wants to do some pub-crawling, tossing caution to the winds, that'll be fine with me. Luckily, in Victoria — unlike Queensland — a lady evidently can have a drink in a bar.

Jimmy Woodser's bar was as noisy as Manila's Army-Navy Club after an Army-Navy game, and for the same reason — a lot of serious drinking was going on. A number of the customers evidently were "sparky" already; everyone Jim saw seemed to be chug-a-lugging. The dark, frothy beer looked delicious, and he followed Albion's advice, asking for "two birthday pots of Old, ta."

Woodser, behind the long bar, said, "G'ddye, Albi. Here y'are, Yank," and slid two 15-ounce foaming glasses over to them.

Melbourne's own Foster's was even more bitter than Brisbane's Fourex, but Jim liked it. Still, Albion surprised him by ordering two more schooners before they were half through their first ones.

"I'll shout for this round," she said.

"Fine. After a cold day in the war plants, warm beer hits the spot. But I'm shouting for our Thanksgiving dinner later."

"Thanksgiving? Well, thank *you.* Will you open the package now, please?"

He broke the string and peeled the newspaper off the soft bundle. It contained a brown tweed jacket with suede patches on the elbows, well worn but still good looking.

"It's the only thing of Dennis's I kept. I'd like you to wear it while you're in Melbourne, if it fits you."

It did, and it felt good. Obviously, Dennis had been as broad-shouldered and tall as Jim. That meant Albion had been able to stand under his chin, too, but Jim did not wish to pursue that thought. In thanking her, he almost said, "You've saved my life." Then he realized that nothing had saved the life of the jacket's owner.

"No worries, Jim. It looks handsome on you. You can return it when you leave. I know you won't need it in Manila."

He had remained seated while he tried on the jacket and fastened the leather buttons, trying not to attract attention. But now the gray-haired man beside him said, "Bonzer, myte! I wish my sheila would rug me up like that. I'd like to shout you both a pot."

As soon as the Australian's gifts of beer were received, Albion whispered to Jim, "You'd better shout him one back, straightaway. It's nearly closing time."

It was only 5:45, but all bars closed at 6:00, she explained, and no more drinks would be served.

"Till when?"

An odd custom, he thought; *maybe they want people to start buying something to eat, for a while. For a lot of these customers, that would be a damned good idea.*

"Till tomorrow morning, from eight to ten." In every state except Queensland, she explained, public facilities could serve alcoholic drinks only in two-hour intervals. The second bar-opening time of day was between noon and 2:00 p.m., and this final period lasted from 4:00 to 6:00. "The churches support the staggered-hours law. They think it cuts down on drinking; but actually, it only compresses more drinking into a shorter time, so it's the people who stagger."

"The churches? The Church of England?"

"Oh, Lord no! We Anglicans never object to a wee drap o' spirit! It's the temperance people — Methodists and Baptists — and we have a bloody lot of them. The politicians don't dare to change to sensible drinking hours, or those wowsers will vote them out of office."

"Holy cow — this shatters my whole impression of Aussies! Till now, I'd been thinking I'd like to emigrate to Melbourne, but I just changed my mind."

She touched his arm — actually, Dennis's sleeve. "I'll launch a protest against the drink curfew, if you'll move down to Melbourne."

Despite the drink curfew, Melbourne's appeal was growing on Jim hourly, even after his beer-buzz began to wear off. He asked Albion to name the most elegant dining room in Melbourne, and as they walked along Collins Street to the Australia Hotel at No. 266, he explained why Americans were blessed with two Thanksgiving Days this year, and today was one of them.

President Roosevelt, attempting to ease the depressed U.S. economy by giving Christmas shoppers a nudge, had decreed that Thanksgiving should be celebrated a week early this year. "But most ManilAmericans are self-made businessmen — that spells Republican. They're furious with the President for tampering with a historic date — so they'll be waiting till next Thursday to do their over-eating."

"I understand. It would be like changing the date for running the Cup to the second Tuesday of November. But any Prime Minister who suggested *that* would be out of office the next day!"

"Well, at least a lot of Republican turkeys will get a week's reprieve. But my mother's crazy about President Roosevelt. She and my dad are having Thanksgiving dinner *today* with High Commissioner and Mrs. Sayre — Frank Sayre was appointed by FDR — at the 'High C's' official residence beside Manila Bay. Our Chinese cook is my pal, though, and I'll bet you two bits, Wing has a turkey tethered in the yard that he's fattening up for a complete Thanksgiving dinner when I'm there next Thursday, just like the Republicans."

"But are you really a Democrat, like your parents?"

"Not my father — he's never forgiven President Roosevelt for taking the U.S. off the gold standard."

"A lot of the New Guinea gold miners would agree with your dad. They hold your president responsible for collapsing the gold market."

"The Philippine mining companies do, too. And *I* was mad as heck when Americans were suddenly forbidden to own any gold. I was thirteen, and I'd saved all the twenty dollar gold pieces my Davis grandparents had sent me for every birthday and Christmas. I had to pack 'em all up — twenty-six beautiful Liberty and Saint Gaudens Double Eagles — and send 'em to the Director of the Mint, Nellie Tayloe Ross, in Washington, D.C."

"Poor lad. Tough cheddar. So you don't vote for President Roosevelt?"

"Oh, men in the U.S. armed forces never vote. We *could* — there's no law against it — but the tradition is that it would be wrong for us to take part in choosing our Commander-in-Chief. The idea seems to be that if the man you voted for lost the election, it might possibly affect your loyalty to the winner. Besides, we have civilian control over the military, so we let the civilians choose who'll be our boss."

In the Australia's dining room, Albion thanked him when he helped her remove her coat and pulled out her chair. "I'd always heard that Yanks have wonderful manners, and now I know it's true."

Turkey was not on the menu, but Jim thought that a steak two inches thick would make a splendid substitute. Doing some quick figuring, he saw that even the most expensive dishes on the menu would not add up to more than one

American dollar for each dinner, so he asked the elderly waiter for a wine list. The waiter, whose English accent exposed him as a "Pommie," suggested a few prewar French vintages familiar to Jim, who had learned about wine from Madame Gladys Savary at her famous small French restaurant in Manila. Jim, however, wanted to try wines from the vineyards here in Victoria state — although the waiter looked askance, and Albion warned that Australian wine was held in low esteem. He ordered a Barossa Valley white burgundy for Albion and for himself a Chateau Tabilk claret, which he thought compared favorably with Chateau Mouton Baron Philippe.

Albion was having an appetizer of Sydney Rocks, and urged him to try one, his first-ever oyster. They were never eaten in the Philippines, and he had always considered them even more repulsive than sea slugs. She was delightfully persuasive, however, and after she speared the glistening object with a small silver fork, dipped it in the red sauce and leaned across the white linen tablecloth, finally he opened his mouth. He did not look at the offering, but looked into her warm, laughing brown eyes with their magnificent dark lashes. Her mouth — slightly open now in her concentration — was infinitely desirable. His sensation, as the moist, delicately saline, cold-hot gift from the sea slid down his throat, was of a sensuality that food had never offered before.

He knew, of course, that in temperate climes oysters had the reputation of Durian fruit in Southeast Asia, or the gall bladder of a black bear in China. *I sure as hell don't need any help in **that** department,* he thought. Nevertheless, the flavor and texture were so indefinably different from anything he had ever tasted that he ordered a dozen Sydney Rocks on the half shell, so he could try to analyze the experience.

Two little boys who had been sitting at a nearby table with their grandparents came over between courses to visit. Their friendliness, frank questions, and accents delighted Jim.

"Bonzer little blokes," he said later. "I'll bet there's never been a shy kid in this country. But all kids are neat, including the shy ones."

"Too right, Jimyank . . . I wanted to have a baby, but Dennis was wiser — he said we should wait till he came back. I never did anything to prevent it, so he always took care of that. Of course, now I'm thankful he did."

She's telling me that she's too smart now to get pregnant. That's swell — but when will there be any chance it could happen?

He wanted desperately to touch her. Beneath the long linen tablecloth, he squeezed her slender calves between his legs. He dropped his napkin, so he could lean over to stroke her knee, find her garter, feel the warm soft skin above her stockings. Her face turned pink, but the corners of her lovely lips formed more of a smile than a frown.

He sat up quickly; the kids were coming back "to talk to the Yank and his sheila," he heard them tell their grandparents.

After the boys left, he told her, "I wish you really were my own sheila, Albi. I like you an awful lot."

He almost said, "I wish I could stay longer," but caught himself because it didn't seem fair. *I was in love with Daphne first,* he thought; *so Singapore gets the priority.*

Truthfully, he said, "I hate to leave you so soon. I wish we could have gotten to know each other better."

"So do I. I like you a lot, too, Jim. They say that in wartime, things get accelerated — like the war production effort — and I feel as if I've already known you for ever so long."

*She said it! OK, Baby, let's accelerate! But how — or where? Damn me for a dumb oaf. Punch would have had her in bed hours ago, but I don't know how to proposition a lady. Besides, I'm breaking Punch's Number One guideline to seduction: He says the most important thing is to keep telling the dame you **love** her — even if it's a lie — because they all fall for that line.*

Albion's unromantic suggestion was to order *pêche Melba* for dessert. He did not demur, though he had eaten peaches only in Texas, and then rarely. Their flavor seemed like an overripe mango, and he had never acquired a taste for them. Although he had learned about French food from Madame Savary, he had always preferred the artistry of Chinese chefs. Now he was expecting a complicated production, but the combination in the stemmed crystal goblet was simplicity itself. Fresh red raspberries, pureéd with sugar to form a thick syrup, gave zest to the golden-ripe peach on its bed of creamy vanilla ice cream. Jim agreed that Auguste Escoffier had created a dessert worthy of the famous coloratura soprano who had adapted her stage name from this city of her birth.

Albion said, "She not only honored Melbourne, but she did herself a favor, too. Surely 'Dame Nellie Melba' sounds more musical than her real name — Helen Mitchell, Mrs. Armstrong. But Melbourne journalists weren't kind to her. Early in her career, they accused her of being 'perpetually soaked in champagne at the Menzies Hotel.'"

"Well, if the Menzies' champagne was as weak as its scotch, that didn't do her much harm — or good."

After his final spoonful of ice cream, he said, "Peach Melba doesn't seem at all French — it's dinkum Aussie. Just like you — unpretentious, fresh, sweet —" He started to describe the raspberry sauce as "sweet and *tart,*" but he had learned not to say that four-letter word in this country, where it spelled the end of romance. "And — just like you — under that luscious exterior, there's a frozen heart."

"Oh, no, Jimyank!"

Albion herself sang in the choir at St. Paul's Cathedral and was active in a Little Theater group, Jim had learned to his dismay, for her commitments would occupy her tomorrow evening and Sunday morning.

Time was slipping away like the oyster, and he knew he must get up his nerve. He ordered snifters of Chateau Tanunda brandy to prolong this perfect scene. Distilled from Doradillo and Grenache grapes, its aroma and body were excellent. However, he thought the addition of "Chateau" to an Aboriginal place-name was a ridiculous, highly uncharacteristic, affectation.

Now or never, he goaded himself. "Uh — Albi — how about relaxing in a hotel room this evening?"

At her look of shock, he quickly added, "I don't mean here at the Australia, where all the 'wowsers' would know about it. Isn't there some small hotel —?"

"'By a wishing well'?" She shook her head. "No. Much as I might wish to be with you, I could never go to a hotel with you — or any man I wasn't married to. Even if nobody I know should see us — and surely someone *would* — I'd feel like a tart."

That word again!

"Albion, you're driving me crazy. I *need* to hold you in my arms."

"I'd really like that, too, Jimyank. . . . I haven't wanted anyone to touch me since Dennis — but I'm terribly attracted to you. But I can't think *where* we could possibly have the right kind of privacy. . . . Unless some friend who has a flat would be leaving on holiday."

"Not bloody likely, is it? And tomorrow, after the meeting with the Prime Minister, will be my last night in Melbourne — *ever.*"

"Jimyank, I'm terribly sorry it's this way." She stood up. "Let's go to the pictures, shall we?"

Handsome Collins Street reminded Jim of pictures of Paris. As they walked in the dappled gold-and-black light of the street-lamps filtered through the branches of the burgeoning trees overhead, the city's charm diverted his mind, if not his body.

Melbourne was all that a city should be, he thought — clean and green, free of slums or crime. And although some of the buildings he had seen were downright ugly, the effort to beautify, to soften and warm the grayness, was everywhere evidenced by the artistic use of wrought iron, draped like black lace on balconies and verandahs, in flowing silhouettes of flowers, trees, animals, and even people. Unlike Manila's ironwork that composed gates, window grilles, and burglar barriers in Spanish style, Melbourne's wrought iron was only for adornment and enjoyment.

"It's like you," he teased Albion. "So pretty — and so unyielding. Hard as nails."

The neon-bright cinema district had its own beauty for a movie-lover; he had never seen so many alluring "dream palaces" on one street. Albion told him there were even more nearby — the State and the Majestic, on Flinders

Street, and the Capitol, on Swanston Street.

"You might like the picture at the Capitol," she said. "It's *You're in the Army Now* with Jane Wyman and Ronald Reagan."

"I managed to avoid that one in Manila. Its major claim to fame is that in one scene Jane Wyman and Regis Toomey share 'the longest kiss ever seen on the silver screen' — three minutes and five seconds. But if I thought it would inspire you to compete for the record, I'd almost be willing to see it."

Albion was a good laugher; *but laughs don't satisfy when you're hungry for something warm,* Jim thought.

The Regent was offering *Golden Boy,* William Holden's debut hit as a boxer who wanted to be a violinist. Barbara Stanwyck was in it, too. "She's kinda like an Aussie girl," Jim said, "sort of frank and gutsy and natural. But oh, how she could turn on the passion in *The Postman Always Rings Twice*! No worry about 'wowsers' for that gal."

At the Plaza, *Dark Victory,* Bette Davis's gripping portrayal of a blind woman, with George Brent as the male lead and Ronald Reagan in a supporting role, was one of Jim's favorites; but he had seen it too many times. The Metro had Reagan starring in the role of a square who inspired the Dead End Kids to better things, in *Angels Wash Their Faces.* Jim had seen all of them, so he decided to see again *The Dawn Patrol* at the Athenaeum. It starred Errol Flynn, Basil Rathbone, and David Niven as daring RAF pilots in the Great War, dogfighting with the German ace of aces, Baron von Richthofen. He knew it by heart, for he had also seen its predecessor, with Richard Barthelmess and Douglas Fairbanks, Jr., several times.

The movie death of the younger brother affected Albion, and she wept quietly. Jim kept his arm around her shoulder and kissed her wet cheek in the dark. The fatal crash seemed more poignant to him this time, seen through her eyes, and he found himself thinking that the boy had died before he'd had time to become a father and pass along his good genes. Like Dennis.

Afterwards they walked east on Collins Street, quiet now. *Manila could teach Melbourne a lot about night life; but at least — with few 'wowsers' around to criticize us — Albi lets me hold her little hand.*

He mused aloud, "Movies *are* educational. It's lucky Errol Flynn and Merle Oberon got jobs in front of movie cameras, or Americans might think Australians look like Martians."

"Merle Oberon isn't really typical. Very few Aussies are Eurasians."

"But I think that Asian strain's what makes her so gorgeous and fascinating. Of course, my mother says it's the Irish in Merle that gives her such charm. But my mother's never forgiven her for changing her name from Estelle O'Brien. Did you see her in *The Scarlet Pimpernel*?"

"Yes. But I loved her best in *Wuthering Heights* with Laurence Olivier as Heathcliff. Does your mother like Errol Flynn because he's Irish?"

"Oh, she adores that broth of a boy. Like most Americans, she thinks all Aussie blokes are like him. And I'm beginning to think he's pretty typical. I understand why he started having affairs with movie stars as soon as he hit Hollywood. It's impossible to have an affair in Australia — too many grousers and wowsers. And after seven years in New Guinea, he deserved all the fun he could get."

"Well, I'm glad you didn't stay in New Guinea that long! Aussies learn from movies, too. We form our mental picture of Yank blokes by the men Hollywood shows us — and you make me think that it's a truthful picture. In you, I can see Clark Gable and Gregory Peck — tall, dark, handsome, and well-mannered. Well, Gregory's polite. Clark acts more like an Aussie."

*Exactly the two I'd most like to resemble! Maybe it's our movies that give Americans our mental picture of **ourselves**.*

Albion's parents had emigrated from Scotland; they were of the Pictish type, small and dark like herself, she told Jim.

"The minute I met you, I knew you were a Pixie!"

They strolled through the Treasury Gardens and into Fitzroy Gardens — six city blocks of smooth lawns, flower beds, and enormous old trees. From the distant northwest corner glowed the stained glass windows of St. Patrick's Cathedral, tinting the evening mist red, blue, and gold. Between the black tree trunks Jim saw the low silhouette of a small cottage, the boyhood home of James Cook, brought from Yorkshire by an Australian philanthropist and rebuilt brick by brick.

"He was looking for a star," Albion said, "and then afterwards he found Australia by accident. When he first set sail from Plymouth in the *Endeavour*, he only intended to observe the transit of Venus from the Pacific."

"I've found Venus right here," Jim said, with his arm around her waist, his chin on her soft hair. "Now we can complete the story. Let's play housie in Captain Cook's cottage."

She laughed, but she would not even sit beside him on the velvet grass; the night watchman might see them. She wanted to show him the possums that climbed down out of the trees at night, but there was no moonlight, and no possums appeared.

A night-bird called.

"That's a little spotted owl — a Boobook. At least, the Abos think it says 'boobook.' To Aussie ears, it sounds like 'more pork.' "

"That tells me the Aborigines are thinking on a higher level than the Aussies. They hear the wise owl saying 'book,' but you blokes are just thinking about your next meal! What the owl is really saying is 'Pixie, kiss Jim.'"

That won him a laugh and a kiss — not a Jane Wyman three-minute smoodge, not even *one* minute, but warm and deep and stirring, and tasting like *more*. He maneuvered her against a giant oak and pressed his body against hers for a fervent, exciting embrace; but he would not exert his strength against her slight frame, and she slipped away once more.

Finally, tense with frustration and desire, Jim walked her to the tram stop. He held her hand along the way, but there was time only for a sweet, quick goodbye kiss before she jumped onto the tram.

Cold shower tonight, he thought, as he walked over to Swanston Street to board the southbound tram.

And I always thought the English were reserved and conventional, while Australians were on the wild side. How wrong could I get? My madcap Daphne would just as soon climb one of these trees while she was wearing a long evening gown, and then toss down her dress — and to hell with the wowsers! Damn the scruples of these enticing sheilas, anyway.

But when I take Daphne to a movie, **she** *chooses which one we'll see. This girl is worth ten of Daphne,* he told himself.

Yes, and if both sides of me were as square as they ought to be, I'd drop the naughty Daphne forever, marry sweet Pixie, and take her back to Manila. But dammit, the side of me that always laughed at Punch's dirty jokes and leered at his dirty pictures — that lowdown, Punchy part of me — is hopelessly fascinated with Daphne.

Part 5 — Barracks Bedtime

Every aborigine fully believes that in the dhoogor or dream (ancestral) times his own ancestors were birds (or animals or plants) like that which is now his totem.
—Daisy Bates, *The Passing of the Aborigines, 1938*

Victoria Barracks
Thursday night, 20 November 1941

Slugger Pell was sitting at a small table in the room he shared with Jim, wearing his pajamas and robe, writing letters. "Have a good time? She seems like a sweet girl — and awfully pretty." He looked up. "How did you manage to get that sharp jacket?"

"She lent it to me — it was her husband's. I'll go say good-night to Captain Ind." As he walked down the chilly hall, Jim hoped Slugger thought he'd been at Albi's place, and that she'd put the jacket on him after a wild passionate tumble.

Dammit, I wish I knew if Slugger's being noble, giving me a chance, by not making a play for Albion himself. Or is he going to serve a surprise ace that's too fast for me?

Allison Ind was sitting up in bed, wearing Lefty Eads's leather A-2 jacket over his robe. With his old portable typewriter on his lap, he was typing the day's notes for his survey of Australia. Lefty was sitting on the floor in a corner, with his papers and their columns of penciled figures spread out before him. He looked up and waved a hand wearily at Jim, who did not interrupt his concentration.

Ind told Jim, "I was so cold that my fingers were too stiff to strike the keys until I got in bed." He seemed to want to stop typing and talk for a while, so Jim sat on Lefty's empty bed and they spoke quietly.

Ind had spent all day at the University of Melbourne with Professor Douglas Copland, "a famous economist who has all the answers I've hungered for. I'll go back tomorrow, to cram all I possibly can. Jim, Professor Copland mentioned another factor that led to the White Australia policy. He says that when the news reached here in 1857 of the 'Sepoy Mutiny' in India, with the massacre of Europeans in Delhi in May and the Cawnpore murder of two hundred ten English women and children in July, and all those horrors, it struck terror in the English colonists here. They realized that if the population of this isolated country ever became predominantly Asian, no earthly power could get here in time to help the white minority in the event of an uprising. A violent anti-Asian panic spread over the few settlers here, and traces of it still affect their thinking."

"Some of the union leaders at one of the factories I toured today told me another reason, besides their fear of unemployment," Jim said. "They say the White Australia policy frees this country from spies and subversion. One of the men told me, 'In Singapore the Pommies have Asiatic servants. Yellow or brown, the bastards hate their bloody masters, and they may be spying for the Japs. Here, nobody has servants; there are no slant-eyes watching, no brown ears listening, and a bloke can trust anybody.'"

"But it's such an unfortunate policy, for so *many* reasons, Jim. If the unions weren't so strong, the country could be stronger. For one thing, they do need more hands to build this country. There are limits to what they can accomplish, with only seven million people. . . . Still — in proportion to their numbers, and the short time they've been here, Australia has developed at a pace that makes ours in the States look sluggish in comparison. She has truly lifted herself by her bootstraps."

"Bonzer blokes. Good-night, Captain, I'll let you get back to work — but don't you two stay up all night."

In bed, Jim's thoughts kept returning to Albion, with the tempting fantasy of having her lovely body in bed beside him. He knew that time was far too short for him to achieve that prize — yet tonight, her kisses had erased a little of the apparent impossibility.

Was he mistaking warm Australian friendliness for something more? No; he was certain that she reciprocated the strong sexual attraction he felt for her.

*But, dammit, she's too nice a girl for a hit-and-run conquest, just so I could cut a notch (the first one) in my belt. If I "make love" to her, I should be **in** love*

Chapter 9 — Part 5 — Barracks Bedtime 233

with her — no matter how temporarily. But do I know that little Pixie well enough, after only one date, to feel real love for her?

It was different with Penny, and her "first date" strictures; she was a play-the-field type, playing according to her own set of rules, which evidently did not include a requirement for love.

Anyway, speculation was academic; Brereton surely would have them on their way north early Saturday morning. Jim told himself he was crazy to get interested in another girl, just when he finally was on his way back to Daphne. By this time next week, he would be with her in Singapore, so why complicate his life with someone here, whom he would never see again?

That leaves me just tomorrow night for a seduction — and I can't move that fast with my first one!

Once again, he cursed his ambivalence. During his teens he had frequently had "crushes" on more than one girl, and he had learned that it was impossible to explain why he was what they termed "unfaithful." It was useless to tell American girls about the dual nature of Geminians, because they all thought astrology was bunk. He had assumed that when he reached manhood he would settle on liking one girl at a time, as most men seemed to do. Yet, here he was: drawn to Albion by a force hard to resist, while July's fierce longing for Daphne still burned inside him.

Do I "love" them both? Or one of them? Which one? Or neither? Do I just yearn to possess their enticing bodies? Is Punch right when he says love is just the polite name for sex?

He assured himself that his feelings were not purely physical; he sincerely enjoyed being with each of them — talking, dancing, laughing, drinking, walking, moviegoing — with all their clothes on. But he could not stop thinking about taking their clothes off. Was his interest aroused, as his body was, just because they were both exotics — the first English girl and the first Aussie sheila he had ever known?

Daphne was the only young woman he knew who understood his divided affections — because, she said, she loved Jim and Robin, too. "No one person can be all the things I like. I love some qualities you have, and some of Robin's, too."

While Jim certainly could empathize, he could not help hating Robin and hoping something would happen to make Daphne prefer *him*.

Strangely, his thoughts floated away from Singapore and back to his enjoyment of the evening, and those sweet, stirring kisses in Fitzroy Gardens.

A little tune for a clarinet began to play in his head, bringing its own lyrics:

I'll be on
Albion,

*Ere I leave
Melbion!*

My mother would give that one a grade of D-minus, he thought sleepily; *she can't stand for her students to use archaic words like "ere" in writing poems.*

Chapter 10

Part 1 —
A Run in the Royal Domain

This will be the place for a village.
— John Batman, anchored on the Yarra River, May 1835

Victoria Barracks
Friday morning, 21 November 1941

Punch's braying laugh woke Jim from his frustrating dream. He had been pursuing Daphne and Albion through dark woods, stumbling on tree roots, lashed by branches, falling clumsily, while they skipped lightly ahead, laughing. Daphne was so far ahead that he could see only glimpses of her hair, bright as a moonbeam. Albion was tantalizingly close, but just out of his reach. Suddenly, he was out in a bright meadow, and there sat Punch on the grass, his handsome head tossed back. He was laughing at Jim while Daphne and Albion bent tenderly over Punch, placing wild-flowers in his golden mane.
Awake, he found himself alone at the visitors' end of Victoria Barracks. The others had left early to wrap up the many loose ends of Brereton's proposals before the most important meeting of all, the culmination of the entire mission. This afternoon the Americans would meet with Prime Minister Curtin to lay out their outrageous and illegal offers and requests. On Curtin's decision hung Brereton's vast conjured network of air-links, still as ephemeral

and unauthorized as a spider's web.

General Brereton had ordered every member of his team to attend the meeting; even Allison Ind must tear himself away from the University and ride the southbound tram. Jim had the morning free, because the only war plants he had not yet toured were too long a train ride from Melbourne to risk getting back late.

The mocking laughter continued. Outside, on a telephone wire, sat five fuzzy brown-and-white birds with their long bills wide open, so saucy and comical that Jim had to laugh with them.

*At last I've seen kookaburras! And they look as unkempt as I am. Let's brush our teeth and our hair, mates, and then we'll see if this day's worth a laugh. If Curtin says it's "curtains" for Brereton's smoke-dreams, **nobody's** going to be laughing on our flight tomorrow.*

It was early; he welcomed the thought of a cross-country run on real turf, after all the miles of concrete factory floors he had trod yesterday. St. Kilda Road extended its broad three-mile length southward from Princes Bridge through such bucolic countryside — grandly called The Royal Domain — that he knew it surely must be home to many species of birds, but he'd had no time to explore until now. He put on running shoes, shorts, and a sweatshirt, thankful for Australian informality that allowed him thus attired to enter the mess hall, to breakfast on eggs and spicy bright red mutton sausages.

The gloomy, chilly, gray stationary front that had hung low over Melbourne since his arrival appeared to be breaking up; the sky was brighter, and the fog was evaporating. Jim, too, warmed up slowly; he first jogged around the green hill below the Observatory and then circled the spacious, handsomely landscaped lawns of Government House. Two roads led to the large, white-columned mansion that resembled Tara in the movie version of *Gone with the Wind;* and he wanted to be sure of entering by the correct door this afternoon.

The mansion's wide-spreading grounds formed a park within a park, a nature reserve that extended to a greensward of contiguous parks on the other side of the river. His small green guidebook (courtesy of the Bank of Melbourne) named the parks north of Government House: King's Domain, Queen Victoria's Garden, and Alexandra Gardens.

Across the Yarra lay Flinders Park, Olympic Park, and Yarra Park with its several cricket grounds. Beyond those, he well knew, were the urban jewels of the Treasury Gardens and 64-acre Fitzroy Gardens. A bloke could run at least six miles, he figured, without stepping off the grass — if he didn't mind swimming across the Yarra. Beautiful viewed from here, within its green curving banks — the Yarra actually was so muddy that Albion had called it "the upside-down river."

He dog-trotted along a walkway that led eastward from Government House and between two lakes. They were surrounded by more than a hundred acres of botanical gardens, meticulously maintained, beneath large trees of many varieties. A multitude of songbirds were saluting the sun's return. Blooming lilies carpeted a small lake from shore to shore with pink and white. The larger lake, a serene expanse of several acres cradled in shady green banks, resounded with the cacophony of waterfowl.

Discreet signs told him that in these gardens 10,000 species of plants flourished, with large sections devoted to native Australian and New Zealand flora — colorful and exotic to him. As he slowed to a walk on the winding path, he heard from the top of a tall tree the clear, silver early-morning chime of the currawong, the bell magpie. Or was it a lyre-bird, imitating another lyre-bird who was imitating a bell bird? Tiny silvereyes fluttered in the budding treetops. Through the lettuce-green new leaves a vista opened to Melbourne, rosy and soft, a vision borne on the mist-band of the Yarra.

Perfection, he thought, breathing deeply, exulting in the strength of his legs. *Perfection can exist, and this is damned close to it.*

Who would have guessed that bottlebrush flowers come in twenty-five flavors, ranging from cream to crimson? And what the hell were they called before brushes for bottles were invented?

Each large bed of sun-warmed flowers gave up its unique invisible pool of scents: spicy, sirupy, tickly — evocative, or surprising. Their odors seemed like solo notes played against a steady background beat: the aromatic perfume of the gum trees.

The gums more properly should be called eucalypts, he learned; he thought that would sound better — and make better sense, since none of their perhaps-600-species produces any gum. By now, he had seen and smelled thousands of those strange trees in all their infinite variety, and while he liked their clean menthol odor, they were, he thought, the ugliest of trees: twisted, dusty, weatherbeaten, some with long, messy tatters of bark flopping from their trunks.

Still, he admired their toughness. Remembering the Ghost Gums that existed in the waterless red desert of the north, he understood why Australians love them. *They're dinkum Aussie trees,* he thought, *rooted in this harsh land, asking no coddling, independent as hell.*

As a contrast, he pictured the banyan: millions of shiny dark green leaves borne on great spreading, shading branches with fascinating aerial roots — always admired and photographed by visitors to the tropical colonial empires. What those visitors to Dutch Java, British Malaya, French Indochina, or the USA's Philippines never guessed was that the banyan is a parasite, a strangler fig that eventually kills its sturdy host.

He knelt to examine calf-high green Parrot's Beak terrestrial orchids and thigh-high, bright blue Sun Orchids. He stretched to peer at high wattle blooms.

The ubiquitous wattles were acacias, he learned, and if the choice were his, acacia seemed a more graceful name. With at least as many species as the eucalypts, they were far handsomer, bearing blossoms that ranged from fluff-balls to spikes, in shades from orange-yellow to palest celery (Bodalla Silver Wattles, Sydney Golden Wattles, Raspberry Jam Wattles, even a Black Wattle). The wattles are the winners, he decided, because, most commendably and incredibly, they grow even in the hellish Interior Desert, where no eucalypt — not even a Ghost Gum — can survive.

West of Government House, crowning the highest hill, the Shrine of Remembrance was visible for miles. As he ran upward toward it, he was grateful for the clear day that gave him his first view of Port Phillip Bay to the west. An ample body of water, deep blue under the first patches of blue sky Jim had seen here, its farther shore and narrow entrance on the south were still beyond his vision.

Albion had mentioned that a friend owned a sailboat they could borrow, if only Jim could stay longer.

Damn Albi's job, he thought; *we should be having a picnic right now!* All the American young women he had known, in San Antonio and Manila — like Daphne and the English girls in Singapore — had always been available for daytime swimming dates, tennis, golf, horseback riding, and picnics, whenever he was free. They lived at home, with plenty of time for fun and sports — except while they were attending college classes or arranging charity benefits — until they married and became immersed in housekeeping and having babies.

Still, to do them justice, all the Manila Army and Navy daughters had been shipped back to the States in May, before Mrs. Sayre had begun her Red Cross bandage-rolling group. Leda and her friends had given up their Monday golf to roll bandages at the High Commissioner's residence. Perhaps the "Service Brats" would have joined in that project, too, if they had not been evacuated.

Even Daphne, the epitome of a good-time girl, had taken some kind of Red Cross First-Aid course in Singapore — although Lady Brooke-Popham complained bitterly about the apathy of most Englishwomen there.

The Army and Navy nurses in Manila were in a class apart: "career women"; but their age and education had intimidated him until this year. Since he had become 21, and a second lieutenant and a pilot, the new batch of younger nurses had begun to look definitely approachable.

Hell, if the U.S. got into a war, American women could probably take over some of the men's jobs, just as the sheilas here have done — but now, there aren't enough jobs for the **men** *in the States. "Rosie the Riveter" probably has six kids, and a husband on Relief, and there aren't enough rivets to occupy many Rosies.*

He had seen flights of roselle parrots and red lowrys — and had heard their harsh voices — been threatened by a diving attack from a black-and-white fighter-pilot magpie; and he was still accompanied by one of the friendly fantails the Australians nickname "Willy Wagtail," when he reached the summit of the hill crowned by the Shrine of Remembrance.

Without today's welcome sunlight, he thought, the classically Greek shrine — set on an extensive base of terraced marble that permitted no softening touch of greenery — would seem unbearably somber and cold. But of course, he reflected, those old Greeks envisioned plenty of sunshine surrounding their temples.

On the entrance side, the windowless square edifice, topped by a truncated pyramid, was relieved by seven columns beneath a carved pediment, and as he mounted the marble steps to the heavy door, Jim saw statues at the corners that added a human scale. He walked all the way around the building to examine each well-sculpted statuary group: Goodwill, Justice, Patriotism, Peace, and Sacrifice. The bronze emblem that emerged from the flat top of the pyramid, he learned, was "a symbol of Glory."

Inside, after the sunlight, it was bone-cold and blind-dark. After his eyes adjusted, he saw the white-haired caretaker seated by the door.

"Too bad you didn't come ten days ago, myte. You missed 'nature's spotlight.'"

Limping, he shuffled over to show Jim an aperture in the pyramidal dome where a shaft of light entered. He explained that each year at the anniversary of the signing of the Armistice ending the Great War, at the eleventh minute after the eleventh hour of the eleventh day of the eleventh month, a ray of sunlight illuminated the Rock of Remembrance. The Rock, a slab of polished black marble, was sunk lower than the floor. "That's so every head must bow, in order to read the inscription," he told Jim.

Jim said, "I guess it's a comfort to the Australians who're in combat now — to know that if they're killed, their country never forgets its war dead." He wondered, however, if a man fighting for his life really would think such thoughts.

"Never forget our ANZACs — win *or* lose. We're the only people who have a national holiday to remember a *defeat*. Most countries try to forget those — sweep 'em under the carpet as soon as they can. But *my* lousy battle, at Gallipoli, is still remembered every bloody year on April 25. That was the day we landed under those goddam cliffs, with the bastard Turks on top, throwing everything they had down on us."

"You were one of the lucky ones who got back."

"'Luck' doesn't half say it, myte. The Blessed Virgin spread her blue cloak over me, and if I hadn't stuck my foot out, I could have brought that back, too. I was one of the lucky seventy-eight and a half thousand wounded. Thirty-three and a half thousand died there — and seven and a half thousand are still listed as missing."

How many of those forty-plus thousand were married, Jim wondered, *and left young widows like Albi?*

"It's for those cobbers of mine that I volunteered to sit in this black tomb every day and freeze my ass off — for them, and for the young ANZACs in the Middle East right now."

"You mean, the ones who are still alive?"

"That's the whole point of *remembering your defeats,* Yank! They're only worth the sacrifice if the fuckin' powers that be make damned bloody sure it won't ever happen again. See, this Shrine is the most prominent object south of the Yarra — nobody can avoid seeing it. Most importantly, the bloke down there in Government House sees this building every bloody day. Whether he chooses or not, the bastard can't escape being reminded of the damned Dardanelles. He remembers about Lone Pine and Hill Sixty, and Chunuk Bair . . . and he swears to himself that Australia will *never* let the British brass send ANZAC troops into a death-trap like that again!"

Maybe they can build another Shrine on the flat top of this one, with a big sign: REMEMBER CRETE.

Jim shook the old soldier's hand, then obediently bowed his head so he could read the words carved on the black marble Rock of Remembrance: *Greater Love Hath No Man.*

Part 2 — John Curtin, PM

After full explanation of what my object was, I purchased two large tracts of land from them — about 600,000 acres more or less — and delivered over to them blankets, knives, looking-glasses, tomahawks, beads, scissors, flour, etc., as payments for the land, and also agreed to give them tribute, or rent, yearly.
       — John Batman's Journal, May 1835,
      written near the future site of Melbourne

Government House
Friday afternoon, 21 November 1941

  Jim felt pity for the man who had stepped into the most important job in Australia only six weeks earlier. Leader of the trade-union based Labour Party, John Curtin had been elected — by one vote — on 7 October, after Parliament's seven unsettled weeks with three changes of government.
  He's hardly had time to find his way to the men's room, Jim thought . . . *but at that, he's been in office since before Brereton and Eubank arrived in the Philippines, less than* **three weeks ago!**
  Curtin did not resemble Jim's idea of a Prime Minister. His open, plain, heavy face and receding, slicked-back brown hair and ill-fitting dark blue suit gave him the look of a trade-union officer like those Jim had met in Melbourne's war plants. Jim liked his unaffected "man of the people" manner,

so different from the English Prime Ministers he had seen in newsreels, Neville Chamberlain and Winston Churchill. Born in Creswick, near Melbourne, 56 years ago to Irish immigrant parents, Curtin now had established his home base at the isolated west coast city of Perth.

He'd be Leda's idea of the perfect combination: a union leader and an Irishman, like her grandfather Hogan. . . . But Curtin sure doesn't look like a man who'd relish having a bunch of bossy Yanks try to push into his newly-acquired domain.

The Prime Minister shook hands warmly with each of the Americans, pausing to tell Jim that his son John was in RAAF pilot training, and to say, "You're about the same age as my daughter Elsie. She's a stenographer out in Perth — a 'Sand-groper,' as Aussies call residents of Western Australia. Too bad you can't meet her."

"Yes, Sir — my tough luck," Jim lied.

Thanks, but I have one too many dames confusing me now. I sure don't need to meet another one! Maybe next time.

In fact, Albion was *here* — to take notes for the Americans. Obviously, she was trying as hard as Jim to appear cool and businesslike; but he was tingling with awareness, hyper-conscious of her little Mona Lisa smile, the curve of her breasts beneath her uniform, her perfect legs. She had mentioned her hope that Merle-Smith might choose to bring her here today, but she had considered it unlikely.

Jim had to struggle to keep from looking at her, and he wondered, *How the hell can I keep my mind on business?*

They had planned on a date, of sorts, for this evening — after she finished her stint of helping backstage at an amateur Little Theater play. When he had complained, she told him, "I had a life here before you came, Jimyank, and I'll have to go back to it after you leave."

Because of the need to keep the Americans' visit secret, the government buildings downtown, north of the Yarra, had been avoided all week. Government House — actually the residence of the governor of Victoria, and not Federal property — provided the ideal seclusion for this meeting that would include high government officials. Brereton and his "crew" were assembling with their Australian counterparts, drinking dark tea from porcelain cups, in a handsome reception room with paneled walls, a huge blue rug, and blue velvet draperies.

Hey, I've seen this scene before — it looks like a rerun of the meeting at General Percival's headquarters in July. Except that, in Singapore, it was the English officers who handled their teacups so gracefully, while we looked as awkward as we felt, displaying our inexperience with tea-sipping. Here, the big hands of the Prime Minister, who got his start in the Timber-Cutters' Union, look as if they'd rather be holding a mug of smoky "billy tea" outdoors

Chapter 10 — Part 2 — John Curtin, PM 243

over an open fire. Hell, so would I.

Allison Ind — devoted to England through his love of English literature — was a good man with a teacup, Jim observed; he held one like an American man-of-the-world, neither effeminately nor bear-paw clumsily.

Ind's conversation with Curtin brought out a facet that Jim would never have suspected: The PM was a reader of poetry for pleasure, and Milton was his favorite. Curtin was telling the Captain, "Sometimes in Parliament, when a member rises to speak, I'm tempted to steal from *Paradise Lost,* and say,

What in me is dark
Illumine, what is low raise and support,
That to the height of this great argument
I may assert eternal Providence —"

Beaming, Professor Ind joined him in the next line:

"And justify the ways of God to man!"

As Jim applauded, Brereton interrupted with a question for Curtin. Sir Keith Murdoch was unable to be here, but he had issued invitations to the Americans to dine with him later at the Athenaeum Club. While Brereton liked the idea of "a shindig," he wondered if it would be safe for the Americans to appear in a group downtown; he was desperately anxious for their presence to remain unreported.

"Your group landed in Darwin ten days ago, and not a word of your visit has been mentioned by press or radio," Curtin reminded the General. "You-lot could go anywhere in Melbourne without endangering your privacy. There's no Fifth Column in this country. We're all the one race — the English-speaking race — and no Aussie would give you away."

Curtin looked into the faces of the three Americans and said quietly, "By the same token, I trust your discretion not to reveal any information that is important to Australia's security." He stared into Jim's eyes with such intensity that Jim felt like raising his hand in the Scout's Honor sign.

He may not look like a leader — but he's got what it takes. . . .

"Murdoch called me just now, to explain his absence," the Prime Minister continued. "Bulletins are pouring into his office from his west coast reporters — all up and down the coast — and he's working alongside his editors to get the entire picture into focus."

Sounds big — but the Japs would never start by attacking that barren west coast!

"Last week, our cruiser HMAS *Sydney* safely escorted north from Fremantle — the port of Perth, my former home city — several ships carrying troops and supplies to Singapore. At the Sunda Strait she turned them over to the British cruiser HMS *Durban* on Monday —"

*So **Zealandia**'s crew made it OK after all their bitching!*

"— twenty-four hours late," Curtain continued. "*Sydney* was due back in Fremantle by yesterday evening, but naturally, she was maintaining radio silence, so her exact location has been unknown. However, the Cunard liner *Aquitania*, which has been in service as a troopship since the war, spotted a rubber raft while en route from Singapore to Sydney about a hundred and fifty miles due west of Carnarvon — that's on our west coast, roughly midpoint between Perth and Broome. Twenty-six Germans were on the raft and were taken aboard *Aquitania*. Upon interrogation, they said they were survivors of a notorious German raider we've called 'Ship 41,' the *Kormoran*, which they said had been sunk Wednesday evening by an Australian cruiser."

*Hooray for the **Sydney**! But why does Curtin look so serious?*

"They say the cruiser had approached them, signaling with flags for identification, and when she was within half a mile the *Kormoran* began firing. Their first salvo, they claim, struck the cruiser amidships and she burst into flames. The cruiser's return fire struck the Germans' engine room. Machinery and water pumps were destroyed, making the resulting fires uncontrollable, and when the flames got near the magazine holding six tons of explosives — they claim they hadn't yet laid any mines on this visit — they abandoned ship. The cruiser's two torpedoes missed; but the Germans say *Kormoran* fired three torpedoes, one of which struck the cruiser forward, and then she — so they claim — blew up. According to their story, both ships sank around midnight."

With a heavy sigh, Curtin continued in a husky voice. "Since then, three more boats full of German crewmen and officers have been picked up by our ships or have beached on the coast — but not a single Carley float from the *Sydney* has been found. So we're hoping that the Germans are lying, and that *Sydney* is all right. We're asking every powerful radio in Australia to transmit to her, asking her to break radio silence, and we're starting an aerial search for her. We're sending an RAAF Catalina from Townsville and another from Port Moresby to the west coast; the Dutch will send a Dornier and two Catalinas down from Java; and the RAAF has ordered seven Hudsons from No. 14 Squadron and five Wirraways from No. 25 Squadron to base at Carnarvon and search from there."

General Brereton held out his hand in a gesture of condolence. "We wish you good luck, Sir."

Curtin managed a brave smile. "She's always been a lucky ship."

Hearty male voices in the entrance hall signaled the arrival of the final contingent of high-ranking Australians who would advise the War Cabinet of their opinions about Brereton's "scheme." They probably came out here on the tram, Jim thought; he admired them for saving rationed gasoline, and for their unpretentious style.

The Prime Minister introduced the Americans to his political rival, the Liberal Party leader, Robert Menzies, who had served as Prime Minister for two years until his resignation in August. It seemed that Menzies temporarily had "retained the portfolio of Minister for Defence Coordination," and that gave him the right to be here. Jim felt sure that Curtin would have been just as happy if Menzies, whose nickname was "Pig-iron Bob," had stayed away from *his* big show. The former PM had a twinkle in his eye — or was it a glint of mischief? Albion had told Jim that Menzies had held office by a one-vote margin, and now Curtin held that same narrow margin, by the vote of that same member.

Jim had heard Menzies's Australian cadences on the radio two years and two months earlier. On 4 September (Pacific time) 1939, it was Menzies who had announced to his people: ". . . in consequence of the persistence by Germany in her invasion of Poland, Great Britain has declared war upon her, and that, as a result, Australia is also at war. . . ."

Lieutenant General Vernon A. H. Sturdee, 51, a native of Frankston in this state of Victoria, held a position in the government that approximated, Jim had been told, Secretary Stimson's in the U.S.: Secretary of War.

So maybe the Aussie military isn't under such tight civilian control as ours, Jim surmised.

Herbert Vere Evatt, 47, portly and jolly-looking, bore an incipient double chin and a thick mop of dark hair turning gray. Curtin had appointed him to the new Cabinet with two titles: Attorney General, and Minister for External Affairs. Dr. Evatt's jovial appearance belied his personality, Albion had told Jim. "He hates the Pommies. He went to university in England — and perhaps they treated him as a wild colonial boy, although he's brilliant. Ambitious, too; he'll doubtless become PM some day."

If that happens, Jim thought, *Evatt probably will make certain that when he's calling the shots, the RAAF commander won't be a "Pommie," like Burnett!*

Jim had met Air Chief Marshal Sir Charles Burnett at Merle-Smith's dinner, and liked him. A balding man with sandy beetle brows and a neat sandy moustache, Burnett definitely was an Englishman, although he had been born in the improbable location of Brown's Valley, Minnesota, 49 years earlier. Brereton, who had met with the Air Chief Marshal almost as soon as he had landed in Melbourne — and continuously since then — spoke highly of his cordiality and cooperation. Still, Jim suspected that despite Burnett's ability and warmth, the 1940 appointment of an RAF officer as Chief of the Australian Air Staff might have rankled some of the senior RAAF officers.

Allison Ind told Burnett, "Last July in Singapore, Jim and I had the pleasure of meeting the staff officers of the RAF and RAAF — and we enjoyed a lovely dinner at the hillside home of Air Chief Marshal and Lady Brooke-Popham."

"'Brookeham' was down here in October," Burnett said. "He told us that while the Japs have superior *numbers* in the air, they're lacking in *quality*."

Funny — that's just what Sir Robert told us in July.

Today's conversation also echoed the buzz of Singapore in July and returned to the same topic: Russia's ancient nightmare come true, the invasion from the West. During July, the stunned and unprepared Soviets had managed to stop Hitler's legions at the Bug River; but many Singapore officers had predicted that the German flood which had drowned Western Europe would soon roll deep into Russia. Most of the Britons had declared that Hitler's boast, "Moscow in six weeks," would be fulfilled; others gave the Soviets two weeks or less.

The "wireless news" reported that General von Kleist's mobile armored force had finally cracked Rostov's defenses and was even now entering the city — a strategic prize. The August attack on Stalingrad had swelled to a million-man battle; the city hung on, but street fighting was reported. German troops were only 110 miles from Moscow.

Jim's father quietly but stubbornly had refused to concede the doom of the USSR. Jim wondered what Alexander was saying now, in the face of today's news. The old man's experience as a member of the little-known American Siberian Expeditionary Force in 1918 obviously had left him with an exaggerated respect for Russian fortitude and fighting ability. Characteristically, Alexander looked back to history — and apparently he equated Hitler's powerful mechanized forces with Napoleon's cavalry!

And of course Leda, enamored of the Red experiment, with wishful thinking believes that Alex will prove correct. And she — the former pacifist — would be delighted if the U.S. would get into the war now, to help Russia.

Like Leda, these Australians of the Labour Party evinced deep sympathy for the besieged Soviet "workers' state."

"Hitler's not satisfied with all the territory he's conquered," Dr. Evatt said. "His mad ambition is nothing less than that of governing the entire world — either by force or the threat of force. And Australia is determined to resist him, to the last man."

Jim felt an implied reproach: *You Yanks are helping Hitler by staying out of it.*

General Sturdee said, "Our men in Malaya are ready to resist an aggressor closer to home. In Singapore, and Darwin, too, the Diggers are becoming restive. They're 'wingeing' because they signed up to fight — not to stew in a tropical camp, clearing jungle or building roads. They want action — they're crying for it. And unless I misread the signs of the times in Asia, they'll have action in plenty before very long."

That's fine with me, just so they wait till I've been to Singapore and had my fling with Daphne. After that, I'll be ready to be a dashing fighter ace, shooting down Japs by the dozen.

"Churchill sent me a wireless last month," Curtin told the Americans, "saying that Japan won't risk war until after the Germans break Russia. And by that time, we'll have an additional strong deterrent — based in Singapore. He's sending two of England's finest warships — escorted by the carrier *Indomitable* — to reinforce the Malay Barrier: the *Repulse* and the *Prince of Wales!*"

"Repulsive" is the word, Jim thought. This news was as shocking to him as it presumably would be to the Japanese; it meant that Daphne's fiance, Robin, probably was steaming toward Singapore right now.

Thank God, I'll get there first, so I can convince her that I'm the one she really loves. If necessary, I'll knock his block off when he steps off the gangplank. No . . . it will be better for her to compare us in the flesh, instead of my trying to compete with her memories and his pretty-boy photo and his English-poet letters to her. That'll make my visit a real challenge. And may the best flesh win — and may it be mine.

Amenities observed, they moved into the adjacent large dining room with its sweeping south views of green hills — including the hill crowned by the Shrine of Remembrance — and were seated around a long table. Before each chair was placed a teacup and saucer, pencil and tablet, and a large bronze ashtray centered with an anchor.

Jim's place was beside Donald Rogers, Curtin's secretary and unofficial advisor, who would take notes for the government record. Rogers previously had worked as a journalist; he seemed quick in mind and body, and Jim liked him at once. The man might have been Albion's brother; they resembled each other in their compact slimness and dark hair, in their compelling presence, and in the impression they gave of knowing everything that was going on. Jim knew that Albion — like the present-day Highlanders — was descended from the fiercely independent clans of northern Scotland; now he surmised that Rogers also might have a Pictish strain. In this "Ivory Soap" country, dominated by large, fair-haired, blue-eyed Irish and Anglo-Saxon types, he found such differences striking.

Rogers sat between Jim and Albion; probably a good thing, Jim thought, knowing that if she were beside him he would have a hard time keeping his mind on the discussion and his hands on the table.

Prime Minister Curtin, at the head of the table, donned rimless eyeglasses that gave him a more scholarly look. His brawny hands extracted a cigarette from a carved wooden humidor and handed the box to Brereton, who did not open it but lighted one of his own cigars. Brereton passed the humidor to Lefty

Eads beside him. Lefty's stacks of papers, covered with his columns of penciled figures, appeared to Jim like an incipient conflagration waiting for a hot ash to fall, but Lefty passed along the box unopened.

Curtin opened the meeting, abstaining from poetry:

"We Australians have long been admirers of Mr. Roosevelt. We have the greatest confidence that he understands fully the critical situation in the Pacific, and that if Japan continues to extend her aggression, America will go right out to meet it. Our honored guests from the Philippines bring welcome evidence that our confidence in America is justified."

Air Chief Marshal Burnett stood to introduce briefly "Major General Lewis Brereton, Commander of the Far East Air Forces based in the Philippine Islands."

It was the first time on this secret mission that an American's military title had been mentioned, and Jim thought it sounded quite impressive. He hoped that Brereton's two stars would add luster to the American plan — although he had seen enough evidence of a "cut-'em-down-to-size" attitude of the egalitarian Australians to realize that any hint of snobbishness could backfire.

The rapport between these two air Commanders evidently sprang from their similar brisk, no-nonsense personal style. Brereton had spoken of the RAF officer as "a remarkable man who conducts a conference more efficiently and with less waste of time than most executives I've met." Now Burnett concisely described the enthusiastic reports he had received from the RAAF Commanders in Darwin, Townsville, Port Moresby, and Brisbane regarding Brereton's suggestions. If he had heard from Rabaul, he did not mention it.

Jim kept glancing at Dr. Evatt's pleasant, plump face, inscrutable behind his black-rimmed glasses. Would this boost by the "Pommie" Burnett automatically turn the Pommie-hater against the plan? Albion had mentioned that Evatt's wife had been born in the U.S.

I hope he likes his wife and her birthplace better than he likes England.

Brereton, with characteristic terseness, outlined the first of his three suggested projects. Starting with the two east coast seaports of Townsville and Brisbane, they would be prepared to handle American freighters carrying crates of U.S. fighter aircraft. After the crates were off-loaded, the planes would be assembled at a plant to be built at Townsville, where maintenance facilities also would function. Brisbane would have a repair depot, training centers, and satellite fields for dispersal, perhaps as far south as Newcastle. The new planes would then be flown to Darwin. That transcontinental flight would necessitate two intermediate airfields equipped for refueling and repairs, these to be established at Cloncurry and Daly Waters. Darwin, the Australian terminus of this ferry route, would be prepared to handle flights departing for the Philippines and also to Singapore via Timor and Java. Estimated cost to the USA: $18,000,000.

*Wow! With eighteen **hundred** bucks, some of the paddy fields around Clark's sod runway could be filled in, so the B-17s could be dispersed.*

Murmurs sounded around the table. Donald Rogers whispered in Jim's ear, "A problem could be that each of our six states is just about its own boss and does what it wants. If any of them didn't want to accept these installations, the Federal Government couldn't force it. But I can't see them objecting to a couple of Yank aerodromes."

Jim could understand why Brisbane might not want to lose any more of that rich farmland, but as for the shantytowns they had flown over in the north — those bleak little ghost towns of the Gold Rush — he doubted if the inhabitants of Daly Waters or Cloncurry would object to an infusion of Yankee greenbacks.

Dr. Evatt seemed affronted by the mention of the money. "We did not initiate these surveys, but you are asking us to relinquish some of our sovereignty. Perhaps there has been too much talk of American aid — aid to Britain, aid to Greece, aid to Russia — and now, aid to Australia? We are not here as petitioners, mendicants, pressing selfish claims. Nor do we speak of the needs of Australia, as though Australians were concerned solely with the defense of Australia. When our men were in the van in Libya, did we speak of the needs of Libya? Did we, when we sent our soldiers to Greece and to Crete, to Syria and to Iraq — when we sent thousands of our airmen to Britain, and our sailors to the Mediterranean — when we sent munitions and equipment overseas, did we ever talk of the needs of those places? No, we talked of *the one need of democracy,* the need of defeating the enemy. If the United States wants to prepare to fight by our side in Australia, you will only be doing what Australia has already done almost everywhere in the world — that is, fighting against the attempts of the Axis to dominate the whole world by force."

Boy! Dr. Evatt sure knows how to put us Yanks in our place.

Curtin smoothed his appointee's ruffled feathers and got the meeting back on track by saying, "Our American visitors are here to discuss strengthening our mutual air power. Our Federal Labour Party, as long ago as 1937, adopted a program supporting aerial defense. Labour has constantly challenged the Liberal Party's policy of naval development — at a yearly cost more than double that of air power — despite the fact that aircraft would be more valuable to us than the warships that would be provided for the same money. With Australia's vast coastline, aerial defense is the only defense within our capabilities. Parliament has approved, in principle, my assurance of a long-range scheme to expand the Royal Australian Air Force to sixty squadrons. However, that goal is still a distant dream. In the meantime, I welcome the American approach."

Now it's the Liberal Mr. Menzies whose feathers are ruffled, Jim thought. *Sixty squadrons! Curtin **is** dreaming. I think the RAAF has all of thirteen* *squadrons operational now — and five of those are only flying Wirraways.*

Former Prime Minister Menzies took the challenge. "The Liberal Party's record of favoring air power for Australia's defense cannot be refuted. I promulgated that doctrine before war broke out, and in a national broadcast the month after we declared war, I again expressed my conviction that air force planning must be given the highest priority. Kindly continue, General Brereton."

Politicians! It must be galling as hell for them to be involved in this — the biggest offer Australia has ever had from any country — and not be able to make a press announcement, taking some of the credit.

Even the Generals, Jim thought, didn't get their stars without playing politics. An officer like Eubank, who would never lick a boot, who treated his subordinates and superiors with the same respect, would probably remain a Lieutenant Colonel for 30 years, although nature had blessed him with the qualities that politicians strive for: magnetism, natural leadership, ease of discourse — still, he was a pilot's pilot, who would rather fly an airplane than fly a desk at Headquarters. Rank was not his goal in life, and he did not claw for it; if it came, it would come by merit alone.

Donald Rogers and Albion were taking notes in shorthand as flowing and mysterious to Jim as Arabic calligraphy.

Hell, I can write in a secret code, too, he thought. He wrote on his own pad in the Cherokee alphabet: *civilian officials all vested . . . good in this frigid climate . . . but Pixie not frigid . . . gold chains across vests across bay windows . . . chastity enforced by absence of privacy . . . neckties choking . . . wowsers strangling. . . .*

Brereton's second request was for a sufficient number of additional airfields to be built, with dormitories and other facilities, to provide space for about half of his Far East Air Force, so that he could rotate Philippine-based squadrons to Australia for training in tactical operations.

General Sturdee wanted to know *how many* airplanes and men.

Brereton assumed, for a working figure, that this would mean: one heavy bombardment group, three fighter groups, three bomber reconnaissance squadrons, and accompanying services.

And this is going to be **half** *of his strength? Hallelujah! Surely I'd be included in that tactical training, and get to stay down here long enough to find* **some place** *where Albi and I could wrap ourselves around each other.* He glanced quickly at her; she was really smiling.

Estimated cost to the USA: $35,000,000.

No one spoke; all seemed to be waiting for Menzies to spring some surprise twist. Albion had told Jim that the brilliant Menzies had lost the election because of his cutting sarcasm; his slashing debating style in Parliament was compared with that of Disraeli. "Even his strong supporters are targets for his mockery. He commands respect, but not loyalty."

The cigarette humidor had come around to Jim again. Each time, he had taken one of the Australian cigarettes, thinking *I'm not really cravin' another Craven-A. I'd rather "Reach for a Lucky, instead of a sweet," but I know I'd look like a Yank snob if I lit one of my own.* He would like to empty his pack of Luckies into the box to give the Australians a treat; but he knew that the gesture would appear condescending. A small gold plaque was inlaid in the top of the humidor: *This wood is from the cruiser HMAS **Sydney**, which sank the **Emden** in the Great War.*

Jim mused, *The **Emden**, the famous "Scourge of the Seas," that put dozens of merchant ships out of business, was an ancestor of the raider **Kormoran** — sunk this week by a descendant of that earlier **Sydney**! It's good that they kept a chunk of the old ship's wood when she was scrapped . . . I hope their new "glory ship" **Sydney** will turn up OK, and when she gets old and heads for the scrap-pile they can make humidors to remember her by.*

After a silence that seemed to express relief, Brereton stated his third request. He hoped that additional operating bases and training bases for bombardment and fighter groups could be established. To start, he had in mind: four bombardment groups, with a bombardment training center, and four fighter groups, with a fighter training center.

The cost could not be estimated until it was decided whether materials and workers could be supplied in Australia, or should be sent from the States.

Jim wondered if the civilians knew the difference between a squadron and a *group*.

Donald Rogers showed Jim the total for the first two "schemes," which he had written on his tablet in Australian pounds: 5,227,845.

General Sturdee said, "The materials are out of my realm, but I can tell you that the manpower will have to come from the United States. Australia has six hundred thousand men under arms. Comparing the size of our populations, if the U.S. had as many men in military service as we, you would have nearly ten million men in uniform. Our civilian population is also stretched to the limit. We have two hundred thousand civilians manufacturing munitions alone. One third of our aircraft workers are women, and the armed forces have an insatiable requirement for women."

Me, too, Jim thought, before the laughter broke out.

Prime Minister Curtin laughed, then added, "Expressed in another way: out of every ten men in Australia, three are wholly engaged in war, as members of the fighting forces or making the munitions and equipment to fight with. The other seven — besides feeding and clothing the whole ten and their families — have to produce the food and wool and metals which Britain needs for her very existence. The proportion is growing every day. On the one hand we're ruthlessly cutting out unessential expenditure so as to free men and women for war work, and on the other, mobilizing womanpower to the utmost to supplement the men. Only the infirm remain outside the compass of our war plans."

Dr. Evatt broke in, as if reproving the Prime Minister, "Nevertheless, we cannot consider admitting American workers, even for a limited time. Our unions would never stand for that! We learned our lesson with the Chinese laborers who were allowed in to work in the gold fields and stayed on to become clever merchants."

And some Americans are black. White Australia would be leery of letting them in.

Curtin nodded. "Perhaps that will need to be taken up with Mr. Casey, our minister to Washington. Meanwhile, I make it clear that Australia looks to America, free from any pangs about our traditional links of friendship to Britain. We shall exert our energy toward shaping a plan, with the United States as its keystone, giving our country confidence and ability to defend itself. You will be our leader, and we will pull knee to knee with you, for every ounce of our weight."

Dinkum Aussie. Honest, sincere, and determined as hell.

Evatt, the last to comment, began with conciliation and ended with a twist. "Preparation in common is the one guarantee of security for Australia, as well as for you in the Philippines. We cannot afford to have defense areas of such weakness as to attract the unwelcome attention of an aggressor. I visualize the formation of a Southwest Pacific zone of security, acting with the colonial powers of Holland, France, and Portugal, as *well* as the United States."

Curtin sighed. "General Brereton, all your suggestions will be presented to the full War Cabinet for their approval."

Flashing his grin, Brereton reminded, "Subject to the final sanction of the U.S. government."

"Too right, General. Your government will be meeting the costs. The final word will come from Washington."

Albion, observing that Jim's ashtray was almost overflowing, had handed her own unused one to Rogers to pass on to Jim. As he did so, Rogers turned it upside down so that Jim would read the engraving on the bottom: *This ashtray is from the officers' dining hall of HMAS* **Australia,** *the flagship of the Australian fleet. Sunk off Sydney Heads in accordance with the Washington Naval Limitation Agreements of 1921.*

Part 3 — A Gift of Time

The Australians have no leaders. Curtin has a schoolboy's mind. They won't introduce conscription to send men abroad. They refuse to allow immigrants to come into their country, because they are afraid of unemployment.
                — Duff Cooper, head of Allied War Council in Singapore, November 1941

Victoria Barracks
Friday evening, 21 November 1941

    Buoyed by strongly favorable parting remarks from the Australian officials, a jubilant Brereton opened his own bottle of Johnnie Walker Red Label and poured three-finger drinks in their toothbrush glasses for all the Americans.
    Allison Ind said, "This is the first time I've felt warm since we arrived in this beautiful, bleak city."
    Brereton sat on the edge of a cot. "All of a sudden, I feel kinda tired." He took a long drink. "You know, I haven't seen enough of this place to know if it's beautiful, bleak, or what. I feel like taking this week-end off, to relax and go sightseeing — head north Monday, instead of tomorrow. Would that suit you fellas?"
    Astonished, thrilled, Jim joined the others in a lusty "Yes, *Sir!*"
    An entire week-end to play! Surely he could — yes, surely he *could*, with

two days and nights. . . . He felt like hugging the little General in gratitude.

Across a movie screen in his mind raced scenes starring himself with Albion: at the races, at the zoo, in a sailboat, on a beach, in a bed. The final scene was obscured by a wide band of print running diagonally across it: CENSORED BY THE HAYS OFFICE.

Lieutenant Colonel Eubank raised his glass. "Here's to your successful mission, General. It was a helluva job, and you accomplished more in less time than anybody since Genesis. Those Aussies were eating out of your hand today."

Brereton grinned his wide, impish grin. "Gene, those blokes don't eat out of *nobody's* hand!" He took another long drink. "Now all I have to worry about are President Roosevelt and General MacArthur. If MacArthur doesn't back up all the wild promises I've made, I'm standing in a heap of trouble. And if this story gets out in the newspapers, Congress will set fire to the President's tail for violating the Neutrality Act."

"Listen, Lewie, the President can take care of his own tail. He's a gambler and a fighter — that's how he got to the White House in a wheelchair."

Eubank's reassurance reminded Jim of Colonel George on the flight back from Chungking in May. George had assured General Clagett that the President would be delighted if Clagett endorsed Captain Chennault's wild idea of bringing American volunteer pilots to China — in utter defiance of the Neutrality Act. Clagett did, and through a secret Executive Order, Chennault's dream now had come true.

Brereton waved his cigar. "Hell, I'm not really worried about FDR. You're right, he wouldn't let this get pinned on him. Congress would accuse *me* of 'acting without authority,' call me a loose cannon, and I'd be a dead duck, with my career shot to hell."

Allison Ind, warmed and mellow with the prospect of two more days in which to complete his survey, quoted Milton again: "Men of most renowned virtue have sometimes by transgressing most truly kept the law."

Damn, I wish Aunt Alice had a phone, so I could call Pixie and tell her we have a whole wonderful week-end to frolic in! How can I wait till after Murdoch's dinner and after the damned Little Theater play is over?

Part 4 — Very Little Theater

Had we but world enough, and time,
This coyness, lady, were no crime.
— Andrew Marvell, *To his coy mistress*

Melbourne, Victoria
Friday night, 21 November 1941

    Albion was already backstage, beyond his reach, when Jim strode into the Princess Theatre on Spring Street. Too impatient to wait for a tram, he had run — after Murdoch's elegant dinner at 83 Collins Street — to the theater opposite the massive Victoria State Parliament Building. He burned to tell Albion the exciting news of their two-day reprieve; his mind was so captured by images of the delights in store that he could not get absorbed in the staged drama. The play, by Douglas Stewart, seemed pallid in comparison with his own romantic prospects (although he liked the title: *The Golden Lovers*).
    This amateur group, St. Martin's Players, had been founded ten years earlier by Hal Perry and Brett Randall, he learned from a bored scanning of the program. Albion, a member of the Players for two years, had never appeared before the footlights; it was Dennis who had been "the bonzer star," she had told Jim.
    Most members of tonight's cast were performing their roles ably, but the

audience was so meager that he wondered how the group had kept going for a decade. He was not surprised that the Players only could afford to rent this theater for two nights, the culmination of months of rehearsals. Albion had told him that most Australians took a dim view of home-grown theater. "Unless it comes from Broadway or the West End, they assume it can't be worth seeing. Just another example of our 'cultural cringe.'"

A lifelong devotee of movies, he formerly had scorned the stage as too confining of action. However, since David's emergence as a star at the Ateneo, Jim had learned to appreciate the immediacy of live performance.

Jim thought Albi should be in the starring role. She was ten times prettier than the big blonde playing the female lead. Albi was more graceful, had a better voice and diction, better legs.

Not so stacked — she's small — but dynamite. The contrast of her dark hair and fair skin would be effective back to the last row. And those eyes! She'd have the "star quality" that can light up a stage.

Or are actors "born" to act? Do they always start early, like David? When we were little kids and copied the movies we saw, I was the director, and he was always an actor. He'll be a great Jesuit priest, dammit — the best sermonizers always have that theatrical flair. Anyway, this gang's lucky to have Pixie behind the scenes: helping the actors change costume, calming them down, telling them they were great. . . . I wish to hell I could see her!

At last the final curtain closed, and he dashed backstage. While the cast took a curtain call, he found Albion and hugged her, lifting her off her feet.

Her brown eyes were as gorgeous as Hedy Lamarr's — and even more expressive, he thought, when he told her of Brereton's announcement. The joy that shone in them was beyond the power of any actress to portray. In a closet used as a dressing room, he kissed her, held her close, and again looked down at her radiant face.

"Oh, *Jimyank!* Stone the crows — I thought I'd never see you again after tonight!"

"That's the best line I've heard all evening."

They sat in the last row in the darkened theater, his arms around her and her head on his shoulder, while her friends set the stage and readied their props for tomorrow night's performance, from which they had excused Albion, after they met Jim. She let him unbutton her blouse and fondle her firm little breasts; her nipples hardened at his touch. Her smooth, thick, dark hair smelled better than the flowers of the Royal Domain; he longed to pull out the hairpins and see it tumbling over her shoulders — her *bare* shoulders.

"Let's hide here and get locked in for the night," he suggested, with a mental eye on the stage set with its couch. "Yeah, I know — Aunt Alice will be worrying, and it's almost time for the last damned tram! Pixie, you've just *got* to think of some place we can go and be alone — or this wonderful week-end will turn into a torture session for both of us. Lord knows, I've tried to look for some secluded spot that isn't a hotel, but I don't know from nothin' around here."

Even if he could smuggle her into Victoria Barracks, and if his roommate, the obliging Slugger, went in to Melbourne to a movie, in the next room Allison Ind, sitting up in bed for warmth, would be tap-tapping on his typewriter almost all night, trying to finish his survey.

In desperation, he had briefly considered taking Albion to Essendon Airdrome and sharing the privacy of the B-18; although — excluding fighter planes and rumble seats — there could be few places on earth or in the sky that would be less comfortable for what he had in mind. *Flying and lust are passions that grab you by the balls and won't let go; but those two mistresses are too damned jealous to share the same cockpit.* He knew also that at the airdrome an observant Australian watchman — or watchwoman — would surely put an abrupt end to a Yank's giving a lady a night tour of the Yank bomber.

When I properly lose my virginity, he had promised himself, *I'm going to do it First Class.*

What he wanted was not only relief of this craving for Albion's body; he yearned for a sublime experience, equal to those that Hollywood always promised were occurring at the top of the staircase, behind the closed bedroom door. He thought again of the rapture on Hedy Lamarr's exquisite face in the famous scene in the wheat field that had been censored from *Ecstasy*. No one whom he knew had ever viewed that scene; perhaps it existed only in men's imaginations — but he longed to see those emotions on a lovely face, as he envisioned it: utter joy, glorious fulfillment, adoring love.

CHAPTER 11

Part 1 — Flemington Racecourse

> *I find that there is no foundation whatever for the opinion expressed . . . that the Japanese have no "air" or "engine" sense. The Japanese are not inferior to Australians or British — they can fly all right. Their only fault, up to the present, is that they take too many risks. . . . Apart from this the Japanese will become equal to the British or ourselves in the air. . . .*
> — W. M. Marks, Member of the Australian Parliament after visiting Japan in 1923

Northwest of Melbourne
Saturday morning, 22 November 1941

    The tootling little train, crowded with jolly racing fans, took only 15 minutes to go from the Flinders Street Station to Essendon Station, but the ride seemed interminable to Jim. Peering through the window, he smiled when he saw Albion, waiting on the platform to ride with him to Flemington Racecourse, only a few minutes farther out.
    Admiring the broad, tree-bordered highway, he told her, "I wish I had my car and some gas, so we could ride out here with the top down."
    "The roadway looks pitifully empty now. Before rationing, there was always a stream of cars heading this way before a race — and, of course, on Cup Day there were *thousands,* from all over Australia."

Chapter 11 — Part 1 — Flemington Racecourse 259

Men and women in uniform were admitted free. It was not the small admission fee that bothered Jim, but the fact that Albion was in uniform and he was not. "I'll come back wearing mine, and the sight will knock your eyes out," he told her.

He seemed to be almost the only man wearing civilian clothes and paying admission, and for a moment he wondered how the track could remain solvent — until he saw the volume of betting ("punting") activity.

Albion said, "I've seen pictures of that long-tailed winner of your Triple Crown —"

"Whirlaway. He's like you — great legs, but no heart!"

The velvet green ellipse, surrounded by acres of brilliant flowerbeds, looked like a worthy site for a world-famous race. Although the sun was out, the air was still chilly enough for the officials to look proper in their gray top hats. With spacious grounds that stretched to misty views of low hills and spring-green hardwood forests, Flemington appeared as stunning in its own way as the famed English tracks Jim knew in Hong Kong and Singapore.

But naturally, he noted, the background lacked the spectacular hills of Happy Valley — and dusty gum trees could not compete with the orchid-draped jungle of the Nature Reserve alongside Bukit Timah (Silver Hill). There at the Turf Club, where Singapore Britons shed some of their inhibitions after attending services at St. Andrew's Cathedral, he and Daphne had sat in the box of the jolly, brandy-nipping Sultan of Johore. At the memory, Jim wondered if he and Daphne could go across the causeway to the Sultan's palace for tiffin next week, and ride his Arabian mares again.

Never, however, had he seen more magnificent horses than here at Flemington. After visiting the paddock to look over the day's contenders, they decided to bet on Colonus, only 7.2 hands tall, lively and graceful. Less than three weeks earlier, the year's Melbourne Cup had been won by Skipton, 7.7 hands, who had run the two miles in 3 minutes, 23¾ seconds. Skipton was not running today, nor was Ajax, whose string of 19 successive wins recently had been broken.

"Even though Aussie children have to go to school on Cup Day, it's like a holiday, because the race is broadcast into all the classrooms," Albion said. "All the schoolgirls are in love with Jim Carroll's voice, and his descriptions really made us *see* every race and feel all the excitement."

Carroll's broadcast over ABC also could be heard now over loudspeakers in every area of the grounds. His dinkum Aussie speech and genuine infatuation with the horses, their riders, and their gallant efforts convinced Jim that if Carroll wanted to emigrate to the States he could easily compete with Bill Stern or Graham MacNamee.

Jim had never seen so many stunning, well-dressed women in one place — and they smiled at him. Jovial punters insisted on shouting him yet another 15-

ounce "birthday-pot" of Tooth's beer, and he shouted back rounds in return. Albion limited herself to five-ounce "ponies." He felt as taut with energy and vigor as a racehorse; everything was fun; he had never laughed so much.

" 'E's ON THE RYLE!" Jim yelled with the crowd, as Colonus made his way through the pack to hug the rail, assuring his victory on the "finishing straight," the home stretch.

Looking down at the track, Jim saw it as a symbol for the sunny, flowering, galloping circuit of these two remaining days. *We're like those healthy young animals, at their peak of vigor and beauty (well, Albi has beauty and I have vigor) — striving to cover distance swiftly. . . . But going nowhere.*

Oh hell — there's always next year. He told Albion, "If Flemington's this exciting on a plain old Saturday, I've *got* to come back for the Cup! Mark it on your calendar, Pixie Doll; we've got a date for the first Tuesday in November, 1942. I'll send you the money, you get the 'tickees' — and give Aunt Alice a vacation in Fiji, for God's sake."

"I'd be delighted! But that's a long year away, Jimyank. You spoke about coming down for your birthday in autumn."

"Too right, the night of fireworks." The Australian way of celebrating Empire Day — Queen Victoria's and Jim's birthday — was with a noisy "Cracker Night."

He squeezed her hand tightly. "Dammit, Pixie. I can't wait till *May,* for *my* fireworks!"

Part 2 —
Royal Park Zoo and Chloe's

I did what I had set out to do — to make their passing easier and to keep the dreaded half-caste menace from our great continent.
— Daisy Bates, *The Passing of the Aborigines*, 1938

North of Melbourne
Saturday afternoon, 22 November 1941

After the races Jim and Albion took another train to Royal Park and the 50-acre zoo, where Jim finally saw marsupials and monotremes, and where a grandmotherly attendant handed him a fuzzy little gold-brown body with wide ears and a flat rubbery nose. He had never heard of a koala nor seen a picture of one.

"You almost lost your chance to see a live one, Yank," the attendant said. "Whitefellow fur hunters nearly wiped out all the koalas — in one year, Sydney alone exported six hundred thousand pelts. But now it's illegal to kill 'em."

What a lousy sport, he thought; *like killing kids.* The sleeping koala smelled like a cough drop because of its diet of eucalyptus leaves, and it seemed perfectly content in his arms. "Walt Disney would go nuts in this country!" he told Albion. "I just wish *you'd* be as snuggly as this creature."

"That creature wasn't trained by my mother to act like a lady in public!"

The attendant joined their conversation. "These females are such perfect ladies, they never take a drink — not even water! They get all their liquid from the gum leaves they eat. And they produce babies only one-quarter of an inch long. Now, what could be more ladylike than that?"

The parrots seemed excessive, in noise and in numbers; including a Golden-shouldered one, there were 57 varieties. "As many as Heinz has pickles," Jim said; then had to explain.

A Golden-fronted Bowerbird tidied up his bachelor apartment stocked with shiny trinkets to entice a female, and a lyrebird imitated the calls of most of the other birds. The Birds of Paradise that he had hoped to see in New Guinea were here in more-than-oriental-splendor: yellow, black, purple, pink, green, orange, olive, and mocha. Here, also from New Guinea, was a bright blue bird nearly three feet long, wearing a lacy crest; Jim had seen Papuan men wearing those feathers of the Goura Crowned Pigeon.

Strange earthbound birds stalked through the dust — cassowaries, emus, and New Zealand's little kiwi, sniffling through its long, probing beak.

Now he saw up close the black whiskers and red faces of the gray brolgas that he had watched with Penny as they performed their "mass minuet" in their marsh habitat near Townsville. Still graceful in their walk, these caged birds seemed to have forgotten their strutting, head-tossing dance.

"Penny and the Brolgas" — sounds like the name of an all-girl Aussie dance band . . . and I'll be in Townsville Monday night, en route Singapore. I hope I can see Penny, and. . . .

You lecherous louse, he accused himself. *You're as disgusting as Punch, going through life with a stiff prick. How can you stand here and sweet-talk this lovely clean girl at the same time you're salivating about screwing two others?*

* * * * *

Downtown Melbourne
Saturday night, 22 November 1941

Even in early-to-bed Melbourne, it was possible to go dancing on a Saturday night, and Bob Gibson's orchestra was playing at a Melbourne version of a night club called Chloe's. Jim was relieved to see that some of the other men in civilian clothes looked as if they, too, had spent the day at the races and the zoo. Albion, in her crisp, dark-blue dress uniform, always looked fresh and perfect for any occasion, he thought. Although she protested that her dancing was rusty, she followed him easily; her slender body against his was an instrument of delicious torture.

Unfortunately, Albion did not know any jitterbug steps, and would not let him teach her any; that would make her feel too conspicuous, she said.

"That's the story of your life — and my frustration," he scolded her, while they sat out Bob Gibson's vibrant interpretation of "In the Mood." "You're losing out on life by never taking a risk. You're so damned afraid someone will see you — going into a hotel with me, jitterbugging — hell, I'm surprised you even took a chance on a couple of horses today!"

"Any Aussie who went to a horserace and didn't punt would feel horribly conspicuous! . . . But Jim, Melbourne's like a small town. I have to live here after you leave, and I don't want to be classed as a 'tom.' Think — have we ever gone anywhere together without seeing somebody who knew me?"

"In fairness, I have to admit you know too damned many people around here." Even in this out-of-the-way night spot, friends of hers had been urging the pair to join their table. "Next time, we'll meet in Sydney and get lost in the crowd."

She smiled. "That's a promise." She was so beautiful that he could not resist kissing her, even though her friends were, indeed, watching.

Chapter 12

Part 1 — St. Paul's Problem

Now if I do that I would not, it is no more I that do it, but sin that dwelleth in me. I find then a law, that, when I would do good, evil is present with me. For I delight in the law of God after the inward man: but I see another law in my members, warring against the law of my mind, and bringing me into captivity to the law of sin which is in my members. O wretched man that I am! Who shall deliver me from the body of this death?
         — St. Paul's Epistle to the Romans 7:20-22

Melbourne, Victoria
Sunday morning, 23 November 1941

Albion was waiting outside St. Paul's Cathedral, and when she saw him, her wistful face became as radiant as a bride's. Behind her, the Anglican cathedral's tall, slender spire had the delicate quality of a wedding dress, he thought, before he checked himself.

But if I ever wanted to get married, she sure would be a swell Aussie wife. They seem to give their men more freedom than most American wives do.

He had wanted to take a picture of her under the curve of a flying buttress, with Princes Bridge and the Yarra River in the background; but after a restless night, he had overslept and had arrived late. He could hear the organ already playing the processional: one of his favorite hymns, Martin Luther's "A

Mighty Fortress."

Anyway, his memory never needed photographs; he knew this sunlit scene was engraved forever in his mind. He wanted only to compose a good picture — and, yes, to be able to show his friends a snapshot of a stunning young woman in a blue Royal Australian Air Force uniform, smiling, with love in her eyes. "This is the girl in Melbourne I almost had an affair with," he'd say.

Attending the service with Albion was only half of the price for a sailboat picnic later — and this was the easier half. After church, she would have to make her every-Sunday visit to see Dennis's cobbers, his close friends now hospitalized with war injuries. Jim had protested that she was wasting so many of his few precious hours — half of his final day! — in following her usual routine. Resentful last night, he had not promised to join her here now, but the prospect of not seeing her until afternoon was worse.

Extending the entire length of the first block of Swanston Street, the Gothic cathedral looked to Jim like the product of at least five centuries; but it had been begun only 50 years earlier and blessed by the Anglican Archbishop of Melbourne only eight years ago, he learned from the service leaflet. Some of the granite columns had been brought from England — a dumb, sentimental waste of shipping space, he thought, when this young city needed so much else. However, most of the edifice was constructed of sandstone from the Barrabool Hills, near Geelong — names, he thought, that you can roll around your tongue. The exquisite tapering landmark spire, echoed by smaller spires, reached heavenward for 314 feet.

He knew Albion well enough now to be aware of a suppressed excitement emanating from the neat blue uniform beside him. He had seen it, when she greeted him; he felt it, sitting in the pew thigh-by-thigh; and he sensed it, in her silent supplication when they knelt in the rite of Morning Prayer; and unmistakably he heard it in her glad voice when they stood to sing.

This kid is bustin' with joy. But why the hell is she? She should be mourning my imminent departure! It can't be because I came to church with her — Anglicans/Episcopalians never try to "save" anybody; they regard evangelism as a rude intrusion of privacy. But she's even happier than she was at the bloody races. Is there, maybe — hey, what an insulting suggestion — some bloke she's crazy about, who agreed to stay out of sight so she could be nice to the visiting Yank? Maybe she has a late date with him tonight. It could be that big Army officer, the lead in the play. Hell, it could be one of a hundred Errol Flynn types who've greeted her, "G'ddye, Albi luv!" everywhere we've been. Or could it be that she's anticipating the hospital visit — maybe she's in love with goddam Dennis's closest cobber? Excuse me, God.

As in Singapore at St. Andrew's Cathedral with Daphne, he was thankful that the Anglican service so closely resembled the familiar Episcopal ritual ingrained in him at Bishop Brent School that he could have followed it without opening the Book of Common Prayer. Today, however, he heard a message that seemed aimed at him — an atypical, un-Episcopalian threat of GUILT.

Avoidance of guilt was the main reason Jim had decided to join his Brent classmates in being confirmed an Episcopalian. It was his father's church, but his mother had urged him to join it, rather than her own abandoned Catholic faith, which David had embraced. One facet of Leda's break with her inherited Irish Catholicism was her repugnance for what she felt was its over-emphasis on guilt; she swore that she'd be damned before she would expose her sons to the childhood agonies of remorse that she had endured.

David, now bent on becoming a Jesuit, never argued about religion and evidently had no trouble with the concept of guilt. Jim had never given it much thought, but he had always felt a vague comfort in the idea that if he ever found himself in a sinful situation, as an Episcopalian he would not be expected to pay for his lapse with what Leda called "great gobbets of guilt."

*Then why this barrage at me today, God? Admittedly, my thoughts are teeming with carnal salaciousness — but I haven't a chance of putting them into action. As Albi would say, "I haven't a Buckley!" But the Gospel reading from Mark speaks of "this adulterous and sinful generation," and that certainly sounds like my generation. The appointed Psalm for today, Number 90, says God sweeps us away like a dream, dried up and withered, consumed in His displeasure, and we are afraid of His wrathful indignation: "Our iniquities You have set before You, and our secret sins in the light of Your countenance." Worse than that, when The Reverend Donald Robertson, in his thundering Aussie monotone read today's verses from St. Paul's Epistle, I felt as if he was directing them right at me. Yeah, lust in the heart or anywhere else is bad, I know. But hell, if St. Paul couldn't cure **his**, why blame me for mine?*

Part 2 —
Royal Melbourne Hospital

Then a big Turkish shell knocked me ass over head
And when I awoke on my hospital bed
I saw what it had done and I wished I were dead.
Never knew there were worse things than dying.
— Australian ballad,
"And the Band Played Waltzing Matilda"

Melbourne, Victoria
Sunday, 23 November 1941

On the northbound tram headed for the Royal Melbourne Hospital, Albion seemed like a bottle of champagne, ready to pop her cork; but when Jim tried to learn the secret behind her effervescence, she only shook her head and smiled her tantalizing "Mona" smile. "I'll tell you when we're in the sailboat," she promised.

He had planned only to walk around outside the hospital in the park-like grounds while Albion made her "lady of mercy" calls; but when she described the loneliness of men whose families lived far away, with no petrol for visits, he relented. Certainly not to visit Dennis's friends — Albion did not want that either — but he agreed to walk through a ward and say hello to any war-wounded man who showed any interest in talking to a bloody Yank.

In the lobby, a world map was marked with clusters of pins showing the locations where 700 Australian Nursing Sisters were serving overseas: not only in Singapore, he learned.

In just a couple of days, he thought, *I'll be drinking* **stengahs** *with that jolly gang again! Or will Daphne want us to be alone every evening? That's fine with me, too.*

To his surprise, the veterans *did* want to talk. A Nursing Sister, tall and young, greeted him warmly. "They'll welcome a fresh pair of ears! They've heard each other's war stories too many times, and they can't listen any more. Come out on the verandah — the wheelchair brigade's having smoke-oh."

He followed her gray uniform through the ward toward the wide door to the verandah. Two physical therapists, wearing tan shirts and skirts, moved along the double row of white cots, one giving massages and the other directing individual exercise. Patients gave him a wave, a grin, or the Churchill V-sign. One gaunt face, however, turned away, blue eyes avoiding Jim's brown ones.

Have I found here the one and only unfriendly Aussie in the entire country? Or — more probably — was he as friendly as all the rest, before whatever hit him happened?

Australian newspapers still shocked him with their daily front-page listing, in a sort of macabre box score, of local men killed and wounded overseas. From the dispatches of Alan Moorehead and others, he had learned what the Diggers were enduring in Syria, Libya, and Tobruk; and for the first time, he had become gripped by that strange, distant struggle against the desert and its wily Fox.

An elderly priest, probably in his seventies, carrying a Communion kit, was walking toward them. Jim was surprised when the nurse introduced him as a bishop, for he wore a plain black suit and a clerical collar.

Well, that figures — nobody "puts on the dog" in this country.

With a warm grin and a firm handshake, Bishop Mannix welcomed Jim in a deep Irish-accented voice, then excused himself to kneel beside one of the cots. As they walked on toward the wide porch doors, the nurse told Jim, "Even the Protestants love him for his humor — and he's a hero to the Irishmen for his demands for independence. He was so active in the time of the Black and Tans that the English wouldn't let him enter Ireland — they sent a warship to intercept the passenger ship he was on and took him off by force."

Out on the sunlit verandah with its ornamental wrought-iron railing, these veterans of the all-volunteer Australian Imperial Forces were the first English-speaking men of his own generation Jim had ever met who had fought in a real war. He regarded them as men, although some were still in their freckled and pimpled teens, and he saw them as heroes, on a pedestal only a little lower than the older Allied pilots of the World War.

Some members of this maimed and disfigured group warmed to Jim at once, seeming aware of his mental salute. Three of the men were "Rats of Tobruk," who had adopted Lord Haw-Haw's radio epithet as their title of honor. They spoke the least and smoked the most, but all showed their enjoyment of Jim's Lucky Strikes.

Reg Greer, a handsome Englishman reared in Tasmania, had been evacuated from Malta, a victim of shell shock. Jim wanted to tell Greer of his admiration for the defenders of the tiny island that Hitler was determined to obliterate — now in its seventeenth month of enduring relentless day and night bombing. But Greer showed no response; his large brown eyes seemed to look right through Jim.

Those who had survived Greece and Egypt were still vehement about their experience. All of them had been on Crete in the week of Jim's 21st birthday, when the German parachute troops began dropping from the blue Mediterranean sky, and had been among the 15,000 in the frantic evacuation to Egypt ten days later on 30 May, when the German parachutes were still descending. These were the lucky ones, they told Jim, a remnant of the 2,000 who got to Alexandria alive. With one voice and many obscenities, they cursed the English leaders and the lack of air protection. Those two factors deserved all the blame for the deaths of their friends, they swore.

A red-haired youth — inevitably nicknamed "Bluey" — had been caught at Piraeus, the port of Athens, when 120 German planes had bombed and strafed his unit for two hours one morning. "And not a fuckin' bloody bastard of a Pommie plane in the air that entire day! Helpless, my God, you feel helpless as a baby. You see that first Nazi bastard come out of the clouds, no bigger than a bush-fly, then you hear it buzzing like a swarm of flies, and before you can take a couple of breaths, it's swooped down over you, dumped its bombs and raked you with its machine guns, and it's gone back in the clouds — that quick. You're there, ass in the air, clawing the ground, with the shit scared into your pants, your mates bleedin' and screamin' and dyin' all around you — but that's not the worst of it. The worst is — if they missed you that time or if they didn't, you know as sure as bloody hell that more of the sons of bitches are on the way."

Jim wondered, how did these wounded men in all their pain endure the months-long journey home in blacked-out ships? Did they sometimes think with envy of those able-bodied ancestral convicts who had survived the stinking prison ships to become Australia's first settlers? "It must have been a hellish trip home, dodging the German raiders," he said.

"Too right — but the fuckin' raiders are gettin' sunk, now that our glamour girl cruiser *Sydney's* on the premises," Bluey said with a grin. "One of our blokes has a mate who's a guard at Murchison — that's the internment camp here in Victoria. They already had twelve hundred Jerries there that we captured in North Africa. He came by this morning to visit his cobber, and he told us Jerry sailors are pouring into Murchison! They're off the fuckin' raider *Kormoran*, sunk by our *Sydney* last week. Their little boats have been coming ashore all up and down our west coast. About three hundred crewmen have already been locked up."

"They've got no right to be treated as POWs," another man insisted. "They're fuckin' pirates. They were flyin' a Dutch flag and gave *Sydney* their name as the Dutch ship *Straats Malacca*."

An older man with a deeply lined face said, "The first sailors that came ashore admitted that. And some said she was flying the flag of Norway — a neutral. But after their Captain and the officers got ashore, the men changed their stories. The bloke from Murchison says one of the officers is from the Gestapo, and he shut the sailors' mouths. At first, some of them even bragged that they sank the *Sydney* with their guns! Sank a bloody cruiser! But the Captain says he couldn't see through the smoke, and he thought *Sydney* sailed out of sight, over the horizon."

"Too right, she did." Bluey grinned. "None of *Sydney's* Carley floats have been seen."

A man at the edge of the cluster of wheelchairs sat with his head bowed as if in prayer; Jim could not see his face. He kept murmuring a sort of incantation, "Souda Bay. Souda Bay. Souda Bay . . ."

"I saw something few have ever seen," a young man, perched on a pillow, his legs off at the hips, told Jim, with a smile. "I saw two squadrons of Pommie fighters and a squadron of bombers in the air over Crete one day."

"Aw, break it down!" his mates hooted. "Don't lie to the Yank!"

"Never again, I admit. But it was a thrill I won't forget."

Jim noted the man's big upper body. *When he had legs, he was probably as tall as I am. Probably played soccer, rode horses, swam. . . .*

". . . wasn't only Aussies there," another was explaining to Jim. "Kiwis, too. ANZACs. Understand, myte?"

Jim nodded, suddenly realizing that they thought of him as a messenger to tell the U.S. their story. "Look, I'm not a reporter or anything. I'm just down from the Philippines, visiting a friend."

"A femyle, right? Helluva long trip to see a sheila! I hope she's worth the trip, Yank."

"Dinkum Aussie," Jim responded, to their laughter.

The patients were unanimous in praise of their new Prime Minister, because Curtin had promised that Australian soldiers never again would be sacrificed by knowingly being exposed to enemy bombers without airplanes to defend them. "Air Co-operation Squadrons" — Australian, not RAF — were being formed, and henceforth, would accompany Australian army units, even as the German air power protected German troops. So their experience had not been wasted, they told Jim; their younger brothers would be spared the unfair match.

"The German air force is *their* infantry's umbrella, advance guard, and artillery," a man with bandaged eyes summed up.

"Those Nazi planes watch over their troops like a bloody Mum," said another Digger. "Any time we were giving their infantry a good fight, they'd just fire off a coupla Very lights, as if to yell, 'Mama, these larrikins are being mean to me!' And pronto! Our boys are getting attacked by the bastard dive bombers again."

When they congratulated Jim for being a pilot in the Yank army, he felt guilty that his body was whole, and that he was not battling the Luftwaffe, their crippler, killer of their best mates.

He felt relieved when Albion came out on the verandah to get him; but he was embarrassed to be able to stand up and walk outdoors with a pretty girl while the veterans watched. The patients, however, took on new life in Albion's presence, and as he departed with her he could hear deliberately loud remarks from the wheelchairs and the cots of the ward.

"Gawd! Don't she smell beaut?" exclaimed the man whose eyes were bandaged. "Does she look that good?"

"She *is* beaut!"

"Lucky Yank bastard, got himself a bonzer sheila, all right. Made in Melbourne — not Manila!"

Part 3 — Port Phillip Bay

U.S. LEND-LEASE AID
TO BRITAIN, CHINA,
RUSSIA, PASSES
$ONE BILLION MARK
— Manila *Clarion,* 23 November 1941

Port Phillip Bay
Sunday afternoon, 23 November 1941

Rebecca, a slender 22-foot copy of a Star class boat, was a pleasure to sail — as soon as Jim could get clear of Victoria Dock and the wharves at the north end of Port Phillip Bay, where the Yarra's brown water faded into the blue of the bay.

Earlier, Albion's description of the sailboat as "Bermudian rigged" had given Jim a few qualms, until he saw her tall mast and hauled up the long mainsail.

"We call this a Marconi rig," he told her. The nickname had stuck since the 1920s, when this type was so overstayed that the mast was said to look like a Marconi radio tower. Lacking the running backstays and peak halyard of a gaff rig, a Marconi was delightfully easy to handle, and while Jim took the tiller, Albion managed the main and jib sheets admirably.

The day was sunny and mild, convincing Jim that spring actually was

Chapter 12 — Part 3 — Port Phillip Bay 273

arriving, even here at the southernmost point of the continent, below the 38th parallel. He and Albion had worn shorts underneath their church clothes, and now he enjoyed pulling off his jacket, shirt, tie, and trousers in her presence and watching her remove her jacket and skirt, revealing her superb legs.

She pleaded, "Can't you work on the rigging or something, while I take off my stockings!"

"There's nothing to do," he lied; for with a Marconi rig, everything was adjustable; there was always fine-tuning to fiddle with. He watched as she unfastened her garters, rolled down her heavy cotton stockings, and then extracted her white garter belt through the waistband of her shorts. She carefully folded his clothes with hers and covered them from spray with a spare jib, known in Australia as a "bag."

She began to remove the "cut lunch" from the dark blue knapsack she had carried all morning like an oversized pocketbook; she called it her "swag."

"I ate breakfast early, and I'm starving — I'll bet you are, too."

"Stop! Before you do anything more — yes, I'm hungry as the devil, but now you've *got* to tell me what you've been smirking about all day, or I'll throw you overboard!"

She looked at him with a radiant, bride-like face, joy in her dark-lashed brown eyes. "Jimyank — fortune has smiled on us! Tuesday's Aunt Alice's birthday, and she's going to spend it at the farm with my parents. She's my mother's sister, you know."

Jim groaned. "Darling, why are you telling me? It's cruel to torment me like that. Or did you forget that I've got to take off at dawn tomorrow morning? General Brereton sure as hell isn't going to give his team another day and night in Melbourne just so I can sleep in Aunt Alice's bed after she finally leaves town!"

"Wait a second — I didn't finish. She went to early Communion this morning so she could catch the nine o'clock train to Bendigo."

"God stone the crows! Do you think she's really *Bendigone*?"

Albion was a good laugher. "I put her on the train myself, and waved goodbye as it chugged away."

"Wow! I'd like to give the dear lady a birthday present. So — is this an invitation, or do I have to break your door down tonight?"

She laughed again. "You couldn't find the door in that block of flats, so luckily for you this *is* an invitation! I'll meet you at the Essendon station tonight — after eight, please, so it will be quite dark — and we can walk to the flat together." •

"Come back here and kiss me, before I go crazy and spin this tiller till we both get dizzy and fall overboard!"

"I'm dizzy already," she said after some deep and prolonged kisses.

His hands were shaking slightly as he lighted a Lucky. He drew deeply and admired the sparkling blue bay, thinking he had never seen one so beautiful; in comparison, even his own Manila Bay faded to gray in his memory. Port Phillip Bay, about 30 miles long and 20 miles wide, was as landlocked as Rabaul's Simpson Bay, with only a narrow entrance, called "the Rip," on the southwest side. If an ancient volcano had formed this bay, it had happened so long ago that its encircling peaks were no longer threatening like those at Rabaul; they had mellowed to green mounds that rose gradually to the Australian Alps northeast of Melbourne.

Albion asked, "Shall we just split a Vegemite sandwich and a stubbie now and have our real picnic on the shore?"

"Only if you'll guarantee that Vegemite's famous B-vitamins will make me the equal of any Aussie bloke in Aunt Alice's bedroom tonight."

"I can't promise you that, because no Aussie bloke — or any other kind of bloke — has ever been *near* Aunt Alice's bedroom!"

She handled the tiller while he ate; she was an excellent sailor. *Rebecca* was as responsive as a polo pony. Her tall sail was ideal to catch the thermal currents from the warming shore, her boom was not bruisingly low, and her rig simplified the continual coming-about.

Jim asked, "Can you imagine sailing a yacht that's one hundred feet longer than this baby? The *Enterprise,* that kept the 1930 *America's* Cup for us, was one hundred twenty-one feet overall, with a beam as broad as this sailboat is long. And our *Rainbow* and *Ranger* are about the same size. Sir Thomas Lipton's J-boat, *Shamrock V,* is one hundred thirty feet, and triple-initial T.O.M. Sopwith's *Endeavour* is one hundred forty. It's too bad England had to let the damn war get in the way of challenging us."

"Well, after the war's over, *we're* going to challenge your stuck-up Vanderbilts, and cut 'em down to size. We'll bring your bloody Cup home and drink Aussie brew from it!"

Jim laughed. "Not bloody likely, my love! England's got some pretty good sailors who've been trying to win it for seventy years. Most recently we've beaten all five of their big *Shamrocks* and out-sailed both of their *Endeavours*. It's not a game for beginners."

They sailed southwest, toward Geelong, then turned east in mid-bay to round the tip of a rocky peninsula that formed the west side of the Rip; it extended into the bay to shape the shoreline into a form that Jim saw with romantic eyes. He told Albion, "From a plane, this bay would look like a blue upside-down heart."

"Oh, Jimyank — spare me a heart that's blue and upside-down! That sounds awful. Sounds like a heart that's about to break."

She told him about the beautiful white ocean liners that steamed to Melbourne before the war. British cruise ships of the Pacific and Orient Line and Dutch ships of the Nederland Line brought rich tourists from Europe and

Chapter 12 — Part 3 — Port Phillip Bay 275

the Americas. En route, they picked up heat-drained Englishmen from Singapore and Dutchmen from the Netherlands East Indies who yearned for a cool holiday — headed for the ski lodge at Mount Kosciusko, northeast of Melbourne, Australia's tallest peak at 7,328 feet.

As *Rebecca* glided alongside little Swan Island, Jim could see southward past the Rip, across Bass Strait to a dim shape that was King Island. King pointed the way to the triangular island of Tasmania, beyond Jim's vision, and out in the tempestuous Tasman Sea.

Bass Strait was where MS *City of Rayville* went down, he remembered learning from Feldt.

Jim asked Albion, "Do you remember the name of the crewman who was killed when that American freighter sank?"

"No, not now, Jimyank. Our own steamer *Cambridge* had been sunk just the day before — at the east end of the Strait — so everybody was badly shocked. If the Bass Strait was a death-trap, ships would have to go all the way down around Tasmania — and mines were found there, too. But both sinkings were kept quiet for a long time, so as not to comfort the Jerries or Japs who'd laid the horrible mines. Why do you ask? Did you know that man?"

"No. But if Japan laid the mine — and if the U.S. gets into a war with Japan — then that Third Engineer would be the first American killed in the war, and his name should be remembered, at least by Americans."

They crossed to the east shore and began tacking northward along the irregular coastline, searching for the perfect picnic spot. *Rebecca* was as happy sailing upwind as downwind. Jim felt great pity for her owner — one of Dennis's mates whom Albion had visited this morning — confined to the hospital on this great day for sailing, while he recovered from war wounds. Albion had told Jim that Roy's wife wanted to sell the boat; but Roy insisted that he would sail again, one-armed.

Albion named each little promontory they passed. "You're a bonzer skipper, Jim. No wonder you Yanks have been able to hang on to your old silver mug for so long — but we'll take it from you one day."

Jim started to laugh, but then he remembered some small neat yachts he had seen in Sydney Harbour. Even while moored and bare-masted, their sharp good looks had caught his eye. *These Aussies may be beginners at building airplanes,* he thought, watching Albion's deft hands, *but they're "wizard" with wind and water.*

The breeze had loosened her hair and she took out her hairpins and let it down; it hung past her shoulders, shining like brown satin in the sunlight.

Might be a sign that she's relaxing her Melbournian prudery, Jim thought hopefully. "That sun's getting nice and hot. I'm going to take off my T-shirt and start getting back my tan. There are hardly any boats on this side of the bay, so why don't you take off your blouse?"

To his delighted surprise, she did. Under the white cotton uniform shirt, she was wearing a sleeveless undershirt; she removed that, too, revealing a lacy white brassiere, but her back was toward him. With his left hand on the tiller, he leaned forward and with his free right hand undid the hooks at the back and caressed her warm shoulders and her small, firm breasts that responded to his touch as readily as *Rebecca* did.

Jim told her, "Let's stop at the next deserted inlet — whether it's scenic or not."

Just north of Mordialloc they found a good spot. They took off their shoes and waded ashore, securing *Rebecca's* line to a tree. Sitting on a smooth, warm rock, they ate their "tucker" with appetites now ravenous, emptied the last drops from the stubby beer bottles, and topped off with apples and "biscuits" — cookies — baked by Aunt Alice.

With one of his hungers sated, Jim said, "I wish your friends — *Rebecca's* owners — had stowed a blanket for us. Lacking that, why don't we spread out the jib on the ground and take a nap?"

"Because, if we did that, someone I know would be sure to sail in here and recognize me — and think the worst! Besides, you have to get back to Victoria Barracks and pack your kit for your flight tomorrow."

"I can pack in five minutes. I want to sail back to the dock under the Southern Cross."

"We couldn't count on getting enough wind. The land breeze dies down at sunset. . . . Will you bring all your luggage with you tonight?"

"I haven't got much — just a B-4 bag and a few souvenirs — like a five-foot didgeridu for my brother. I could ask Slugger to take my gear to the airport for me — but I don't want to put him in a position where he'd have to lie. He's a Scout's-honor bloke. I think the best way to work it is for Slugger to tell the others in the morning — *truthfully* — that I woke up early and went out to Essendon airfield before they got up. So the answer to your question is, yes, I'll bring everything to your place tonight."

"Jimyank . . . something else you need to bring. You won't forget to stop at a chemist shop, will you?"

Chemist shop — drug store! "Don't worry, Pixie. I'll come well equipped. I wouldn't leave you with a little Yankee souvenir."

"Thanks, cobber. I don't need a baby to remember you by — I'll never forget you."

Part 4 — Decision Time

> . . . *where before we were troubled in clearing the ground of great Timber, which was to them of small use; now we may take their own plaine fields and Habitations, which are the pleasantest places in the Countrey. Besides, the Deer, Turkies and other Beasts and Fowles will exceedingly increase if we beat the Salvages out of the Countrey.*
> — Captain John Smith in Virginia, 1622

Victoria Barracks
Sunday night, 23 November 1941

No one was in the lavatory, so Jim carefully opened his wallet and took out the blue envelope that said "Jimbo" in Daphne's bold handwriting.

She had given it to him in the cool living room of her father's home on Penang Island, on the afternoon of the night that was to see their love affair consummated — the night that had turned to smoke dreams.

"Proud products of my father's plantation," she said as she handed him the blue envelope. "Only the best latex is used to make french-letters."

He had brought the envelope on this trip with the hope of going on to Singapore, a dream that was about to come true. Only four days of flying remained: the hops from here to Townsville and thence to Darwin and Batavia, Java. As a symbolic joke, he had planned to hand it back to Daphne for a laugh

— a rueful laugh over that wasted night and the promise of a new night that would *not* be wasted. He had not actually intended to use one of these same items that had been in the envelope all this time; he knew that Daphne would be able to get plenty of fresh samples produced from Mr. Light's rubber plantation.

Lucky I had these. I guess Pixie was so excited she forgot that no "chemists' shops" would be open on a Sunday night. Dennis probably did his rubber-shopping early in the week. But even if a shop had been open, I don't feel capable of asking a grandmotherly clerk for a condom, or a package of them, or however they're sold. It would be different if you were married — but the old wowser of a clerk would know that I'm a lewd Yank bachelor. The scandal would be all over "Proper" Melbourne before morning, and the reputation of American officers would be zilch. Anyway, she'd probably say, "They're rationed, myte. There's a war on, and Australia needs more bybies."

Still, Daphne had given him the blue envelope in August, and now November was nearly over. *How long,* he wondered, *do these items keep their . . . vitality?* He turned on the water in the washbasin, took a condom out of the envelope and began to fill it with the always-cold water.

Someone was opening the door from the hall, and Jim quickly stepped inside a stall. His burden jostled and bounced, but did not break, and he managed to keep from laughing as he sat holding it in his lap until the other man had gone. As he poured out the water, he thought, *Daphne's dad's latex is tough enough; I don't need to test the others.*

He was whistling while he walked down the hall, "I'd Like to Get You on a Slow Boat to China." But by the time he reached his room his tune trailed off. His lungs felt emptied of air. Thinking about Daphne had broken into his amorous fantasies of sharing Aunt Alice's bed with Albion. He would be in Singapore with Daphne before the week was over.

*Punch would think it was fine to sleep with two girls in one week — five or six would be even better, he'd say. But dammit, how can I "make love" with Pixie in my arms, if Daphne's in my thoughts? Could I close my eyes tonight and pretend she's Daphne? Of course not; for one thing — no, two — Daphne's voluptuous breasts. And how will I feel when I'm with Daphne, a few days from now, having just come from rolling in the clover with Pixie? I'll feel like a double-dyed rat tonight, when I trivialize the gift that Pixie's offering from her heart. And I'll feel like a bed-jumping snake in Singapore, if I give back the blue envelope to Daphne with one item missing — or **don't** give it back. And I'll feel like a complete heel during the days and nights between here and there, after betraying two women who trust me.*

As Jim furiously stuffed his clothes into his B-4 bag, he longed to talk to Slugger about his dilemma; but he knew that Slugger would never have gotten himself into such a mess, and he would not understand. *He'd despise me,* Jim thought. *But I really haven't done anything despicable — yet. Is there time to get out of this without hating myself, and without hurting anyone?*

Which would be worse: to cynically use Albion as a playtoy, en route to Daphne's bed — or to weasel out of tonight's date? I could invent a face-saving excuse: tell her that Brereton ordered me to stay up all night scrubbing the latrine with a toothbrush. That's the only gentlemanly thing to do. I like her too much — dammit, maybe I really love her, because it hurts when I think about treating her unfairly.

He looked at his watch. If he left right now to catch the Essendon tram, he would be at Albion's station before she arrived there on foot at eight to meet him.

When she sees me without my baggage, she'll wonder. Then I'll explain that it's going to be impossible for me to spend the night, that Brereton's given me all these chores.

But as he began to rehearse this *beau geste* scene, he saw Albion's luminous face, her glad smile of greeting, and those brown eyes looking up at him as he spoke. His scenario crumpled.

I can't tell her in person, I'll have to do it by phone. . . . Oh, goddammit to hell — she has no telephone!

Chapter 13

Part 1 — Farewell to Australia

Farewell, Australia! you are a rising child, and doubtless some day will reign a great princess in the South: but you are too great and ambitious for affection, yet not great enough for respect. I leave your shores without sorrow or regret.
— Charles Darwin, *The Voyage of the Beagle*, 1845

Essendon Aerodrome
Monday, 24 November 1941

Jim left Australia with sorrow, regret, and crushing guilt. On the Essendon tram en route to the airfield, after the worst night of his life, he had closed his eyes in agony of mind and spirit as the tram clicked past Albion's station. But inside his eyelids he saw her small, sweet image, waiting in the dark for him last night. The self-loathing that had grown within him through the night now threatened to choke him. He wondered how many hours she had waited.

No matter how much you hate me, I hate myself worse. If I get killed in a plane crash today, I deserve it.

Now he shivered in the gray pre-dawn as he strode restlessly back and forth between the B-18 and the Douglas which would return the Americans to Brisbane, there to pick up the Fortress that would take them, finally, to Singapore. But that prospect was tarnished now; the place was only a Malay fishing village, overrun with Chinese merchants and arrogant Pommie bas-

Chapter 13 — Part 1 — Farewell to Australia

tards, he told himself.

Merle-Smith's official car drove onto the runway, and Brereton and Eubank got out. Jim caught his breath; in the dim light, the driver in her WRAAF uniform resembled Albion, just for an instant. He gave her the bundle he had addressed to Albion, containing Dennis's jacket, with a note to her in the pocket.

Although he had torn up several notes he had laboriously written on typing paper borrowed from Allison Ind, he knew that this final effort was scarcely better than nothing. Unable to explain about his decision to "wait for Daphne," he had invented a lie about running into General Brereton as he was trying to sneak out of Victoria Barracks, and being ordered to stay in his room until morning. His *apology* at least was sincere, as was his plea to Albion for her forgiveness. His postscript, intended to serve as a balm, now seemed so weak that it was worse than nothing: "P.S. Pixie — I realize now that I really do love you."

Burnett of the RAF stood by with Australian air officers, as Brereton, appearing vigorous again after his two-day rest, said goodbye to them with his broad, tight grin and brisk handshakes. "Sir Charles, you were extremely hospitable — as, indeed, was everyone we've come into contact with. As we leave this great continent, I must say that everywhere we landed, Australian enthusiasm at the sight of an American aircraft has been most gratifying. I am glad I can assure you that more American planes will soon be arriving, and will stay longer than *we* could."

Brereton then wheeled to face the Americans, and dropped his bombshell: "Over the weekend I've had some time to re-think my schedule. I'm eager to get back to Manila and conduct tactical inspections of the FEAF units. By now they've had three weeks of the intensive training I ordered."

Jim thought of his squadron-mates in the 20th Pursuit Squadron and their handsome, harried Commander, Joe Moore. *The poor kids — sweating their balls off, while I've been playing Don Juan, and doing it lousily.*

"— I want to spend a week checking on improvements in pilot readiness, in airplane maintenance, in airfield construction, and the early warning network before I go to Singapore and Java. So I'm postponing that survey till next month."

Of all the fucking luck!

"— That'll give you blokes time to get your civilian suits cleaned and your socks washed, because I want each one of you to go with me to Singapore on Monday, 8 December —"

Daphne, darling, I'll get there yet!

"— and now Gene Eubank will tell you how he's going to get us back to the Philippines. There's not another pilot in the world I'd trust to try the route!"

Eubank explained, "Ever since we first mapped out the ferry route for our

Forts from Hawaii to Luzon, via the top of Australia, I've been wondering if it would be possible to fly directly to Clark from Port Moresby. I'm thinking about the 7th Bomb Squadron and other new squadrons that'll be coming out to the Philippines soon. If they could eliminate the stops at Townsville and Darwin — saving three landings and two days — we could of course reduce crew fatigue, and save a helluva lot of gas."

*Don't tell me **we're** going to try to get back to Clark via Miserable Moresby!*

Eubank continued, "On the other hand — you've all seen the tail of the mountain spine of New Guinea, and had a taste of its quick-changing weather —"

And no weather stations to warn you if you're heading into the teeth of a New Guinea Special that tops out at seventy thousand!

"— Believe it or not, the mountains at the Dutch end of the island are even worse than the Owen Stanleys," Eubank went on. "They're snow-covered all year. There really will be no place to land till we get back to the pineapple plantation on northern Mindanao. So — after we pick up our 'Seventeen in Brisbane, we'll head back to Port Moresby and see if we can make it to Clark from there, nonstop. So, that gives us about eight hundred fifty miles to Brisbane and thirteen hundred from there to Port Moresby today — and about twenty-eight hundred more miles to get us home tomorrow."

Oh, my aching ass. Back to "Port Lessby." No stopping in Townsville. God sure is punishing me for my "sins of omission."

Part 2 — Bad News in Brisbane

The Japanese are . . . masters of the Far East. . . . Japanese spokesman have declared more or less publicly that neither Great Britain nor the United States is any longer capable of protecting by force of arms its territories in the Western Pacific.
— Hector Bywater, *Sea-Power in the Pacific*, 1934

Monday, 24 November 1941

On Brisbane's tarmacadam runway, Jim said a regretful goodbye to Slugger Pell, who would fly the B-18 back to Clark Field by the Townsville-Darwin route. To add to Jim's gloom, there would not be time for lunching at Lennon's; mutton sandwiches must suffice.

The RAAF officers who met the Americans brought a piece of paper that infuriated General Brereton: the transcript of an English-language broadcast from Radio Tokyo that had been intercepted by Commander Feldt's listening post in Townsville. The Japanese announcer gave a comprehensive description of each visit by the Americans to the locations in Australia, New Guinea, and New Britain.

"General Bellerton's" secret plan, "in flagrant violation" of the U.S. Neutrality Law to establish U.S. air bases "to complete the military encirclement and economic blockade of Japan, in conjunction with the expansion of the white empires," was condemned. This General's "reckless scheme" for Australia was but another example of the U.S. belligerence which Premier Tojo and Foreign Minister Togo would tolerate no longer; they were determined to force America and England out of East Asia.

The broadcast named every member of the "high-ranking band of conspirators," including *Second Lieutenant James T. Davis*. Although Jim regretted the breach of security, his spirits were boosted slightly at the thought that the Kempei Tai regarded him as an accessory to a threat.

Brereton swore. "We didn't succeed in fooling anybody — the Japs have their agents everywhere! I just hope all the plans we've set up here can materialize before it's too late. . . . But what the hell — if General MacArthur doesn't approve of all the commitments I've made, I'm in worse trouble than Tojo and Tweedledum can dream up."

Jim hoped the Japanese spies didn't know their route north. *If one of their planes from the Carolines decided to intercept our high-ranking band over the wilds of Dutch New Guinea, no one would find our Fortress for about a hundred years!*

After the B-17 took off from the best runway in Australia, various RAAF aircraft accompanied it northward for a while in a friendly, informal escort: Avro Ansons, Tiger Moths, Wirraways, and Fairey Battles.

CHAPTER 14

Farewell to New Guinea

Preparations are becoming apparent . . . for an early aggressive movement of some character although, as yet, there are no clear indications as to its strength or whether it will be directed against the Burma Road, Thailand, the Malay Barrier, the NEI, or the Philippines. Advance against Thailand seems the most probable. I consider it possible that the next Japanese aggression might cause an outbreak of hostilities between the United States and Japan.
— Message from President Roosevelt, 26 November 1941,
to High Commissioner Sayre in Manila

Airborne
Tuesday, 25 November 1941

Hours before the B-17 finally overflew Vogelkop, the head of the New Guinea-bird, Eubank and Brereton had decided that no pilot ever should attempt to fly that northwest route again.

The huge island just south of the Equator thrust itself upward, out of steamy swamps and jungled river canyons, into dazzling white peaks that threatened the airplane's domain. Jim had never seen snow; now he learned that it existed permanently above 16,000 feet, and he found its vertical white masses, shadowed in blue, awesome, ominous, and menacing. A mountain named for little Dutch Princess Juliana rose to 16,700 feet; the one bearing the name of her mother, Queen Wilhelmina (now in London, a refugee from Hitler) peaked

100 feet higher; Mount Cartensz topped out at 17,700 feet.

Three years ago Richard Archbold had led an expedition inland from Humboldt Bay and had discovered the Grand Valley — an area unknown to the Dutch colonists — home to 60,000 New Guinea tribespeople. Elsewhere, except for a few tiny Dutch settlements on the coast, the island remained in its primeval state, the wilderness home to unknown tribes.

Keeping safely west of the Japanese-held Carolines, Eubank flew low over the Moluccas, the fabled Isles of Spice held by the Dutch. Jim thought those green magnets that had drawn the ships of the white world for centuries looked singularly inhospitable to aircraft the size of a B-17. Between here and the big island of Mindanao, the only spot even remotely possible to set the Fortress down on was the tip of the upflung tail of the northernmost island of the Celebes; but it looked to him as soft as a monkey's tail.

In the Philippines the only field south of Clark that could take the weight of a four-engine bomber was the vast Del Monte pineapple plantation on the north coast of Mindanao. Although Eubank intended to fly all the way to Clark, 500 miles north of Del Monte, it was somewhat heartening to Jim to know that the plantation could serve as an alternative. Even Eubank's careful fuel-weaning could be foiled by strong headwinds. And if Clark Field was socked in tonight by weather — well, Mindanao and Luzon seldom had storms simultaneously.

Over the Celebes Sea, Jim was serving a turn in the right-hand seat, keeping his "eyes skinned," as an Australian would say, for the coast of Mindanao.

Colonel Eubank said, "Dammit, Jim, Del Monte's too far from Australia — sixteen hundred miles north of Darwin — to be the only emergency field on our proposed ferry route. I'd sure like to have another field on Mindanao that's closer to Australia — and to Borneo. Wouldn't you?"

"Yes, Sir, any pilot would — even with four props turning."

"Zamboanga would be an ideal location, down on the tip of that eastern peninsula. But they tell me it's too low and swampy for heavy ships like this one."

"Yes, Sir, Zambo's even wetter than Manila."

"Well, you've lived down there; got any ideas?"

Jim visualized the peculiar elephantine shape of Mindanao, with Zamboanga like a peanut held in the tip of the trunk. Davao, representing the elephant's undersized penis, was swampy and worse: It was the abode of a colony of Japanese, estimated to number 30,000. Lake Lanao, like a huge sapphire set in the pachyderm's circus collar, sat high atop a volcano: ideal for seaplanes. Southward, beside the Moro Gulf, Cotabato was total swampland. But in between, on the elephant's chest . . .

"Sir, just south of Lake Lanao there's a Moro settlement they call Malabanga. It's well above sea level, and fairly flat."

Chapter 14 — Farewell to New Guinea 287

"Sounds good. I'll ask Colonel Casey to fly down there from Del Monte and take a look. We're gonna need a helluva lot of auxiliary fields on Mindanao — out of range of the Jap bases on Formosa — to handle all the planes they're sending us from the States."

Malabanga rang in Jim's memory like the brass gongs of the Muslim Moros who inhabit the region. When he was ten years old his parents had lived beside Lake Lanao at Camp Keithley, helping their friend Frank Laubach teach the adult Moros to read. Jim Davis and Bobby Laubach had been best friends; they also joined the effort to prove Dr. Laubach's developing theory of literacy training: "Each One Teach One."

The place name "Malabanga" contains the five most-used consonants in the Moro language. When Jim had taught a Moro to recognize that word (with each consonant imaginatively decorated to suggest a bird or animal), he knew that the man soon would be a reader, and later, a teacher.

But if war came, he didn't know if these fierce Muslims would side with them, the paleface "infidels" and the Christian Filipinos — or with non-Christian Japanese. If Japan promised to give them their dream — Mindanao as an independent Moro-ruled sultanate — how could they resist?

The clunky forty-five was designed for Pershing "to subdue the fanatics," because a thirty-eight couldn't stop a Moro determined to win his ticket to Paradise by killing Christians. But no matter how many damned forty-fives you tote, or how quick-on-the-draw you are — if a Moro sneaks up behind you and slices your head off, you're a dead cowboy. Right now, if Japanese forces should hop westward from the Carolines to take Mindanao, with its size and resources equal to Pennsylvania — and if the Moros should welcome them — Japan could take Borneo and New Guinea; God help Luzon, and farewell forever, Australia.

Eubank interrupted Jim's grim thoughts. "I'm sleepy as hell. I won't have any trouble keeping awake, once we make landfall — but until I can see something besides water down there, you'll have to talk to me. Don't worry — I'm not asking you to tell me about you and your Aussie girlfriend, though she seems like a peach. Here's a timely topic: Captain Ind told me that you know Kurusu; tell me what you think of the fellow."

"Sir, he's a fine person. Of course, I was only about one year old when he was Japan's Consul-General in Manila. But my parents got to know him well then — and I met him when he came through Manila on the *California Clipper* a couple of weeks ago."

"I just missed him, didn't I?"

"Yes, Sir. November 6th. Everybody'd been wondering why the *Clipper* was delayed at the Kai Tak ramp in Hong Kong for two days. Afterwards, we heard that the U.S. State Department asked Pan Am to hold the *Clipper* till Special Envoy Saburo Kurusu could be sneaked out of Japan and put aboard, before Japanese militarists discovered that he was on a peace mission to Washington. They probably would have assassinated him."

"They're good at that. But his stopover in Manila wasn't kept secret."

"Not at all. In fact, Consul-General and Mrs. Yoshida gave a ritzy reception for him at the Nippon Club. But most of the ManilAmericans stayed away, to show their anger at Tojo's anti-American ravings."

"Then why'd you go?"

"Well, High Commissioner Sayre's such a man of peace himself, he couldn't stand to have 'the Emperor's Peace Ambassador' snubbed in Manila. He asked my parents and me to go to the reception as a personal favor to him. He didn't know we'd have gone anyway. My mother — who's a tough judge of character — likes Kurusu's American wife, Alice, a lot. And my dad says if *anyone* can prevent a war, maybe Kurusu could; though my dad thinks the chances are about one in ten thousand. He's the world's worst pessimist. Kurusu's so Americanized, and he really understands Americans and respects them. He was stationed in Chicago for a long time, in the Consul's office — that's where he met Alice, and their son was born there — and he learned a lot of American slang, and speaks English fluently."

"But that's what the newspapers said about Nomura, when he took over as Ambassador. They said he knew Washington because he'd served there as a naval attaché during the World War; he'd made close friendships with lots of Americans; he had a fine understanding of the U.S.; and he had a sincere regard for the country, blah, blah, blah."

"Yes, Sir, if *anybody* could make Secretary Hull like the Japs, it was supposed to be Admiral Nomura."

In February, the Japanese liner *Kamakura Maru* had docked at Pier Seven in Manila Bay, bearing Kishisaburo Nomura to the U.S. to assume his diplomatic duties. Manilans had welcomed him with high hopes, and invitations to the Yoshidas' reception for him were eagerly sought. Jim had felt lucky to be in the long line waiting to shake the hand of the tall, jovial, moon-faced, slightly deaf, one-eyed Admiral. (Earlier, a bomb planted by a Korean patriot/revolutionary had half-blinded Nomura.)

Jim continued, "A friend of mine, Commander Frank Bridget, went to language school in Japan and knew Nomura there and liked him. He told me that Nomura likes American whiskey, cigarettes, and poker as much as Cordell Hull himself. We all thought they'd become bosom buddies in Washington, and patch everything up."

"What the hell went wrong?"

"Kurusu told my dad that Ambassador Nomura's deafness is getting worse, and he can't understand old Hull's Tennessee twang. Hull can't understand Nomura's English, and he hates all Japs, anyway. He calls Nomura a 'piss-ant' while he's still in the room — Nomura's not too deaf to hear that."

Chapter 14 — Farewell to New Guinea

Eubank laughed wryly. "*Some* diplomacy! But you really think Kurusu can do what Nomura hasn't been able to do?"

"Yes, Sir. I'm sure of it. He's so intelligent and likable and sincere. When he says, 'All over Tokyo, no taxi,' with those sad brown eyes peering through his glasses, you realize that they don't just need oil for their armed forces — they need it to *live*. He says Japan's willing to withdraw from China, though they can't be forced to apologize to Chiang. They'll just leave some troops in north China to help Chiang keep the Reds under control. But he says they can't withdraw from Manchuria after ten years of investing in factories there, because that would mean economic disaster for Japan, and if Japan pulled out, the Red Chinese army would spread Communism to all of Asia."

"Does he think Hull has forgotten that Kurusu himself signed the Tripartite Pact with Italy and Germany last year, while he was Ambassador to Germany? How does he get around that promise to go to war for them?"

"My dad asked him about that. He said they can't act as Judas and renounce the Pact, but the Emperor would never project the people of Japan into war at the behest of any foreign power. He said he'll inform Hull that an understanding between Japan and the U.S. would outshine the Tripartite Pact."

"So a verbal agreement outshines a signed document? I'm glad I never craved to be a diplomat!"

"He said Prime Minister Tojo told him, 'I'm praying to the gods that some way we'll come to an agreement with America.'"

"Tojo sure has a funny way of praying. Maybe the gods are confused by his daily diatribes against us."

"Kurusu said the people of Japan and the Emperor all want peace, but the military leaders have a loaded gun in each hand, determined to shoot. He said that the U.S. embargo against Japan, and denying their ships access to the Panama Canal, have made peacemakers unpopular with some strong factions there. His highest hope, he told my dad, is to see President Roosevelt alone, without Secretary Hull."

"What could he say that he won't say to the Secretary of State?"

"Colonel, I'll bet you my next month's flying pay that he was given secret instructions from the Emperor for a backdown that'll lead to a compromise. He told us, 'It's far easier to start a war than to end one, and we must do everything in our power to prevent one.'"

"Well, I hope to hell he can do it."

"Sir, I'm positive he will."

Chapter 15

Clark Field Confrontation

As they flew, the ploughman in the field stopped to gaze, and the shepherd leaned on his staff and watched them, astonished at the sight and thinking they must be gods who could thus cleave the air.
— *Bulfinch's Mythology*, The story of Daedalus

Tuesday evening, 25 November 1941

Fourteen hours and 2,765 miles after taking off from Port Moresby, with only 200 gallons of gasoline left, Eubank set the B-17 down at Clark Army Air Field.

Captain Ind had been airsick most of the way; he looked pale and wobbly. "I'm deafened by the tireless roar of those four engines," he murmured to Jim, "but so grateful for their tenacity."

Jim nodded assent. He thought no place he had seen on the journey was more beautiful than this, his own assigned airfield, with all its lovely silver planes glowing in the light of a spectacular Philippine sunset.

Colonel Lester Maitland, the jovial, Nordic-looking airfield Commander, famed as the first pilot to fly from California to Hawaii, was waiting to greet the weary group, together with Headquarters officers, squadron Commanders, and others alerted by the plane's radio contact.

As General Brereton's feet touched the sod field, he seemed to explode. Hands on hips, brown eyes hard as marbles, he barked, "Gentlemen, I have

Chapter 15 — Clark Field Confrontation

just seen this field from the air. Fortunately for *you* — and for all who depend on us — I wasn't leading in a hostile bomber fleet. If I had been, I could have blasted the entire heavy bombardment strength of the Philippines off the map in one smash!"

He clenched his jaw and his eyes drilled into each startled pair of eyes in the circle, in turn. With a wide gesture that encompassed the clusters of parked B-17s and the perfect straight lines of wingtipped P-40s, he demanded, "Do you call that *dispersal?* It's absolutely, carelessly, insanely *wrong* — and such sloppy practices will have no place in the functioning of this field, or any other field under my command. This condition will be rectified at once — *tonight* — and you will never permit it to occur again. Do we understand each other, gentlemen?"

Jim looked at the ground, unable to bear the sight of the officers' humiliated faces. Reared by his *amah,* Saadra, to respect every person's *hija* (a Filipino concept more inclusive than "face" or pride), he was shocked that Brereton would berate Colonels, Majors, and Captains in front of their subordinates.

Chickenshit! He sure jawed himself out of The Dad Game — forever — with that exhibition of chewing ass en masse. The Japs are too smart to try to attack this field. And, anyway, Kurusu and Nomura are still talking to Secretary Hull in Washington, so nothing's going to happen.

Epilogue

Clark Army Air Field
Luzon Island, Philippines
Noon, Monday, 8 December 1941
(7 December in U.S. and Hawaii)

"*Good God Almighty!*" *screamed Jim's crew chief. "Yonder they come!"*
Captain Joseph H. Moore, Commander of the 20th Pursuit Squadron, raced his P-40 down the runway to lead his pilots off the ground before the Japanese bombs fell. Following in train were Second Lieutenants Randall Keator, Edwin Gilmore, and Jim Davis.
Behind them on the runway their squadron-mates, Second Lieutenants Lowell Mulcahy of Portersville, California, Jim Drake of Dallas, Jesse Luker, a Californian, and Max Louk of Lawrence, Kansas, were caught on the ground and killed in their cockpits as their gasoline tanks exploded.

Aftermath

Most of the U.S. airplanes in the Philippines were destroyed on the ground in the attack that occurred a few hours after the Japanese struck Pearl Harbor. General Brereton was evacuated to Australia, where the plans he had set in motion in November proved invaluable. He went on to command U.S. air forces in Java, India, and Europe. Colonel (later General) Eubank also led air units in Europe. Allison Ind worked in Australia with the Allied Intelligence Bureau.

In January 1942, all American and Filipino units on Luzon were forced to withdraw to the Bataan peninsula, where Jim Davis and other pilots fought as infantry against the invading Japanese.

On 19 February, flying his P-40 in defense of Darwin during a surprise attack by Japanese planes, Floyd "Slugger" Pell, 28, was shot down and his body strafed in his parachute. The Australians named a wartime RAAF airfield, south of Broome, in his honor.

Starving and malaria-ridden, the remnant of U.S. and Philippine forces on Bataan surrendered in April, followed by the exodus from Bataan that became known as the "Death March." As prisoners of war, they endured more than three years of inhuman conditions in prison camps in the Philippines or as slave laborers in Japan. A few escaped to the mountains, formed guerrilla bands, and became Coastwatchers, sending valuable information by radio to General MacArthur in Australia.

Commander Feldt's earlier advice proved useful to Jim when he set up his guerrilla transmitter behind Japanese lines.

Sources

As this is not a reference work, I'll spare the reader a bibliography of my sources — which include more than 40 volumes about Australia on my own shelves — but I could not have attempted to reconstruct the scenes without these eight books:

Brereton, Lewis H. *The Brereton Diaries* (New York: Morrow, 1946).
Edmonds, Walter D. *They Fought with What They Had* (New York: Little, Brown, 1951. Reprinted by Zenger).
Feldt, Commander Eric A., RAN. *The Coastwatchers* (New York: Oxford University Press and Melbourne, Australia, 1946. Reprinted at Garden City, 1979).
Gillison, Douglas. *Royal Australian Air Force 1939-1942* (Adelaide, Australia: The Griffin Press, 1962).
Goerner, Fred. *The Search for Amelia Earhart* (New York: Doubleday, 1966).
Ind, Allison. *Bataan: The Judgment Seat* (New York: Macmillan, 1944).
Lightbody, Mark and Tony Wheeler. *Papua New Guinea* (South Yarra, Victoria, Australia: Lonely Planet Publications, and Berkeley, CA, 1985).
Montgomery, Michael. *Who Sank the Sydney?* (New York: Hippocrene Books, 1983).

Permissions to Quote

The author thanks the following persons, agents, publishers, and companies for granting permission to reprint copyrighted material:

Walter D. Edmonds and the Air Force Aid Society for use of his hand-drawn map from his book *They Fought with What They Had,* published in 1951 by Little, Brown and Company, Boston. Copyright © 1951 by Air Force Aid Society, Arlington, VA.

Doubleday, a division of Bantam, Doubleday, Dell Publishing Group, Inc., for an excerpt from *Ramparts of the Pacific* by Hallett Abend. Copyright © 1941 by Hallett Abend and published by Doubleday, Doran in 1942.

Carl Fischer, Music Publishers, for the first verse of "The U.S. Air Force" by Robert Crawford. Copyright © 1939, 1942, 1951 by Carl Fischer, Inc., N.Y. Copyrights renewed. All Rights Reserved. Used by Permission.

Greenwood Publishing Group, Inc., for excerpts from *The Passing of the Aborigines* by Daisy Bates. Copyright © 1938 by John Murray, London, and published in 1967 by Frederick A. Praeger, Inc. Reprinted by permission of Greenwood Publishing Group, Inc., Westport, CT.

John Hawkins & Associates, Inc., for excerpts from *The Brereton Diaries* by Lewis H. Brereton. Copyright © 1946 by Lewis H. Brereton, and published in 1946 by William Morrow and Co., N.Y.

Random House, Inc. for an excerpt from *Suez to Singapore* by Cecil Brown. Copyright © 1942 by Random House, Inc., N.Y.

Houghton Mifflin Company for an excerpt from *Sea-Power in the Pacific* by

Hector Bywater, published in 1934 by Houghton Mifflin Company, Boston.

Bantam, Doubleday, Dell Publishing Group, Inc. for excerpts from *The Coastwatchers* by Eric A. Feldt. Copyright © 1946 by Oxford University Press and published in 1979 by Bantam Books, Inc., N.Y.

Little, Brown and Company for "The Kangaroo" by Ogden Nash. Copyright © 1942 by Ogden Nash and published in 1942 by Little, Brown in *Verses from 1929 On*.